D1552836

IN HARD TIMES

IN HARD TIMES

REFORMERS AMONG THE LATE VICTORIANS

HERMAN AUSUBEL

GREENWOOD PRESS, PUBLISHERS
WESTPORT, CONNECTICUT

The Library of Congress has catalogued this publication as follows:

Library of Congress Cataloging in Publication Data

Ausubel, Herman.
    In hard times.

    Bibliography: p.
    1. Social reformers--Great Britain.   2. Great
Britain--Social policy.   I. Title.
[HN385.A84 1973]   322.4'4'0942   72-9826
ISBN 0-8371-6600-4

Originally published in 1960
by Columbia University Press, New York

Reprinted with the permission
of Columbia University Press

First Greenwood Reprinting 1973

Library of Congress Catalogue Card Number 72-9826

ISBN 0-8371-6500-4

Printed in the United States of America

For Anne, Kenneth, and Jesse

ACKLOWLEDGMENTS

My chief debt is to the keepers and assistant keepers of manuscripts who gave me permission to use the documents in their care. I am particularly grateful to the following: Dr. Frank Taylor and Miss Glenise Matheson of the John Rylands Library; Mr. Sidney Horrocks of the Manchester Central Library; Miss Hilda Lofthouse of Chetham's Library, Manchester; Mr. J. M. Carty of the National Library of Ireland; Mr. Herbert Cahoon and Miss Mary M. Kenway of the Pierpont Morgan Library; Dr. John D. Gordan, Mrs. Charles Szladits and Miss Beatrice Landskroner of the Henry W. and Albert A. Berg Collection; Mr. Robert W. Hill, the late Edward Morrison, and Miss Jean R. McNiece of the New York Public Library; Miss Alice H. Bonnell and Mr. Kenneth A. Lohf of the Columbia University Library; Mr. Garry Ryan and Mr. Daniel T. Goggin of the National Archives, Washington, D.C.; Dr. David C. Mearns and Mr. John de Porry of the Library of Congress; Miss Kathleen Cohalan of the American Irish Historical Society, New York; Mr. John Alden of the Boston Public Library; Mr. Robert D. Newkirk and Mr. Howell J. Heaney of the Free Library of Philadelphia; and Mr. Alexander P. Clark and Mr. Alexander D. Wainwright of the Princeton University Library.

I also wish to thank the Fulbright authorities who enabled me to spend a year at the University of Manchester as a visiting research professor. And for two research grants I should like to express my gratitude to the William A. Dunning Fund of the History

ACKNOWLEDGMENTS

Department of Columbia University and the Columbia University Council on Research in the Social Sciences. As a believer in self-help, however, I look forward to the time when academic salaries will permit scholars to meet their own research expenses.

Finally, I owe much to several friends who were good enough to criticize this book in manuscript: Salo W. Baron, A. S. Eisenstadt, Ruth Emery, John A. Garraty, Joseph D. Huntley, Vergene F. Leverenz, Richard B. Morris, Lawrence Ritt, and Harold C. Syrett. I also wish to thank Frank Taylor for having read this book in proof. And I thank the staff of Columbia University Press for having made this an enjoyable—and educational—publishing experience. To R. L. Schuyler I owe a long-standing debt that I can never adequately acknowledge.

HERMAN AUSUBEL

Columbia University
August 10, 1960

CONTENTS

x CONTENTS

IN HARD TIMES

PROLOGUE

Late Victorian England—the England of the last third of the nineteenth century—was what it was for hundreds of reasons, some of which historians will never know. But it owed its distinctive character to two facts above all: the enfranchisement of most adult male workers in 1867 and 1884; and the staying power of a baffling economic crisis. The English of the late Victorian era were a democratic generation—the first in the history of their country. They were also a depression generation. And they had hardly begun their experiment in democracy when serious economic difficulties set in.

Although the late Victorian age was a time of troubles for every major section of the population, it was an inspiring and exhilarating period for reformers of many kinds. Advocates of temperance, educational reorganization, social welfare legislation, land reform, socialism, bimetallism, tax and tariff revision, imperial reconstruction, and Irish home rule, among other causes, saw countless evils to expose, analyze, and remove. Far more important, they found that political and social conditions favored them in their criticisms of the old order. They had a multitude of new voters to arouse. And because of the widespread economic distress they could more easily reach and interest both old and new voters. For reformers the late Victorian period turned out to be almost a golden age—a time not only of challenge but of fulfillment.

{ I }

1688-1788-1888

Desperate men made the Glorious Revolution of 1688, but they had little faith that their efforts would succeed. Accustomed to the upsets that marked so much of seventeenth-century history, they looked to a future as insecure as the past, and for years they expected their work to be undone. The notion that there would ever be a centennial celebration of their actions would have struck them as preposterous.

The anniversary did come, and the instability of 1688 had given way to the stability of 1788. As the centennial drew near, so keen an observer as Adam Smith pronounced the younger Pitt's Government as firmly established as any British Ministry could possibly be; and Smith noted the conspicuous absence of public discontent or agitation. As the celebrations of 1788 progressed and Britons gloried in their ancestors who had resisted arbitrary government, patriots justifiably repeated Smith's description of a stable, safe, and satisfied society. An octogenarian clergyman, despite his age, preached "with a spirit which seemed to be derived from the occasion." Those who heard him included not only men of property but "a hardy, yet decent and attentive peasantry; whose intelligent countenance shewed that they understood, and would be firm to preserve that blessing, for which they were assembled to return thanks to Almighty God. . . ." The chairman of the committee on the celebration of the jubilee of the Glorious Revolution even expressed the hope—not too fantastic at the time—that the

English constitution would be "transmitted unimpeached and un-impaired to our latest Posterity." [1]

While the English were celebrating with prayers, speeches, il-luminations, fireworks, and hogsheads of ale, the French were also rejoicing. Louis XVI had consented to revive the Estates-General, and it seemed that at last the French were having the good sense to imitate the English form of government. During the summer of 1789, however, this notion was speedily dispelled by the anti-aristocratic measures that the National Assembly adopted. Worse still, it became clear by the early 1790s that the French Revolution was for export and that almost everywhere in western and central Europe there were small groups of men determined to import it.

In England the friends of the French Revolution were quick to organize, but the enemies of the Revolution acted with no less haste. Typical of dozens of antirevolutionary societies was the ad-mirably named Manchester Association for Preserving Constitu-tional Order and Liberty as well as Property against the Various Efforts of Levellers and Republicans. Seeking to thwart those mal-contents who wished to "subvert the happy Rights and Liberties equally enjoyed by all Descriptions of Persons under the auspicious Protection of a long experienced and universally venerated Con-stitution of Government composed of King, Lords and Commons," the members of the Association viewed it as their mission to "un-deceive such Persons as may have been misled by the Sinister and inflammatory Insinuation of designing men." The Association ostentatiously offered rewards to those who gave evidence against traitors, and it searched out the ingrates who attempted to cir-culate subversive doctrines among soldiers. Familiar with the so-cial habits of their compatriots, members of the Association worked closely with innkeepers who were in a favorable position to detect and prevent seditious meetings. [2]

During the Napoleonic period and its aftermath, the English enemies of French radicalism acted through a network of Pitt Clubs that aimed to "Check the Contagion of Opinions which tended to dissolve the frame of civil Society." Glorying in their monarchy and what they hoped would be their immutable con-stitution, Pitt Club members held banquets at which they did much toasting, and their toasts disclosed the anxieties that had dislodged the hopes of 1788:

May the genius of Britain ever triumph over the demon of Jacobinism.
May the Dream of universal Suffrage and annual Parliaments no longer
disturb our Repose.
May the Liberties of England never be diminished by the unprincipled
violence of demagogues.
The Constitution of England as it is, and may it, and the world, fall together.
Confusion and disgrace to all Preachers of discord.[3]

Unfortunately for Pitt Club members and other traditionalists,
the meeting of the Estates-General in 1789 inaugurated not one but
two generations of revolution and more than two generations of
fear of revolution. Political upheavals became so frequent in Europe that by 1815 a hardy English gentleman could properly insist
that he would not change his travel plans because of so ordinary
an occurrence as a revolution. And even after the disastrous failure
of the Revolutions of 1848–49 the expectation was general that new
upheavals would soon take place. "We ought to remember that,
with the exception of England and Russia," wrote freedom-loving
Richard Cobden, "there is hardly a throne in Europe worth ten
years' purchase, and we should therefore avoid dynastic alliances
as much as possible, and take care at least to retain the good will
of the *peoples* who will last when dynasties are forgotten." Cobden,
an indefatigable defender of freer trade as a means to domestic
stability and international peace, watched Continental developments closely, and his prediction of new revolutionary outbreaks
was widely believed by both friends and enemies of the old order.[4]

II

By the time of the bicentennial celebration of the Glorious Revolution the most optimistic Victorian would have scoffed at the
notion of transmitting the English constitution "unimpeached
and unimpaired to our latest Posterity." Unrest was widespread,
and agitation for change had become perhaps the most striking
feature of English public life. In 1885 Mrs. Annie Besant, the
impassioned socialist orator, called the social and political environment as "unsettled and stormy as the weather," and her description applied not only to 1885 but to many other years during the
last third of the nineteenth century. Young George Santayana,
fresh from Harvard on a visit to England, was reinforced in his
conviction that the admirable English temper had been achieved
by avoiding breaks with the past. But few English traditionalists

would have agreed with him: they had witnessed too many breaks in the last two decades, and they saw worse ones threatening. The popular novelist Ouida, overflowing with upper-class sympathies, exaggerated the insomnia of the people she admired when she wrote in 1888 of the dread of popular uprisings driving away the sleep from "rich men's couch, from monarch's bed." But George Gissing, the socially conscious novelist and embittered ex-socialist, spoke for many of his frightened contemporaries when, after gathering literary material at a radical meeting, he remarked: "a more disheartening scene it is difficult to imagine,—the vulgar, blatant scoundrels! . . . May we not live long enough to see Democracy get all the power it expects!"

Traditionalists found late Victorian England in a deplorable condition that was steadily becoming worse. Some detected the origins of their troubles in the first great Reform Act, which in 1832 had redistributed seats in the House of Commons and extended the right to vote to large sections of the middle classes. Some traced the beginning of the end to 1846, when the repeal of the corn laws assaulted the special privileges of the agricultural interest and, according to embittered Tories, politicians became lackeys who did the work prescribed by the latest agitators. But all traditionalists saw their woes intensified in 1867 when the Reform Act gave the right to vote to many urban workers, and political democracy, which traditionalists equated with mobocracy, Jacobinism, and Chartism, began its official career in England.[5]

III

In 1848, the last great year of the Chartist agitation for democracy, Richard Cobden received a remarkable anonymous letter: "The Chartist Demonstration is put down—clean smothered think the Whigs. Let them take care they are not mistaken. I wonder what the Devil they take this Chartism to be. They must think it some cutaneous disease. They see the eruptions plain enough but are stone blind to the cause." Cobden's correspondent, though an acute analyst of the wretchedness that lay behind Chartism, turned out to be wrong about the future. The years following the Chartist collapse of 1848 saw no further movement of importance for the attainment of democracy. Lord John Russell's disheartening but accurate description of the political environment of the

1820s applied equally well to that of the 1850s: "the corrupt are too much interested and the people too indifferent to expect great things at present." Indeed, when a group of English democrats addressed their American counterparts, they had every reason to indulge in self-pity: "On your side of the Atlantic the interests of the multitude were not clipped and crippled by old hereditary powers. Among you all *our* principles have grown strong, which here are comparatively weak. We are proud of you as fulfilling many of our aspirations." [6]

The outlook for democracy was bleak, for both the Whigs and the Tories, as James Buchanan, the alert American minister to Britain, pointed out in 1853, were really aristocratic parties. It is true that Buchanan anticipated that the next struggle would be between democracy and aristocracy, but he wisely qualified his prediction with the remark that this conflict would probably not become serious for a long time because the working classes still viewed their superiors with awe. Richard Cobden was even more discouraged by the lack of movement in the political world. He looked eagerly for a large-scale agitation to enfranchise workers, but the painful truth was that he did not receive a single invitation in 1857 to attend a Yorkshire reform meeting. "The operatives and their employers are doing well," he wrote, "and as usual there is little political feeling." Depressed by the servility of Parliament, the lack of earnestness in public life, and the unwillingness of young men to work for political and economic reforms, Cobden— the great symbol of Victorian urbanism—spent as much time as possible in the countryside. In short, conditions had changed markedly since 1848, that unforgettable year of revolutionary hopes, when Charles Dickens, after congratulating a French friend on the overthrow of the government of Louis-Philippe and the establishment of the Second Republic, had fittingly added, "Meanwhile, we are in a queer position ourselves, with great distress in the manufacturing towns and all sorts of public bedevilments." [7]

Reformers like Cobden and his parliamentary colleagues John Bright and John Benjamin Smith were pessimistic about the prospects of a democratic suffrage in what they viewed as their wretchedly misgoverned island; but old-time Chartists despaired. Many of them had sacrificed both income and career for their political principles. Yet, had they come all the way for this? In 1859 a Halifax Chartist reported despondently that since there was no Chartist society in his town, or in any of the nearby villages, it was impossible to raise funds for reform. Many active Chartists had emigrated, and those who remained, he confessed bitterly but accurately, "have become so thoroughly disgusted at the indifference and utter inattention of the multitude to their best interests that they too are resolved to make no more sacrifices in a public cause." Chartists in other parts of the country had the same tale of working-class apathy to report. The exhilarating days of immense meetings, indescribably enthusiastic receptions, and deafening acclamations belonged to the remote Chartist past.[8]

IV

In 1865, after decades of trusting that people would calm down and stay calm, the antireform Whig, Lord Palmerston, died. Reformers, to be sure, had long looked forward to his disappearance from the political scene. "As for Palmerston," John Bright, the fiery democratic orator, wrote in 1862, "he is the last link connecting us with a past generation, and when his time is out, we shall enter on a new and I believe a better time." Once the hope became a reality, democratic reformers rejoiced openly and unashamedly that their arch opponent could no longer restrain them, and they reassured themselves that, despite the nonsense that was appearing in obituary notices, Palmerston would be forgotten in a month. "What of his doings are worth remembrance except as warnings for the future?" John Benjamin Smith, Member of Parliament for Stockport, asked John Bright. Both Smith and Bright knew the answer.[9]

But since Parliament and the country were filled with lesser Palmerstons, the prospects of democracy did not seem promising. Contemporaries, in short, found nothing inevitable about the coming of the Reform Act of 1867. "Our Reform movement advances," Bright wrote cautiously to Horace Greeley in 1866, "but we shall not see much of the future before the meeting of Parliament." Reform groups were organized, leaflets distributed, and meetings and processions held. And the public was reminded that even Bismarck's newly formed North German Confederation had a democratic suffrage. Workers were warned to conduct themselves properly in order to show that they were worthy of the position in the state that they were claiming; and they were begged to appear at demonstrations in order to prove that they were not indifferent to reform. The veteran Chartist leader, Ernest Jones—the long-tried friend of the working classes—gave countless speeches; and he was even urged to bring out a new edition of his poems because he was receiving so much publicity in the press.[10]

Yet the old apathy remained oppressive. Bright spoke and wrote enthusiastically about the great question that faced the country, and he remarked correctly that the coming session of Parliament was arousing "more political feeling than we have seen of late years." He doubted, however, that the past and the present could "be made to *slide peacefully* into the inevitable future." That was his hope, but, as he put it, "We did not make the past—and we can only partially mould the present, and prepare for the future." Bright was impressed by the obstacles in the way of the cause -particularly the unawareness of the middle classes of the extent to which they suffered from aristocratic domination. "I am not confident that anything really great and good will be done without some movement almost of a revolutionary character," he confessed. "I do not think the prospects of the country are cheerful." [11]

Many democrats shared Bright's gloom. A Gloucester reformer reported that his town was sadly backward in public spirit. He found a great deal of local party feeling but great indifference to all important issues. "I am sick of it!" he told Ernest Jones. Similarly, an official of the Liverpool branch of the National Reform League informed Jones that people were very slow to join. And a reformer from Peterborough was impressed by the desperate need for some of the old Chartist passion. All these people would not have believed it if they had been told that by September banquets would be held to celebrate the passage of the Reform Bill of 1867. It seemed far more likely that the House of Commons would continue to be elected by about one-fifth of the male population and that workers would continue to be "treated as children, fit only to be placed under the political guardianship of the wealthy." [12]

Working-class indifference to the extension of the suffrage helps to explain the bitterness of standpatters about the Reform Act of 1867. The measure was not the result of pressure exerted by a large and strong group in the country on a powerful party in Parliament. "It really is very hard that the respectable public of about 2 millions," the ultra-Tory Robert Curzon told an ultra-Tory friend, "is to be bullied by the thieves and rogues about 30 thousand in number on the false pretence of a reform bill, which is an utter humbug, being of no use or advantage to any body." Things were done in the England of 1867 that would have made Nebuchadnez-zar ashamed, scholarly Curzon insisted. Indeed, he was convinced that it had made more sense to worship the Babylonian's image than that of the brash politicians and labor leaders of the Victorian age. Thomas Carlyle was also outraged, and he released some of his fury in *Shooting Niagara*. Walt Whitman, among many others, was provoked by Carlyle to assert the virtues of democracy; but there is little evidence that anyone became convinced of a belief he had not held before.[13]

What traditionalists considered a thoroughly detestable reform bill became law because of the very type of factional fight that so many people of principle denounced in nineteenth-century Eng-lish politics. "Dizzy is pushing the Bill as hard as he can," John Benjamin Smith noted happily. Yet if Smith reported himself in a state of acute anxiety, the reason was that Disraeli's disgruntled Tory colleagues were saying, "We don't know where we are, or where we shall be, thank God there is yet the third reading to come on, when we can throw it out altogether." The old Tories failed, and they never forgave Disraeli for his degradation of the aristo-cratic dogma.[14]

V

The experiment in political democracy began in 1867, but the fear of it pervaded English life for the rest of the century, and important sections of Curzon's respectable public—regardless of party affiliation—remained unreconciled to it. They did not know that, despite the Reform Act, England would remain in many ways oligarchic and that politics would continue to be dominated largely by the class that went to Oxford and Cambridge. They did not know that as late as 1895 a large number of important towns would elect peers as mayors. Inevitably, they thought, democracy would bring such disasters as corruption, Boss Tweedism, medioc-rity, demagogy, weakness, the subversion of religion and property, and the vulgarization of morals and manners.[15]

Traditionalist fears were often hysterical, but, irrational or not, they were widely held and savagely expressed. Admit the principle of the popular will, said an ultra-Tory in 1869, and there was almost nothing to prevent a rascal of a minister like Gladstone from dissolving Parliament, promising the masses of poor voters a redistribution of property, and procuring a constant majority in the House of Commons to support his depredations. In the introduction to the second edition of *The English Constitution* (1872), Walter Bagehot, that genius among political analysts, confessed that he was terrified by the ignorant masses of the new constituencies, and with no embarrassment or self-consciousness he cautioned the aristocrats in the House of Lords and the wealthy in the House of Commons to stop quarreling and form a united front so as to keep spokesmen for the lower classes in their place. Like Bagehot, Anthony Trollope saw painful signs of the democratic influence everywhere. Fresh from reading Greville's gossipy *Memoirs* in 1875, he denounced it as a vile piece of work that reflected the disappearance of the gentlemanly spirit from the new England.

It is instructive that as late as 1884—when the suffrage was extended to agricultural workers—James Russell Lowell, American minister to Britain, felt called upon to justify democracy to an audience in Birmingham, and he did so with vigor, exposing many of the myths that had come to cluster around the word. It is no less instructive that Mark Twain, visiting England in 1897, was convinced that the enfranchisement of the masses had ruined their manners and made them "Americanly uncourteous." For Mark Twain, a hero in the democratic tradition, this was an extraordinary remark, but it was no surprise that antidemocratic George Gissing had Henry Ryecroft record in his *Private Papers* (1903): "I am no friend of the people. As a force, by which the tenor of the time is conditioned, they inspire me with distrust, with fear; as a visible multitude, they make me shrink aloof, and often move me to abhorrence." To Ryecroft—and a prominent section of the late Victorian respectable public—democracy was a national apostasy, a repudiation of the faith in which the English had achieved their greatness.[16]

The first important result of the enfranchisement of the urban working classes was the victory of the Gladstonians in the election of 1868—an election in which all the politically conscious world was interested because of the emergence of a new power in English society. "You should apply yourself to politics in these stirring times," an aged reformer fittingly advised a friend. Adherents of all political factions competed in guessing which institutions would be shaken. Many were, and the stereotype of the English was again upset. These were not people whose love of tradition and patient endurance of anything old prevented them from changing an institution. That self-styled "roaring Tory," Lord Zouche (formerly Robert Curzon), was not the only traditionalist to complain that "the Queen signs anything that Gladstone orders her to sign, without even a squeak, while he is sawing off one leg of her throne after another." [17]

The achievements of Gladstone's first Ministry (1868–74) were impressive by any standard. The Anglican Church in Ireland (the Church of Ireland) was disestablished and partially disendowed— an act that traditionalists saw as the triumph of Jacobinism and the prostration of the Church at the feet of the rabble. Irish tenants were given new rights and privileges in their economic relations with their landlords—a measure that propertied groups denounced as the victory of communism. The purchase of commissions in the army was abolished. Trade unions were given an improved legal status—a sign of that tyrannization of society by labor and the newly founded Trades Union Congress that the comfortable classes were to protest against increasingly. And the system of open voting was replaced by the secret ballot—an action that traditionalists condemned as the ruination of national character and the legalization of political cowardice, but one that reformers since the time of John Cartwright, the eighteenth-century pioneer of English democracy, had considered essential to free elections. Now it would no longer be possible to complain, in Cartwright's elegant words, about "the notoriety that the tenantry, the retail traders, the working manufacturers, and all other persons whose very bread depends on their Landlords, their Employers, or their Customers among the more wealthy classes, are liable to be ruined if they be not slavishly subservient to those on whom they so depend. . . ." [18]

Most important of all, the elementary schools were shaken up during Gladstone's first ministry, and a major step was taken in 1870 to wipe out the fiercest indictment that Cobden, Bright, and a host of educational reformers had leveled for years at the old ruling groups: that *"the masses of this country are the most illiterate of any protestant people in the world."* Other Education Acts followed, and by 1884 Florence Nightingale, thinking of workers' children now required to attend school, could go so far as to proclaim the elementary schoolmasters the most important group in the new England.[19]

VI

What Gladstone's first Ministry did to alter old institutions was bad enough to traditionalists, but other threatening movements were gaining strength during the aftermath of the Reform Act of 1867. John Stuart Mill and an ardent band of followers, obsessed with the unfavorable status of women in English society, were insisting that only political power would end female subjugation and provide security against oppression. Tiny cliques of Irish republicans—Fenians—were perpetrating acts of violence and seeking martyrdom in order to draw attention to the grievances of their countrymen. And eager groups of English republicans were proclaiming the monarchy an expensive, wasteful, inefficient, and antiquated institution without which England—like Spain and France—could manage admirably. "Rather discouraging times for thrones or Bishops!" wrote an alarmed traditionalist in 1870.[20]

Victoria, though queen for more than thirty years, had not yet become venerable, and Disraeli had not yet begun the public relations campaign that would make her one of the most profoundly loved figures in the history of the monarchy. The time was still far off when most of the population of England could say that they had been born in the reign of Queen Victoria and had never known another ruler. The Victoria of the late sixties and early seventies was still mourning the Prince Consort, and by her long retirement from public life was damaging the popularity of the Crown perhaps as much as the most profligate of her predecessors.

Professor Henry Fawcett, the economist and women's rights advocate, founded a republican association even at Cambridge, and other reformers organized societies elsewhere. The art critic William Michael Rossetti, when asked about a proposed republican journal, thought it best not to contribute, for he was an assistant secretary in the Inland Revenue Office; but he was sure that some of his friends who were "all more or less decided republicans"—

Algernon Swinburne, William Morris, William Allingham, Ford Madox Brown, and Edward Burne-Jones, among others—would support the venture. The Positivist leader, Frederic Harrison, just become a father, announced proudly that his son already exhibited marked republican traits. And the young politician, Sir Charles Dilke, having proclaimed himself a republican, was to be plagued for years afterwards with the necessity of explaining to the Queen that what he had in mind was simply a theoretical preference for republicanism in new countries.[21]

In 1871 even Walter Bagehot's *Economist* recognized the existence of a republican party, and it urged that the ideas of this new group be discussed. The fact was, however, that no single republican party existed. English republicans, though few in numbers, differed widely among themselves. Some thought a republic would do most good in a social sense; some found it desirable mainly for economic reasons; some considered it justifiable above all on political grounds; and some favored it chiefly as a prelude to religious change. But the republicans, after an initial spurt, did not win much support even among advanced reformers. And the severe illness of the Prince of Wales in 1871 put an end, for all practical purposes, to the republican agitation. "We are not Republicans yet notwithstanding the Dilkes [etc.]," wrote an ardent English monarchist, rejoicing in the loyalty to the throne evoked by the illness of the Prince. Joseph Thompson, the humanitarian and educational reformer, gave perhaps the best explanation of the failure of the republican movement. He himself believed that a republic would have more disadvantages than the English monarchy. "But whether or no," he added, "it is very unwise to agitate such a question when so many important matters need settling." [22]

Gladstone—despite what his enemies said of him—had no sympathy with the republican movement. In response to it, in fact, he became all the more impressed with the importance of the activities of the Prince of Wales. "What we want," he told the Queen's private secretary, "is not to supply him with the means of filling a certain number of hours: we should seek to give him a central aim and purpose, which may though without absorbing all his time gradually mould his mind, and colour his life." It was no accident that the future Edward VII was to become famous for his humanitarian activities.[23]

VII

The gloom among traditionalists in the years after the Reform
Act of 1867 was impenetrable—the more so because they thought
of Gladstone's Government what Disraeli had believed in 1850 of
Lord John Russell's: that it would do "anything but go out." They
viewed Gladstone as an opportunist whose politics consisted in
achieving office and not being defeated over such trivial issues as
those bearing on the survival of the Church or the State. Robert
Curzon, that inveterate traveler, was sure that England was the
least merry country in Europe: "All these reforms and improvements look bad for poor old England. What with strikes, Fenians,
reform, and other leagues, etc., there is no security left." His diag-
nosis was that England was "very rich, and gouty and shaky, and
coming near her end, with lots of quack doctors about her, which
is always a bad sign." At least one depressed country gentleman
found the debates and divisions in the House of Commons so revolting that he tried to think and read of them as little as he could.
And another depressed country gentleman, contemplating in 1869
the extinction of his family with his own death and that of an unmarried cousin, noted: "This is perhaps a small misfortune in the
general ruin that I fear impends over the heads of all the Gentlemen of England whether titled or untitled. Protestantism is abolished in Ireland, perhaps proscribed and shortly to be persecuted.
Religion in England will share the same fate. Property will next
follow. It is the inevitable course of events; and Revolution is at
hand, if it is not bloody it will be only that it is unresisted." Few
traditionalists had any sense of the amount of free, rough, and rude
treatment that the English constitution could bear. And few had
the balance or wisdom that one of their literary gods, Robert
Southey, had achieved in his last years: "We learn that the good
which we expect, or the evil which we apprehend from public
measures and great political events, generally falls far short of our
anticipations. . . ." [24]

Ernest Jones, among others, had predicted that the extension
of the suffrage would make outdoor agitation much less important
than it had been. Jones did not live long enough to see himself
proven wrong; he died in 1869 shortly after he made a speech in
Manchester announcing that he had strength for the work of re-

form that lay ahead in the House of Commons. Outdoor agitation, contrary to Jones's prediction, took on increasing importance, and Members of Parliament found themselves subjected to pressures that would have been unthinkable in the pre-democratic age. To judge by the incoming correspondence of late Victorian politicians, it would seem that almost every individual and group—and their numbers grew each year—wanted the backing of a Member of Parliament for something or other. There is particular point in what R. J. Muir, the witty Scottish novelist and school inspector, wrote in 1900 to a friend:

Lord Salisbury passed through Montrose the other day and of course I was at the station. What passed between us, you will excuse my mentioning even to you. But *this* you are at Liberty to quote as a *Fact*. The New Minister of Education is not to be.

Yours faithfully

R. J. Muir

P.S. I really forget what passed between us. I have an impression that a Railway Porter did.[25]

Reformers in the last third of the nineteenth century had enormous advantages. First, they had plenty of predecessors on whose experience to draw and from whose mistakes and wisdom to learn. Second, they had the newly enfranchised voters to whom they could appeal for the changes they favored; for the first time in English history, as an English single-taxer hopefully told Henry George in 1885, "we have a permanent majority of 1,000,000 working men on the Electorate who will judge all things from the workers' standpoint." Third, reformers could increasingly reach the new voters through the written word, for the Education Act of 1870 and subsequent legislation worked to wipe out illiteracy. Above all, however, reformers had the business cycle on their side, and this proved to be an inestimable blessing.[26]

The combination of a reform tradition, an enlarged and increasingly literate electorate, and a prolonged economic crisis made the reformers a powerful force among late Victorians—a force dedicated to transmitting a different kind of society to subsequent generations. The men of 1688 and 1788 would have been appalled by the aspirations of many of their descendants of 1888.

{ II }

THE LONG TRIAL

As members of the most advanced commercial and industrial society in the nineteenth-century world, the English people had
more experience with prosperity and depression than any of their
contemporaries. From their long familiarity with the ups and
downs of the business cycle, at least one fact emerged unmistakably: economic conditions were always changing. But the trouble
in the last part of the century was that they always seemed to be
changing for the worse. How to explain this and what to do about
it—these were disturbing questions.

In history books depressions (and wars) always come to an end.
In life, too, they always end, but with the difference that people
living through them never know how long it will take for that end
to come. In the early 1870s—during Gladstone's first Ministry—
the English were enjoying an unprecedented prosperity: "the magnitude of our riches at times makes me tremble," a humble Englishman confessed to an American economist. The one serious complaint of businessmen was that labor costs and the prices of other
sellers' products were unduly high. In 1873, however, a world economic crisis began; prices and profits started to fall and, with some
exceptions, they continued their decline almost until the end of
the century.

Judging from experience, Englishmen who lived during the
Great Depression of 1873–96 constantly expected reverse tenden-
cies to come into play. Rising prices and profits, they hoped and
thought, were imminent. Prices, as a discouraged businessman

wrote in 1878, were about as low as they could possibly go. Except for occasional slight upturns, however, prices did not increase. Nor did profits; and "profitless" became a much used word in the vocabulary of late Victorian businessmen. Indeed, to understand how contemporaries responded to the Great Depression, their conviction that economic forces would shortly correct themselves is of central importance. In the end they did, but the process took considerably longer than even the wisest economic observers anticipated.[1]

What made the depression particularly hard for businessmen to bear was the memory of the phenomenal economic growth of the early seventies. Then everything was on the increase: revenue returns, traffic on railways, clearing-house returns, bank dividends, job opportunities. Business was growing so rapidly that one entrepreneur after another ostentatiously told his correspondents that he lacked even the time to write—he was so rushed trying to keep up with orders. Reports from Lancashire stressed the healthy state of industry, and the expectation was that the commerce and manufactures of the thriving Manchester area would assume larger proportions than ever before. The Cotton Supply Association, founded in 1857 because of the fear of English dependence on American cotton and the desire to guarantee other sources of supply, announced that the time had come to end its special work. By 1873 there were even hopes of remissions of taxation. "The brilliant surplus is scented afar off," the economy-minded free trader, John Benjamin Smith, wrote to the Chancellor of the Exchequer, "and claimants are lying in wait, like beasts of prey, to pounce upon the precious carcass."

Soon a different view of the economy of the early seventies emerged: it was an unhealthy economy based on excessive production and overtrading. The get-rich-quick spirit had spoiled both capital and labor, The Economist insisted, adding that inordinate profits had encouraged a shocking recklessness that could end only in disaster. "The exceptional and inflated—unnatural—prosperity of almost all industries from about 70 to 73," wrote a well-informed peer, "is working out its results and until the poor bubbles that were floated then have burst and the consequent distress been got over, we shall not do much." The consensus of contemporaries was that over-confidence in prosperity had caused prices to rise unduly, and now they were being rectified both naturally and inevitably. Time and thrift were the great cures for what ailed the economy.[2]

II

After 1873 bankruptcy and the threat of bankruptcy became massive realities, even for well-established enterprises. "A failure at anytime of life is awful but at near 60 years of age it is worse," wrote George Burgess, a melancholy merchant who went bankrupt in 1875 after more than thirty years in the consignment business. "All our efforts are needed to keep our body and soul together," Louis Mallet, a civil servant and free trader, told an American economist. In 1876 the Manchester Chamber of Commerce anxiously pointed out that the India trade had been carried on in recent years at a bare margin of profit and that losses had been inevitable. In 1877 the disheartened chairman of the Chatterley Iron Company, Ltd., deploring the depression in the coal and iron trades during the last three years, noted that the selling price of ironstone was less than its cost of production. And a Lancashire businessman remarked ominously that in recent years few or no cotton mills had been built in any of the manufacturing towns except Oldham.[3]

If the mid-seventies were hard, the late seventies were much harder. "Here we are becoming worse than we have been," John Bright wrote to Cyrus Field, the American businessman, in August, 1877. A month later, Bright, who watched business trends more closely than perhaps any other Member of Parliament of the time, visited his home in Rochdale, and what he saw made him sick: "Trade here is terribly depressed, and mills generally are lessening their time of working." It was no consolation to international-minded Bright that the whole world economy seemed out of joint.

But even worse business conditions lay ahead. A well-placed estate agent, preparing his report for 1878, emphasized the almost unprecedented distress of the coal and iron trades and almost all other industries. American consuls in Britain found all branches of business dull and depressed. The medical celebrity and acute social observer, Dr. Elizabeth Blackwell, fresh from a trip, could not believe what she had seen: "Just think of the old mining industry of Cornwall being utterly ruined!" And *The Economist,* reviewing recent business history, summed up laconically but accurately: "1878 has been as much worse than 1877 as 1877 was worse than 1876." By 1879 earnest John Bright had every reason to tell Cyrus Field that there would be much that was unpleasant for them to talk about the next time they met. And humane Thomas Hughes was not writing fiction when he reported to an American correspondent that the English were in great trouble.[4]

For all kinds of complicated and trivial reasons there were exceptions to the general distress. As the annual report of the Scottish Provident Institution so forcefully put it: "In spite of commercial depression everywhere, we have to record a splendid year's business for 1879." Despite the exceptions, however, the Manchester Chamber of Commerce was right when in 1879 it called the depression "great, prolonged, and increasing." There was no doubt about it; the English were at last feeling the harsh effects of the growth of world production and the lag of world purchasing power.[5]

III

The gloom of the late seventies continued, with only minor interruptions, until almost the end of the century. Complaints about falling prices, shrinking profits, and unemployment were legion. Coal and iron prices were so low, the American consul in Birmingham reported in 1880, that they barely sufficed to keep the mines in operation. Everyone, he remarked, groaned about "hard times and nothing doing." An American banker, visiting London in 1882, found business entirely at a standstill. He exaggerated, of course, but it is instructive that he could make such an overstatement. A Yorkshire politician had no doubt by 1885 that the biggest single problem facing the country was unemployment. And in 1886 the Manchester Chamber of Commerce, as it had done for years, bemoaned the decline in prices and profits that had gone on for so long and gave no signs of stopping. It was easy, of course, for some relatively impartial observers to suggest that the remedy for falling prices was limited production. But few businessmen could afford to risk such an expensive solution.[6]

Though conditions improved in the late eighties, they again deteriorated in the early nineties, and the opinion was often expressed that the depression might be chronic. In 1892 the Manchester Chamber of Commerce bewailed once more "the unsatisfactory conditions of trade which have existed for so long without there being any prospect of alleviation in the future." Three years later the Chamber pronounced the coal, iron, and cotton industries hopelessly depressed, and in 1896 the president of the Macclesfield Chamber of Commerce reported the silk industry to be moving from bad to worse. In these circumstances it is no surprise that Henry Adams, having spent years studying tables of English, French, German, and American trade balances, came to some somber conclusions. Viewing the depression as a result of the increased rivalry of the capitalist countries—a rivalry that lowered the profits of both industry and capital—he predicted that this competition and the economic distress that accompanied it would continue until they produced revolution and ruin in western Europe. The decline of the relative economic position of England, Adams guessed shrewdly, meant that sooner or later the United States would have to come to her aid.[7]

IV

Late Victorian businessmen would have given almost anything for the return of the time when they could say that business was never better—the inspiring time when John Stuart Mill told Thomas Carlyle of the staggering number of railroad projects that consumed all those parts of the daily newspaper that were not filled with gossip, the exhilarating time when Richard Cobden marveled at the number of new carriages with impressive horses and attendants that crowded the streets of prosperous English towns. As each year ended, late Victorian businessmen were thankful that another year of sorrow was over. As each new year started, they trusted that brighter times were at last returning. "The beginning of 1878," reported an American consul, "found the majority of shrewd Bradford business men hopeful that the year would see a revival of business—that peace would bring prosperity—that the cloud of despondency would pass away as it always had before, leaving the commercial atmosphere clear and healthy; but I am sorry to say their too sanguine expectations have not been realized." John Bright, writing during Christmas week in 1878, acknowledged the low spirits in the country, but he added that with the coming of spring he anticipated signs of revival. In much the same spirit George Burgess, confessing how difficult to bear the last years had been, told an associate in 1879 that he expected that business would improve in the near future. Indeed, when portraits and photographs of late Victorian businessmen showed anxious and worried faces, they faithfully captured the dominant mood of their subjects—the confused victims of a baffling price and profit revolution.[8]

Statistics, though often inadequate for the period, make clear the nature of the depression, but all standard economic history books include long lists of such figures. What has been lacking is unself-conscious testimony as to the countless ways—often trivial— in which the hard times entered into the private lives of both eminent and obscure late Victorians.

The illustrations are often moving. The depression compelled young men to search for relatives who might help them to find work. It led well-wishers to hope that their friends were "prospering more than the Coal and Iron Trades." The depression discouraged a publisher from running the risk of bringing out an anthology of American poetry; and it prompted Wilkie Collins, advising Charles Dickens's relatives about an edition of his letters, to urge them to keep the price low. The depression caused the American poet and Anglophile, E. C. Stedman, visiting England in 1879, to be shocked by what he observed and to predict that in the future England would be "more of a Museum, Park, Picture Gallery, for the world at large to visit than anything else." [9]

The depression inspired a group of titled ladies, who hoped to revive the economy of Bradford, to form an association to popularize ladies' goods made of bright English wools. It compelled a longtime and dedicated director of the Manchester Chamber of Commerce to resign his office in despondency. And it led George Gissing to report in 1886, "They tell me it is a poor season; nobody has any money; no parties, etc." The depression forced proud Ouida, though she was convinced that her reputation was greater than ever, to accept sums from her publisher that she considered outrageously low. And it impelled the kind-hearted Christian Socialist, Thomas Hughes, to urge the wife of a bishop to use her influence to secure funds for poor country parsons, "the worst sufferers in these late hard times." [10]

The depression encouraged an alert journalist to vary the character sketches in his magazine by including for once a profile of an unsuccessful man—a man who at the age of seventy-five was poverty-stricken. It compelled the Dean of Salisbury to apologize for the smallness of the amount he could contribute to a worthy memorial. "The bad times have reduced my means greatly," he confessed in 1893. The depression confronted Henry Lunn, beginning his career as a travel agent, with numerous cancellations. It moved the water-colorist Augustus Hare to sell drawings to help support a home for the genteel poor. And it led a professor to remind an English publisher that the number of Scottish university students who could afford to buy books was very small.[11]

v

All classes of Englishmen through all recorded history have had two main topics of conversation: the weather and the state of their health. During the late Victorian period a third was added: the depression. There were many attempts to account for it—to set forth what Michael Davitt, the Irish land reformer and single-taxer, called *"the right causes."* But, as even such a relatively homogeneous group as the Manchester Chamber of Commerce recognized, no report on the distress could adequately present the varied views of its members.

Every explanation of the depression was a call to action, or to inaction, which is action, too. The social reformer and economist Philip H. Wicksteed, convinced that traditional political economy was fallacious because it could not account adequately for depressions, announced to Henry George in 1882 that he had been converted to the American's theories by his analysis of hard times in *Progress and Poverty*. On the other hand, Thomson Hankey, after a lifetime devoted to studying banking and finance, could not explain to his own satisfaction the universal price decline. And the conscientious economist, W. Stanley Jevons, having spent twenty years analyzing business fluctuations, thought only in 1878 that he was perhaps beginning to see light—or rather sunspots. But few of the contemporaries of Jevons and Hankey had either their scholarly humility or the disarming discretion of the American consul in Bradford who remarked that since his superiors in judgment and experience differed so widely as to the causes and cures of the depression, he could give his own opinions only with great hesitation.[12]

Nevertheless, several facts are clear. One is that throughout the period it was particularly popular to blame the ministry in power for the economic hardships of the time. This type of explanation frequently had no connection with the "sound" views that professional economists wished to make influential in practical politics; but many people—even many intelligent people—believed in ministerial interpretations of the depression, and so, though often false, they are important for an understanding of the late Victorian generation.

In the early 1870s admirers of Gladstone insisted that there was a causal relationship between the prosperity of the time and the wisdom of Liberal policies. Gladstone's enemies saw no such connection. On the contrary, they insisted that the so-called prosperity was a myth, and that the high cost of labor, meat, coal, building materials, and almost everything else—"so entirely out of all reason"—could be traced to "the action of Mr. Gladstone and his party—action which, if unchecked, will sooner or later lead to the utter ruin of our country, and the destruction of all that has preserved us from the convulsions that have at some period or other shattered the nations of Europe." The bitter estate agent who wrote these words confessed himself to be ignorant of politics, but he was unalterably convinced of the accuracy of his view of Gladstone's baneful influence on the economy; and he was not alone.[13]

The economic crisis began in 1873, and Disraeli's Conservative Ministry (1874–80) was quickly blamed for it. Tories insisted, of course, that their Government was not responsible for the hard times and that the depression was, after all, not confined to England or even Europe but was world-wide. It was simply another of those waves of depression that periodically passed over the country; it would soon end and the prosperity cycle would soon begin. This reasoning did not convince the Liberals, who saw a close connection between the economic troubles of the late seventies and the militant foreign policy of Disraeli (Lord Beaconsfield after 1876). "Trade has suffered very much during the past two years from the inconsistency—the secrecy—or the contradictions of members of the Government," John Bright wrote to Gladstone in

1877. A year later, Bright, again impressed by the anxiety in Rochdale over bad trade and unemployment, once more singled out Beaconsfield's diplomacy and its adverse effects on the economy. Similarly, the Manchester Chamber of Commerce, urging British neutrality in the war between Turkey and Russia, cautioned the Government that the commerce of Lancashire was in large measure disrupted because of the menacing character of foreign affairs. Indeed, every good Liberal, whether moderate or advanced, insisted that what the country suffered from was "the blight of the Beaconsfield curse." In the memorable words of Edwin Waugh, the popular poet of the north:

> Let England remember the days of old,
>   When the Liberal leaders ruled her,
>   Ere she squandered in bloodshed her hard-won
>   gold,
>   And a Beaconsfield be-fooled her;
> When peace and plenty went hand in hand,
>   And her toilers lived in clover,
> And the aim of those who ruled the land
>   Was justice the wide world over.
>
>   Oh, Weep for the Hour
>   Oh, Weep for the Hour,
>   When to place and power,
> The Dark Lord Beaconsfield with false vows
>   came;
>   Sweet Peace fled away,
>   With hope in dismay,
> And wept behind the clouds o'er the country's
>   shame.
>
>   Then the game began,
>   Which for six years ran,
> When every morning brought the land some
>   new foul scare;
>   And peace and plenty's room,
>   Were filled with famine, war, and gloom;
> And ruined traders clenched their hands in
>   black despair.[14]

During Gladstone's second Ministry (1880–85) the Tories returned to the attack. An unreconstructed Anglican clergyman, unable to forgive Gladstone for the disestablishment of the (Anglican) Church of Ireland, warned his compatriots that Protestantism

and prosperity were inseparable and that to support those who pandered to popery was to invite national calamity. Gladstone's Ministry wrecked everything it touched; and inevitably the lament of
depression was raised throughout the land. How long would it
take people, the clergyman wondered, to link cause and effect?
The results of a Liberal Ministry, declared the vigorous Tory Member of Parliament, Sir William Bromley Davenport, were business
disasters and an overtaxed nation. Doubtless many things contributed to the depression, Davenport conceded, but one of the chief
causes was the vicious Liberal legislation that "tended most dan-
gerously to disunite the ties which connect one class with another."
Furthermore, said Davenport, one of the main sources of the present distress lay in people's uncertainty about the future intentions
of the Gladstonians: "men walk in fear and know not what tomorrow's legislation may produce." The return of a Conservative
Ministry to power, Davenport concluded, would mean the restoration of confidence between individuals and classes and the rebirth
of prosperity.[15]

The Tory leader Lord Salisbury headed a Ministry from 1886 to
1892, and then it was the turn of the friends of Gladstone to as-
cribe England's economic woes to the enemies of Gladstone. By
the time of the election of 1892 voters were told by the Tories to
vote Conservative if they wanted trade increased, and that if they
preferred hard times to vote for Gladstone. Liberals told voters to
do the opposite. And so the process continued rhythmically until
the depression lifted by the end of the century.[16]

VI

Along with the minister who headed the government, the favorite whipping-boy of the depression generation was the foreigner.
There was, to be sure, nothing new in this. Long before the late
Victorian period some Englishmen had attributed their economic
difficulties to foreign competitors, and it is edifying that even
international-minded reformers had used the example of foreign
rivals to incite the English to greater efforts. Young Richard Cobden, writing from Saxony in 1838, suggested that the Germans
there were possibly the most industrious and thrifty people in the
world. Experts in the production of broadcloths, merinoes, lace,
silks, ginghams, and stockings, they were "rivalling and indeed

superseding us in many articles of manufacture." And as Cobden
thought of the changes in transportation and communication that
would take place increasingly in the future, he was convinced that
the English had to prepare to meet the challenge of increased competition from Continental peoples. In 1838, too, young John
Benjamin Smith drew up a petition to the House of Commons
for the Manchester Chamber of Commerce. The manufacture of
cotton goods, he pointed out, was now not only taking place in
other countries but increasing rapidly, and it would continue to
grow. With such major advantages as cheap food and the latest
models of machinery, the foreigner was already able to compete
successfully in the production of many fabrics and "even in various
instances to undersell, and thus to supersede British manufactures
in foreign markets."

More than a generation later Smith was still drawing attention
to foreign competition. When the clamor for tax reductions and
remissions was increasing during the prosperity of the early seventies, Smith urged that it was far more important to pay off the national debt. Foreign competition was growing. The United States
was turning from agriculture to the development of her coal, iron
and other resources, and her economic progress, Smith noted, was
even more extraordinary than that of England. Her energetic, en-
terprising, and rapidly growing population, the increase of her
railroad mileage, her outstanding coal deposits—equal to the sur-
face of all England—promised a phenomenal future. Already the
English Government was buying coal in the United States to supply the foreign depots of the Royal Navy because it was cheaper
than in Newcastle. In these circumstances, Smith told the Chancellor of the Exchequer, the wise economic policy was to reduce
the national debt so that the English would be in a stronger position to deal with the increased foreign competition that inevitably
awaited them.[17]

With the coming of the depression, the fear of foreign rivals
grew, and as the depression extended from year to year that fear
became more intense. Back in the twenties, Samuel Taylor Coleridge had declared it impossible for anyone to be with him for any
period and in any friendly relationship without feeling an attach-
ment for Germans. But by the time John Galsworthy published
The Man of Property (1906) vast changes had taken place. Old

Jolyon, Galsworthy's standard late Victorian patriarch, could not stand Germans, and it is revealing that he called all foreigners Germans.

It was painful for the English no longer to be able to say of people of all countries, as a patriot had said of the French in 1869, that in all useful things they were very far behind. As late as 1875, when the Sultan of Zanzibar addressed the directors of the Manchester Chamber of Commerce, he spoke the words that English businessmen loved to hear: "We are poor and you are rich; we are as children, you as grown up men in civilization; and we therefore look to you to provide the capital and to initiate the organization which shall develop the resources under our rule. . . ." But the trouble was that in the last part of the nineteenth century the counterparts of the Sultan of Zanzibar looked increasingly to people other than the English, and this was, to put it mildly, humiliating. As the American consul in Bradford shrewdly reported in 1878, "It is hard—perhaps because unpleasant—for Yorkshire merchants and manufacturers to realize that, on account of largely increased home manufacture, the demand from the United States, Germany and other Countries can never again be what it has been, and they almost feel that in manufacturing ourselves we are infringing upon their prerogative, and that in failing to buy of them we are failing to perform our bounden duty." Two years later the same consul noted with his usual perspicacity, "Any country naturally and properly fights against losing commercial supremacy and while I am not at all ready to prophesy that England is doomed to drift toward the position of Holland,—her mineral resources are too varied and great for that—still I believe that the center of commercial and financial gravity is moving westward, nor must England expect to be forever the distributing station for the world's commerce." [18]

VII

The list of the rivals of the English was ample, and it allowed room for many nationalities. A spokesman for the Manchester Ship Canal, urging the people of Salford to help to bring the project to completion, pointed out that not only the United States and Germany but France, Holland, Belgium and Austria were twenty-five years ahead of England in their canal systems. "All these places are developing their home resources, and enter the markets against us," he warned ominously. Among many others, there were frequent lamentations that the English economy was being undermined by the activities of Russians in Persia and Central Asia, Indians in China and Japan, Austrians in Rumania, Italians in Turkey, Japanese throughout East Asia, Americans in Latin America, and Frenchmen—especially with their silks—everywhere. In 1876, when Alfred Waterhouse was designing a large room for the Manchester Town Hall, he planned twenty-eight panels in each of which would be emblazoned the arms of a representative town with which Manchester had close ties; but the brutal truth was that by 1876 those towns were trading significantly with areas other than Manchester and countries other than England.

George Gissing, visiting Italy in 1889, had the impression that Continental peoples, in contrast with the English, were constantly aware of other nations in the world besides their own; but Gissing's image of his countrymen was false. If ever there was a time when the English were conscious of other nations, it was in the age of the Great Depression. It was no accident that by the early twentieth century Alfred Marshall, patriot, humanitarian, and the finest economic mind in England, described the focus of his work as "national industries in relation to international trade." [19]

Above all, it was German and American competition that frightened people in late Victorian England. With obvious pride the American vice-consul general in London sent along to Washington in 1880 an alarmist English newspaper article that emphasized the extent to which the energy and persistence of Americans were making it possible for their products to enter every market in Europe. The American consul in Birmingham, spending week ends visiting neighboring towns and country places, rejoiced to find shops filled with American products. "Canned meats, hominy in sacks, scissors and small tools, sewing machines and watches, fresh meat and salted meats, peaches and other canned fruits, and apples in barrels are to be found every where," he reported cheerfully in 1880. But he also noted grimly, "Everybody finds his income reduced; and everybody blames America for the reduction." And German consuls made a similar discovery. By the nineties the "Made in Germany" label and the photograph of the American millionaire had become powerful foci of English resentment.

It was bad enough that German and American products were supplanting English goods in the markets of the world and the colonies. Worse still, they were bulking larger and larger in Britain itself—and this in a time of severe depression. Bret Harte, American consul in Glasgow in the early 1880s, spent part of his time drawing up statements of the chief imports from the United States, and what Harte did other American and German consuls did, and the lists of articles and the statements of quantities they compiled were impressive. Germans and Americans were moving rapidly into the chemical, electrical, and other relatively new industries. And they rivaled the English in such old industries as coal, iron, and cotton, sending coal to Newcastle, iron to the Midlands, and cotton goods to Lancashire. "In all branches of machine work," an American businessman and economist insisted in 1883, "we may surely produce the cheapest goods at the highest relative wages." Solely in the handicrafts, he predicted, would Europeans continue to have advantages over Americans.

Only a few decades earlier a Member of Parliament for Bolton had proudly arranged for Lord John Russell's visit to Lancashire to include a tour of factories with machines of the newest and most improved construction. But now the most modern factories were increasingly to be found abroad. Even Sir Henry Bessemer acknowledged that the man who had done the most with his process was Andrew Carnegie; and the inventor marveled at the extent to which the United States had been enriched by Carnegie's extraordinary spirit and commercial enterprise.[20]

Reports of American and German economic and technological advances were everywhere. "We have just had a wonderful invention here called the 'Telephone,' " wrote George Gissing from Boston to his brother in England in 1876; and even Queen Victoria was impressed by this product of American mechanical skill. Cyrus Field, urging Gladstone to visit the United States, assured him that American railroads were not only comfortable but luxurious and that they made traveling a pleasure rather than a chore. W. S. Gilbert, staying in New York in 1880, was impressed that even chorus girls were paid £3 a week. William T. Stead, an inveterate reader of American magazines, reveled in their illustrations, with which the English could not compete. The manager of an English journal requested an American editor to send him patented clasp envelopes; he could not find their equals in England. The secretary of a famous English Technical and Recreative Institute took pride in his American desk, with its large number of pigeon-holes, which made it easy for him to file and find his papers. The author of *Hints to Carriage Buyers* (1893) conceded that American buggies, sulkies, and sleighs were vastly superior to English-built vehicles. Almost everyone marveled at American typewriters. Josh in Arthur Morrison's *A Child of the Jago* stole not just any clock but a nickel-plated American product. And a leading English journalist visited the United States in order to study the technical organization of its daily newspapers.[21]

VIII

In these circumstances it became increasingly a tendency for the depression generation to compare English ways unfavorably with German and American practices. As early as 1879, one outraged patriot, deploring all the talk of decay and decline, wrote to a newspaper editor: "I fear nothing so much as the sentiment of despondency, the feeling that England has passed the summit, that henceforth she is to decrease whilst others take the lead; a sentiment neither wise nor patriotic, nor founded on any wide review of our real position, nor worthy of a high-spirited Imperial race." But the continuation of the depression strengthened the defeatist spirit. "Englishmen just now [are] being rather self-depreciating and despairing—especially in industrial comparisons with us," the American bookman R. R. Bowker noted in his diary in 1880. Even the learned historian Edward A. Freeman had the impression that the United States was the only country where any money could be made.

Germans and Americans came to be regarded as economic supermen—people with fabulous drive and incredible ingenuity. They were viewed, moreover, as practical people who, unlike the English, did not make it a point of honor to object to innovations or to belittle them. Bowker, living in England in the early eighties, noted that many English manufacturers would say: "O, yes, we quite know you can do this or that better in America!" His own impression was that American machine-made products were generally cheaper and better than their English counterparts, and he rejoiced that many shops were selling American novelties.[22]

Both Englishmen and foreigners grumbled repeatedly that English businessmen were slow to get things done. The novelist Robert Murray Gilchrist complained in 1891 that it took a month to have a photograph developed and printed in Sheffield; and the American editor Albert Shaw was discouraged by the amount of time required to receive English documents in the United States. In contrast with English slowness was American speed. Bowker recorded in his diary in 1881 a story he heard of some American tourists at a hotel in Brighton. They wanted an early bath, but on Sunday the baths were not opened until 10:00 o'clock. They hastened to lease the baths from 8:00 to 10:00, publicized the new arrangement to other guests, and proceeded to make a good profit, which they contributed to the collection at church. The minister, Bowker remarked, now prayed for another invasion of Americans.[23]

"Ei komens mei 71st year," said Eizak Pitman in 1883, "under the most favorabel auspises of the Divein Providens, as tu the great and nesesari Reform which ei have been favored tu begin. . . ." But though Pitman's shorthand was winning many converts, other devices were not. The English were particularly inept in the use of one business technique that both Germans and Americans were employing with considerable skill: advertising. An American in London in 1892 complained that omnibuses were so crowded with advertisements that she had trouble finding the sign indicating their route and destination. George Gissing, on the other hand, with his profound sense of what the status of a writer should be, was horrified that a friend had consented to write advertisement-poetry for a soap company. "A nice pass this for a literary man!" he groaned. And H. S. Foxwell, the tough-minded economist, remembered proudly that he was taught as a child never to buy a product that was advertised. As late as 1917 he pointed out condescendingly, "Most of our best people never, or very rarely, advertise." [24]

The growing tendency in the age of the Great Depression was to depreciate things English and to exalt things foreign; but there were noteworthy protests. Julian Hawthorne, a perceptive American Anglophile, argued that by and large the English still had more comforts than Americans. And Lincoln Steffens, then a young American student in Germany, found Germans unbearably slow and phlegmatic, complaining that they did not get things done. Walter Crane, the socialist artist and book designer, conceded that commercialism and an eagerness for new appliances were more widespread in the United States than in England, but his impression was that Americans (because of their difficult and exhausting climate!) had less energy than the English, and nowhere in the United States did Crane find the vitality he associated with London. Fussy Mrs. Craigie, seeing an American edition of one of her novels through the press, wished that American printers would be less careless. And Rudyard Kipling, living in Vermont in the early 1890s, thought that the excess of individualism in the United States made "everything—workmanship, roads, bridges, contracts, barter and sale and so forth—all inaccurate, all slovenly, all out of plumb and untrue." In much the same spirit an obscure miner recalled that when he left England for the United States in the early twentieth century he was imbued, like most Englishmen, with the idea of English superiority in all technical matters. And as late in the history of the industrial United States as 1916, Bernard Shaw, who had had many dealings with American businessmen, proclaimed them hopeless people who "never understand anything, never return anything, never can find anything, though their filing systems are the wonder of the universe." [25]

In other spheres, too—especially the arts—the English had their outspoken defenders. Sir Arthur Sullivan was convinced that during the last half of the nineteenth century music had made such remarkable progress in England that it was no longer necessary, as in the past, for students to go abroad for technical studies. And young John Masefield, writing an introduction to the catalogue of the Wolverhampton Art and Industrial Exhibition of 1902, insisted that the artistic outlook for England had never before been so promising. Indeed, English cultural chauvinism grew markedly as English economic leadership declined.[26]

IX

"There is not a port in the world which the ships of Great Britain do not visit; *to* this island all the world pays tribute—, and *from* this island all the world receives benefits and blessings!" So wrote that ardent patriot and Benthamite, Dr. John Bowring, in the late 1830s. It is no surprise that by the late nineteenth century the world paid less tribute to England and received fewer of her economic benefits. What is surprising is that it took so long for English economic supremacy to be challenged—that Americans and Germans and other peoples were so slow to develop their

economic resources. The likelihood had existed for decades that
they would follow the English example. As Horace Greeley aptly
pointed out in a lecture on *The Crystal Palace and Its Lessons*
(1852): "America and Russia, France and Austria, Belgium and
Spain, have here their Commissioners, their Notables, their *sa-
vants*, earnestly studying the Palace and its contents, eager to carry
away something which shall be valued and useful at home." [27]

Once the United States, Germany, and other countries began
seriously to develop their resources, they could accomplish in a
short time what it had taken the English decades to do. Even Henry
Adams, a critical historian not easily impressed, found the emergence of an industrial America especially staggering. Contemplating the world of the end of the nineteenth century, he wrote: "the
greatest revolution of all seems to me to be that astounding economical upheaval which has turned America into the great financial and industrial centre of the world, from being till now a mere
colonial feeder of Europe." And by the early twentieth century the
young Austrian economist, Joseph Schumpeter, fittingly suggested
that every economist should see the United States at least once. [28]

If the English were not challenged even more than they were in
the late Victorian period, one reason was habit: so many customers
had bought English goods for so long that they preferred to continue
to buy them. Another reason was the English reputation for honesty. John Ruskin could proclaim two-thirds of English businessmen pickpockets of the worst sort; George Gissing could dismiss
English traders as persistent liars and swindlers; and young Arnold
Bennett could rejoice in a new manservant who terrified thieving
London tradesmen. But purchasers of goods all over the world insisted that they had never known businessmen as honest as the
English.

Finally, if the English did not fare worse than they did in competition with foreigners, a main reason is that they did learn—
however slowly and however great their sense of humiliation—to
draw on the experience of their rivals. There is much point in an
advertisement run by a dental surgeon of Leeds in 1876: "Mr.
Rhodes, *being in constant communication with America and the
Continent*, is enabled to supply every real improvement in ARTI-
FICIAL TEETH." [29]

⁊ III ⁊

THE NEW MASTERS

The urban working classes took on an importance during the late Victorian period that they had never before had. Their enfranchisement in 1867 made their opinions on all kinds of subjects count in a way that they had not in the past. And the Great Depression, with its severe unemployment and even more severe underemployment, focused unprecedented attention on the conditions under which workers lived. Even so, old stereotypes persisted with remarkable tenacity. To the respectable public, workers remained semi-savages—brutal, dirty, ignorant, lazy, untrustworthy. As late as 1906, the thoughtful economic historian William J. Ashley, serving on a local government committee in Birmingham, recognized that since he spent so much time with manufacturers, he had to be on guard against adopting their unflattering views of the working classes.

Anxiety over labor distress became acute by 1878. In that year Beaconsfield's humanitarian and dedicated Home Secretary, Richard Cross, requested borough officials to provide him with information concerning the extent to which labor was suffering from the depression as well as the extent to which local measures were adequate to cope with the crisis. The invaluable replies that he received left no doubt that working-class life was grim in the England of the late seventies—even by the harshest standards of the age. The mayor of Birmingham, though he thought that the amount of destitution in his town was less than in other large industrial centers, reported a great deal of poverty and distress and many cases of severe hardship. Because of the long-continued depression, wrote the mayor of Gateshead, large sections of his town's working classes had been reduced to unspeakable misery. The workers of Burnley, reported its mayor, shared in the depression that was affecting the whole country, but they were not so badly off as the people in other cotton towns such as Bolton, Blackburn, and Preston. The distress in Morpeth was the worst the mayor had ever known. The main difficulty in Wolverhampton, the town clerk noted, was that almost all industries were working at only a portion of their capacity and that even those who had work were suffering keenly from underemployment. On the other hand, the mayor of Luton anticipated that because of the interest of the Prince of Wales in the straw hat industry the town would soon be prosperous again; but most borough officials would have agreed with the statement of the mayor of Manchester that it would be hazardous to predict the probable duration of the hard times or whether they would get worse.

Yet the impressive point is that borough officials, however cautious, expected that the depression would soon end, and they informed the Home Secretary that the emergency steps they were taking would suffice. Most towns—Birmingham, Bristol, Hull, Leeds, Liverpool, Manchester, Oldham, Rochdale, and Sheffield, among others—adopted special local relief measures, and on a large scale. Barrow-in-Furness employed labor in improvement projects. Darlington provided women with sewing work and distributed bread and soup. Jarrow gave coal to the unemployed and hired workers for stonebreaking and road repairs. Manchester employed labor to clear away snow and ice. And Sheffield offered children's dinners, soup, and grocery tickets to the poor.[1]

Yet it is revealing that despite the great use that was made of local governmental aid borough officials stressed the generosity with which the wealthy contributed to special relief funds. And they fittingly praised local newspapers for playing an important part in stimulating, especially in the winter months, individual acts of benevolence. It was one thing for the well-to-do to bemoan the ordeal of the weather; they did so constantly and, whenever possible, spent the winters out of England. But it was quite another thing for the poor to complain about the weather, for they had often pawned their clothing and bedding; and winter meant that they desperately needed blankets and coats. There were, to be sure, people like the mayor of Newcastle-under-Lyme who feared running the risk of pauperizing the working classes and "of removing the natural stimulus to self-reliance, exertion, and prudence by over-readiness to assist and an undue amount of assistance." The intensity of the distress, however, kept this type of attitude in check.[2]

II

While some years during the eighties and nineties were worse than others, unemployment and underemployment remained persistent problems. As young Rudyard Kipling described the occupation of prostitute in one of his *Schoolboy Lyrics* (1881):

> It's a terrible up-hill strife,
> Like all professions—too filled.

It is unfortunate that unemployment figures for the late Victorian period are grossly inadequate. What matters, however, is that regardless of the job opportunities at any given time unemployment and underemployment were constant working-class preoccupations. In the stirring words of Edwin Waugh, the Rochdale poet, some of whose best friends were workers:

> But when a mon's honestly willin',
> And never a stroke to be had,
> And clemmin' [starving] for want of a shillin'
> No wonder that he should be sad.
> It troubles his heart to keep seein'
> His little birds feeding o' th' air,
> And it feels very hard to be deein',
> And never a mortal to care.

There were, of course, people who cared; and they worked hard at getting other people to care about the jobless. Kind-hearted Mrs. Gladstone, alarmed that England was overpopulated, tried to impress Mrs. Andrew Carnegie in 1885 with the urgency of finding temporary employment for large numbers of the poor. Asking not too subtly for funds, she wrote: "I would do anything to help these poor people who are patiently waiting for *work*. . . . They only ask for *work work*." Even self-centered Ouida came up with a solution for at least some of the jobless. Enraged by a literary critic who had insulted her, she insisted that if she were back in England she would hire some of the unemployed to give the scoundrel the beating he deserved.

Anxiety over unemployment reached a new high in the mid-eighties. An inhabitant of Preston observed that its streets were never so crowded with beggars. "Life," he lamented, "is miserable to all but the hard hearted." The English working classes were starving, Sir William Bromley Davenport declared in an election address in 1886, and he raged at the foreigners who enjoyed the work that he thought properly belonged to the English. There were so many jobless about in London in 1887 that young Helen M. Gould, daughter of the wealthy American financier, hesitated to go sightseeing. She was reassured that mounted policemen were guarding Trafalgar Square to keep demagogues from inciting the great numbers of unemployed to revolt. But much-publicized rows between the police and the unemployed did take place. It was, in fact, entirely appropriate that Edward Bellamy had the hero of his American utopian classic, *Looking Backward,* read a newspaper of 1887 which grimly decribed English labor conditions: "Great suffering among the unemployed in London. They demand work. Monster demonstration to be made. The authorities uneasy."

The uneasiness would have been even greater if there had been more workers with the spirit of John Burns. Obsessed with the injustice of unemployment, Burns noted angrily in his diary during a visit to depressed Nottingham in 1888 that women were busy at work replacing men. Deploring the extent to which his class was daily haunted by the uncertainty and insecurity of employment, he was convinced that if socialism did nothing except regularize work it would be worth fighting for. Indeed, Burns described approvingly a conversation that he had with a policeman who had abandoned his former trade because he could no longer bear the anxiety of unemployment. "His opinion based upon experience was that the poor are getting poorer, and work more precarious than ever. Apprehended serious trouble soon if depression continues." [3]

The depression persisted and so, too, did unemployment and underemployment. Plato E. Draculis, a Greek socialist in England, was so overwhelmed by working-class distress in 1891 that he considered an uprising of the poor inevitable. The Scottish clergyman and novelist S. R. Crockett, writing to his English publisher in 1893, explained that he was too busy to give much attention to his literary work, what with "mills running half time and the pit-men out." Even indefatigable John Burns could not keep up with his writing commitments. "You will be angry with me I know," he apologized to the editor of the *Nineteenth Century*, "but the necessity of me attending daily to the unemployed in my district and helping to organise the sweeping of the ice in Battersea Park which with other work has meant over 200 men employed daily and a total of 1200 employed during the frost has prevented me writing the article as I intended to do." Borough officials received innumerable special representations concerning the hard times, and Members of Parliament received petition after petition urging the need to deal with the unemployment problem.

The London unemployed acquired a particularly nasty reputation—and not only in England. Indeed, it is not without humor that when W. T. Stead described the London unemployed and the American Coxeyites as similar groups, Albert Shaw, his American colleague on the *Review of Reviews*, protested strongly. Shaw argued, although not very convincingly, that the Coxeyites were buoyant, lighthearted, and prankish, and almost not at all distressed or desperate. What above all distinguished the London unemployed, to Shaw and to many contemporaries, was their despair.[4]

III

Many late Victorian employers blamed the workers themselves for the hardships they underwent. They argued that workers—and other English consumers—constantly and thoughtlessly bought foreign goods and did not sufficiently buy English. If English consumers, who spent more than £300,000 on foreign matches in 1888, bought instead Bryant and May's products, as a widely circulated advertisement pointed out, jobs would be available for large numbers of the unemployed in East London. Arthur Morrison, noting in *A Child of the Jago* how hard it was to secure match-box work, cogently presented the same argument: "As the public-spirited manufacturers complained: people would buy Swedish matches, whereas if people would Support Home Industries and buy no matches but theirs, they would be able to order many a twopence-farthingsworth of boxes more."

In another way, too, workers were accused of playing into the hands of foreigners and bringing on hard times. By clamoring for factory legislation, they were told, they forced up production costs and drove customers away from English goods. In fact, every time new factory legislation was proposed manufacturers pointed to the much longer hours of work that existed in other countries and produced appalling statistics concerning the cheapness of foreign labor. Unless English workers wanted the depression to become even worse, they must be wary of further legislative restrictions on the length of the workday.[5]

In even more important respects workers were charged with being the authors of their economic troubles. Employers and the respectable public in general singled out labor unrest, strikes, and trade unions as among the main causes of the hard times. Their reasoning was that strikes and unions, by forcing up wages and the cost of production, made it impossible for English producers to compete with foreigners who paid cheaper wages and had a much lower cost of production. There was nothing new, to be sure, in this type of argument—nor in the answer to it. As the perceptive author of a letter to the editor of the Manchester *Chronicle* wrote as early as 1833: "It is evident that we should not be under the necessity of meeting foreign competition so extensively if we could *ourselves* consume our manufactures, and the best way we can consume them is, to give the productive classes such wages as will enable them to purchase them. At all events, to meet a foreign market out of the starvation of our own countrymen is neither founded on sound policy nor the dictates of humanity."

The high-cost-of-labor argument continued to be advanced vigorously for decades, but without the desired effect on working-class demands. Even Mortimer Grimshaw, the unsentimental agent of the National Association for the Prevention and Settlement of Strikes and Lock-Outs, acknowledged that workers simply did not read the books, pamphlets, and newspaper articles that aimed to teach them to be moderate. Grimshaw's Association, founded in the early sixties, had as its objects, therefore, not only to collect information about strikes and to prevent and settle them, but to enlighten workers, through the use of lectures, tracts, and meetings, as to the principles governing wages. "We have a settled conviction," Grimshaw hopefully told an employer in 1864, "that if we only receive fair support we will not only frustrate the deep laid schemes of Trade Unions and interested delegates but kill all 'Strikes' and confer lasting benefit upon the country at large."

The efforts of the Association were no more successful than previous attempts to counteract what employers considered to be unreasonable demands. Nevertheless, other publicists continued to urge workers to be cautious if they wished to serve their best interests. In a tract of the late sixties that aimed to demonstrate "the beauty and excellence of the divine laws governing workmen and employers" as well as the folly of all efforts to raise wages through violence and strikes, the pamphleteer warned once more that other countries were becoming nations of shopkeepers and that strikes and the high price of English labor were playing into the hands of foreign competitors.[6]

The depression helped to make the high-cost view of labor's guilt even more popular among the comfortable classes. William Lovett, the elderly working-class leader, believed in 1877 that labor spokesmen were striving in a progressive spirit to reduce class antagonisms and promote class harmony as well as prosperity; but few members of the respectable public shared his belief. Workers, they insisted, had brought the hard times on themselves. One of the clearest statements of this position came from the country gentleman and social reformer Barwick Baker. In a letter explaining the origins of the depression, he wrote to an American friend in 1877:

There were not men sufficient for the work required; they got high wages but were not satisfied, and struck for more. The masters raised the wages but also raised the prices. Your countrymen and Foreigners continued to employ us for a time but at last gave us up and our mills now give employment to each man for two or three days in the week. Our workmen are now very poor but they can't believe that trade is gone from them and they linger on hoping for "something to turn up."

By 1878 labor conditions were worse, and a marked increase in vagrancy and crime had taken place. Baker again wrote to his American friend, elaborating subtly on his explanation of the plight of the English working classes:

About 1870 there was immense commercial activity. All nations came to England for goods. The manufacturers could not get workmen enough to supply the demand, wages rose naturally, the men struck for higher wages and raised them unnaturally. The masters raised their prices and our customers naturally left us. Now the men are out of work they find that striking will not help them, they don't like to think it is their own fault, and they can't find who's fault it is, and they are poor and discontented and hence a terrible rise in petty larceny.

To Baker—and many members of the respectable public—the moral was clear: England could remain a great country only if she continued to supply other lands with industrial products, and this was possible only if she could turn out goods more cheaply than her competitors. In short, English workers had better be careful.[7]

IV

Baker was unvenomous—even kind—in his statement of labor's responsibility for the depression. So was the mayor of Maccles-field, who, noting that the silk industry and all other trades were in trouble, deplored the conflicts between capital and labor that were causing work to be sent elsewhere. But some of the contemporaries of Baker and the mayor of Macclesfield were much less restrained. At least one aristocrat, convinced that trade unions went out of their way to further ruinous struggles between masters and men, wished that he could whip a few labor leaders. And many irate witnesses before the royal commissions that looked into the causes and course of the depression expressed no less violent feelings. Such labor heroes as George Potter, Robert Applegarth, Tom Mann, and John Burns were often held up as scourges who were destroying the English economy.

During a strike of engineers, back in 1852, Charles Dickens had expressed the opinion that workers were unfortunate in their choice of leaders. "Honorable, generous, and spirited, themselves," he wrote, "they have fallen into an unlucky way of trusting their affairs to contentious men, who work them up into a state . . . and are the greatest Pests their own employers can encounter on earth." Dickens's view would have won quick approval from many middle- and upper-class late Victorians. By 1878 public-spirited John Bright, who ordinarily never hesitated to give advice to his compatriots, would not even take part in the discussion of the relations of capital and labor. "I do not know that anything but experience and perhaps suffering," he said, "will teach the working men what is their true interest in regard to their dealings with their employers." And the American consul in Bradford, pointing to the widespread strikes of the late seventies, assured the Assistant Secretary of State that the United States did not have a monopoly of the riotous elements in the world.[8]

Despite the active hostility to trade unions that marked the England of the late nineteenth century, unions enjoyed a more secure position than they had ever before had. Partly this was the result of the political rights which the working classes exercised after 1867. Partly, too, it was the result of humanitarian sympathy for underdogs and the weapons they were using to improve their condition. "Of course the men are in the right," said John Ruskin to a disciple during a strike in 1875. "The Masters have been villainous slavemasters—and their slaves are just finding out their strength." Even penny-pinching George Gissing, who scorned and feared the English working classes, contributed two shillings in a single day in 1888 at strike meetings of Bryant and May's pathetic match-girls.

Elderly J. M. Ludlow, the Christian Socialist pioneer, went so far as to insist that the most remarkable change in opinion that he had witnessed in his lifetime concerned trade unions; and he rejoiced in 1886 that he had lived long enough to see the labor leader, Henry Broadhurst, made Undersecretary of State for the Home Department—an event that would have been unthinkable a generation before. But Ludlow exaggerated the extent to which unions had won acceptance. It is true that Plato E. Draculis, noting the shocking things that happened in Greece, found it inconceivable that an English judge would upbraid the police for not having killed the unionized strikers they had been sent to put down. But as late as 1896 George Jacob Holyoake, the old-time advocate of cooperatives as a panacea, found it necessary to justify workers' combinations by pointing out that lawyers, doctors, and Anglican clergymen were, in effect, unionized. And in 1899 a member of the Amalgamated Society of Engineers insisted that the county court judge who heard his claim for workman's compensation was prejudiced against him because he was a trade unionist.

The point is that many influential late Victorians still agreed with Thomas Carlyle's description of unions as "tending Hellward (Downward let us say?) for all (that is, Towards getting more and more wages for work however done)." Even Thomas Hughes, the Christian Socialist and long-standing supporter of the working classes, complained in his old age that unions had "become so absurdly bumptious, and mischievously wrong headed" that he was almost always against them; and workers, he feared, were rapidly becoming as despotic as any king or oligarchy. Indeed, it was mainly the recently acquired political rights of workers that compelled anti-unionists to restrict their hostilities largely to words.[9]

The depression made labor leaders people to be feared, but so, too, did their own growing self-confidence. Claiming to speak for large masses of workers who now had the right to vote, they could not easily be ignored. When George Potter, founder and past president of the Trades Union Congress, requested that labor representatives be given tickets for the Queen's special Jubilee services of 1887, he proudly called attention to the importance of his position among the working classes. As unlikely a figure as Cecil Rhodes was eager to meet John Burns. "Do not be alarmed," W. T. Stead reassured Burns in 1892, "there is absolutely nothing in this beyond merely the desire which the Prime Minister of the Cape has for making the acquaintance of the most eloquent leader of the British Democracy."

There are other evidences of the new position of labor leaders in late Victorian society. In 1887 a motion was introduced before the Manchester Chamber of Commerce to permit union officials to become members. And in 1892 an Australian labor official cautioned John Burns to be wary of royal garden parties and breakfasts. "You must forgive me for thus presuming to advise you," he pathetically told Burns, "but I have lived to see so many real true men ruined by these things that I fear for all." [10]

V

If factory legislation, strikes, unions, and labor leaders were blamed in an important way for the depression, so, too, were working-class drinking habits. This was inevitable, for concern over the liquor traffic had been widespread in England for centuries and intense for decades. Gifted George Cruikshank had sought for years to use his art to make the bottle an object of abhorrence; and members of the United Kingdom Alliance and other organizations committed to the total and immediate legislative suppression of the liquor traffic had tried to arouse a sense of shame in their compatriots by pointing out that drunkenness had made Englishmen notorious among the nations of the world. Not that intemperance was a problem confined to men. It was pointless, as an official of the Catholic Total Abstinence League in Liverpool noted, to encourage men to stop spending their money on drink if their wives were free to squander it.[11]

The coming of the depression inspired the advocates of temperance to greater efforts. If funds spent on liquor were diverted to more socially desirable objects, there would be fewer periods of distress and workers would be in a better position to tide themselves over such times. "How comes the depression which exists in the cotton trade?" William Hoyle, the Manchester manufacturer, asked rhetorically in 1876. The answer was plain: excessive expenditure on drink. Anticipating a further falling off in foreign trade and intensified foreign competition, Hoyle was impressed with the importance of building up the English home market. But this could be done only if the English reduced considerably their large expenditures on liquor. As Hoyle told the members of the Manchester Chamber of Commerce in 1877, the continuing depression would end only when workers—and other classes—stopped spending such a large portion of their income on drink.

Like Hoyle, many other advocates of temperance exploited the depression to further the movement that they thought promised salvation. They constantly undertook money-raising campaigns and sought new recruits. They even tried to win over hedonistic Wilkie Collins, that self-described "miserable infirm worn-out old devil," but in a masterly letter of refusal he indicated that while he respected the sincerity of members of temperance organizations he was unable "to associate himself with the opinions which those Societies represent." Unlike Collins, many late Victorian celebrities did join the anti-drink crusade, for they saw in it a sure way to improve working-class conditions.[12]

Though the chief trait of temperance advocates was often their self-righteousness, it is a mistake to suppose that they lacked compassion and humility. Professor Leone Levi, the statistician and social investigator, prided himself on never having needed either alcohol or tobacco for his work. But he was profoundly disturbed by the numbers of people in Liverpool committed for drunkenness, and he recognized the importance of seeking accurate explanations without undue moralistic intrusions. "Is the uncertain character of employment connected with shipping, or bad dwellings, or want of the habit of saving, or what at the bottom of it? Or is it the large number of Public Houses and Beer Houses?" he asked humbly and scientifically.[13]

The omnipresence of taverns impressed almost everyone. George Eliot was not alone when she remarked bitterly in 1875, "My gall rises at the rich brewers in Parliament and out of it, who plant these poison shops for the sake of their million-making trade, while probably their families are figuring somewhere as refined philanthropists or devout evangelicals and ritualists." Impressed by the difficulty of making workers temperate, she confessed humbly that she had not found any satisfactory answer: "One moves despairingly in a circle: they can't leave off drinking till they have something else to cheer them, and they can't get a taste for that something else till they leave off drinking."

If Englishmen were disturbed by the drinking of many of their compatriots, foreigners were overwhelmed. After church services, an American clergyman called in 1879 on a Presbyterian minister in London to congratulate him on his sermon. *"His breath, as I inhaled the fumes, told a tale not to be mistaken!!!"* he noted. The same American, lunching with an English Presbyterian professor of theology in London, was outraged not only because his companion ordered stout but because he dared to offer him a drink. Another shocked American noted in his journal in 1880 that it was not unusual in England to see women "sillily intoxicated"; and even Julian Hawthorne found the amount of drinking in England astounding. The contrast with the United States was striking. There the cause of total abstinence was gaining ground, as the American showman and reformed drinker P. T. Barnum announced proudly to an English temperance leader in 1882. And since Barnum had no doubt that drinking was "the parent of nearly all the crime, poverty and misery of Great Britain," he prayed that the practice would end there soon.[14]

The energy of English temperance people in late Victorian times was staggering. In a six-month period in 1882 Charles Leach of the Gospel Temperance Union conducted or participated in Blue Ribbon Missions at which more than 130,000 people signed the pledge. "Splendid meetings and *Grand Success,*" reported another temperance agent. "My meetings are always well attended and great ~results by God's grace follow," William Dunn, the music-hall entertainer, remarked, rejoicing in the statistics of pledges he had accumulated. Salvation Army officials gave particular attention to alcoholics, and other religious groups tried to deal with the problem of drink. The Church of England Temperance Society was filled with such rabid enthusiasts that an eminent aristocrat, though he approved of the movement, refused to join owing to the violence of the language that some prominent leaders used at meetings. Even the House of Lords set up a Temperance Committee, headed by the Duke of Westminster, to examine the question.[15]

Despite the relentlessness of the friends of temperance, the drink problem remained serious. John Ruskin, always alive to suffering and pain, insisted that the oppression most common among the English was that of drunken men over their families. George Gissing, visiting the Continent in 1889, was impressed that since he left England he had not seen a drunkard. "Sufficient for the day is the whiskey whereof," the poet Ernest Dowson quipped to a drinking companion; but Dowson dreaded the day when his father and his father's foreman were away and he had to pay "obdurate and drunken iron men, all clamoring for more than their due." And as late as 1900 Florence Nightingale told some nurses that if the average London working-class mother were asked what she had fed the sick child she had brought to have examined, her answer would be that the child had had the same as the rest of the family. "Yes, often including the gin," said Miss Nightingale, appalled that this was happening in a city where good milk—of which she was a staunch advocate—could more easily be had than in the country.[16]

VI

Workers were criticized for frittering away their income on tobacco and gambling as well as liquor. And on all sides they received the advice that a Yorkshire poet gave them in 1876:

> Be industrious and honest, making progress each day,
> And waste not your earnings in a frivolous way.

Some moralists went so far as to favor stringent legislation that would make gambling a severely punished crime. As George Moore accurately and humanely remarked, however, gambling brought hope to people who were otherwise hopeless. In that masterpiece of a working-class novel, *Esther Waters,* he wrote movingly: "The dear gold came falling softly, sweetly as rain, soothing the hard lives of working folk. Lives pressed with toil lifted up and began to dream again. The dear gold was like an opiate; it wiped away memories of hardship and sorrow, it showed life in a lighter and merrier guise, and the folk laughed at their fears for the morrow and wondered how they could have thought life so hard and relentless."

Indignation over working-class drinking and gambling always reached a high point during holidays, when the industrial masses sought relief from what the author of a guide to Southport appropriately called "the monotonous and exhaustive nature of their employment." George Gissing expressed the horror of many of his comfortable contemporaries in a devastating description he wrote in 1882 of workers on a bank holiday:

[They] rush in crowds to some sweltering place, such as the Crystal Palace, and there eat and drink and quarrel themselves into stupidity. Miserable children are lugged about yelling at the top of their voices, and are beaten because they yell! Groups of hideous creatures drive wildly about the town in gigs, donkey-carts, cabbage-carts, dirt-carts, and think it enjoyment. . . . Places like Hampstead Heath and the various parks and commons are packed with screeching drunkards, one general mass of dust and heat and rage and exhaustion.

Nor was Gissing's feeling of revulsion restricted to critics of the working classes; the friends of labor were no less appalled by what happened on bank holidays. Workers, far from benefiting from them, said Plato E. Draculis, got drunk and spent any money they might have; much too often, he conceded, the day of rest ended in a police court.[17]

In *Period Piece* Gwen Raverat, of the Darwin family, recalled the many restrictions that were placed in late Victorian times on the conduct of young people of the comfortable classes. The reason was, of course, that they were supposed to set a good example for the laboring classes and help to lift them up from semi-savagery. Some of the prudery associated with Victorianism was, in fact, an attempt to civilize the lower orders—to teach them how to behave. For workers were the new masters in politics but in not much else. In the light of the image the respectable public continued to hold of them, their enfranchisement stands out all the more as a marvel.

{IV}

THE UNPEACEFUL COUNTRYSIDE

Robert Burns, engaged in a farming venture in 1788, found himself so worried and tense that his muse "degenerated into the veriest prose-wench that ever picked cinders, or followed a Tinker." Fortunately, the farmers and landowners of the late Victorian period did not, as a rule, try to write poetry. They were so "harrassed with care and anxiety"—to use Burns's words—that they would either have been unable to write at all or they would have written poems about why they abandoned agriculture.[1]

Like merchants and manufacturers, farmers and landowners of the depression generation expected the falling prices and profits of the middle and late seventies to end soon, and they frequently used equivalents of the phrase, "the depression out of which we are now emerging." Time and again their expectations were proven wrong, and the distress from which they suffered lasted until the end of the century.

What obscured the nature of the agricultural depression, especially in its early stages, was the weather. The English, of course, have for a long time excelled in jokes about their weather. Robert Curzon, with his proud upper-class bias, was sure in 1870 that the clerk of the weather was a tradesman, for he always took the side of the clothing and umbrella manufacturers against the farmers and country gentlemen. Two years later Curzon (by then Lord Zouche) reported the occurrence of an incredible event: "the Sun has come out. I write it down immediately, lest he should have gone in again." Even Gladstone—famous for many things but not for his wit—was credited in 1875 with the remark that Englishmen should never abuse their weather; they should be grateful that they had any weather at all.[2]

After a succession of bad seasons, however, the weather was no laughing matter. "We have just had one of the most destructive hail-storms I can remember. Hailstones as big as marbles!" a distraught landowner reported in 1877. "Our winter has set in earlier than usual with sudden changes and every conceivable variety of bad weather," another disheartened landowner noted in 1878. The following year was the worst of all; and estate agents submitted reports that rivaled one another in grimness: "The excessive rain has much impeded farming operations and rendered the prospects of corn crops very unpromising, wheat and oats having suffered much. The quantity and yield will, I fear, be much below the average. Pasture lands are becoming very bare on account of the cold wet weather, and feeding stock and sheep are not doing well."

R. D. Blackmore, creator of *Lorna Doone* and an enthusiastic and dedicated fruit farmer, had a particularly pitiful story to relate in 1879: "I have suffered very severely from the terrible hail, and I cannot put my loss under £100, which is no trifle in so barren a season. About 1500 squares of glass are gone; but worse than that is the damage to the small and disconsolate survivors of the fruit-crop. Pears by the thousand—and a thousand this year is as much as ten thousand sometimes—are cut in two, or excavated; I have seen some with a leaf driven into the hard flesh. Of course all even *bruised* must rot instead of ripening; so we do not know a tenth part of the mischief yet."

Nor did the mischief end in 1879. Blackmore complained in 1880 that farmers needed rain as much as the year before they had needed sun. And in 1881 Englishmen heard heartbreaking accounts of floods and diseases of sheep and cattle. Sympathetic John Ruskin, considering in 1881 the severe seasons of the last years, properly called them altogether unprecedented in his lifetime—and, as he added, he was getting old.[3]

The weather of the late seventies was so conspicuously bad that it is understandable that farmers and landowners saw it as the main cause of their troubles. Bad weather meant poor harvests; when the weather improved, they reasoned, harvests would be plentiful, and the depression would be over. As a large land-owner told a group of farmers in 1879, they should not feel despondent because of the present condition of affairs; true, they had been through several bad seasons, but nobody could seriously suppose that disastrous weather conditions would last forever.

It irritated patriotic James Russell Lowell that even poor harvests were sometimes attributed to the wicked influence of American democracy; but more often it was English governments that were blamed. First Disraeli's Conservative Ministry was abused for the bad weather—although every Tory would have been happy to have the Liberals in power forever could they have guaranteed fine seasons. Then, when Gladstone returned to office in 1880, it was his turn to be charged with the disasters that befell agriculture. To improve relations between the farming classes and the Ministry, the ordinarily unsnobbish John Bright urged Gladstone to create some baronets and knights from among people concerned with agriculture; farmers, Bright pointed out in a masterpiece of understatement, "have been taught by some that you and I and our friends are not their friends." [4]

II

Already in the seventies, some contemporaries were aware of something peculiar about the agricultural depression. In the past poor harvests had meant smaller quantities of farm products than usual and therefore higher prices. But this time poor harvests brought falling prices. The weather, in other words, was insufficient to explain the depression. If prices were declining despite the meagerness of English produce, the main reason was that foreigners, especially Americans, were delivering abundant supplies of commodities and forcing prices down. An American who visited the House of Commons in 1880 and heard a debate on the importation of American cattle could dismiss it as dull; but the subject of the debate, quite without reference to the level on which the discussion took place, was of vital interest to English farmers.

For years Americans had pointed with pride to the foods of American origin ("cheese—cheese from America") that they found in England. In 1877 an American diplomat pasted in his diary a newspaper clipping about four steamers with cargoes of food that had left the United States for Britain in a single day. "We are now feeding England to a very considerable extent," he wrote exultantly, though prematurely. But two years later John Bright reported a conversation with a former official of the Illinois Central Railroad concerning future American supplies of food to England. "Some of his facts," said Bright, "would alarm our farmers, and would not be a comfort to our landowners." [5]

The growth of railroads, the improvement of long-distance shipping, and the development of better techniques of food preservation meant inevitably that Americans and peoples in other fertile farming countries would be exporting more and more of their produce. "The importation of fresh meat is now an established thing and can be increased to almost any extent," a merchant engaged in British-American trade remarked without exaggeration in 1876. And Dr. Elizabeth Blackwell, noting in 1877 that Americans were already sending strawberries from San Francisco to New York, insisted that there must be ways of sending perishables to London in a good state of preservation and at a moderate price. There were ways, and they came into use increasingly in the last decades of the century, making possible what Sir Horace Plunkett, the Irish agricultural reformer, accurately and gracelessly called "the opening up of the world market by rapid transit and processes of refrigeration and preservation." [6]

Even when the weather improved in the eighties, the agricultural depression continued. "I can see no prospect of anything but low prices for wheat. Abundance all over the world, as far as known," wrote an alert businessman, who for years had marveled at the quantities of agricultural commodities arriving from so many distant countries and who for years had wondered what would become of English farmers. And many an estate agent apologized to his employer for not being able to present a more satisfactory balance sheet. Although mild winters encouraged hopes of brighter prospects for agriculture, the hopes were repeatedly and tragically dashed.

An American businessman exaggerated when he declared in 1882 that American competition had virtually destroyed English landlords as well as those English institutions which depended on the land, such as the Established Church and the old universities. And a Yorkshire politician also exaggerated when he spoke in 1885 of the ruin that was rapidly overwhelming the agricultural classes. But William E. Bear, a leading English writer on American agriculture, acutely related the lamentable condition of English farming to the growth of American production and competition. And officials of the British legation in Washington wisely began to show great interest in the publications of the American Bureau of Agriculture.[7]

The plight of rural England was clearly reflected in food prices. The young American intellectual John Fiske, living in London in 1883, reassured his wife that even in expensive restaurants food was inexpensive. And George Gissing, an inveterate bargain-hunter, noted delightedly in his diary in 1888: "meat and two vegetables for 8d., and really of very decent quality." Yet the low prices of the eighties went even lower in the nineties. In St. Ives, Gissing wrote in 1892, "we had a dinner: two cold joints, vegetables, apple tarts with 1/4 lb. of Cornish cream, cheese,—and all for 1/2 each." And in Birmingham Gissing found that he could manage very well with merely a shilling a day to pay for all his meals. In the light of such prices it is not strange that any farmer who heard of the book *English Farming and Why I Gave it Up* (1894) could sympathize readily with its author, Ernest Bramah. It was bad enough that he had been losing money for years; worse still, the future promised only more of the same.[8]

And so it did—at least for another few years. The landed interest was "probably in a worse position than it has ever touched in modern history," the unsentimental economist H. S. Foxwell accurately remarked in 1895. And even tired Gladstone, by then the most famous old man in England, was moved to act in behalf of one of the institutional victims of the depression. The Bodleian Library, he pointedly told his friend Andrew Carnegie in 1897, was suffering from the general distress affecting landed endowments. The University of Oxford could not help the Library much because it was a poor body, and the wealth of the colleges, Gladstone explained, had been considerably reduced by the deplorable condition of agriculture.[9]

III

The prolonged distress forced the two dominant rural classes— landowners and tenant farmers—to make unpleasant changes in their traditional way of life. Landowners liked to think that they had the right to do what they wished with their own, but the depression made it increasingly difficult for them to act as they

OUR SAVAGE TRIBES.
WAR DANCE OF FENIANS AND LAND-LEAGUERS, AND GENERAL DEFIANCE OF EVERYBODY.

Fun, June 22, 1881

liked to think. They remembered the time when they could set high standards for their tenants to meet—when they could insist on pleasant and congenial farmers who could keep men and things orderly, take advice, adopt improvements, and hold the right political and religious convictions. As late as 1877 a member of an old landowning family demanded that his tenant farmer be a member of the Church of England and preferably a Conservative in his politics.

But in the late nineteenth century it was less possible to be so particular about a farmer's qualifications. "I think I may say you knew my father as a good farmer and one that brought his children up to hard work," wrote an eager applicant for a farm in 1877; but such tenants became rarer and rarer. Landowners were happy to find almost any farmer—as long as he was honest and reliable and not given to idleness, drunkenness, and quarrels. In the years when their estate agents were announcing that they had no farm at liberty at Lady Day next, landowners could be hard to please. But as early as 1873 a perceptive estate agent informed a large landowner, "I anticipate some little difficulty in letting the two very large farms, for I find that there is not the competition for large farms which there used to be: men possessing the necessary capital preferring to invest it in commercial pursuits yielding a larger return than farming does, or, as I think ever will do again." During the depression it was increasingly hard to let farms. Falling agricultural prices made them one of the worst possible investments, and thousands of acres went out of cultivation.[10]

The complaint that rents were never worse paid was repeated frequently in the late Victorian period, and rental-book entries in the column marked arrears carried forward were often transferred to the arrears irrecoverable column. More and more the estate records of the time—with their summaries of rental totals and memoranda of alterations in rentals—were filled with the distressing item "rent reduced on revaluation." Landowners, however, were never sure how their actions would be received. One group of grateful farmers wrote touchingly to their landlord: "We, the undersigned tenants on your Woodford estate, humbly beg to present to you our sincere thanks for your kind sympathy towards us in these distressing times, in presenting us with a return of 10 per cent. on the present half-year, and pray that heaven's blessing may ever rest on you and your honorable house." But a very different kind of letter came from a disgruntled and outspoken farmer: "I thank you for what you have done for me, still I do not consider you have done anything more than was necessary to meet these bad times, and I shall feel it an injustice if you do not return me the percentage as long as this depression continues." [11]

With rents unpaid or lowered, landowners had to be cautious about their expenditures. As an estate agent politely but bluntly told his employer: "I hope you will reduce matters in 1882 so that you may see your way to be in a better financial position in time. As it is, matters are going the other way and if some reduction is not made at once, it will be a serious question in a year or two's time." Landlords cut their expenses by eliminating alterations in their country houses, entertaining less, stopping repairs on the cottages of their tenants, making fewer charitable contributions, and in countless other ways.

The income of landowners kept shrinking, but because of the depression the demands on them kept growing. Whether the times were good or bad, Little Lord Fauntleroy's grandfather had a fit when any of his tenants dared to need help. But in hard times even landowners who were kind and generous found that there were limits to what they could do. Mary Gladstone, thanking Andrew Carnegie for a donation to one of her favorite causes, remarked disappointedly that English landowners had failed to contribute. And Barwick Baker, himself a country squire, found it hard to raise money for humanitarian purposes. Landowners had been leading contributors in the past, but now, Baker feared, the future promised "probable heavy loss to all and entire ruin to many." Convinced that the ranks of the country squires were to be sadly thinned, Baker was grateful at least that his son and grandson would suffer less from the depression than most landowners, for his land was unmortgaged and he owned some property in London which he thought would probably increase in value in a generation. But he told an American friend that when she next came to visit him she would find him in a smaller house. "Alas," he added, "I fear many of our good squires will be worse off." [12]

And so they were. Some were forced to sell parts of their estates or even all of them. "What a number of fine old places have changed hands within the last three years," a large landowner noted in 1882. Because of the commercial and industrial depression from which merchants and manufacturers were suffering, however, landowners rarely received what they regarded as a satisfactory price for the land they sold. And they ran into other difficulties. An agent who drew up an advertisement for the sale of an estate strongly recommended the omission of any reference to the country family disposing of it. If this were not done, he shrewdly remarked, potential purchasers from the merchant and manufacturing class might not apply, fearing "to lay themselves open to the banter and chaff of their local associates of having aspired to leave their own for another class." [13]

The articulate old Tory, John Temple Leader, was one of many country gentlemen who grieved over the accounts he read in the newspapers of old English families which had been forced to abandon their country seats because of the hard times. By 1887 Leader feared that there was no remedy for the condition of landowners. Many of the weakest had already disappeared, and even the strongest, he suspected, would eventually vanish. "Great merchants and manufacturers, Jew and Gentile, successful speculators, and American corn, cotton, gold, silver, and oil men will take their place; perhaps, in future generations, they will take also the old family names and pretend to be descended from them."

Such was Leader's image of the future—and not at all an unusual one among late Victorian landowners. By 1894 even William T. Stead, the fearless journalist and friend of the urban underdog, was moved by the plight of "Our Splendid Paupers" and alarmed that they were in danger of being swallowed up by American millionaires like Astor and Carnegie. His strong-minded American colleague, Albert Shaw, objected to Stead's obsession with the rich Americans who were buying English property; and he reminded Stead that the invasion of England by American millionaires was minor compared with attempts of Englishmen to buy large tracts of American farmland and run them as absentee landlords. Nevertheless, after a close investigation of the condition of English landowners, Stead concluded: "The economical revolution that has been brought about by the fall in the prices of agricultural produce has been far more serious than most people imagine." [14]

IV

Landowners and farmers joined to denounce declining prices, disastrous seasons, foreign competition, labor costs, and high taxes, but there was little else on which they united. Nevertheless, rural orators constantly urged them to work together and to ignore the agitators who were trying to stir up trouble. In the present crisis, as an eminent aristocrat said in 1879, landowners and farmers should be friendly in their feelings for each other, for they would stand or fall together.

Farmers, to be sure, received countless expressions of sympathy for the losses they sustained—despite their hard work and long hours. They had suffered the most in the recent long period of unfavorable seasons and depression, many landowners conceded. Yet the trouble was that landowners tried to keep up rents as much and as long as possible, and farmers, fearing to dip into their rapidly diminishing capital, tried to force rents down as much and as soon as possible. The rents that resulted were rarely satisfactory to either. Too low, said landowners. Still too high, said farmers. And while English farmers deplored the violence that Irish peasants were using against their landlords, they longed for the low rents that the Irish were securing. Since there were, as a rule, more farms to be let in the late Victorian period than tenants seeking them, farmers were often masters of the situation. What matters, however, is that they did not think so, and they expressed their opinion often. More than one exasperated landowner suggested that his farmers would be happy only when they had the land rent-free and landlords took care of all repairs.[15]

Falling prices made it necessary for farmers to pay not only low rents but low wages as well. Again they ran into difficulties. If they were not to lose their agricultural laborers, they had to pay them wages sufficient to hold them. Farmers, in short, were squeezed, and their ideal of what economic life should be was shattered. They had to pay higher rents and wages than they could afford, and they received low prices for what they produced. "It is impossible to go on long as we are," an Essex farmer wrote in 1879. An American consul, visiting the countryside surrounding Birmingham in 1880, noted: "Everywhere I heard of farmers having become bankrupt; or of other farmers having given up their farms because they could no longer make them pay; and in many of these cases I have been told that those farmers have gone to America." By 1888 Gladstone, writing critically to Mrs. Humphry Ward about a character in her novel *Robert Elsmere,* used a revealing simile that was peculiarly late Victorian: "It is like a farmer under the agricultural difficulty who has to migrate from England and plant himself in the middle of the Sahara." [16]

John Ruskin once complained that the superintendent of his experimental community was too much concerned with the usual farmers' questions of market price. Of course, Ruskin's Guild of St. George subsidized the community, and its products were, in any case, to be sold at low prices to the poor. Unlike Ruskin's superintendent, however, the mass of English farmers had every reason to worry about prices. Their problem was to devise ways either to force them up, to keep them from declining, or to prevent their fall from ruining their lives. They were slow to adapt themselves to the depression as long as they thought of it mainly as a consequence of disastrous seasons. When improved weather failed to bring rising prices and farmers came to understand that they could not compete with foreigners in the production of certain staples, they shifted increasingly to the cultivation of crops that had fallen less in price than wheat, rye, and oats. Thomas Hughes, referring to a friend who was experimenting with fruit trees, noted approvingly, "I am sure it is the right thing to do looking to the prospects of agriculture here." And the *Farmers' Herald* and a host of other agricultural publications also encouraged farmers to raise new products.

But the process was slow and painful, and some farmers could not change their ways. As late as the end of the century John Lockwood Kipling, father of the writer, wondered why English farmers did not have the good sense of the French. Impressed by French horses, fruit, fowl, eggs, cheese, and cider, he wished his countrymen would turn more to such products. But they were "idle, extravagant, careless of small economies, ruined by a false ideal of respectability, by conceit, ignorance, and religion," he argued. Kipling, of course, failed to understand the psychological difficulties of English farmers, and so, too, did many of his contemporaries. If ever there was a time in the history of agriculture when farmers needed such rare human qualities as ingenuity, efficiency, flexibility, and a willingness to experiment, it was during the late Victorian period. It was a time that tried farmers' habits as well as their souls and pockets.[17]

V

Farmers and landowners had many opportunities to describe their hardships during the course of the governmental investigations of the agricultural depression. So, too, did agricultural laborers, but the pictures that emerged from their testimony differed markedly. Landowners and farmers insisted that of all rural classes laborers had suffered the least from the depression. Laborers and their spokesmen insisted that this was nonsense. Landowners and farmers, they argued, could afford losses much more than they could, for laborers were so poor initially that any further losses meant disaster for them. Both sides were right.

In the years before the depression there had been much discontent among farm workers because the wages they received barely kept them alive. It was to this pre-depression period that Joseph Chamberlain referred in 1903 when he remarked that laborers were still "frightened by the traditions of the old time when they were indeed on the verge of starvation." In the early seventies Joseph Arch and others formed agricultural trade unions to fight for higher wages, and their success, though limited, was a symptom of the unrest that existed in rural England.[18]

Estimates of membership in the agricultural trade unions that were organized vary; at most only a tiny portion of the total rural labor force joined. What is important is that agricultural trade unionism raised laborers' expectations of what was economically desirable and possible for them. At the same time, the spread of unionism—and the fear of its further spread—served to embitter farmer-laborer relations even more and to intensify rural unrest. Strikes, lockouts, threats, and counterthreats were the legacy of the early 1870s, and the rural community that soon found itself forced to deal with a severe and prolonged depression did not remotely resemble the one, big, happy family that lovers of country life liked to think existed. W. Harrison Ainsworth, the popular historical novelist, who was constantly looking for topics in the past that would have contemporary interest, significantly chose Wat Tyler and Ket's Rebellion as likely subjects.

The biggest item in the cost of living of laborers was food. Since food prices fell almost uninterruptedly during the Great

Depression, workers benefited—a fact that farmers and landowners harped on before governmental investigating committees. But workers were interested in wages more than prices, and while the purchasing power of their wages increased in a setting of falling prices, they insisted that their nominal wages were still absurdly low. Thomas Hardy, whose understanding of village conditions was extraordinary, wrote in *Tess of the D'Urbervilles* (1891): "The staple conversation on the farms around was on the uselessness of saving money; and smock-frocked arithmeticians, leaning on their ploughs or hoes, would enter into calculations of great nicety to prove that parish relief was a fuller provision for a man in his old age than any which could result from savings out of their wages during a whole lifetime."

What helped laborers perhaps above all in their economic bargaining was their discontent. Farmers repeatedly and often justifiably pleaded poverty; but enough dissatisfied laborers left the countryside so that those who stayed behind profited from the smaller supply of available labor and the occasional labor shortages that resulted. "This is the busiest time of the year," complained R. D. Blackmore in July, 1883, "and I have not even an under-gardener to whom I cd. trust for half a day." Blackmore's complaint was frequently repeated by other farmers in the late nineteenth century. Nevertheless, agricultural workers continued to grumble at the lowness of their wages, especially in comparison with those of urban labor, and they pointed out that they worked harder and longer and had less time off than their urban counterparts. While their real wages increased appreciably in the late Victorian period, their money wages mounted only slightly.[19]

VI

Even in the early stages of the agricultural depression there were contemporaries who recognized its connection with the commercial and industrial distress. The Tory Member of Parliament and landowner, William Bromley Davenport, often emphasized that rural England was hurt not only by the weather and foreign competition but by the depression of the towns. And Davenport was not the only rural spokesman who saw the relationship. Yet just as rural England suffered because urban England was in trouble, so urban England felt the effects of rural hardships. For English merchants and manufacturers—and their workers—became more and more dependent on the home market during the late Victorian period. English carriage-building, as a spokesman for the industry acknowledged in 1893, was feeling severely the depression of the rural community. And what he said of his business applied to almost every other enterprise.[20]

The impoverishment of farmers and landowners and the limited purchasing power of farm laborers were major urban problems as well as major rural problems. The difficulty was, however, that the new political masters, the urban workers, did not think so, and they were the people who decided the course of elections. In the bitter—and typical—words of one rural partisan: "the lowering of the franchise only adds to the power of all except those who live by the land in comparison. The towns and the never-to-be-forgotten, everlasting 'working classes' who have been so much pandered to by politicians of late years—but who are very well able to look after their own interests if fairly treated and let alone—are getting more and more influence in parliament every year." And as another disheartened agricultural spokesman put it, "And yet what can we hope from our new Electorate?"[21]

{ V }

DOING GOOD

Young John Stuart Mill, after some years of involvement in reform activities, came to the conclusion that doctrines made their way best when they were presented in relation to a subject in which the public had an immediate interest. Mill's impression was repeatedly confirmed in the England of the late nineteenth century. With large sections of the population—businessmen, urban workers, and the rural classes—deeply concerned over the Great Depression, reformers had circumstances on their side as they pressed for the changes they favored.

During an earlier economic crisis Richard Cobden had wisely observed that "we all find fault with something or somebody when we are in distress and difficulty." The fault-finding that Cobden referred to flourished luxuriantly during the late Victorian depression. "The unfortunate condition of England's trade is so continually reviving old questions and theories, or bringing new ones to the front, that an almost weekly comment is necessary to keep pace with events," the alert American consul in Bradford pointed out in 1879. "It is astonishing what a movement is abroad, preparing for the new advent of Christianity—the selfish and luxurious are shaking in their shoes," Dr. Elizabeth Blackwell wrote ecstatically in 1884. "All sorts of empirical remedies are being put forward," an English disciple of Henry George informed his master two years later, and many of them, he correctly added, were making remarkable headway. Strongly urging George to visit England, he suggested that the single-tax leader plan lectures on such topical themes as why men starve, why work is scarce, the tariff question, and the coming revolution. Similarly, John Stuart Mill's stepdaughter, Helen Taylor, never more hopeful about the course of public affairs, remarked in 1890 that so many reform movements were flourishing that she felt herself to be living in one of the great ages—an age when a remarkable quickening of conscience was taking place.[1]

Some reformers, to be sure, had been actively agitating long before the depression began, and they found in the prolonged hard times further justification for the changes they favored. But the point is that never since the Puritan Revolution had such an intensive reexamination of the structure and processes of English society taken place. And never before did humanitarianism thrive to such an extent. By the end of the century George Gissing, with his scorn of the masses, feared that the English were in "danger of losing all that was best in the old regime whilst fostering thoughtlessly all manner of evils disguised beneath the humanitarian spirit of the new." On the other hand, Sir Walter Besant, the humanitarian novelist, rejoiced that when future historians studied the reformers of late Victorian England they would view them as worthy of favorable comparison with the *philosophes* of prerevolutionary France.[2]

II

It is impossible to estimate how many reformers there were in late nineteenth-century England, but what matters is not so much their number as their extraordinary quality. An aged reformer, justly proud that his life had spanned the age of Dickens, Cobden, Bright, Gladstone, and Ruskin, wrote deferentially and movingly in 1897: "I am often impressed with the thought of the many good and great men who have lived since I saw the light, and what an honour it is to have been their contemporary—a dim unknown unit among the crowd above which they towered so grandly." And another respectful and thoughtful reformer, noting in 1902 that the English had recently had such giants to speak to them as Ruskin, Arnold, Mill, Carlyle, Spencer, Browning, Huxley, Darwin, Bradlaugh, Bright, and Gladstone, had every reason to doubt that the twentieth century could possibly compare favorably with the nineteenth.[3]

Reformers, to be sure, differed widely in their aims. But they had one main characteristic in common: they were people whose desire to be useful members of society amounted to a compulsion. Like John Bright, they thought it their duty to point the way for voters and Parliament to follow; and, like Matthew Arnold, they believed in the importance of advancing even several steps in the proper direction. Few of them would have gone so far as John Stuart Mill when he argued in 1867 that reformers were obligated to struggle to advance *every* opinion that they held deeply. Certainly, however, their favorite expression was "to do good." And, like Thomas Carlyle and the author of a poem in memory of the great crusading journalist William Cobbett, they had faith in the power of the earnest and dedicated individual to accomplish much:

> Then learn, ye Many, from this master-mind—
> Whose boast it was, from you to take its rise—
> What true Sincerity may sacrifice
>   For humankind;
> What GOOD may by a single hand be done,
>   What GLORIES may be won! [4]

Disenchanted George Gissing had Henry Ryecroft prize as a virtue his ability to live solely for his own satisfaction and not to worry about the world. But to reformers this attitude was the height of irresponsibility, and they worked constantly to combat it. Like Arnold Toynbee—whose early death in 1883 was a serious loss to many causes—they had a passion for the common people and for their material and moral improvement. Indeed, in the tradition of William Cobbett, reformers were forever hunting down oppressors. "You are always at work either smiting the guilty or vindicating innocence," a politician fittingly teased W. T. Stead.[5]

Moved by a sense of the hardness of life for large sections of the late Victorian population, reformers had to communicate their awareness to others. "The misery of the masses weighs upon me," Dr. Blackwell confessed, adding that she had no choice but to work for the remedy she saw in Christian Socialism. Even the cynical novelist, R. Murray Gilchrist, referring to a relative whom he dreaded to visit, explained, "He always struggles (vainly) to raise my moral tone and to excite me into emulation of such strange spirits as Mrs. Beecher Stowe, etc., etc., who work for the world's good." Naturally, Gilchrist always hoped that his cousin would be out when he called on him.

But reformers did not permit themselves to be easily avoided: they needed to do good and to arouse others to good works. "You know my passionate fad for making people happy—even by main force," wrote the creator of Little Lord Fauntleroy, Frances Hodgson Burnett; but any number of reformers could have written the same words. For, compared with helping to improve the conditions of the downtrodden, they viewed most activities in life as unworthy of serious attention. It was symptomatic that, when Florence Nightingale told a friend that nobody had ever received a finer Christmas present than the one he had sent her, she was referring to a series of maps that she could use in her campaign to promote better public health measures for India.[6]

Reformers were not easily satisfied. Like Thomas Clarkson in the years of the antislavery agitation, they were endlessly aware of how much remained to be done. A friend noted in 1875 that George Jacob Holyoake, though sick and old, was still determined to serve the cause of social reform; a generation later—in 1904— Holyoake was as determined as ever. And in 1877 John Bright fittingly congratulated Edward West, the veteran free trader, for the great interest he continued to take in great public questions. George Cruikshank, always eager to agitate for temperance and education, was a frequent attendant at meetings of humanitarians even as an octogenarian. And Vansittart Neale, the Christian Socialist advocate of cooperatives, devoted himself absolutely and endlessly to what he considered the greatest cause of the age. In these circumstances, it is not strange that John Galsworthy had a late Victorian character in The Man of Property complain that the country was eaten up with sentimental humanitarianism. Nor is it strange that antireformers often deplored the growth of what they regarded as a morbid propensity for doing good.[7]

III

The biggest single influence that made people reformers in the late Victorian period was still religion. As in the time of the prison reformer John Howard—"My Hope is in Christ"—and the anti- slavery crusader William Wilberforce—"May the Almighty direct us right"—the religious and the reform impulses still went closely together. To function as a reformer was to do God's work in this world and to expose and correct abuses that were unpleasing to Him. Indeed, many of the leading late Victorian reformers were clergymen or devout laymen, whose activities cannot be understood except in the light of their ideal of service to God; they were engaged in holy causes. Florence Nightingale, though far from orthodox in her religious views, significantly thought of Christ as the father of the nursing profession. Barwick Baker, thankful for his successes as a penal reformer, declared after the fashion of Mrs. Harriet Beecher Stowe that they were God's victories, not his. Arnold Toynbee always insisted that a religious regeneration had to form the basis of any permanent social reformation, and so did Henry George and his British followers. "Once, in daylight, and in a city street, there came to me a thought, a vision, a call—give it what name you please," George confided to his Irish disciple, Father Dawson. That was the beginning of *Progress and Poverty;* and, since the publication of the book, George added, the feeling had never left him that the fate of his work was in the hands of God. In much the same spirit W. T. Stead confessed that it was during church services that he often received his inspiration for a new crusade against injustice. In fact, it was typical of Stead's thinking that when in 1888 he consoled Mrs. John Burns, whose socialist husband had been imprisoned, he wished her "God speed in the name of our Lord who like your husband suffered for the cause of our brethren." No doubt about it, late Victorian reformers were endlessly turning to God for guidance as to the next steps to be taken; and progress had meaning for them, as for Gladstone, only in the framework of Christianity.[8]

In combination with religion, family influence and tradition had much to do with making people reformers. Many had been reared by parents who upheld humane standards and values similar to those which the mother of Little Lord Fauntleroy preached: "only be good, dear, only be brave, only be kind and true always, and then you will never hurt any one, so long as you live, and you may help many, and the big world may be better because my little child was born. And that is best of all, Ceddie,

—it is better than everything else, that the world should be a little better because a man has lived—even ever so little better, dearest."

There are countless real-life illustrations of the role the family played in fostering the reform impulse. Mrs. Josephine Butler, eager for her children to meet William Lloyd Garrison, told the American abolitionist in 1877: "I so deeply desire that they all three should embrace the cause of humanity and labour for it." Barwick Baker, apologizing for his strong sense of family pride, promised an American friend that when she came to England he would show her portraits of his ancestors and tell her of what each had done in the service of humanity. "Looking round at them, I was bound to *try* to do something," Baker humbly remarked— the more so, he added, because it had pleased God to give him an unusually long life. But just as Baker's family conditioned him to do good, so the families of many other reformers prepared them to adopt causes. Helen Taylor, like her stepfather, John Stuart Mill, worked actively as a reformer. And so did members of the Arnold family. Even self-immersed Ernest Dowson, fresh from reading a book by Mrs. Humphry Ward, was struck by the dedication and passionate seriousness of the Arnolds.[9]

Reformers, by doing what they did, tried to make peace not only with God and their families but with themselves, for unless they were working for what they regarded as progress, they found life barren. Humanitarian activities provided reformers with a sense of purpose and direction. "Depend upon it," George Gissing advised his sisters, "there is nothing like forgetting oneself and working for the good of others. It is the only way to be happy."

Gissing did not follow his own prescription, but many reformers kept discovering it independently. To be happy they needed the reassurance that they were improving the welfare of others. "The complacency I have in being liked and the pleasure of being useful," John Ruskin wrote in 1875, "are the chief things now left to me as the strength of life diminishes." A year later Ruskin, confessing to his tremendous need for affection, told a young admirer, "Oh me, if I only could come to be petted every day. But then one wouldn't be a martyr and a reformer." Ruskin may have analyzed himself—and some others—correctly; but there were many reformers who, having had the love that Ruskin lacked, felt all the more profoundly the need to come to the aid of the downtrodden.[10]

IV

Reformers were so convinced that their views were correct that they tended to be impatient of opposition. When Thomas Hughes said of one of his reform proposals that no one could examine it without concluding that it was absolutely right, he spoke not only for himself but for a generation of reformers who had few, if any, doubts about what should be done. Cardinal Manning, discouraged by the slow progress of the campaign to secure pure water for London, consoled himself and other reformers with the thought that old countries, like old men and old wagons, moved sluggishly. But Manning's patience was not typical. Reformers were rarely willing to follow the traditional advice about making haste slowly; they found it hard to learn how to wait and work to overcome their opponents' dread of the consequences of precipitate measures. Indeed, reformers devoted much of their time to trying to prove that their demands for change were eminently reasonable, that their opponents were irrational, and that the new steps they urged were thoroughly English and had ample precedents in English history. "There is nothing," said a perceptive advanced Liberal, "like showing the Englishman and Scotsman, that *it is done* and is not 'out of your head.' " [11]

Nathaniel Hawthorne, serving as American consul in Liverpool, was infuriated by the reports he received of the activities of American abolitionists. In an unusually harsh letter to one of the antislavery crusaders, he wrote angrily and profoundly in 1857: "I do assure you that, like every other Abolitionist, you look at matters with an awful squint, which distorts everything within your line of vision; and it is queer, though natural, that you think everybody squints except yourselves. Perhaps they do; but certainly *you* do." What Hawthorne thought of abolitionists antireformers thought of reformers. They viewed them as eccentrics and cranks who were plotting mischief against the welfare of society and hatching schemes against the public peace. "All my life long," W. T. Stead confessed with his usual candor, "I have been told that I am lacking in stability." In fact, the more desirable the reform he proposed, the more emphatic was the charge that he had been seized by the devil or gone insane.[12]

Stead himself had an affinity for what he affectionately called "cranks of all sorts." In general, however, reformers were highly sensitive about being called unstable or eccentric or being ranked with the cranks. Yet this did not restrain them from dismissing as unstable those reformers with whom they disagreed. "The man is mad evidently," said Mrs. Josephine Butler of a temperance reformer who linked rheumatism with drink. Erratic Sir William Harcourt meant well, Barwick Baker conceded of Gladstone's Home Secretary, but his rashness and thoughtlessness were dangerous; for, if he saw or fancied an evil, he rushed to eradicate it, without thinking about what would replace it.

While Stead and others often urged reformers to cooperate, their words were conspicuously wasted. One of the leading accusations against bimetallists was that no two of them agreed on any point. This was an exaggeration, of course, but it had an unmistakable element of truth. Even Auguste Comte's English followers—the Positivists—were badly split. Richard Congreve, one of their leaders, could insist that the forces making for unity among them were so great that even their blunders did not matter. And when a number of them became enthusiastic vegetarians, another leader could urge the desirability of permitting many such little divergences. But some of the differences that developed were not little. When in 1888 several disciples planned to publish a statement of the Positivist creed, Professor Beesly and others refused to endorse it. Not that Positivists confined their antagonisms to their countrymen; they also fought angrily with their colleagues in France. All the while hostile outsiders sneered at their divisions—and ridiculed them as eccentrics.[13]

Most reformers had some particular cause to which they gave priority, and they were constantly distressed that what took first place with them did not assume the same place with politicians. England's foreign and imperial involvements particularly vexed the reformers. "I hope," said the determined women's rights advocate Mrs. Josephine Butler in 1879, "there is no chance of this horrid Zulu War occupying all the evenings for Debate and putting off this Question and others." And Henry George and his followers were chronically upset by English embroilments in foreign affairs. Determined that politics should be more than a struggle for place, they wanted—by focusing on land reform—"to project a blast of common sense into the unreal atmosphere." Yet just as reformers resented the parliamentary hours given to foreign and imperial policy, so they begrudged the time the Irish question consumed during the late Victorian years. Longing for a non-Irish session, some of them were willing to make almost any concessions in order to make sure that the other island would no longer divert attention from domestic English reforms.[14]

V

The energy of the reformers was one of their main sources of strength. Florence Nightingale, that specialist in overwork, justly remarked in 1895 that for some forty years she had not known the meaning of leisure. And what Miss Nightingale said any number of reformers could have said with equal justice. Dr. Thomas Barnardo, crusading fiercely for the establishment of homes for orphaned and destitute children, was indefatigable. "Till lately," Thomas Hughes noted in 1877, "I have been able with impunity to run down in the morning to a northern town, speak or lecture and run back by night to work in the morning without feeling the strain." Emily Faithfull, the aptly named philanthropist, had so much to do that her pen was always in her hand. "It is my business," said the Positivist Frederic Harrison, "to teach our doctrines in season and out of season," and Harrison rarely lost sight of his business. Nor did that other leading Positivist Richard Congreve, who was constantly exhausted from overwork. Indeed, a member of the staff of the *Review of Reviews*, having cautioned W. T. Stead that he desperately needed a rest, knew that he was giving advice in vain: Stead would soon be off on some new crusade.[15]

In addition to energy, reformers had the ability to concentrate on their commitments. "We who know what we want have a big advantage over the folks that don't," Henry George rightly remarked during one of his English campaigns. "Strive on then," Barwick Baker advised a disenchanted American reformer, "strive on with your noble work and don't feel discouraged; though things may be bad at present they are not so bad as our case was a century ago and we had been enduring it for a thousand years." Indeed, reformers often believed that the same admirable results would flow from their efforts that Darwin and his fellow-scientists thought would come from theirs.[16]

Ernest Dowson, chronically disgusted with life in general and in particular with life in his "Protestant, respectable, democratic, hopelessly inartistic country," remarked to a friend, "I suppose certain lucky people aren't so constantly conscious of the general futility of things." Among the fortunate people to whom Dowson referred reformers figured prominently. With minds neatly packed with settled convictions, they could work, with a minimum of self-doubt, for the changes they favored. In fact, much of their importance and influence grew directly out of their vigorous anti-futilitarianism. James Thomson, the morose author of *The City of Dreadful Night,* could doubt that all the efforts of the reformers "availed much against the primeval curse of our existence." George Moore could ridicule the democratic orator who promised "poor human nature unconditional deliverance from evil." And Thomas Hardy could never escape from the conviction that regardless of what humanity tried to do "there remains the stumbling block that nature herself is absolutely indifferent to justice and how to instruct nature is rather a large problem." Reformers, however, viewed such utterances as unwarranted surrenders to pessimism. Certain that the human lot could be considerably improved, they dismissed as unfounded statements of despair concerning man's fate, and they made one of their main sources of strength and power out of what futilitarians considered their softness.[17]

To be sure, reformers grumbled constantly about the indifference against which they had to contend, and they were repeatedly shocked by the ability of many of their countrymen to resign themselves to conditions that they found appalling and to accept injustices that they considered outrageous. They wanted to be able to shout that all England demanded this or that reform, that there was a madness in the country for this or that measure. But while they rarely had difficulty in gaining support for Polish and Jewish victims of Russian persecution, American freedmen, or sufferers from a disaster like the Chicago fire, they often found it hard to win sympathy for Englishmen in distress. "Blessed are they who expect nothing; they shall never be disappointed," W. T. Stead wrote bitterly in a moment of discouragement. And all reformers at one time or another reacted similarly, complaining that their difficulty was less wrong-headedness than inattention and indifference. "The most terrible thing about unjust social enactments," Henry George wisely remarked, "is not the physical suffering they cause, but the mental and moral degradation they produce."

As a rule, however, late Victorian reformers had remarkable powers of recuperation; and mass indifference, far from stopping them, inspired them to even greater efforts. Compared with earlier reformers, moreover, they had an easy time of it. The growing literacy of the population, the extension of the suffrage, and the prolonged depression were weapons that they put to effective use.[18]

VI

There was nothing new about the chief methods late Victorian reformers employed to draw attention to the changes they urged. They formed societies; they made indoor and outdoor speeches; they wrote articles, pamphlets, and books; they sought publicity in the press; they curried the favor of rich people who could finance their activities; they tried to win converts among clergymen, writers, journalists, women with leisure, and energetic young people; and they brought pressure to bear on politicians and governmental investigating committees. While their methods were not remarkable, the scale on which they applied them was.

Reformers were, on the whole, great joiners, but there were notable exceptions. Thomas Carlyle thought societies produced "nothing but fun, dinner-oratory, newspaper-puffery, under various figures—wind." Florence Nightingale avoided reform organizations—even at the risk of offending John Stuart Mill. And Leslie Stephen prided himself on not being "an associable animal." Yet the proliferation of organizations during the late nineteenth century—Thomas Hughes belonged to so many that in 1868 he felt obliged to refuse to give his name to any more—demonstrates how eager reformers were not to stand alone. Almost invariably their societies were tiny, and frequently they were short-lived. But they tried to create the impression that they spoke for vast numbers of people. And they testified to the belief of reformers that by concerted action they could accomplish much.[19]

Reform organizations promoted their views through a large-scale use of public lectures and meetings. Already in 1869 the inhabitants of the parish of St. Martin-in-the-Fields called attention to the annoyances to which they were exposed by meetings in Trafalgar Square. Unfortunately for the complainants, however, conditions in the Square were idyllically quiet in 1869 compared to what they became during the course of the late Victorian period. And what was true of London was equally true of other towns, many of which had their lively counterparts of Trafalgar Square and Hyde Park.

Reformers had a faith in speech-making that was often pathetic. For few of them had the oratorical gifts of a Charles Bradlaugh or a Mrs. Annie Besant—the gifts that young Winston Churchill considered to be so rare, so precious and so impossible to acquire. Yet the semi-literacy of the working classes left reformers little choice. "Speaking and talking—talking and speaking until there was nothing left of him but a cough," a friend said of W. T. Stead in 1893; but the remark applied to many others. If reformers often exaggerated the attention and interest span of their listeners, the main reason was doubtless that they had to think that others were as earnest and committed as they. Self-critical Bret Harte, delivering speeches in Britain, could be devastating in his comments on his audience: "Young ladies and gentlemen flirted openly—taking the lecture as an occasion. It was only by staring respectfully but ardently at the best looking, that I got any attention. Everybody, however,—particularly them who hadn't listened—told me afterwards that it was a good lecture." For reformers, however, Harte's brutal realism was impossible: lecturing helped them to think that they were accomplishing something.[20]

The difficulties that middle-class reformers had in reaching working-class audiences were much less pronounced when they wrote for them than when they spoke to them. Indeed, it is not odd that the literature of reform in the late nineteenth century is filled with masterpiece after masterpiece of clear, simple, and direct prose. Reformers worked so hard at form because they cared so much about content. "You are dreadfully difficult to understand; and that is really a sin," Carlyle once told Robert Browning. And reformers showed in their prose their agreement with Carlyle's strong views on clarity. To be understood was their aim, and repetition was their favorite literary device. Barwick Baker, sending a friend some papers on penal reform, explained that since he was not one of those who could strike a powerful blow that would worry his countrymen into attention, he devoted himself to a perpetual hammering and steady boring—repeating the same ideas tirelessly and tiresomely. Baker's conclusion was that his writings showed how donkey-like persistence "may have effect in eight or ten years where the far greater power of a clever man, if not carried on, would fail." [21]

For all their efforts to gain the widest possible audience, late Victorian reformers, like those of the predemocratic age, still concentrated mainly on winning the support of the opinion-leaders of society. "I have an idea that extension of social acquaintance is not without its uses to our cause," said the American Minister to Britain during the Civil War. And just as Charles Francis Adams visited country houses with an ulterior motive, so, too, did reformers. Their method was admirably summed up in the title of a pamphlet by the clergyman G. W. Bower: *An Address Chiefly Directed to Those Who Occupy Influential Stations in Life.*

Richard Cobden had guessed in 1852 that 800,000 was a generous estimate of the number of people who were vitally interested in public affairs. To what extent this figure—if correct—grew by the end of the century, it is impossible to determine, but the point is that reformers directed their efforts above all at this section of the population. Thoughtful people, John Bright once complained, were a small minority in every country; and it was the thoughtful people, despite the smallness of their number, whom reformers tried to convert. The veteran Christian Socialist Charles Kingsley, appalled in 1872 by the scenes of dissipation at the Chester races, told an eminent aristocrat: "These matters are not to be set right by a profligate Press, and noisy public meetings, but by honest Gentlemen taking counsel from, and with, each other." [22]

Nor was Kingsley's an isolated attitude. For two generations Florence Nightingale excelled in winning over the élite to reform. "Please you who see everybody and who have already done so much for us, make the Blue Book known as much as possible," she begged an aristocrat in her enthusiasm for some public health measure. "If I had twenty copies," she told the author of a paper on hospital reform about which she felt deeply, "I could place them well—abroad and at home." In much the same spirit, when Barwick Baker came upon a publication of which he strongly approved, he distributed it among the "men of weight" whom he knew. Henry George went out of his way to see that British celebrities received copies of his writings, and he met as many of them as he could during his visits. Similarly, W. T. Stead tried to reach what an associate called "every conceivable person of any note," and so did the fervent bimetallist Moreton Frewen.[23]

VIII

In an outburst of enthusiasm, Dr. Elizabeth Blackwell argued in 1883 that money was "the smallest item in reform," but she exaggerated, to put it mildly. Certainly reformers wanted the prestige that went with the names of the rich, hoping that they would make more respectable the particular reforms they urged. Thus Thomas Hughes, encouraging a wealthy aristocrat to become a member of the Cooperative Guild in 1877, recognized the desirability of getting "some ballast in from above." But it was not simply prestige that reformers sought. Nearly all the time they desperately needed financial aid, and so they hunted endlessly for rich and open-handed converts. It is true that W. T. Stead often complained to Andrew Carnegie that the wealthy were rarely receptive to new ideas. But Stead diligently searched for exceptions, and he found them in Carnegie himself and Cecil Rhodes. Still Stead kept looking, for there was no end to the reforms he thought necessary. Obsessed during the Boer War (1899–1902) with the need to further the arbitration of international disputes, he urged an American colleague at the Hague Conference to watch for "millionaires running round loose." It was inevitable, of course, that Andrew Carnegie, a constant visitor to Britain, should be a favorite target of reformers. Even the young socialist, H. G. Wells, sent him a copy of the new edition of *Anticipations* (1902) in the hope that Carnegie might speed up the coming of the world of the future.[24]

Reformers played constantly on the guilt feelings that they

thought the rich had or ought to have. Little Lord Fauntleroy's mother reminded him repeatedly that the wealthy must always remember the poor. And reformers preached the same message. As proselytizing Professor Benjamin Jowett told George Eliot, herself a generous contributor to humanitarian causes, every businessman should amass a fortune and then use it for noble purposes. And as a minor poet expressed the thought in a Christmas annual:

> O rich one in your happy home,
> Think of the poor who houseless roam.

Indeed, if the wealthy recognized their responsibilities, reformers told them often, they would have a future and the social problem would no longer threaten to engulf them. "We are the guardians of Property, both against selfish plutocrats, and revolutionary levellers, who alike imperil it," an ardent Positivist said bluntly.[25]

Nor is there any doubt about the success of many of the appeals that reformers made. "It is a saving feature in modern society that the rich are taking a greatly increased personal interest in the poor," said a toughminded Tory Member of Parliament in 1883. "There has been no period of time in which wealth has been more sensible of its duties than now," James Russell Lowell insisted in Birmingham a year later. Gladstone vigorously endorsed Andrew Carnegie's gospel of wealth, and he hoped that many monied people would adopt it and learn to disgorge with as much gallantry and enlightenment as his friend. Indeed, Frederic Harrison teased Carnegie about the rate at which he was distributing his wealth to worthy causes, suggesting that he would soon not have enough left to give his friends a meal or a drink.[26]

Reformers sought converts not only among the rich but among energetic, enthusiastic, and idealistic young people and leisured women who had the time to devote to causes. Above all, however, they besieged journalists, writers, clergymen, and politicians. These were the chief opinion-makers in late Victorian society— the men of weight whom reformers had in mind when, like Carlyle, they declared that agitators were needed. For these opinion-leaders, by the nature of their occupations, had access to large numbers of voters; and they often had it in their power to decide how much and how fast reform was to take place. They could make noise; they could stir up issues and keep them alive; and they could translate talk into action.[27]

❧ VI ❧

ABIDING INFLUENCES

Reformers owed much to their religious and family backgrounds; but they were also products of what they had read. And, having been shaped in many instances by earlier writer-reformers who had felt profoundly the burdens of society, they tried to do for their generation what their predecessors had accomplished for theirs. By far the most influential of these earlier writer-reformers were Thomas Carlyle and John Ruskin; and to trace their impact in any detail would be to write an elaborate intellectual history of late Victorian England.

Carlyle and Ruskin were important not so much for any of their specific ideas. Their importance lay, above all, in their unlimited capacity for moral indignation. Not only angry men but very angry men, they communicated to their followers the sense that to be worthy of the status of a human being a person had to be outraged by unjust institutions and practices. "God help a generation of men bred on Macaulay and a generation of women on Miss Strickland" (the conservative writer of popular histories), moaned a discouraged mid-Victorian reformer. By the end of the century antireformers had reason to repeat the invocation, but to substitute the names of Carlyle and Ruskin for those of Macaulay and the much maligned Agnes Strickland.

Carlyle, to be sure, belittled reading, insisting that the silences and actions that the contemplation of nature stimulated in man were better for him than all the books ever written. And Ruskin strongly urged at least one undergraduate not to waste time reading his writings or even those of Carlyle. To reformers in late Victorian England, however, life without the works and words of Carlyle and Ruskin to draw upon would have been unthinkable. Just as no economist could adequately estimate his indebtedness to Adam Smith and David Ricardo, so no reformer could accurately express his obligation to Carlyle and Ruskin.[1]

II

As early as 1820—when he was only twenty-five—Carlyle had augured a long period of nothing but evil in public life. A generation later—during the Crimean War (1854–56)—he complained that the British world, ever since he knew it, had been one vast Balaklava. When he died, in 1881, he had not changed his mind. Yet in the six intervening decades Carlyle, though he hated teaching and insisted that his proselytizing impulse was never irrepressible, made himself one of the most powerful teachers and proselytizers of his age. And the message that he drove home brutally and relentlessly concerned man's obligation to expose and denounce abuses.[2]

Although Carlyle had noted glumly in 1820 that few eminent writers had yet emerged to arouse and inspire public thought, he himself contributed heavily to make the complaint invalid. "When you are weary," Ralph Waldo Emerson wrote to Carlyle in 1835, "believe, that you who stimulate virtuous young men, do not write a line in vain." Carlyle, to be sure, could advise a correspondent who regretted that she was unable to love the world to let it go its own silly way; but neither he nor his disciples could remain aloof. This world, despite all its shortcomings, was still a place of hope and work for him and for them.[3]

Henry Wadsworth Longfellow thought of Carlyle as a man who deprived himself of happiness because of his mania for work. But the evidence suggests something else. Carlyle needed his work as an outlet for his abundantly stocked store of aggressions; and what happiness he knew was inseparable from his work and the peace he found in making war with words. When Matthew Arnold described Carlyle as "part man of genius—part fanatic—and part tom-fool," he came much closer to the truth than Longfellow. Yet this is not to suggest that it is easy to distinguish the parts that made Carlyle both whole and holy.

Carlyle had an overwhelming—almost an embarrassing—need to inflict pain and to attract attention. He bemoaned endlessly the wretched state of his spirits; "very sad—and very lonely," as Ruskin plaintively described him. As a frantic young man he thought of founding a misanthropic society; throughout his adult life he inveighed against the blockheadism of people; and as a weary old man he rejoiced that his work and time were done and that he would soon leave the unmanageable world. Indeed, the conclusion is inescapable that many of his forebodings concerning the condition of English society were projections of the tortures of his inner life.[4]

Through all his private trials Carlyle argued heroically that a person could be ruined only *"by his own consent, by his own act, in this world."* He considered the role of the individual decisive, and the event that he thought deserved to be called great occurred when the noblest of human beings were put in charge of a country's affairs. This did not happen often in either English or any other history, he granted, but it did happen now and then, and it could happen. And if the English were to have much more of a history, the great man would have to appear soon. It was especially important, therefore, Carlyle believed, that the English appreciate Oliver Cromwell, the noblest governor they had ever had. If he could help them to do this, his "poor dry-bones of a compilation [might] prove to be a better 'Poem' than many that go by that name!" What impressed Carlyle particularly about Cromwell and the Puritans was their "practical Contact with the Highest," for this, he was convinced, could be imitated and emulated by all men.[5]

Caution was a quality for which Carlyle had no respect; he worshiped earnestness and passion. When he praised Ebenezer Elliott the reason was that the working-class poet struck him as "a *Man* and no *Clothes-horse.*" And when Dickens, who admired Carlyle greatly, praised him for his manliness and honesty, the novelist singled out traits that meant much to his friend. Without "toil and pain, and all sorts of real *fighting,*" as Carlyle told Robert Browning, a man could achieve nothing.

Cant was the great enemy, and though Carlyle gave much energy to denouncing it, he was convinced in 1848 that it would be dissipated by the labor question. Governments would either have to do something about the horrors of working-class conditions, he said at the time of the establishment of the Second French Republic, or they would collapse one after another. Carlyle despised the anarchy embodied in such expressions as leave it alone, time will mend it, and it will mend itself. He hated these slogans with such intensity that he greatly exaggerated the extent to which they held sway in his "sorry sloppy epoch." Historians and other scholars, taking his strictures to be accurate, have often given an unwarranted importance to the theory and practice of laissez-faire in Victorian history.[6]

Year after year Carlyle waited for a new Cromwell, but none came. Instead, there was a long line of politicians like Disraeli and Gladstone, all of whom Carlyle dismissed as hypocrites and imposters. And so he spent a lifetime hoping that each new head of the Government "would have the goodness to take himself away!" The last complete Ministry through which he lived was led by Disraeli, whom he regarded as a master of pranks and nonsense and lies.

Yet if Carlyle did not appreciate Disraeli, Disraeli was big enough to appreciate Carlyle. Hailing him as one of the heroes of the age, the Prime Minister tried to bestow honors on him. Carlyle not only refused them, but, though he prided himself on not reading newspapers, he rejoiced to hear rumors that the Prime Minister was seriously ill. "The state of the world, with Dizzy at the top of it," he wrote in 1879, "appears to me abundantly ominous but also abundantly contemptible and I say to myself always, What have I to do with it more." [7]

III

In 1881 Mary Carlyle informed her uncle's few surviving intimate friends that his funeral was to take place at Ecclefechan. To contemporaries the idea of an England without Thomas Carlyle to criticize and uplift it was difficult to imagine. From time immemorial, it seemed, he had been preaching government by the wisest and the duty of man to his fellow-men while denouncing hypocrisy, mammon-worship, and irresponsibility.

The publication of James Anthony Froude's edition of Carlyle's *Reminiscences,* with its juicy indiscretions, caused a brief anti-Carlyle reaction. As one irate Carlyle authority put it to another in 1881, "What a woeful mess Mr. Froude has made of it by his want of tact—raising a storm of antagonistic feeling against the grand old master that might have been avoided by the deletion of a score or so of sentences that were sure to provoke indignation and to give the enemies of Carlyle . . . the opportunity for which they were longing." But the effects of the *Reminiscences* wore off quickly. By 1895 a movement was well under way to raise funds to purchase Carlyle's house in Chelsea, and a year later Cheyne Row had become a shrine for pilgrims from many parts of the United Kingdom and of the world. "With the present Carlyle boom," the author of a book on Carlyle expectantly told his publishers, "the circulation of a cheap edition ought to be considerable." [8]

Carlyle inspired a host of reformers. "You have made it possible for me still to believe in truth and righteousness and the spiritual significance of life while creeds and systems have been falling to pieces," James Anthony Froude wrote to Carlyle in 1874. "What you have been to me you have been to thousands of others," he added. "Do you ever read Carlyle?" the young socialist Robert Blatchford asked a friend in 1885. "I am getting to hate that man with a bitter and undying hate, ah! I cannot help reading his infernal books—yet they always make me as if I have just been through a mangle. . . . Tommy Carlyle's works are wholesome medicine—but they are very strong."

If Blatchford could not escape from Carlyle, neither could any number of other reformers. When the band of humanitarians who were preparing a working-class version of the New Testament wrote their autobiographical sketches, many pointed to the reading of Carlyle as one of the decisive events of their lives. And when W. T. Stead disagreed with an American about the interpretation of labor conditions in the United States, he attributed their difference in opinion to the fact that he had been brought up on Carlyle and the American had not. It is probable, however, that the finest compliment ever paid to Carlyle came from the Irish reformer and writer, AE. At the height of the Irish literary renaissance of the early twentieth century, AE insisted that what Ireland needed above all was a Thomas Carlyle.[9]

IV

John Ruskin, like Carlyle, was cross, disheartened, and melancholy during a great part of his adult life. "I would wish you a happy Christmas if my wishes were the least good—which they never are," he said typically in 1872. Almost twenty-five years younger than Carlyle—he was born in 1819—Ruskin lived on until 1900; but during his last years he suffered from the acute mental illness that had long threatened him.

Already in his mid-thirties—in 1855—Ruskin described himself as a person "whom many untoward circumstances of life have had too much power to harden and darken into deadness and bitterness." But in the light of his upbringing, the humiliation of his marriage, and his disastrous friendship with Rose La Touche, the remarkable thing is not that he broke down but that he held up as long and functioned as well as he did. "I have had to do all my books, since 1858 in this pain—and am used to bear it," he confided to a disciple in 1873.[10]

Worse times lay ahead. Though he urged a friend in 1876 not to worry about him because he had already been through too much to be in danger, there was every reason for concern. "My time to me now is as gold, beaten thin," he wrote in 1879. Two years later he bemoaned the severe attacks of illness that he had recently sustained. And in 1884 he deplored the power that the emotions had to comfort or to paralyze the brain. By 1885 he was sure that he had reached the end, but he did not dare to tell this to his devoted cousin, Mrs. Severn, who had seen him recover so many times from earlier attacks. Ironically, this was the same year that he brought out a new edition of *Dame Wiggins of Lee, and Her Seven Wonderful Cats,* which he recommended for the Christmas fireside, because it had nothing to do with either sadness or ugliness. By 1886 Ruskin referred to himself as "poor old crazy me" and as "the mere slave of weather and diet and sofa and bed." In 1887 he was determined to make an effort to recover, and on New Year's Day, 1888, he found his mind quieter and stronger than it had been in years. But soon he was again in a state of severe depression and "much bewildered with the question . . . of what to do and where to live—if I *can* live, without falling into these dark fits again." [11]

v

Ruskin's interests were much broader than those of Carlyle, but to his contemporaries he was for a long time primarily an art critic.

While it is true that he repeatedly stressed the social implications of art, it is often forgotten that he had strong doubts as to the good that art could do. On the one hand, he despised connoisseurs and insisted that poor and illiterate people were far better judges of art. On the other, he believed that before his contemporaries could adequately appreciate art they first needed moral and physical education, a sympathy with humanity, and a love of nature; and it would take a long while for them to acquire these prerequisites. At the same time, however, Ruskin was grateful to have had the opportunity to inaugurate the teaching of art in England and on the university level.[12]

Like Carlyle, Ruskin combined humility with a strong authoritarian strain. "Mr. Ruskin is a clever odd sort of fellow," astute Robert Curzon noted, "but I believe he never was at school to have the natural self sufficiency kicked out of him, so he lays down the law with a loud voice, on subjects which his hearers may understand better than him." Curzon had in mind Ruskin's views on art; but Ruskin could be equally dogmatic on political and social subjects. "By the bye," he wrote to Elizabeth Barrett Browning in 1855, "I hope you give up those rascally radicals now. I am very liberal—and in most senses very Republican—but in heart and head entirely Louis Napoleon's and a great advocate for Slavery, of a wholesome kind and in the right place." [13]

Contrary to a widespread impression, Ruskin did not regard writing as his proper vocation. He confessed to Mrs. Browning in 1859 that he was never happy when he wrote and that he never wrote for his own pleasure. He would have much preferred to spend his time collecting stones and mosses and reading science books. Increasingly, however, he found his days for art and literature past, and he dealt with the social questions that faced what he thought of as his "ineffably ridiculous Country." When he brought out *Unto This Last* (1860), he expected that because of its relevance people would receive it with much more enthusiasm than they did *Modern Painters*. "Finding them spit and scream at it," he told a disciple, "I gave them more—always more and so was drawn in and on to leave my other work." [14]

The future, he wrote in 1868, would be difficult, but no one could lessen suffering without in some degree sharing it. "Until I know something more than I do of the laws of this present life," he bluntly told a clergyman, "I indulge in no dreams—however beautiful—of another." This was the same Ruskin who in order to reassure his mother about the condition of his mind had read religious books to her—and with feeling, so as to show that he liked them. Yet Ruskin never overcame the religious training to which he had been exposed. God's will, he insisted in *The Future of England* (1869), was that people should be righteous and happy both on earth and in heaven. In every English community, he declared, there must be helpers and comforters for those who need help and comfort.[15]

VI

Ruskin's main intellectual effort in the latter part of his life—the years when he justifiably regarded himself as a ruin—was *Fors Clavigera*, the first number of which appeared in 1871. It is revealing that he distributed many free copies of the early issues and that he pointed out to potential subscribers that they would find on the cover information about how to get further numbers if they wished to do so. When he was asked by admirers which of his writings he preferred, he insisted that he had no favorites but that *Fors* was the work they should study.

In it Ruskin announced the establishment of St. George's Company, explained its purposes, and sought contributors and companions. "It is *not* to be *Communism:* quite the contrary," Ruskin told a friend. "The old Feudal System applied to do good instead of evil—to save life, instead of destroy. That is the whole—in fewest words." To become a soldier for good a person had to give a tenth of his income, or—if he had no income to speak of—to promise to donate the tenth if he ever had it to contribute. Although in 1873 Ruskin gave the membership as all of eight, he made it clear to potential recruits that absolute obedience to him —the Colonel—was a condition of joining. He could get little done if he had to discuss matters with his troops.[16]

Ruskin did not mind public ridicule and hostility; on the contrary, he enjoyed them. For he regarded the hatred of the wicked and the scorn of fools as sure signs of his usefulness. By 1874, however, his sense of the misery and stupidity that surrounded him became so overpowering that he doubted the wisdom of the gentle and quiet measures he had been advocating. He suspected that he would be compelled to take desperate steps and repudiate all conventions and even take to preaching from a hillside: "For this is no ordinary time. It is like speaking in the midst of a mob. No use speaking in ordinary tones of propriety or even in shouting against their shout. One must Do something." It is no surprise, then, that when he sent successive issues of *Fors* to some of his favorite young girls he cautioned them not to be shocked. Overflowing with "cold and hard and horrid things to say and do and think of," he could be useful only by swearing at everyone. George Gissing once referred to *Unto This Last* as Ruskin's "contribution to—or rather, onslaught upon,—Political Economy." To describe *Fors*, however, even onslaught is a tame word.[17]

Several of Ruskin's companions made the offerings that he sought. Mrs. Frances Talbot, his chief backer, in 1874 offered him grounds and houses that were exactly the kind of property that he wanted most for his St. George's Company. In 1876 he thought that the organization might even become rich, and as a man who always sided with the poor he felt embarrassed. Three years later, however, he spoke much less confidently; the Great Depression was having its effects. By 1881 he complained that the companions were poor and few, and he urged them to try hard to overcome these disadvantages. Applicants still wished to enroll and spend their time in the company of noble spirits and in the pure and refined atmosphere that *Fors* enjoined. But the members Ruskin needed above all were those who had money to donate. Of course, he tried actively to recruit all kinds of candidates—especially young girls. He even attempted to enlist aged Thomas Carlyle as a member, but while Carlyle considered Ruskin entirely sane in his view of the Guild, he doubted that the experiment would fulfill the millenarian hopes of its founder.[18]

Ruskin was convinced that St. George's work would go on as long as he kept his health. But the severity of his illness in the 1890s crippled the Guild's activities, one of the reasons being that no one but the Master could admit new members. After Ruskin's death in 1900 some of the companions, concerned that the Guild had been dormant for some years, tried to give it new life. A meeting was held in Sheffield, but only nine companions attended, five of whom came from Liverpool. The properties of the Guild were declared to be in a satisfactory condition; but it was plain

that the organization was doing almost none of the work for which
it had been founded. The Liverpool contingent, determined that
the Guild should be a monument neither to Ruskin's folly nor
to their own lack of loyalty and drive, tried to carry on St.
George's work, but the response they evoked was disheartening. The companions did not cooperate.[19]

VII

Ruskin shared Carlyle's overwhelming sense of the dignity and
worth of labor. He abhorred smoking because it made men content to be idle. He despised lawyers. Labor that society scorned
Ruskin often found praiseworthy. "If I saw any good to be done—
or useful thing to be learned, by doing so," he wrote in 1869, "I
would tomorrow without the least pain or concern—sweep any
crossing in London the whole day or any number of days in a
ragged coat—asking for pence." He could do this, he said, because
sweeping gave him no sense of shame; what would make him feel
embarrassed was an inability to do the work properly.[20]

Despite his constant assertions of the dignity of labor, Ruskin
often insisted that he would willingly give up all his work to spend
his time with his "divine girlies." He revolted constantly against
his involvement in social questions, for it caused him undue grief
and toil. "I long to rest and amuse myself anyway I can," he wrote
in 1874, "all my work for others is hateful to me." At the end
of a day, he said in 1875, "I have only a jaded feeling of being overworked—not the least of having done *right* in writing political
economy—and yet—heaven knows I do it for other people's sake,
not my own—but then I can't help doing it—and have no more
sense of satisfaction in it than a dog who barks himself hoarse
without waking anybody in the house while the thieves are getting
in at the window." [21]

Sometimes Ruskin thought of himself as playing a role in his
time similar to that played by St. Francis and St. Dominic in theirs.
Carlyle and others even suspected that he would finally turn Roman Catholic and become a monk of Assisi. For the most part,
however, Ruskin thought of himself as another Rousseau. In fact,
he sometimes believed that he was Rousseau come to life again
—with some advantages of wealth but even greater hard luck.[22]

Ruskin could refer to himself as "poor old crazy me," and some of his contemporaries dismissed him with similar phrases. Leslie Stephen was more moderate than a number of other critics when he called him an insane genius. But Ruskin rejoiced in his critics and enemies—the more so because he had an articulate and energetic group of followers who saw him as a latter-day saint pointing the way to a wholesome reconstruction of society.

"I always *am* serious—if only people would attend to what I say," Ruskin pointed out in 1889. Some people did, and they accepted as articles of faith and keys to action his attacks on competition, his exposures of malice and folly, and above all his admonition—since his whole life was a worship of beauty—to make God's world more beautiful by caring for its inhabitants. Oscar Wilde did not exaggerate too much when he wrote to Ruskin: "There is in you something of prophet, of priest and of poet, and to you the Gods gave eloquence such as they have given to none other, so that your message might come to us with the fire of passion and the marvel of music—making the deaf to hear, and the blind to see." Even captious George Gissing admired Ruskin and considered his strictures against modern civilization valid. Gissing went so far as to urge his brother Algernon to join the Guild of St. George, and he told his sister Margaret: "It matters little that his immediate schemes are impracticable; to keep before the eyes of men the *ideal* is the great thing; it does its work in the course of time." [23]

Nor did Ruskin's influence stop with his death. The young Liberal and historian Herbert Fisher considered the artistic repercussions of Ruskin's career thoroughly wholesome. "Among all the movements of our time," he wrote in 1906, "there has surely been none which has exerted an influence of unalloyed goodness comparable to that which has flowed from the Artistic Renaissance of which Ruskin was, I suppose, the prophet, and William Morris the most versatile exponent." Even the stubborn Tory and imperialist W. E. Henley, who deplored Ruskin's influence and prided himself on having escaped it, conceded that it was impossible to deal with many subjects "without Ruskinizing." [24]

VIII

Although Carlyle and Ruskin were the chief older writer-reformers who swayed the humanitarians of the late nineteenth

century, others were also important: Robert Owen, Christian
Socialist Frederick Denison Maurice, John Stuart Mill, Herbert
Spencer, and Matthew Arnold—not to mention Mrs. Harriet
Beecher Stowe and William Lloyd Garrison. Above all, however,
the earlier writer-reformer who—next to Carlyle and Ruskin—
had the profoundest influence on the late Victorian generation was
Charles Dickens (d. 1870).[25]

Thomas Carlyle, a close friend of Dickens for almost thirty
years, found him a "quietly decisive, just and loving man," and
Carlyle's sympathetic image of him was widely shared both before
and after Dickens's death. Ouida, to be sure, was convinced that
it would have been better for English literature if Dickens had
never lived; but no writer, Henry Wadsworth Longfellow rightly
insisted, was ever so widely loved and missed as Dickens. It is true,
of course, that temperance reformers objected to the novelist's
drinking habits. And churchgoers complained that he did not go
to church. But even the Bishop of Oxford praised him for his
services to the cause of morality—and with good reason. As Dickens himself remarked, "I have seen, habitually, some of the worst
sources of general contamination and corruption in this country,
and I think there are not many phases of London life that could
surprise me." Almost always, however, Dickens dealt with what
he saw in a reformist spirit—something could be done about it.
To Dickens, as to Carlyle, the enemy was cant.[26]

While he was still alive, Dickens received many testimonials to
the influence of his books on the life and character of his readers,
and he considered it both a privilege and a reward for a novelist
to succeed in awakening in his audience noble feelings and a
hatred of cruelty and pretentiousness. Indeed, throughout his
career Dickens saw it as one of the main purposes of literature to
lift up the wronged and suffering multitude. He never wrote
simply to amuse; literature without a purpose he considered an of-
fense against God. In the fitting words of the obituary notice that
appeared in 1870 in the *Daily News:* "For everything which tends
to elevate the low or enlighten the ignorant, or rescue the outcasts
of society, he not only had an enthusiastic admiration, but could
communicate it to his readers." [27]

Edward Bellamy went so far as to have a character in *Looking
Backward* (1888) rate Dickens the outstanding writer of his age,

not because of the distinction of his literary gifts but because of the depth of his sympathy for the victims of social injustice. "No man of his time," wrote Bellamy in an outburst of enthusiasm, "did so much as he to turn men's minds to the wrong and wretchedness of the old order of things, and open their eyes to the necessity of the great change that was coming. . . ." Bellamy cast his vote for Dickens. Other reformers cast theirs for Carlyle, and others theirs for Ruskin. Regardless, however, of how they ranked the masters, all late Victorian reformers were, in varying degrees, Carlylized, Ruskinized, and Dickensized.

VII

WRITERS PROTEST

In historical perspective it is clear that the late Victorian generation produced no social critic of the stature of Carlyle, Ruskin, or
Dickens. This, however, was not at all clear to some people living in the last third of the nineteenth century. There were those—
young and hypercritical Bernard Shaw among them—who considered William Morris a comparable figure. And there were those
who judged Henry George incomparable—the prophet for whom
they had been searching for years, the Columbus of political
economy and social science. The reading of Henry George, as
the smitten proprietor of the Bradford *Observer* wrote in a typical
outburst, "changed my whole outlook on Political and Social
affairs and altered my angle of vision towards all Economic
questions." Even Bernard Shaw acknowledged that the socialists
he knew in the early eighties were drawn into the movement
mainly by *Progress and Poverty;* and it was one of his ambitions,
Shaw confessed in 1904, to do for young Americans what Henry
George had done for him and his British colleagues.[1]

Other late Victorians placed the unorthodox socialist poet
and master of plain English, Edward Carpenter, on a level with
the giants of the past. They insisted that *Towards Democracy*
(1883), Carpenter's frequently revised and expanded volume of
poetry, was the greatest book in many decades, and they reveled
in his other criticisms of modern English life—of its economics,
politics, provincialism, clothing, and sexual behavior. Nor were
they alone, for even Tolstoy proclaimed Carpenter a worthy suc-

cessor to Carlyle and Ruskin; and a host of Carpenter worshipers descended on the vicinity of Sheffield to pay their respects and take instruction.[2]

In addition to Carpenter, George, and Morris, there were, of course, other thinkers—the humanitarian political philosopher T. H. Green, the Master of Balliol Benjamin Jowett, and Arnold Toynbee—whose admirers ranked them with the greatest of recent times. Among working-class people, however, one writer-reformer stood out above all others: Robert Blatchford, the author of the stirring plea for socialism, *Merrie England,* and the editor of the brisk socialist journal, *The Clarion.* Blatchford, to be sure, could refer to himself jokingly as the most popular and influential socialist in England, but he simply spoke the truth.[3]

Although the late Victorians brought forth no Carlyle, Ruskin, or Dickens, they produced a host of extraordinary writer-reformers who worked for the elevation of "the millions." Sometimes these reformers tried to arouse public opinion and public indignation through novels, poems, and plays, and sometimes through works of nonfiction. Mainly, however, they served their causes through newspapers and magazines. In fact, an impressive number of the most important reformist books of the time began as journalistic enterprises. By 1884 James Russell Lowell, addressing a Birmingham audience on the theme of democracy, went so far as to express doubt that Parliament sat in Westminster: it seemed to be moving, he shrewdly suggested, to the editors' offices of the leading journals.

As a passionate defender of democracy, Lowell gloried in the power of the press to further reform movements. But antireformers were constantly—and understandably—alarmed by what they read in reformist newspapers and magazines. Just as on the eve of the Reform Act of 1832 a reformer like William Cobbett acclaimed the influence of the press and an antireformer like Charles Greville prayed that people would be too tired and worn out to listen to the trouble-making reformist press, so in the late nineteenth century reformers and antireformers had similar responses. The difference was that by the last decades of the century the population, the reading public, and the world of journalism were considerably bigger.[4]

"A cheap and free Press conducted on intelligent and moral

principles," John Bright earnestly told an editor in 1883, "is of priceless value to the Country." Always, however, the difficulty was that reformers and antireformers could not agree as to what policies were intelligent, much less moral. Charles A. Cooper, the high-minded editor of *The Scotsman,* argued that those who ran newspapers should not strive for titles and other rewards that might threaten their impartiality and lessen their influence. But Cooper had no doubts about the integrity of newspaper proprietors and editors. Young and rebellious Robert Blatchford, on the other hand, saw corruption everywhere. "The press is senile and decrepit and morally out at elbows," he said bluntly in 1886 in words that could have come from his captor, Thomas Carlyle. "The average journalist is fat and lazy and of easy virtue, with no more soul than suffices to keep his bowels in motion and no more intellect than is needful in the daily task of spinning flimsy copy. Let us then do some little good or be for ever idle; let us speak the truth or develop diligently a talent for dumb silence." For Blatchford, however, there was really no choice to be made. Like Carlyle, he was not the quiet type.[5]

II

The proliferation of newspapers and magazines in late Victorian times had many important effects. For one thing—and this has often been overlooked—it brought about the decline of the pamphlet. As early as 1872 the socialist journalist and politician Louis Blanc, visiting England, noted the great difficulty with which pamphlets were sold; they were "downright *killed* by newspapers," he reported with some exaggeration. Pamphlets—and some impressive pamphlets—continued, of course, to be published, but their role in the communication of reformist ideas was much less than it had been for centuries.

Far more important, the growth of the press greatly intensified the rivalries among both old and new newspapers and magazines. This was doubtless inevitable, for in a period of prolonged depression most publications were threatened with short life and sudden death. William Blackwood was not merely engaging in shop talk when he expressed concern in 1885 for the fate of his almost seventy-year-old magazine: *Blackwood's* had formidable rivals. The competitive spirit affected other prestige publications

as well. Bernard Shaw considered the *Westminster Gazette* under the editorship of Liberal J. A. Spender the only paper he
could read with the feeling that he was in decent company. But
even Spénder, vacationing in Venice, sharply cautioned one of
his subordinates that the *Gazette* was quoting too heavily from
and therefore calling too much attention to—the Manchester
Guardian.[6]

The running of a daily newspaper, Robert Southey once remarked, was the most arduous of all literary tasks. By the last
decades of the century Southey's comment was more relevant
than ever. To survive was the important thing, and thus many
proprietors and editors encouraged their writers to specialize in
scoops and sensations. The tendency was marked long before
Alfred Harmsworth founded his *Daily Mail,* whose circulation of
250,000 made Arnold Bennett, among many others, gasp in 1896.
Not many decades earlier young Disraeli could write a gossipy letter
to his father and assure him that he now had heard all the secrets
that not ten people in the country knew; but with so many scoop-
minded journalists omnipresent secrets could no longer be so
easily kept. Furthermore, as Ouida rightly noted in 1897, anonym-
ity did for journalists what the wig and gown did for barristers:
it gave them an air of importance.

Sir Charles Dilke complained bitterly to Gladstone in 1884
about the serious leakages of confidential information that were
taking place, but it was not only politicians who deplored the invasion by the press of their privacy. Gilbert and Sullivan, for
example, regarded the reasons for the ending of their collabora-
tion as no concern of the public, but journalists thought otherwise. The much pursued Ouida reached the conclusion that the
sole purpose of the English press was to spread lies about her.[7]

The multiplication of newspapers and magazines was a godsend
to writers, most of whom could not support themselves on the
income from what they regarded as their serious work. "We rarely
have a good manuscript from a lord, or even from the class of
landed gentry," remarked a publisher's reader in 1897. He might
have added that for years many of the people who wished to get
ahead in the world of letters could have said, with H. G. Wells,
that they were incredibly poor, or, with George Gissing, that their
symbol of England was the workhouse, towards which they were

repeatedly drifting. Indeed, the part of his work that status-conscious Gissing considered most important and characteristic was that which dealt with "a class of young men distinctive of our time—well educated, fairly bred, *but without money*." [8]

Baron Corvo, no victim of low self-esteem, insisted that, though he was not rich, he would never humble himself by doing trifling magazine pieces. And the ambitious literary critic Edmund Gosse confessed that, if a philanthropist left him £500 a year, he would damn journalism and dedicate himself to pure literature. For poets, however, who discovered on their own the truth of Leslie Stephen's warning that the writing of poetry was not a lucrative occupation; for those who were aware that it took thirty years even for Tennyson to win a well-paying reputation; for novelists who found out for themselves what Wilkie Collins discovered when he contrasted his sales with those of the royalty-laden author of *East Lynne*—for these writers journalism offered pecuniary advantages as well as a stepping-stone to other literary efforts. [9]

The growth of the press alarmed some writers—especially those who, unlike Gissing, had no need to write "for sheer bread and cheese." George Eliot, convinced that superfluous literature was the calamity of the age, deplored the time that people wasted on magazines. And Henry James had no doubt that the reading of newspapers was "*the* pernicious habit, and the father of all idleness and levity." Conscience-ridden W. T. Stead, on the other hand, was so concerned that people lacked the time to keep up with the journalistic outpourings of the age that he founded in 1890 the inexpensive *Review of Reviews* to make life simpler and richer for them. Despite Stead's heroic efforts, however, the problem of quantity remained. As a contributor to the *London Quarterly* put it in 1900, "Perhaps the difficulty nowadays is less to find writers prepared to write than readers with leisure to read!" [10]

III

Reformers went out of their way to win journalistic support. For, as Gladstone advised Edward Burne-Jones during one of his campaigns for the cause of art, there were very real advantages in working up a lively discussion in the press. Often, however, reformers ran into difficulties. In the words that Francis W. Newman, the high-minded social and educational reformer and brother of the Cardinal, wrote in 1877 to the editor of the *Contemporary Review:* "I constantly am thought extreme and impracticable, because I think new lines of action must supersede the old grooves; but this circumstance is apt to make me a very unacceptable writer to those in high places, whether of the State, of the Church, or of certain Professions."

Newman would not ask an editor to risk irritating his readers on his account, but few reformers had such misgivings. Mary Carpenter constantly tried to draw public attention to her plans for the reform of education and the treatment of criminals and juvenile delinquents by planting items in newspapers and periodicals. The artist William Holman Hunt sought the help of Sir John Millais in winning press support for the reform of legislation concerning illegitimacy. And a leading English single-taxer, explaining the spread of Henry George's ideas in England, attributed it, among other reasons, to the increased discussion of social questions in the press.[11]

It is true that Florence Nightingale sometimes complained angrily that the *Times* had it in its power virtually to destroy her proposals, but she found out early in her career that its enthusiastic support of a particular reform could do inestimable good. "An *early* article and a continuation of articles in the *Times* makes all the difference," she conceded. And experienced Herbert Spencer knew what he was doing when he scolded a friend in 1894 for bringing out an article in an obscure journal instead of one of the leading monthlies. For the prestige that the *Times* enjoyed among newspapers the *Nineteenth Century, Contemporary Review,* and *Fortnightly Review* enjoyed among periodicals.

Punch, to be sure, was in a class by itself. As the notorious Governor Eyre put it, "People are influenced by ridicule when they are scarcely affected by sound argument—and everybody sees *Punch.*" Reformers, however, rarely found comfort in its pages during the last decades of the century; those—like Eyre—who wrote letters of thanks to its staff were almost invariably anti-reformers. Nevertheless, reformers always hoped that the wrong lords of the press, whether of *Punch* or any other publication, would make way for the right ones. As Michael Davitt, the land reformer and anti-imperialist, wrote when he heard during the

Boer War that the *Daily News* was to take on a new editor and drop its jingoism, "That *would* be cheering news for all good causes!" [12]

Reformers looked for allies not only among journalists but among other writers as well. Back in the early 1830s—at the time of the agitation for the regulation of child labor and for the abolition of slavery in the colonies—William Wordsworth was asked to support these reform movements, but he refused because he would not add to public unrest. Like Wordsworth, some late Victorian writers preferred to remain silent on the big public issues of their times; and others considered their intervention futile. George Meredith, for example, whose opinions were generally those of the Liberal Party, doubted that his name would help the causes he favored. Nevertheless, writers were subjected to endless appeals from innumerable reformers to lend the prestige of their names to countless causes. Justin McCarthy, journalist, historian, and Member of Parliament, pointed out proudly in his *Irishman's Story* that home rulers included George Meredith, the painter Ford Madox Brown, and the dramatist and actor Dion Boucicault. And John Redmond, Parnell's successor, rejoiced that the outspoken anti-imperialist poet Wilfrid Blunt—as well as his wife—were great friends of Ireland.[13]

Writers—especially the successful ones—were also bombarded with requests to contribute money to a vast variety of causes. A friend remarked of the humanitarian-novelist Charles Reade that his philanthrophy was boundless, and what was true of Reade was true of other writers. Tennyson did not exaggerate when he noted that the calls on his purse were discouragingly great. Mrs. Craigie, without knowing it, testified to the energy of late Victorian philanthropists when she complained in 1897, "What with American Diamond Jubilee Testimonials, Greek Ambulances, Aged Catholic Orphans who have lost both parents, Social Evenings for the Catholic Poor, etc. etc. etc.—I have scarcely the price of a Jubilee bonnet."

In other ways, too, writers aided humanitarian causes. Thomas Hardy asked those who requested his autograph to send contributions to hospitals for the poor. Lewis Carroll brought out in 1886 a special edition of *Alice,* the profits from which were to go to hospitals and homes for children. And W. S. Gilbert often allowed performances of his works to aid children's hospitals and similar institutions—at least until Lloyd George's "Spoliation Budget" of 1909 outraged him to such a point that he refused to help any cause that aimed to benefit the working classes.[14]

IV

No writer-reformer of the late Victorian period pinned so many hopes on the press—and on professional writers—as W. T. Stead. Through the *Northern Echo*, the *Pall Mall Gazette*, and the *Review of Reviews* he tried to awaken his readers to the need for a staggering list of reforms. "I shall greatly prize any opportunities I may have of ascertaining from you where and how I can be most useful to the cause," Stead wrote to Gladstone in 1880. Although Gladstone sometimes changed his opinion about his journalistic ally as Stead moved from project to project, he valued him as one of the most reliable of men in the worst of crises. Cardinal Manning considered Stead so important that he urged him to visit the Pope to discuss Irish home rule. And Cecil Rhodes wrote to Stead from Cape Town to send along books that he thought the South African statesman ought to read.[15]

The son of a clergyman, Stead was an irrepressible crusader who viewed the press as the greatest pulpit in world history. He never tired of calling attention to what he regarded as abuses, and while he exhausted his colleagues, his own energy rarely lapsed. Antireformers were often appalled by the fervor of his convictions, but they envied the courage—even recklessness—with which he defended what he believed was right. From the time he was imprisoned during the course of his struggle to expose white slavery in England, he never lost his faith in prison as a road to success for the reformer. "I am secluded almost as if I were the Grand Lama," he wrote in 1885; but the attention he attracted during his imprisonment helped to assure the passage of the Criminal Law Amendments Act.

Although Stead did not scorn logic and reason in journalism and even worried at times about his tendency to be too didactic, he conducted his enterprises on the assumption that both individuals and nations were swayed above all by appeals to their emotions. He defied even the Archangel Gabriel to do a clever piece on bimetallism, but there were few subjects on which Stead

could not write a lively and moving article. When Mrs. John
Burns read distressing reports in the *Pall Mall Gazette* that her
husband's health was suffering from his imprisonment, a friend
assured her: "I know Stead likes a bit of sensation. It helps the
paper." [16]

In 1890 Stead left the *Pall Mall Gazette;* its proprietor, he explained, "has discovered that he can not sleep easy at nights when
I go prancing round." Stead then founded his magazine for busy
people, the *Review of Reviews,* from which he expected extraordinary results. By 1891 he told his American editor that it was
catching on well: when he traveled to different British cities he
was received with such enthusiasm that he had to conclude that he
was "almost the next greatest man to the Prime Minister of the
Country." Stead was convinced that he had "got hold, with both
hands, of the most vital elements in the nation; that no one else
has a position that can be remotely compared with the *Review of
Reviews,* and that, if health only holds out, and we are true to
our calling, there is no knowing what we shall not be able to do."
Designed above all to further Anglo-American harmony, the
Review became a vehicle for dozens of Stead's other schemes, both
trivial and grand: the employment of the police for charitable
work; the promotion of trade unions; the use of the bicycle to
further harmony between the classes; the Christianization of social and economic life; the furtherance of welfare legislation;
Irish home rule; the arbitration of disputes between nations.[17]

Because Stead welcomed suggestions from people in high
places, he sometimes came to be viewed as a puppet whose strings
were manipulated by Gladstone, General William Booth, Cardinal Manning, Cecil Rhodes, and Andrew Carnegie, among others.
But Stead was no one's sycophant: he worked with the highly
placed because he was interested in the lowly. Always he sought to
drive home to ordinary and previously indifferent readers the importance of reform. While he sought to be widely read by clergymen, lawyers, doctors, teachers, politicians, businessmen, and
women with leisure, his main ambition was to use the press as a
device by which to overcome the apathy and ignorance of the
masses and immerse them in the great reform movements of the
age.

Some of his colleagues insisted that there was no market for philanthropic journalism and that the public, eager for news and amusement, did not want newspapers and magazines that aimed at the regeneration of mankind. But Stead would not accept the role of a mere conveyor of information and provider of entertainment. He compromised to the extent that he recognized that he could not get the public to listen to anything serious during a holiday. Fortunately, however, holidays were few in the course of the year.[18]

Stead was alarmed that the millions of people who had been taught to read as a result of the education acts passed from 1870 on did not understand or care about the big questions of the day. Many avoided the morning papers, reading the evening papers for their sports news and such miscellanies as *Tit-Bits* and *Answers* for their frivolous matter. When the first half-penny morning newspaper made its appearance in London in 1892, Stead pronounced it worthless; and he did not expect the second to be any better. Indeed, it was inevitable that Stead, with his sense of mission concerning journalism, would find the state of newspapers and magazines scandalous.[19]

Stead's faith in the power of the press in the fight for reform was shared by other editors. Dedicated Percy William Bunting, obsessed with the need to extirpate all kinds of social evils and to elevate the masses, considered it the function of the press to stimulate in readers a great rush of moral feelings. For years Bunting, as editor of the *Contemporary Review,* sought to encourage that rush. And so did an impressive number of other editors, whose aims were very different from those of Bunting. In the much prosecuted and persecuted *National Reformer* Charles Bradlaugh and Mrs. Annie Besant clamored for converts to atheism, birth control, and a host of other reform movements. William Morris's literate *Commonweal* and Robert Blatchford's lively *Clarion* pressed hard for the cause of socialism. The *Freeman's Journal* bluntly attacked landlordism in Ireland, England, and Scotland and urged the doctrine of the land for the people. The journals of Henry S. Salt, Jr.'s Humanitarian League movingly decried a wide variety of cruelties, whether against animals or people. Robert Donald's *London* boldly emphasized the need for the moderni-

zation of local government. And W. E. Henley's *Scots Observer*
and *New Review* eloquently preached empire-mindedness and
imperial reform.[20]

V

The press was important in its own right in promoting ideas of
reform, but it also played a prominent part in publicizing books
that urged the revamping of particular institutions. Almost every
such book that attracted considerable notice in the late Victorian
period owed its success in no small measure to the attention it
received in newspapers and magazines.

Ouida insisted that books which could not survive without the
help of a middle-man ought to die, and she and many of her
contemporaries in the literary world—Charles Reade, Thomas
Hardy, George Meredith, George Gissing, George Moore, Marie
Corelli—protested against the power they thought the press had
in determining the success of a book. But even Ouida rejoiced
that no one ever saw a paper in which she was severely criticized.
And other writers tried brazenly to use the press for their own
advantage. One aspiring man of letters, sending along a volume of
his poetry to a leading citizen of Liverpool, requested that he do
what he could to have the book reviewed in the daily papers. "I
ask this of all my acquaintances," he wrote, "as only by their
aid can one extend one's name as a writer in these days; and
every notice, however small, is significant and valuable, especially
in the large towns." [21]

As with writers of imaginative literature, so with writers of
reform literature. While they often resented the influence of the
press, they still went out of their way to curry its favor. Young
H. G. Wells, though he granted that all the socialist papers were
alive to him, prided himself on never using his friends in the
world of journalism to promote his works; but Wells was an exception. When Plato E. Draculis, a socialist refugee, brought out
a book in England, he sought access to W. T. Stead in the hope
that he could be induced to publicize it. George Jacob Holyoake
consoled his publisher that his latest book would sell well both
in England and the United States because he had many important friends in the press. And Canon Samuel Barnett, a fervent
Christian Socialist and housing and educational reformer, as-

WRITERS PROTEST 103

sured his publisher that among his old friends in the London press were luminaries on the *Daily News,* the *Westminster Gazette,* the *Chronicle,* the *Telegraph,* and the *Morning Post.* Indeed, the fantasy of every writer-reformer was to have said of his book what was said of Stead's volume on Chicago—that it received more publicity in the press than almost any book in history.[22]

VI

Reformers and antireformers alike were often alarmed by the censorship to which they were subjected by the intolerances of the late Victorian age. Wilkie Collins and George Moore were particularly outspoken in their criticisms of the proprietors of the large circulating libraries, who decided which books were moral enough to be made available to the public. Sometimes Collins called Charles Mudie an "ignorant fanatic" and sometimes a "fanatical old fool," but always he raged because Mudie stood between him and the public and controlled the circulation—or lack of it—of his books. "English writers," George Moore similarly protested in 1885, "were subject to the censorship of a tradesman who, although doubtless an excellent citizen and a worthy father, was scarcely competent to decide the delicate and difficult artistic questions that authors in their struggles for new ideals might raise: questions that could and should be judged by time alone."

In a sense both Collins and Moore were unfair, for Mudie was not an isolated figure. His spirit and outlook pervaded the staffs of magazines and publishing houses as well as the public. As George Du Maurier confidently remarked of *Peter Ibbetson* in 1891, "It will be better in Book form; many gentle blasphemies and sweet innocent little indecencies had to be left out in the magazine—especially towards the end!" And R. Murray Gilchrist wrote indignantly in 1893 of a novel he had just completed: "Methuen's wrote t'other day asking me to expunge a certain passage. 'They were not prudish themselves—but the critics and the public'!!!" This was the same Gilchrist who insisted that if the Venus of Milo came to dwell among his fellow-citizens of Sheffield she would have to wear a woollen petticoat and shawl.[23]

Public squeamishness had countless repercussions on late Victorian literary history. It had much to do with Arthur W. Pinero's admiration for the crusade of the Bancrofts to produce realistic plays, and it had much to do with the respect in which Pinero himself was held by his fellow-playwrights. It had much to do with Ernest Dowson's doubts about the acceptability of his poetry; with Thomas Hardy's abandonment of the novel; with young Somerset Maugham's wish not to be typed as a novelist of the George Moore school; and with the commercial failure of George Gissing's novels, the constant criticism of which was that they were squalid, depressing, and offensive. It had much to do with the Oscar Wilde affair. And it had something to do with Bernard Shaw's difficulties with his Unpleasant Plays, *Widowers' Houses* (1892), *The Philanderer* (1893), and *Mrs. Warren's Profession* (1894). Small wonder that George Gissing, attending a dinner in honor of Anthony Hope, that eminently safe novelist, the author of *The Prisoner of Zenda,* fumed at the money-making—and inoffensive—writers with whom he spent the evening: "To mingle with these folk is to be once and for ever convinced of the degradation that our time has brought upon literature. It was a dinner of tradesmen, pure and simple."

While public squeamishness mattered a great deal to writers of imaginative literature, it also seriously concerned writer-reformers, many of whom dealt with subjects that were, by the standards of the time, delicate. Mrs. Annie Besant and Charles Bradlaugh with their daring publications on birth control; W. T. Stead with his powerful account of prostitution in *The Maiden Tribute of Modern Babylon;* women's rights advocates with their blunt repudiation of the Old Woman and their enthusiastic endorsement of the New Woman; housing and temperance reformers with their morbid exposures of the degradation and brutality of life in English slums—all shocked their contemporaries. But they also accustomed them, however grudgingly, to the public discussion of themes that had often been hushed up. Indeed, the increased freedom of expression that writers of imaginative literature came to enjoy by the beginning of the twentieth century owed much to late Victorian writer-reformers who spoke up courageously about touchy subjects. Young Arnold Bennett, then assistant editor of a woman's magazine, used a revealing infinitive when he told a friend about his first novel, *A Man from the North.* Its purpose, he wrote in 1897, "is to 'expose' a few of the hardships and evils of the life of the young celibate clerk in London." [24]

Writer-reformers, determined to reach not just "the Cultured Few" but the largest possible audience, constantly sought to keep down the prices of their books. The poet and anthologist Francis Palgrave could bemoan the decline of typography in a time of literature for the many; Henry James could object to having his work appear in cheap form; and George Moore could abhor inexpensive books, insisting that they ruined both publishers and authors. But writer-reformers had no doubt about the wisdom of the low-price policy. As one of them cogently put it, "I wished it to be got up in a cheap form, as I wished the working classes to read it." [25]

Nor were reformers wrong—especially in an age of depression —to insist on inexpensive editions. Ruskin was constantly told by his admirers that his books were priced too high. As a clergyman with an income of £100 a year wrote to him, "I think it is a fact, and a serious fact, that thousands of those who would turn your teachings to the best purposes are utterly unable to procure your works at their present prices." With a more than comfortable income Ruskin was able to distribute many free copies of his works: "If people won't buy,—yet *will* read, I think it is best to extend one's influence as one can." But few writer-reformers could afford to be so generous. Like Keir Hardie, the socialist labor leader, they were convinced that there was a demand for good books among a section of the working classes, but because of limited income this demand could not be satisfied. The solution, therefore, was low-priced editions. It was much easier, as an experienced socialist bookseller was to remark, to sell a thousand volumes at sixpence each than a hundred at a shilling each. [26]

Enthusiastic writer-reformers, lacking George Eliot's conviction that the world was already suffering from a vast oversupply of superfluous books, published hundreds of works during the late Victorian period. Unlike George Eliot, they considered themselves teachers; and, like Mrs. Craigie, they wrote books not for art's sake but because they wanted them read. "It is one of my chief pleasures in life," as Matthew Arnold confessed to an ad-

mirer in 1884, "to find that my books have had the right readers
such as yourself—readers to whom, in the unsettled and trying
days in which our life passes, they have been of use, and a support." [27]

Many writer-reformers thought that their books would revolu-
tionize English life, but only a tiny number of their volumes received the attention their authors believed they deserved. By far
the greatest successes were four books that dealt directly with the
baffling problems of the depression: *Progress and Poverty*, Henry
George's appeal for land nationalization and the adoption of the
single tax; *In Darkest England and the Way Out*, General Booth's
invitation to a large-scale war on poverty; *Merrie England*, Robert
Blatchford's plea for the establishment of a socialist society; and
"Made in Germany," Ernest E. Williams's call for state help and
self-help to meet foreign competition. And the dream of every
writer-reformer was to outdo—or at least to equal—Henry
George, General William Booth, Robert Blatchford, and Ernest
E. Williams.

VIII

When *Progress and Poverty* was published in the United States
in 1879, Henry George assured his father that it would ultimately
be recognized as a great book and that it would be brought out in
both hemispheres. With a journalist friend, he was more restrained: "I believe it will be much of a success. The time is certainly propitious." But George was not of a temperament to wait
for things to happen; he had to try to make them happen, and so
he distributed copies of his book to British celebrities who might
be able to help it along. As early as January, 1880, Professor John
Stuart Blackie, the eminent Scottish classicist and land reformer,
thanked him for the volume, adding that he thought it especially
useful for the new colonies; but an old country like England,
Blackie suggested, required measures of a much more moderate
kind. Blackie then proceeded—unpardonably—to refer George
to an article on the land question that he had just published in
the *Contemporary Review!* George, concerned that his book did
not seem to be attracting attention in England—"the center and
radiating point of Anglo-Saxon thought"—asked Sir George Grey,

the New Zealand political leader, to use in its behalf any influence he had in England.[28]

In January, 1881, Kegan Paul and Company brought out an English edition of *Progress and Poverty*, but it had a slow start: "When they first got it out no one would touch it. They laughed at the idea of selling an American book on political economy. It was a long while before they got rid of twenty copies." George consoled himself with the thought that works on political economy simply did not sell either in the United States or England, and that relatively his was doing very well. At least it was reassuring that the Leeds *Independent* proclaimed *Progress and Poverty* a book for every English worker to read. "Pretty soon the economists will be forced to notice it," George hopefully told a friend. Impatient for fame and a mass audience, he fumed at critics who stigmatized his book as incendiary and communistic, and he reveled in every flattering comment he could find. The eminent scientist and socialist A. R. Wallace, he proudly reported, was endorsing the book as "undoubtedly the most remarkable and important work of the present century." [29]

At last in February, 1882, one year after the book's appearance in England, his publisher told him that *Progress and Poverty* was "the most astonishing success he *ever* knew." Although George recognized that he had accomplished "something utterly unprecedented in the history of economic literature," he remained insatiable. He lectured indefatigably in England, Scotland, and Ireland in the hope of winning converts to the cause of the single tax; and he complained angrily that the English press did not pay sufficient attention to him, his book, and his lecturing activities. His disciple Helen Taylor encouraged him to believe that there was a journalistic conspiracy against him—that the press avoided mentioning him for fear that people would go to hear him. And this caused him great anxiety, for England was central to his plans. If the single-tax movement caught on there, its success would be furthered in other countries—including the United States. As he ended his first visit to Britain, he assured his leading American financial backer that he had "done a bigger work (or rather started bigger forces) than any American who ever crossed to the old country." [30]

George's British friends constantly bolstered his morale. Helen Taylor told him in October, 1882, that she saw the six-penny edition of *Progress and Poverty* almost everywhere. The editor of the *Contemporary Review* told him that his audience was growing bigger and better and that he was attracting the attention especially of the thinking classes. Michael Davitt and other British Georgites also reassured him that more than any other book *Progress and Poverty* was making the cry of the poor heard.

If by March, 1883, George was jubilant, the reason was that his book was doing admirably in many places but best of all in England: "All over the country *Progress and Poverty* is being discussed in lectures and debates and in the Mock Parliaments, of which they now have so many. Every few days I get English provincial papers containing long reports of such discussions." By January, 1884, George called himself "the best advertised man in England," and he told his wife, "I can't begin to send you the papers in which I am discussed, attacked and commented on—for I would have to send all the English, Scotch and Irish papers." Always, however, the vexation remained that George's critics misinterpreted and distorted his views and linked him—because of his Irish disciples—with explosives.[31]

IX

George's achievement was the envy of all writer-reformers, and with good cause, but it was almost a decade before another reformist book caused anything remotely resembling the stir that *Progress and Poverty* had made. Such a book was General William Booth's *In Darkest England and the Way Out* (1890). "You will be pleased with it," an English single-taxer told Henry George. "It seems to me the most important thing that has occurred for some time." The economic historian William J. Ashley, apologizing to an American editor for the length of his review of the volume, explained that it was, after all, an exceptional book and that it was attracting a vast amount of attention in England. W. T. Stead, who had helped General Booth with the book, used his press connections to publicize it as well as the appeal it contained for funds to further the Salvation Army's scheme of social salvation. Stead thus had every reason to take pride in the success of *In Darkest England*. "General Booth's book has gone to 200,000 copies, and 100,000 copies of the 1s. edition are ordered," he noted in January, 1891.

Apart from Stead, the General had other illustrious and articulate supporters who endorsed his call for increased state help and increased private charity to lift up the downtrodden in society. But the General also had some illustrious and articulate enemies —Thomas Henry Huxley, whose agnosticism made him suspicious of anything connected with the Salvation Army; and the president of the Charity Organisation Society, Charles Loch, who doubted the desirability of multiplying and duplicating the facilities for private charity. The upshot was that while the General was gratified by the attention his book received, he was startled by the intensity of the hostilities that his scheme of social salvation awakened. "The Church, the Conservative, the brewing and drinking interests and gambling and unclean businesses, together with the Ultra-Radical and Socialist parties appeared to have joined hand [*sic*] to slay the infant," he reported to Henry George.[32]

x

The controversy over the General's book had not ended when Robert Blatchford's *Merrie England* (1894) achieved the fame of which writer-reformers dreamed. *Merrie England,* unlike *Progress and Poverty* and *In Darkest England,* received relatively little attention in the press, and Blatchford, like Henry George for a while, was bitter about what he regarded as a conspiracy on the part of newspapers and magazines to ignore his work. Even so, *Merrie England* quickly reached a mass audience, a good fortune not enjoyed by some other recent socialist books, for example *The Fabian Essays* and William Morris's *News from Nowhere.* In the words of a circular advertising Blatchford's masterpiece:

This Book is intended to explain in a simple and interesting manner the reasons why the many are poor, the way in which they .can escape from poverty, and the reasons why they should try to receive a better state of things for themselves and their children.

It explains Socialism and answers all the chief arguments commonly used against Socialism. It deals in a plain way with poverty and drink, the factory system, capital and labour, property and land.

It shows why England ought to grow her own wheat, and shows how she could do it.

It is the very book a working man can read and should read. It explains and clears up in a series of short and easy essays nearly all the questions which seem so hard and so dry to the average reader.

It is easy to read and easy to understand, and has already enlightened many readers who have perused it in the columns of *The Clarion*.

It was designed for purposes of popular education, and promises thoroughly to fulfil the purpose.

The advertisement did not lie. No doubt about it, *Merrie England* is a joy to read. But this is not to say that it was a joy to write. For, like Ruskin, Blatchford derived little pleasure from his pieces on social questions. "Work of the 'Merrie England' kind is laborious and painful and gives me no personal satisfaction," he confided to a friend, and if he had his way, he "would never write another line of social thought." In short, Blatchford was a frustrated literary man who could hardly control his passion to write artistic pieces. Like William Morris, however, he felt that art could not flourish in a society in which poverty abounded, and so, however reluctantly, he played the part of a recruiting officer for socialism. A letter he wrote to A. M. Thompson, the co-editor of *The Clarion*, is especially revealing:

A week or two since the yearning for artistic work had got so strong a hold on me I felt like giving in and letting the other work alone. And then I was in Manchester drinking in the Exchange and there came a little match girl, and I looked at her and saw the pretty child face and sweet feminine soul of the baby already half deformed and the flame of rage, that such a sight always lights in me, began to burn and I felt like a traitor who had gone over to the flesh pots and left the tiny ones to be trodden down and savaged by the Ghouls.[33]

George Gissing often complained about his inability to make his moral indignation marketable, but Blatchford had no such trouble. For life without indignation was impossible for him. In a remarkable piece of self-analysis, he confided to a friend: "I used to think that it was because I had been hungry and sickly and unhappy as a boy that I was impelled to fight for justice and toleration. But perhaps if I had been a duke I should have been a Socialist and a rebel. We must be born so." Indeed, when Blatchford joked that by not becoming a clergyman he deprived the church of a fine parson, he did not exaggerate. His sincerity, his idealism, his Carlylesque hatred of cant and sham, his profound sympathy for the poor, his wariness of Shavian brilliance and straining for effect, and his love of simple and strong language—

all helped to account for the success of the masterpiece that took him, he estimated, a month to write.[34]

The reception of *Merrie England* also owed much to the support of a number of prominent labor leaders. As Blatchford told John Burns in June, 1894: "I have written a book called "Merrie England," which is making converts wholesale. I mean to get out a popular edition, at cost price, and I want it spread all over England. You can do a great deal. Will you do it?" Burns and other socialists helped, and so did the ubiquitous Stead. Pointing out in December, 1894, that he had made *Merrie England* the book-of-the-month selection for the *Review of Reviews,* Stead explained: "It is a phenomenal 1d. socialist manifesto of which 700,000 copies have been sold, they expect to reach a million by the new year, and the size of the book and the shape of it, and the cheapness of it, and its extraordinary circulation, demand attention." By the early twentieth century Blatchford estimated that the book had sold nearly two million copies in England and the United States, and that it had been translated into eight languages.[35]

XI

The last of the super-sellers by a late Victorian writer-reformer was Ernest E. Williams's vigorous and often funny *"Made in Germany"* (1896). Like *Merrie England,* it began as a journalistic venture; and, like Blatchford, Williams was a socialist, although this fact never emerges in his pages. The success of the book owed much to the deterioration of Anglo-German diplomatic relations in the late nineties and to the alarm caused in England by German economic and naval expansion. The book itself, however, though it was often misinterpreted and distorted, was not a piece of alarmist literature. Its main thesis was that the relative economic decline of England could be stopped. Although foreign competition threatened them, the English had it in their power to improve their position considerably. But they had to act—and act soon. Among other things, they had to revamp their antiquated consular system, abandon free trade, reorganize their educational system, stop their uncritical worship of old economic practices and habits, and learn to venerate and welcome economic innovations.[36]

In addition to *"Made in Germany," Merrie England, In Darkest*

England, and *Progress and Poverty,* there were other influential books by writer-reformers that struck some late Victorians as seminal: John Seeley's *Expansion of England* (1883), an extraordinarily successful attempt to inspire empire-mindedness; Herbert Spencer's *The Man Versus the State* (1884), a devastating attack on the growth of state intervention and the decline of the spirit of self-help; Edward Bellamy's *Looking Backward* (1888), an ingenious American romance about a golden age without hard times, unemployment, waste, insanity, and suicide; *The Fabian Essays in Socialism* (1889); Edward Carpenter's *Civilization, Its Cause and Cure* (1889); and *If Christ Came to Chicago* (1894), W. T. Stead's moving plea—"the general judgment is that it is the best book I ever wrote"—for the improvement of conditions in urban slums.[37]

For every book by a writer-reformer that attracted attention, however, there were hundreds that made only a slight impression. That they were written and published in such quantities is what matters. Filling many shelves in the great libraries of the world, they testify to many things: to the vitality of the reform impulse in late Victorian England; to the importance at the time of what a publisher's reader called "the philanthropic public"; and to the sense of obligation that so many writers had that they must bear —and lessen—the burdens of the society in which they lived.[38]

VIII

FIGHTING ECCLESIASTICS

Along with writers, clergymen were invaluable converts to the cause of reform. Their social prestige and their ability to attract publicity in the press were major advantages, but their chief asset was their easy access to their parishioners. Clergymen, to be sure, sometimes protested that they had no regular holidays, insisting that they and their parishioners would be better off if they had occasional breaks in their monotonous relations. Nevertheless, it was the very closeness of these ties with their people that made them important opinion-leaders. It was quite natural for Charles Darwin to wish that clergymen would engage more in instruction than in exhortation, but it was this very power to exhort that endeared them to countless reformers.[1]

When Quaker John Bright grumbled to Gladstone in 1874 that Roman Catholics voted as priests told them to vote, he doubtless exaggerated priestly power. But the influence that Bright ascribed to the Roman Catholic clergy other reformers attributed to other clergymen, and so they gave particular attention to gaining their support. It is revealing that Henry George went out of his way during his stays in Britain to meet ministers who might be persuaded to preach the gospel of the single tax. Hopeful, for instance, about the results of a lengthy session in London with an impressive and receptive group of ecclesiastics, George assured an American financial backer in 1882 that things were really moving. In Ireland, too, George worked tirelessly for priestly support, and while he proved to be overoptimistic in the long run, he did not exaggerate when he reported that his ideas were making headway particularly among the younger clergy. In fact, British ecclesiastics repeatedly raised George's hopes. "Without doubt the light is spreading quickly," Stewart Headlam, the spirited Anglican minister and irrepressible Christian Socialist, told George in 1882, adding that he heard *Progress and Poverty* discussed on all sides. What is more, the Georgite campaign to win over clergymen continued for years. As late as 1889, when George was planning another lecture tour in Britain, Sidney Webb, the best organized and most efficient socialist of the time, urged him to remember the clergy: "remind all your committees to bring you into contact with all the ministers round." Not that George needed the reminder! [2]

As with George, so with other reformers. The Manchester and Salford Sanitary Association petitioned the Archbishop of York in 1890 to use the power of the Church to promote sanitary reform, and two years later the Church of England Sanitary Association was formed. Thomas Hughes worked persistently to recruit clergymen for the cooperative movement. As he proudly told the wife of the Bishop of Ripon in 1887: "I am glad the Bishop means to throw his hat (though it is a three cornered one) into the ring for cooperation. By the way we score another Bishop (the fourth or counting your husband the fifth) at this year's congress." Of all late Victorian reformers, however, it was W. T. Stead who pursued the clergy most relentlessly in his efforts to apply Christian ethics to the conditions of English life. No one was safe from Stead—not even the Pope; and clergymen often found it easier to say yes to him than to be subjected to the type of barrage he could deliver.[3]

Politicians also actively sought the aid of the clergy in order to advance particular reforms. Gladstone's Home Secretary Henry Austin Bruce, seeking publicly respected members for a committee to reexamine the legislation concerning prostitution, urged the Reverend Thomas Binney to serve because he had the confidence of the Dissenters. And Gladstone himself, having appealed for adherents to Carnegie's gospel of wealth, reported to his American chief that Cardinal Manning had expressed his strong support of the doctrine shortly before his death in 1892. Even more important, Edward White Benson, the Archbishop of Canterbury, was enthusiastic about the scheme, and he was communicating his fervor to his clergy, Gladstone told Carnegie. Not that this was a surprise, for Benson had served as a member of the House of Lords committee that investigated "sweating"; he had defended the extension of the suffrage, insisting that the Church could trust the masses; and he had repeatedly upheld the idea of reform from within.[4]

Some clergymen—and their wives—continued to hesitate to express their views on public issues, doubting the wisdom of committing themselves and alienating some of their co-religionists. The Bishop of Bath and Wells refused to become a patron of the YMCA for fear of endorsing the general policy of the organization. And Catherine Booth, wife of the founder of the Salvation Army, told Henry George that privately she would further his ideas as much as she could but that her position made it impossible for her to advocate his views publicly.

Such reticence, however, was increasingly unfashionable. Late Victorian clergymen—and their wives—took sides with much more frequency and much more daring than their predecessors. The social question, declared Herbert Mills, the outspoken Unitarian minister and socialist, "is much more in need of trusty workers than any religious question—if indeed they be not identical." English methods of dealing with the children of the poor required drastic revision, Henrietta O. Barnett, wife of the Anglican minister and social reformer, told everyone who would listen as well as those who were reluctant to listen.[5]

II

The increased involvement of clergymen in reform activities was closely linked with the protracted depression. For ministers, much more than any other professional group, saw at first hand the suffering that went with hard times. "It was always my wish to be *at work* and amongst the poor," Father Dawson reported from Liverpool to his master Henry George; but much of the work that Father Dawson and other clergymen did was the direct result of the lack of work of their parishioners. In the words of a Dissenter who was alarmed by the plight of his co-religionists in a small town in Durham: "The great difficulty with which they

have to struggle is *extreme poverty*. Many are out of work altogether and those who are in work have very low wages, with a
further reduction . . . about to take place."

Since many clergymen were exposed daily and hourly to scenes
of almost unbelievable misery and degradation, it is understandable that they were especially susceptible to the appeals made by
reformers. Long before W. T. Stead brought out *If Christ Came
to Chicago,* clergymen were saying in much the same indignant
tone that Jesus would be appalled by social conditions in any
number of English urban and rural communities. By 1892, in
fact, Stead was able to alert his American editor to an important
statement that many of the leading clergymen not only of England
but of the Empire were about to issue:

> We rejoice exceedingly to note the quickened interest of men of all Parties
> in questions relating to the amelioration of the conditions of existence among
> the masses of labouring men and women, and their evident desire to use the
> authority and influence of the State on behalf of the Poor, the oppressed,
> and those who have no helper. To promote industrial peace in place of in-
> dustrial war; to secure to every toiler one day's rest in seven; to protect the
> orphan, and to provide for the aged; to humanize the conditions of labour,
> and to remove the great physical evils and social plagues which render family
> life almost impossible to many of our fellow men. All these are Social aspira-
> tions which owe their origin and their inspiration to the Christian ideal.

The increased involvement of clergymen in reform activities was
also due to their fear that if they remained aloof unbelievers would
capture the reform movements. If, on the other hand, clergymen
played an active role in the groups, they could control them.
W. T. Stead, eager for a united Christendom, noted proudly that
his conception of religion was so elastic that he would include in
the ranks of Christians people whom most others would brand
as heretics. But few clergymen shared Stead's broad view of Christianity, and they feared the damage that might be done if the
wrong people directed reform movements. As the Reverend H. J.
B. Heath, assistant secretary of the Land Nationalisation Society,
bluntly put it to Henry George: "In such a movement there will
be many workers of varying shades of thought, but the lofty
religious tone which has pervaded those of your speeches which
I have been privileged to hear, has strengthened my conviction
that to win the goal it is of imperative importance that the real
leadership should be in the hands of Christian men." [6]

III

The increased participation of clergymen in reform activities owed much to the Great Depression, but it was also in part a result of the general religious history of the time. In this history, to be sure, Darwinism, higher criticism, agnosticism, and atheism figured prominently, but scholars have greatly exaggerated the influence of these movements in late nineteenth-century England. It is true that they had a profound impact on the lives of some intellectuals. Young W. E. Henley wrote poetry in which he tried "to set forth the reckless despair, the wild sorrow of an age that believes and hopes nothing, that finds no pleasure in the thought that there can be an Hereafter and no consolation for the fact that there is not save in a frenzy of sensuous enjoyment." Old Cardinal Newman deplored "the tyranny under which we at present lie of a 'science falsely so called,' which is so shallow, so audacious, so arrogant, and so widely accepted." Ouida was staggered by the growing number of scholars to whom Christianity was simply one of many passing phases of belief. And Thomas Hardy envisaged lives of chronic melancholy for people who had lost their faith. It is striking that even William Holman Hunt, who held steadfastly to the whole scheme of Christian revelation, proclaimed himself notoriously behind the times; but he and Frederic Shields continued to try in their paintings "to illustrate some new truth of the infinite sided story of God's loving care of His children to be found around us plainly enough." [7]

While it is unmistakable that Darwinism, higher criticism, agnosticism, and atheism were central influences in the lives of some intellectuals, their importance for the late Victorian population as a whole has been greatly overstated. Indeed, it is edifying that as late as 1879—twenty years after the publication of *The Origin of Species*—Charles Darwin told a French correspondent: "It has delighted me to find that you are not shocked at the belief that man is a modified and wonderfully improved descendant of some lower animal-form. . . . Throughout Europe, with the exception of France, the great principle of evolution seems to me to be now fixed on a sure basis; *though very many yet demur to man being included in the same category.*"

The late Victorians remained a church-going population. Swinburne could declare that Christianity seemed almost lifeless. Bernard Shaw could quip that God had gone out of fashion in the London of the seventies and "had not been heard of there since." Mrs. Annie Besant could contend that if there were a God, "how one would hate him for making things in such a muddle"; and she could devote her energies to trying to prove that atheism and morality were not antithetical. And the friends of Thomas Henry Huxley could argue from his exemplary life that agnosticism and goodness could coexist.[8] But, for all the efforts of critics of traditional religion, England was filled with people who, like John Ruskin's mother, constantly anticipated the coming of the end of the world; who, like Edmund Gosse's mother, distributed religious tracts and labored for souls; who, like General Gordon and Gladstone, endlessly called on God for help; who, like William Holman Hunt, expected divine intervention against the Russians as a punishment for their pogroms, for "there is a God in Heaven who rules the world by means somewhat more pointed than the principle of the survival of the fittest"; who, like Bishop Wordsworth, nephew of the poet, rarely completed a railway journey without rendering thanks to God for a safe return; who, like the members of young Norman Angell's family, never engaged in sports, games, or amusements on Sunday, but after church spent the day reading religious books; who, like the country gentleman W. H. G. Bagshawe, objected to a prospective son-in-law because he was not a decided Christian; who, like Angel's father in *Tess*, saw no point in a university education if it was not to be used in the service of God; and who, like the critics of the Roman Catholic Modernist Father Tyrrell, did not hesitate to defame a priest who dared to tamper with traditional beliefs.[9]

The militant atheist Charles Bradlaugh, proud that he had achieved "a certain sort of notoriety," liked to announce that he had no religion and knew nothing of religious needs. But Bradlaugh spoke for only a minute segment of the population. And the vigor of the opposition that he met during his lifetime—especially during his long and melodramatic struggle to take his seat in the House of Commons—is proof of the hold that traditional religion still enjoyed in the late nineteenth century. Even people who thought it as a rule hateful to persecute a man for his opinions were willing to make an exception in Bradlaugh's case, for they saw atheism as a threat to the very foundations of family and social life. Indeed, when Bradlaugh died in 1891, the story was widespread that at the end he had changed his theological opinions. And it is significant that, despite his daughter's repeated denials, the rumor lingered on.[10]

IV

Cardinal Newman deplored the religious unbelief and indifference of the England of his old age, but to clergymen of the late Victorian period the great menace was not so much unbelief as apathy. To increase church attendance was, therefore, one of their main preoccupations. "Our congregations are steadily growing; but they are not yet what they should be and must be," a Baptist minister reported characteristically in 1882. In obituary notices of clergymen few accomplishments were lauded so much as skill in filling once empty churches. And in appeals for funds few arguments were used so often as the need to reach the indifferent. An appallingly large number of young adults, the money-raising leaders of the Congleton Town Mission declared, were totally apathetic about their eternal state; instead of going to church on Sunday, these people spent their time flying pigeons, betting, and playing cards. This type of complaint recurred often in the late nineteenth century.[11]

Indifference was the enemy—and especially among the working classes. Slum-dwellers, as the authors of an exposure of *Squalid Liverpool* (1883) said, most needed the comfort, the enlightenment, and the feeling for humanity that religion could give; and yet they simply did not seem to care about religious values. In short, to fight indifference and win workers to God it was not enough to use spiritual arguments; it was also necessary to change the conditions under which the poor lived. Spiritual and social reform—the Gospel and the social gospel—were inseparable. Arthur Morrison wisely remarked that rainy Sundays in particular inclined the slum-dwellers of the Jago to go to church, where they could keep warm, look at pictures and flowers, hear music, and listen to a brief and undemanding sermon. Morrison had his doubts about churchgoing under these circumstances, but many a clergyman considered almost any kind of appeal justified if it brought people to God.

Never before did English clergymen harp so much on the application of the Christian spirit to worldly matters. "I can never forget," Charles Kingsley noted in 1870, "that while both Church of England and Calvinists were forgetting it, the Early Friends preached the broad gospel of humanity, and acted up to His own preaching by being foremost in all good works." During the last decades of the nineteenth century, clergymen of other religious groups caught up at last with the Friends. Political and economic problems, they insisted, must always be dealt with according to the law and spirit of Christ; it was absurd to divorce the discussion of wealth from that of ethics. At the same time, they emphasized that secular reform without religious regeneration was futile. It was impossible, as General Booth told Henry George, to do "very much for the welfare of men *here* to say nothing of hereafter without the direct recognition and interposition of God."

Like Tolstoy, clergymen preached endlessly the doctrine that belief in God and His love could relieve workers of their sufferings, and that worldly reforms had meaning only in so far as they brought people to God and the Christian spirit to every department of society. On the one hand, clergymen idealized the poor in the spirit of the lines of Walter Savage Landor: "None can confer God's blessing but the poor, / None but the heaven-laden reach His throne." On the other, they worked to lessen the hardships of the poor in the spirit of the words of a Liverpool minister:

> Go, preach the Gospel to the poor,
> Go, to their haunts of sin and grief;
> Those scenes of misery explore—
> Prompt to administer relief.

To achieve results with the poor, clergymen had to be able to gain their confidence, and this ability came to be particularly esteemed. Charles Kingsley, praising a young minister, emphasized that he won the love not only of the rich but of the poor. The Archbishop of Canterbury, strongly recommending a clergyman to Gladstone, stressed his great capacity for making the upper classes and the lowliest of the poor care for one another. And the author of an obituary notice of the Bishop of Sodor and Man praised him especially for the vigor with which he brought the church to the masses. "Good God," Charles Dickens once exploded at a High Church group, "to talk in these times of most untimely ignorance among the people, about what Priests shall wear, and whether they shall turn when they say their prayers!" Dickens's complaint applied less and less during the age of the Great Depression.[12]

V

Many efforts were made in the last decades of the century to bring Christianity to workers through labor churches and settlement houses. But the most ingenious late Victorian attempt to Christianize the working classes took the form of a translation of the New Testament into everyday English. Begun independently by the wife of a Congregational minister and the grandson of a Swiss Reformed preacher, the undertaking speedily won the enthusiastic backing of W. T. Stead, who put its originators, Mrs. Mary Higgs and Ernest Malan, in touch with each other. Stead publicized the venture in the *Review of Reviews*, attracting to it additional enthusiasts who were willing to serve as translators.

The participants consisted of laymen, clergymen, and former clergymen, all of whom felt that, although the Revised Version was a great advance over the Authorized Version, it retained, nonetheless, far too much archaic language; and this, they insisted, was unfortunate, for the working classes could not understand what they read. "I am inclined to think," one of the participants, a Congregational minister, wrote in 1893, "that few things have repelled the multitudes of artisans and manual labourers from the Churches more than the artificial aspect given to Christianity by the old-world language, the antique clothing given to the truth." Christianity, he added, was undergoing a severe trial, and unless it penetrated all phases of the nation's life, it would die. If it was to live and rule, it could not remain a curiosity. The new translation, in a word, was not for the educated but for the masses—artisans, laborers, and young people leaving school. Indeed, the aim of the collaborators emerged clearly in their discussion of a title for their work. Before they finally decided to call it The Twentieth Century New Testament, they considered such possible titles as The New Testament in Every-Day English, The New Testament in Present-Day English, The New Testament in Modern English, The New Testament in Current Language, The New Testament in the English of To-Day, and The New Testament, People's Version.[13]

The chief bond of the translators was their strong belief in the social responsibilities of the Christian. Mrs. Higgs was active in philanthropic work for destitute women and girls, and she started the movement to beautify Oldham. Mrs. S. Elizabeth Mee, the wife of a Methodist clergyman, was a vigorous temperance worker as well as an admirer of Edward Bellamy, General Booth, and W. T. Stead. Several of the contributors were outspoken Christian Socialists. E. D. Girdlestone, an ex-curate, helped to found the Clifton and Bristol Christian Socialist Society and the Birmingham Fabian Society, and he wrote and lectured constantly on socialist topics. Henry Bazett, another former clergyman, was a socialist who engaged actively in the organization of trade unions among women. Ernest Malan, on the other hand, was suspicious of socialism and convinced that its adherents were often hostile to religion and lacking in morality. "As long as human selfishness continues in both master and man," he told one of his clergymen-translators in 1893, "so long will it be impossible to much ameliorate the lot of the community; the oppressed will merely become the oppressors and so on ad infinitum. No, we want the power of the Good News to help the 'kosmos' and may our present labors tend towards that happy end!" [14]

Despite illnesses, disagreements, financial difficulties, and the pressures of other commitments, all of which made the progress of the work seem slow to many an ardent participant, the contributors succeeded in bringing out the tentative edition of their New Testament between 1898 and 1901 and their revised edition in 1904. Whether it achieved the results they expected from it among the working classes is doubtful, but they publicized the work with skill. They distributed circulars, sent presentation copies to local editors, circulated leaflets in trams and trains, and used posters and window bills on a large scale. They won the support of the Salvation Army and a number of prominent ministers of different sects. And their work still stands as one of the most notable attempts to make the New Testament read, as Christ spoke, "not in the language of 'the schools,' not in a peculiar ecclesiastical phraseology . . . but, as far as possible, in the very language of the market-place and the street." [15]

VI

Like other reformers, clergymen often quarreled with one another. Their disputes, which were above all sectarian, took place on several levels. To start with, Protestant and Roman Catholic clergymen denounced one another freely. On the eve of the election of 1892, for instance, an organization known as the Protestant Alliance issued a list of candidates who could be recommended for their religious beliefs, and in order to keep Protestants on guard gave them the names of Roman Catholics who were running for office. What Joseph Mazzini during his frequent stays in England had called "Papacy and its deadly influences" was, of course, a favorite theme of Protestant clergymen; so, too, were what other publicists had long been calling "the enormities and gross contradictions of Romanism" and "the open encroachments of popery." Rome, Charles Kingsley wrote characteristically, "is utterly of the Devil, and . . . not only she, but all which approaches to her, is to be held anathema by every one who does not intend to give up not merely his status, but his very feeling, as an Englishman."

Charles Dickens had belittled fears of papal aspirations in England, looking forward to the time when the papacy would "wear itself out and wear out the endurance of mankind." He found it incredible that "any human creature should seek at this time of day to set up the tottering monster in England here!" The English, he asserted in 1869, "are in unconquerable opposition to that church. They have the animosity in their blood—derived from the history of the past, though perhaps unconsciously." But few of Dickens's Protestant contemporaries and successors shared his confidence. They thought of Catholics as a well-disciplined flock that was always ready to do what the "old gentleman in Rome" told it to do. Samuel Smiles, the author of the best-selling *Self-Help*, provided material for many a sermon in the early seventies when he brought out his history of the Huguenots and showed "what certain parties did, not so very long ago, when they had the power." [16]

In part, the fear of Roman Catholicism was due to the extraordinary attention given to celebrities who became converts. George Santayana, visiting Oxford for the first time in 1887, remarked that Catholicism was in high favor and that conversions were frequent. And an ardent Anglican minister, surveying the religious situation in 1888, was ashamed to be living in an age when so many people were "being deceived by Romanism." Such impressions were current because Roman Catholic clergymen rarely permitted conversions to take place without publicizing their spiritual victories. While their behavior reflected their own insecurity in a hostile religious setting, it also served to make the setting even more hostile.[17]

Cardinal Manning served as the favorite target for the anti-Catholic prejudices of the late Victorians. "He seems a very old man, so wizened that he can scarcely grow any older," a contemporary observed in 1881. But Manning lived on until 1892—long enough, among other things, to petition for the canonization of Joan of Arc. In fact, his last years were in many respects the most fruitful of his life, especially in his attempts to apply Christianity to social problems. Lionel Johnson, the poet and convert, had the greatest respect for him, as did his fellow-poet and convert Aubrey de Vere; but devout Protestants—Gladstone among them—could not forgive Manning for the steps he had taken in the years since he had announced his general approval of the Oxford Tracts and his implicit belief in the principles they upheld. Henry George, W. T. Stead, Joseph Chamberlain, and even Gladstone sought his aid as a reformer, but Protestant clergymen preferred to pretend that he did not exist.

Even within the Roman Catholic Church Manning was often under suspicion and isolated, for his eagerness for social reform exceeded that of many of his fellow-priests. "I heartily wish that all Catholics appreciated as clearly as you the great significance of the Holy Father's Encyclical," he told W. T. Stead shortly after the appearance of *Rerum novarum,* the pronouncement of 1891 on the application of Christian principles to the relations of capital and labor.[18]

VII

While Protestant clergymen joined to criticize Catholics, they themselves rarely stood together. Anglicans and Dissenters carried on their centuries-old conflict, the former refusing to alter the position of the State Church, the latter continuing to assert the righteousness of disestablishment and disendowment. Many a Dissenting clergyman could have said, like the Reverend J. G. Greenhough: "I was brought up a Calvinist of the olden type, with a fear which always troubled me more or less that I might not be one of the elect, with a wholesome horror of Rome, priests and theatres, with a belief that the prayer book and the Romish Missal were not far apart."

It was striking, however, that many Protestant clergymen, who could agree on little else, joined forces to condemn the most important new development in late Victorian Protestant history: the emergence of General Booth's Salvation Army. "My whole life," the General aptly remarked in 1891, "has been one continued fight with obstacles of one class or another, and my opponents have ever been those who have professedly sought the same end as myself." Fortunately for General Booth he always felt the Hand of the Lord on and with him; fortunately, too, he had Mrs. Booth to bolster and console him. Indeed, until her death from cancer in 1887, she played a vital role in the Army. General Booth did not exaggerate when he told a correspondent who was alleged to have a cure for cancer that his wife's life was "a very valuable one not only to us as a family, but to the church and the world." [19]

The hostility to General Booth and his officers—of whom there were almost five thousand by 1899—was largely emotional. Salvationists, specializing in devices to attract the religiously indifferent, worked on the assumption that some people had been so beaten down by misery that they had wandered from God. The world, Robert Burns once remarked in a period of discouragement, "sits such a load on my mind that it has effaced almost every trace of the image of God in me." Salvationists tried to lift some of the pressures on the downtrodden and in the process to awaken or reawaken their feeling for God.

To get the wretched to listen was their biggest practical problem, and much of the notoriety of the Salvationists grew out of the unusual audio-visual aids they employed. In 1879, for example, they caused considerable commotion in Manchester. "For some days before the first service was held," a contemporary observed, "the walls of the town were placarded, in a sensational manner, with the announcement that 'Captain Booth and the Salvation Army will attack Beelzebub every evening, in the Salvation Temple, Grosvenor Street,' and that he would be assisted by the 'Hallelujah Brass Band,' the 'Champion Pigeon Flyer,' and 'a band of Hallelujah Lasses.' " Hoodlums appeared at meetings, and the police of Manchester were kept busy. A year later an

American visitor, having heard Mrs. Booth in Glasgow, noted in his diary:

She brought down the house in a very un-religious roar at her descriptions of Army devices to attract attention. Two of them came one night into a town in the snow—one had lost his voice at a shouting the night before, nor could the one with a voice get a hearing. So they planned that one should lie down in the snow as if dead, and the other should stand by and stare at him without saying a word. Presently came a small boy, who ran into a public-house and told them of the extraordinary sight. They rushed out and, the man continuing standing and silent, a great crowd gradually gathered. Then —"Up and at 'em, Jim!" said the fellow, and they had a rouser! Another pair brought four yards of clothesline, made a noose for the neck of one, whom the other dragged about the streets until he got a crowd after them.[20]

Nor was this all. At the time of the Oxford-Cambridge boat race of 1881 Salvationists set up their outposts and paraded with placards bearing such inscriptions as "Let us therefore run the race that is set before us." By 1891 there were probably few urban slum-dwellers who had not had an adventure with Salvationists similar to the one Plato E. Draculis described in a private letter: "I had two attacks, one by an Officer and one by a Salvation Army lass for the purpose of saving me. They assured me that I could be saved that very night. They exercised all their persuading powers to get me to go to the front and be saved. I was unable to get rid of them until I solemnly declared that I had direct dealings with God who duly assured me that I for one can not possibly be saved except through a life time effort." Such jokes about the Army were widespread in the late Victorian period.

Increasingly, however, the impressive achievements of the Salvationists were appreciated. Even Robert Buchanan, notorious for his attacks on his fellow-writers, wrote a poem sympathetic to the Army. "I see all the follies and absurdities of the movement," he confessed in 1892, "but I try to show that it may get hold, through its very tumultuousness, of natures inaccessible to all other influences." Buchanan's conclusion was shared especially by temperance reformers, who were often convinced that no other group was so responsible for so many new abstainers and so many fewer public houses.[21]

VIII

The disputes among late Victorian clergymen-reformers were mainly sectarian, but they were also partly personal: some ministers simply could not stand others. And their cleavages were also ideological, for while most clergymen favored only moderate reforms, some were outspoken socialists. Herbert Mills, the Unitarian minister and socialist, shrewdly summed up the difficulties he was having in 1889 with a land settlement scheme: "We are obliged to carry on our work judiciously. If we look for the means of starting a colony amongst the avowed friends of Socialism we cannot possibly raise the money we need so as to be independent of commerce and if we put the socialistic aspects of the experiment into the very front of our advocacy we shall offend many who might have helped, amongst those who desire to help the poor but who have an unreasonable fear of Socialism."

While Christian Socialists still had a hard time of it in the last decades of the nineteenth century, their difficulties were fewer than those faced by F. D. Maurice, J. M. Ludlow, and Charles Kingsley when they undertook their campaign to Christianize socialism and socialize Christianity. Yet just as Kingsley had protested bitterly in 1851 about "the ignorant and dishonest attempt to identify Christian Socialism with Communism," so later upholders of the cause had the same complaint. And just as Maurice was bitterly attacked—even persecuted—for the theology that underlay his Christian Socialism, so, too, were his late Victorian counterparts. Indeed, Thomas Hughes in his old age recalled mournfully and accurately that Maurice "was quite unable to think of any good times he had ever had or good he had done, but only of the wretched mess the poor old world had blundered into, which he had been sent specially to pull her out of and hadn't done it." [22]

Christian Socialists believed that they knew what Kingsley liked to call "the real meaning of the Bible," and while Kingsley himself had decided by 1870 that he could contribute most by devoting his remaining years—he died in 1875—to the popularization of physical science, other Christian Socialists continued to focus their attention on the Bible as *the* guide to the organization of social life. When the Bishop of Manchester predicted in 1877 that the principle of cooperation would figure more and more prominently in the economic life of the English people, he voiced a great hope of the Christian Socialists. For socialism, as J. M. Ludlow always insisted, was simply "the 'ism' of being social or partnerly," and it embraced all cooperative enterprises.

As late as 1885 Ludlow refused to say to what extent Christian Socialism had succeeded or failed, but he noted that it had served as "a leaven—that is, as modern science teaches us, a living germ, —capable of reproduction *ad infinitum.*" While he could detect its influence operating profoundly in many people who were unaware of the fact, he feared that the latter-day Christian Socialists had lost the zeal of the earlier movement. Indeed, he was convinced, though unjustly so, that the late Victorian Christian Socialists were almost entirely unfamiliar with the writings of F. D. Maurice and the other early pioneers.[23]

IX

In 1868 John Bright protested angrily that the members of the Anglican hierarchy were remiss in their obligation "to expose or to remedy the grievous ignorance, sufferings, and poverty of so many of our people." The last part of the century, however, was the age of Edward White Benson—a time when Anglican and other clergymen concerned themselves so much with the relations between Christianity and social conditions that the charge was often made that they could have little time left for their own spiritual improvement, to say nothing of that of their parishioners. The aged Dean of Salisbury, noting in 1894 the preoccupation of young clergymen with the social implications of religion, confessed that if he was not disposed to be hard on them the reason was that he himself as a young man had undergone the influence of Maurice, Kingsley, and other Christian Socialists. By the end of the century it was so ordinary for clergymen to stress what Bishop Westcott called *The Social Aspects of Christianity* (1887) that young G. K. Chesterton, examining in 1899 the manuscript of a novel of faith and doubt and of capitalism and socialism, reported to the publisher for whom he was serving as a reader, "The question is—do people want any more of them?" For his part, Chesterton was convinced that "most thinking people" had long since come to the conclusion that "real Christianity was a misunderstood Socialism." [24]

{ IX }

POLITICIANS UNDER PRESSURE

If reformers rejoiced when they drew journalists, writers, and clergymen to their ranks, they went ecstatic when they won the support of politicians—particularly Members of Parliament. For the sooner they converted them to their cause, the greater was the likelihood that the particular abuse they condemned would speedily receive what that pioneer humanitarian Thomas Clarkson liked to call a "death-wound from the British Parliament." Thus almost all the roads reformers traveled led to Westminster —and especially to the lobby of the House of Commons, where, Thomas Hughes remarked, much of the important business of Parliament was transacted.[1]

When reformers lashed out at politicians—"those old muffs in the Upper House," as Hughes once wrote angrily of the Lords —almost invariably the reason was that they had been unable to convert them. In fact, from the time of Thomas Carlyle and Charles Dickens to that of William Morris and Rudyard Kipling, some of the sharpest critics of Parliament were reformers who had been balked by unreceptive politicians—reformers who found to their distress that the zeal of the impassioned did not necessarily pave the way for the legislation of the wise. Indeed, Carlyle and Dickens refused to serve in such a cockpit as the House of Commons—it was, they thought, far too depressing an arena. In at least one outburst Kipling dismissed most Members of Parliament as "best dead and dee little use any way." And in his socialist novel *News from Nowhere* (1890) William Morris had the

Houses of Parliament converted into a storage place for manure.[2]

Reformers made the lot of politicians difficult at best. As Sidney Webb remarked of the sturdy Gladstonian Liberal John Morley, during the eight-hour agitation, "Some strong medicine is being administered to him, but he must have a good deal more from all sides." What Webb tried to inflict on Morley, other reformers— from lively antivivisectionists to grim bimetallists—tried to inflict on other politicians. It is not strange, therefore, that Members of Parliament often complained that they were hopelessly busy, that they needed extended respites from the strain of parliamentary work, that they used up their strength, as the old Tory Colonel William Bromley Davenport wrote,

> In elbowing through divisions
> And arguing Bills of ungainly length
> Full of wearisome provisions. . . .

Davenport, a character straight out of Trollope, even took to daydreaming:

> Last night in St. Stephen's so wearily sitting,
> (The member for Boreham sustained the debate),
> Some pitying spirit that round me was flitting
> Vouchsafed a sweet vision my pains to abate.
> The Mace, and the Speaker, and the House disappearing,
> The leather clad bench is a thoroughbred horse,
> 'Tis the whimpering cry of the Foxhound I'm hearing,
> And my 'seat' is a pig skin at Ranksboro' Gorse.

To listen to the complaints of late Victorian Members of Parliament is to wonder why they were willing to serve at all. Prestige and the need to exercise power certainly had much to do with it, but so, too, did something else: like Davenport himself, many Members would have argued that, while they had nothing to gain in a personal sense, they were determined at almost any cost to keep worse men out.[3]

When reformers did not get their way—and this was much of the time—they struck out especially at the prime minister who had thwarted them; and, looking forward to a change of government, they returned with ardor to winning the kind of mass support that might force politicians to listen. "The more quickly we can afford Lady Beaconsfield the felicity of possessing the exclusive attentions of her husband the better will it be for the Nation!"

wrote a frustrated reformer in 1868. "So long as the Tories are in power," a crusader for the reform of the laws relating to prostitution predicted in 1876, "we shall not carry our point, but when the day for a Liberal government to be returned comes, we shall be on the winning side"; in the meantime, he added, the important thing was to get the public to understand the problem of prostitution and become familiar with ways to solve it. Mrs. Josephine E. Butler, similarly obsessed with the need to abolish what was in effect legalized prostitution, also recorded her exasperation with Disraeli and the Tories. "We, like you," she told Gladstone, "have been driven from any dependence upon Parliament, at least as it is at present constituted, to base our hopes upon the awakened conscience of the people at large." [4]

Just as disappointed reformers denounced Disraeli as an imposter and a charlatan, so, too, they condemned other prime ministers. "Gladstone has been our ruin and I wish all the women of England would join the Primrose League to keep him and his party out of office for ever," wrote Frances Power Cobbe, the fiery and disheartened women's suffrage advocate. "I do not at present like the state of things in England," Helen Taylor impatiently told Henry George in 1883; Gladstone, she charged, was holding back reform by insisting that his small measures were the most that could be secured. George, for his part, consoled himself with the notion that politicians would "follow the leaders of thought when the latter have made for them a following." And George's disciple, Michael Davitt, reassured himself that the cause of reform could best be served by indoctrinating and organizing the working class, for Parliament would then have no choice but to follow popular opinion. [5]

II

There was nothing unusual about the ways in which late Victorian reformers tried to reach politicians: they swamped them with letters, petitions, and resolutions, and they sought frequent interviews with them. When a library reformer reported that he had sent heaps of letters to Members of Parliament, he spoke not only for himself but for many of his fellow-reformers whose incessant recourse to letter-writing helped to make the collected papers of late Victorian politicians bulge.

Along with the passion of reformers for correspondence went their passion for petitions and resolutions. Indeed, reformers in chambers of commerce, trades unions, farmers' organizations, temperance leagues, women's rights societies, and a host of other formal groups became experts in the drawing up of such documents and in arranging for other reformers to submit similar documents. The Government should adopt the metric system and revamp the consular service, the Manchester Chamber of Commerce urged repeatedly. The Government should extend the eight-hour day to all works under its control, and the London County Council should establish depots for the sale of coal to the working classes, the Battersea Branch of the Amalgamated Society of Engineers petitioned. The Government should make more adequate provision for secondary and technical education, the Technical Instruction Committee of Cheshire pleaded.[6]

Writer-reformers, to be sure, had an easy way to attract the attention of politicians: they could send them copies of their publications. The only question was whether busy Members of Parliament would bother to read the literature they were sent. As Francis W. Newman reported gloomily in 1870, "An M. P. dissuaded me in January from printing 2000 copies and sending a copy to every legislator, by saying that it would inevitably go into the wastepaper basket." While the prospect of adding to the quantity of parliamentary refuse deterred Newman, it had no effect whatever on dozens of other reformers. Henry George sent *Progress and Poverty* to Joseph Chamberlain; the bimetallist Moreton Frewen sent *The Economic Crisis* to Arthur J. Balfour and to Chamberlain; J. A. Spender sent his book on old age pensions to John Morley; H. R. Fox Bourne sent the publications of the Aborigines' Protection Society to dozens of politicians; and when in 1894 Beatrice Webb rushed an advance copy of *The History of Trade Unionism* to John Burns, she begged him to bring it to the attention not only of trade union officials but also of Members of Parliament. "Do boom it in the Lobby!" she urged.[7]

Calling on politicians was another favorite device of reformers. While Charles Stewart Parnell and his Irish cohorts made it a point not to go on deputations to members of the Government, other reformers prided themselves on the frequency of their calls.

Go-getting Mrs. Josephine Butler was such an inveterate deputy that politicians tried to shun her, but they underestimated her patience and her determination. And Mrs. Butler's traits were widespread among her colleagues. It is revealing that when a group of tireless marriage law reformers requested a meeting with Gladstone, Joseph Chamberlain urged him strongly to see them. "These people are influential and can make a great deal of noise," he cautioned. Chamberlain was particularly alive to the desirability of listening to suggestions from organized groups. "Of course when a representation is made to me by so important a body as the Manchester Chamber of Commerce," he remarked characteristically in 1885, "I am bound to give it the most serious consideration. . . ." [8]

III

On the eve of the Reform Act of 1867 and during its immediate aftermath reformers looked above all to one politician: John Bright. Traditionalists, on the other hand, considered him a man to be both watched and stopped, for they viewed him as a latter-day preacher of the Gospel according to St. Robespierre—a demagogue who encouraged the poor to believe that, since they were angels and the rich were scoundrels, they had a right to the property of the rich.

The real John Bright bore little resemblance to the traditionalist stereotype of him. It is true that he always liked to point out that when Englishmen went to other countries they did not refuse to make adequate provision for the education of the masses. Nor did they create peerages, state churches, and lands laws designed to protect the privileged classes. For all that, Bright was willing to acknowledge the greatness of the monarchy, the aristocracy, and the Church. His main contention was that as long as the masses were poor, ignorant, and degraded, the established order was in danger. Indeed, if ever a man respected private property, it was Bright. But the memory of his ferocious and fearless attacks on the corn laws, landlordism, the game laws, the restricted suffrage, imperialism, and the abuse of Ireland made him a superlative target for traditionalists. [9]

By the time Gladstone ended his reform-laden Ministry in 1874 he had replaced Bright as the scourge of standpatters and the darling of reformers. And because he lived so long—he died in 1898—more reformers brought more pressure to bear on him than on any other politician in the last part of the century. Such was Gladstone's stature that even his lukewarm approval was enough to make reformers glow. George Gissing shed his traditional melancholy when Gladstone praised *The Unclassed* and *Thyrza* as worthy examples of the didactic novel. And W. T. Stead could barely contain himself when Gladstone based his last speech in the House of Commons on Stead's *Fifty Years of the House of Lords*. Even tough-minded bookmen were convinced that a statement from Gladstone—flattering or hostile—would sell a book; and they sought his comments with such persistence that by 1898 an American novelist suspected that Gladstone's words were falling flat because of excessive repetition.[10]

There was almost no cause that Gladstone was not asked to support. William Morris, acting in behalf of the Society for the Protection of Ancient Buildings, requested him to sign his name to a petition opposing the rebuilding of the great façade of St. Mark's in Venice: "we well know that no one outside Italy has so much influence there as yourself." Scottish farmers memorialized him to promote legislation that would counteract the ruin brought on by the prolonged agricultural depression. Temperance reformers and the eight-hours people went at him frequently. And that one-man army of reformers, W. T. Stead, gave him no peace. Stead sought his views on marriage—it was the fortress around which "the great battle of belief would be fought," Gladstone answered. During the Jubilee of 1897 Stead even tried to win his support for a movement to halt the splitting of the English language into a host of confusing dialects.[11]

The power of a minister to decide what should be "the engrossing questions"—a power that Gladstone had extolled as a young Tory frightened by the reform agitation of 1832—was his for much of the late Victorian period. In the light of the bombardments to which he was chronically exposed, however, it is no surprise that he was often compelled to tell reformers (in stately language, to be sure) either that he regretted that it was beyond his strength to further their excellent purposes, or that he doubted the practicability at an early date of some particular reform—whether it was land nationalization, the eight-hour day, or temperance. The truth is that after 1886 Gladstone was so obsessed with the Irish home rule question that he regarded all other reform proposals as trivial and superficial. Even when in 1893 he

PEACE AND PLENTY.
A BRIGHT AND GLAD •••• PROSPECT.
Fun, January 23, 1869

urged the revamping of the House of Lords he did so in order to further the home rule cause.[12]

IV

Although Gladstone was the most hounded politician of the last third of the century, there were many other Members of Parliament whom reformers pursued with vigor: Disraeli, Joseph Chamberlain, Sir Charles Dilke, Lord Randolph Churchill, Sir John Gorst, John Morley, James Bryce, Jesse Collings, Anthony John Mundella, and Henry Broadhurst. Of all late Victorian politicians, however, it was Chamberlain who for a time stirred up the greatest hopes in the ranks of reformers. As early as 1873 John Bright told Gladstone that Chamberlain deserved close watching: "he is an able young man, and will before long I doubt not be in the House, and has been a leading speaker on the Education question in Birmingham and other towns." A passionate municipal reformer and defender of the idea of government help, Chamberlain gloried in the changes that made the Birmingham of the seventies the most forward-looking town in the Kingdom: "if you can spare a day or so," he told Gladstone, "I should be proud to show you our Schools, our Improvements and some of the Manufactories which I feel sure would greatly interest you." [13]

By the early eighties reformers looked eagerly to Chamberlain to lead them to a variety of promised lands. From the Queen down, however, traditionalists had no doubt that the former mayor of Birmingham was easily the most dangerous man both in Parliament and in Gladstone's cabinet. Gladstone's ideas were bad enough, but Chamberlain's were unspeakable. "The Tories have always had a Bogey; and they seem inclined to promote me to the position just now," Chamberlain told Gladstone in 1881. Nor did he misstate the role he came to play. For, when traditionalists were guarded, they called him Robespierre and the brummagem dictator; when they spoke freely, they called him unprintable names.

"My proposals may be right or wrong," Chamberlain protested more than once, "but they are not to be answered by slander and fraudulent misrepresentation." That his proposals usually were grossly distorted is easy to understand: he had become by the early eighties the symbol of a new-style demagogue who, traditionalists feared, would incite the masses to plunder the comfortable classes. A real estate agent, explaining in 1883 why he could not find a buyer for a piece of land, wrote to a disappointed squire: "Unfortunately many other people besides yourself have the same feeling of distrust as to legislation regarding land which this radical government seems bent upon carrying out and in addition to this trade is far from good. . . ." If Chamberlain had his wicked way, an old Tory told an old Tory friend, the results would be catastrophic: all the fine old places of England would be made national property and become clubs, libraries, and museums for the working classes.[14]

All that was bad enough. But the point is that Chamberlain was also feared for what was considered his ungentlemanly conception of politics: he simply did not act like a member of the Club. Arthur J. Balfour refused interviews to journalists, insisting that there were no incidents in his life that would interest their readers; and when he did express his views publicly he avoided any excess of candor. Lord Rosebery boasted that he would never willingly permit his speeches to be reprinted in book form. Another aristocrat insisted that people in official positions should not write at all on political, social, and legal questions. And still another aristocrat assumed that when he made a speech he had to be a model of caution in what he said. Chamberlain, on the other hand, was critical of delicacy and restraint in politics; and he was rarely complimented for speaking in good taste or with tact. As he bluntly told Gladstone, who both on his own and at the suggestion of the Queen had tried to moderate him: "Popular government is inconsistent with the reticence which official etiquette formerly imposed on speakers, and which was easily borne as long as the electorate was a comparatively small and privileged class, and the necessity of consulting it at meetings infrequent and limited." [15]

The actual Chamberlain was very different from the ruthless, arrogant, and destructive man and politician that antireformers made him out to be. He had, in fact, the deep humility of a person who has experienced severe trials. Shattered in 1875 by the death of his second wife, he went through years of indescribable suffering. "She was so intimately identified with all my public work as well as with my private life and thought," he confided to Bright, "that I have not a hope or interest which is not crushed by my bereavement." Chamberlain saved himself, though he doubted that he could do it, by losing himself in his work. He drove himself in a way that late Victorian politicians rarely did; and in large measure it was his combination of earnestness, capacity for work, and general indifference to either praise or blame that made him so formidable a figure.

But for an alleged demagogue Chamberlain was remarkably uncompromising. Far from rushing about to curry favor, he constantly asserted his independent-mindedness—and this was true both before and after his break with Gladstone over the issue of Irish home rule. He loathed—and avoided—public dinners. He did not hesitate to alienate labor leaders. And at a high point in the Irish land war, when anti-Irish sentiment in England was intense, he dared to spend an evening with Henry George. Instead of bidding for attention, moreover, he often went out of his way to avoid it. He even refused to write the preface to a reprint of John Stuart Mill's *Principles of Political Economy,* insisting that such work was altogether out of his line.[16]

Chamberlain's ideas were much less threatening than traditionalists imagined. Far from aiming to subvert English institutions, he sought to secure them by modernizing them. Men of property, he said repeatedly, had not only rights but obligations, and the more they met their obligations, the safer their rights would be. Shipowners should welcome concessions to their crews; landlords should encourage the multiplication of small owners; the wealthy should carry a greater share of the tax load; and the whole community should back futher social legislation to assist its poorer members. Always Chamberlain's purpose was to preserve. Indeed, it is revealing that when he thanked Henry George for sending him a copy of *Progress and Poverty,* he pointed out that he could not admit that the state had a right to confiscate land without compensation. Similarly, he told Moreton Frewen of his wariness of state ownership of railroads: "I fear the pressure of the employed would interfere with the satisfactory and economical management of the undertaking." Small wonder that William Morris and other socialists thought that Chamberlain did not go nearly far enough. And disappointed Henry George reached the fantastic conclusion that Chamberlain had nothing of the reformer about him.[17]

V

The role Chamberlain played in the Liberal Party in the early eighties was similar to that of Lord Randolph Churchill among the Tories. Convinced that dedication to the needs of the masses was "absolutely essential to any permanent success for the Tory Party," he tried to give new life to the paternalistic doctrines that Disraeli had preached for decades in his speeches and letters and in such novels as *Sybil* and *Coningsby:* the people could trust the Tories, and the Tories could trust the people; and the Tories, recognizing not only their rights but their obligations, should strive to befriend and uplift the downtrodden and promote class harmony.

Disraeli's critics had often argued that his conception of the aristocracy bore no relation whatever to reality—it was a sycophant's glorification of an irresponsible class and an attempt to reconcile people to its privileges and pretensions. To Churchill, however, there was nothing absurd or impractical about Tory democracy. Proud of the social legislation enacted during Disraeli's great Ministry (1874–80), he insisted that these measures should mark a beginning, not an end. In an age of economic crisis and of almost universal manhood suffrage, he argued repeatedly, Tory survival required the enthusiastic application of Tory democracy. The monarchy, the aristocracy, the Church—these and the rest of the establishment would last forever if the Conservatives acted according to Disraeli's social philosophy. If not, the future belonged to others.[18]

By the mid-eighties it seemed that Churchill might have his way. By harassing and embarrassing Gladstone both in and out of Parliament, he won an incredible amount of publicity, emerging as a David-like hero in the English press. Even the Goliath in his life acknowledged in 1885 that the Tory Party had Churchill "in its bosom and to a great extent in its Leadership." And old Tories feared all the more for the future because they considered Churchill as much of a menace as Joseph Chamberlain. But Gladstone and the anti-Churchill Tories underestimated Churchill's impetuosity as well as Lord Salisbury's determination to stop the young man in a hurry. For, when Churchill submitted his resignation from the cabinet in 1886 over what was a minor issue, Salisbury accepted it—and relieved the anxieties of traditionalists.

While it is easy in retrospect to say that Churchill wrecked his political career by his impatience, this was not at all clear at the time. In the late eighties it seemed almost certain that he would bounce back. What prevented his political resurgence was something unforeseen by contemporaries: the prolonged illness that killed him in 1895 at the age of forty-six. Indeed, the memory of Churchill's speedy rise and fall made some of those who knew his young son Winston fear that he might suffer a similar fate. "I believe in him," the Irish reformer Sir Horace Plunkett wrote in 1902, "provided the high pressure at which he is driving the machine does not wear it out as it did in the case of his unhappy father." [19]

VI

The presence of Chamberlain among the Liberals and of Lord Randolph Churchill among the Conservatives shows what catchalls both major parties were in late Victorian times. Indeed, it is a mistake to think of Conservatives and Liberals as significantly different from each other. Both consisted of three kinds of members: a small group of standpatters, a large group of supporters of mild changes, and a small group of advanced reformers. Conservative and Liberal standpatters, Conservative and Liberal moderates, and advanced Conservatives and Liberals had more in common with each other than they had with other members of their own party. And Churchill and Chamberlain were closer to each other than they were to most of their colleagues.

This confusion of parties enraged people like Herbert Spencer who wanted their political distinctions neat and clear. And it infuriated socialist labor leaders like John Burns and Keir Hardie, who, though they preferred the Liberals to the Conservatives, felt that neither party offered enough to the working classes. The great fact is, however, that the confusion of parties prevented either from claiming a monopoly on progress. Whenever an election approached, each tried to outdo the other in its rhetoric of reform—in its assertion of its contributions to the welfare of the many and not just of the few. Every measure that would help to relieve the burdens of the working classes would have his cordial support, said one Liberal politician after another.[20]

But as with the Liberals, so with the Tories. The historical novelist J. H. Shorthouse and other Tories liked to call themselves members of the Stupid Party, but they fooled no one. The revealing title of a circular distributed during the election of 1885 was *Some Great Tory Reforms: A Legislative Review of Measures Expressly Beneficial to the Working Classes.* And when the Sheffield *Telegraph* issued a broadsheet concerning the labor legislation of the late 1880s, it stressed that the measures demonstrated the aim of Toryism to promote, in a practical way, popular welfare. Similarly, during the campaign of 1892 the Conservative Central Office issued such remarkable leaflets as *Conservatism: Past and Future* and *The Poor Man's Pocket, What the Conservatives Have Done,* which sought to justify their right to be called the friends of the lower classes.

Tories pointed with pride to what they had done for the cheap breakfast table, the improvement of labor legislation, the reorganization of local government, the encouragement of allotments, the erection of artisans' dwellings, and the spread of education. And they promised that they would work in the future to increase small holdings, extend workmen's compensation, improve public health, and promote Irish prosperity. To vote Tory, people in the North Eastern Division of Derbyshire were told in 1892, was to help to shorten the work week and to benefit all classes. The Tories, a representative Member of Parliament pointed out in 1895, could be counted on to press for those social reforms that the changing conditions of the country required.[21]

Nor was Disraeli, the Queen's "dear and ever lamented friend and great Minister," forgotten in all this. The Primrose League, founded to honor and perpetuate his memory, tried to combat class antagonisms and win workers to the Tory fold. And dozens of speeches and publications reasserted Disraeli's Tory Democracy. When a Conservative publicist brought out a penny life of Disraeli, he explained that he wrote the book in the hope that it would "make an effective instrument for educating the masses of our people in sound and progressive Conservative principles." Certainly, however, the best testimonial to Disraeli came from

Joseph Chamberlain after the great Tory defeat of 1906. Chamberlain, long since estranged from the party of Gladstone, told a parliamentary colleague his prescription for the Conservatives: Tory policy should be that advocated by Disraeli in *Sybil* and *Coningsby*.[22]

VII

The rhetoric of reform that Liberals and Conservatives used so freely—even wantonly—had its foundation in dozens of laws passed during the late Victorian age. As early as 1882 an American professor who had carefully examined this legislation claimed that England provided the most striking example anywhere in the world of the power of the state over the individual. He went much too far, of course, but another close student of English affairs—W. T. Stead—did not exaggerate when he pointed out a decade later to readers of the *Review of Reviews* that more and more government was regulating the way of life of the citizen.

Not that Stead's audience needed to be told of the trend, for it had been prominent both nationally and locally for years. Businessmen were compelled to seek out barristers and solicitors who were expert in Board of Trade and related matters. And despite their loud protests against needless and vexatious controls, they were constantly informed that some new law required special registers, age certificate books, abstracts, and other documents. Government officials, working to minimize the leakage of assessable earnings, reminded taxpayers of their responsibilities; and the rates, as George Gissing noted during a stay in Birmingham in 1892, were a topic of perpetual grumbling.[23]

Just as tax collectors descended on citizens, so, too, did a host of other government officials. Inspectors forced one of Galsworthy's Forsytes as well as thousands of nonfictional late Victorians to install drainage systems and other sanitary improvements. And other inspectors justly prided themselves on what they had done to improve conditions in factories. Indeed, Thomas Hardy knew what he was about when he had a character in *Tess* frightened by a visitor who, she suspected, might be "some gaffer sent by Gover'ment." Some civil servants even came to look forward to a time when their superiors would tire of sending them to conduct investigations all over the Kingdom. Other officials insisted that their salaries be raised in keeping with their new duties. "It is obvious," remarked an overworked magistrate, "that the Increase of Responsibility in Consequence of the exclusive Jurisdiction over the cases of Employer and Employed . . . and the new School Board Cases constitute a fair Claim for Increase." It is no surprise that country squires felt threatened, fearing that they were soon to become an extinct race. "The tide is setting strong against us," Barwick Baker reported accurately, "and an army of officials hold it to be very mean of us to do the work without pay, which would give pay to more of their staff." [24]

VIII

The point is that the rash of legislation passed during Gladstone's great Ministry of 1868 to 1874 set the pattern for the remainder of the century. Antireformers were, of course, unaware of this, and they were relieved, to say the least, when the Conservatives triumphed in 1874. "It is a wonderful change," wrote one of them, "and I hope we are now in for a quiet steady government, able to attend to the business of the Country without being forced to count the votes of extreme sections."

The irony was, however, that the faith in legislation grew during Disraeli's Ministry; and owing to the hard times that became harder as each year of the Ministry passed, the calls for fresh legislation became more numerous. Even ordinarily self-reliant William Bromley Davenport favored laws to lessen the distress of the agricultural classes; yet it was he who only a short time before—during Gladstone's Ministry, to be sure—had suggested that it "would not be a bad thing if some able Member of Parliament were to bring forward a short bill proposing that for the next three or four years no Act of Parliament should be passed at all—unless it be to rescind other Acts which have been recently passed." [25]

The success of reformers in winning politicians to support more and more government intervention helps to explain the gloom of those Englishmen who still had faith in self-help. Sir Louis Mallet, the veteran free trader, remained convinced that progress could be assured only "by giving the freest play to private and personal agencies, and by restricting within the narrowest possible limits the interference of the State with all commercial and social enterprises," but already in 1873 he deplored the growing tendency among younger liberals to press for government aid and regulation. So, too, John Bright mourned the decline of faith in self-help among Liberals. Criticizing a colleague for the unsoundness of his views on social and economic matters, he complained in 1875 that this Member of Parliament did not care about expenditures and that he was "fond of Factory Bills and the rotten legislation which has come so much into favor of late years." [26]

As the depression deepened, the appeals for state help—what Mrs. Josephine Butler called the "regulationist madness"—grew impressively. Charles Rowley, Jr., the author of a booklet on *Social Politics* (1885), noted that even George Goschen, the eminent banker and Liberal Member of Parliament, had pronounced laissez-faire dead. And a year later the solid Gladstonian James Bryce contrasted the lip service paid to the doctrine of self-help with its practical neglect. It is no surprise, then, that Herbert Spencer, Barwick Baker, Charles Bradlaugh (who in economic matters had become "almost too respectable"), W. H. Mallock, the Duke of Argyll, Auberon Herbert, and the members of the Liberty and Property Defense League and the Charity Organisation Society felt desperately the need to reassert the virtues of self-help and to denounce what Richard Cobden had liked to call "bungling legislation." Herbert Spencer went so far as to argue that the greatest urgency in political life was to dispel the myth that the majority had unlimited powers—that it had "a right to dictate to the individual about everything whatever." Barwick Baker warned repeatedly that to do too much for the poor was to make them depend on others and therefore become slaves. The Duke of Argyll deplored the ignorance even among the educated of the laws of political economy. And Auberon Herbert, opposing the interference of the state in religion, education, health, labor, the professions, insurance, poor relief, trade, banking, marriage, drink, and taxation, condemned what he regarded as the bribes with which politicians tried to tempt voters.[27]

Yet the great fact about the individualists was their defeatism: they knew they did not stand a chance. "I have now pretty well done with political writing," Herbert Spencer told Andrew Carnegie in 1885, shortly after the publication of his masterpiece

on *The Man versus the State*. And the main reason for his decision
was his conviction that his protests were in vain—there was little
that could be done. To be sure, he encouraged others to write with
a view to results in the future, but for the present he regarded
the trend as unmistakable. "The wave of opinion carrying us toward Socialism and utter subordination of the individual is becoming irresistible," he declared repeatedly.

A wreck of a man—an insomniac suffering from "nervous per-
turbation" and a host of other disorders—Spencer found late
Victorian society as sick as he was. Politics—his involvement in an
anti-imperialist campaign—had shattered his health. And politicians were ruining the health of England. Like other staunch
individualists, Spencer ascribed the condition of public affairs
to cowardly Members of Parliament, especially Liberals, who
could not resist the pressures to which they were subjected by the
wrong kinds of reformers.[28]

⁅ X ⁆

SCRAPPING THE OLD

The socialists were the reformers who took the fullest advantage of the Great Depression in order to impugn late Victorian insititutions. John Burns spoke for all of them when, having read the Royal Commission report of 1886 on the depression of trade, he hopefully called it "the funeral oration over the grave of English monopoly and commercialism." And Alfred Russel Wallace also spoke for all his socialist colleagues when he declared that the greatest of all the crimes of society was its failure to organize itself in such a way that everybody could live decently and well by his labor. As long as a single willing worker was unemployed, Wallace insisted, society and government were criminals.

Socialists, to be sure, differed among themselves, but all of them used the hardships of the unemployed—especially during the winter—as a weapon with which to agitate for the national ownership of the basic means of production. At gatherings of the unemployed and at meetings which they themselves organized, they insisted that only socialism could end unemployment and depressions. And in their newspapers and in hundreds of pamphlets and circulars they emphasized the same point. "Buy this pamphlet, love, it will do you good!"—these were words that many late Victorians were to hear from socialist salesmen who were convinced that they knew how to end hard times forever.[1]

If a socialist movement did not develop in the very early years of the Great Depression, one reason was that contemporaries expected the hard times to end before long. Another reason was that socialism had been discredited by the failure of the Parisian Communards in 1871; and it had come to be regarded in England as a foreign doctrine. Thus, as late as 1878, when Bismarckian Germany was vigorously combating socialists by prohibitive legis- lation and other means, there was nothing even remotely resem- bling a socialist movement in England.

There were, to be sure, some individual socialists. As an old Tory Member of Parliament crudely described them in 1874, "We have got a number of gentlemen among us who call them- selves Communists and Socialists, who think that everything should be subdivided, and everybody have an equal amount of property." But such people were few in number, and they were mostly foreigners like Karl Marx. It is true that some English intellectuals were reading about socialism: George Eliot, for instance, recorded in her diary in 1879 that she was studying what John Stuart Mill had to say on the subject. No one supposed, however, that in a remarkably short period of time the socialists would be creating a great stir in England.[2]

Even Karl Marx's death in England in 1883 was hardly noticed. H. M. Hyndman, Marx's leading English disciple, was outraged by the silent treatment that the event received in the English press, although he acknowledged—as a former Tory—that the obituary notices in Conservative papers did more justice to Marx than those in publications of "the beastly Capitalist-Liberals." Within a few years of Marx's death, however, socialist agitation developed rapidly, and by 1886 a young and alert American economist was already lecturing on the new English reformers in the United States.

What gave the socialists their opportunity was the persistence of the depression. "The Period of Apathy," as Bernard Shaw later called it, was over, and dozens of little socialist organizations were formed—branches of the Social Democratic Federation, the Social- ist League, and the Fabian Society, Christian Socialist units, and unaffiliated groups of various names. Although none of them grew to any great size or won a commanding position, they made their contemporaries aware of their doctrines, and, in the apt words of Edward Carpenter, they "deeply infected the views of all classes, as well as general literature, and even municipal and imperial politics."[3]

II

The original purpose of Hyndman's Democratic Federation
was to find an answer to the Irish Question and to further a
variety of social reforms. But some members of the Federation
were socialists; George Gissing, for instance, reported in 1881 that
he had joined the society and was preparing, for delivery at workers' clubs, a lecture on the practical aspects of socialism. Gissing
was to make great use of his experiences in his novels, but he
quickly discovered himself out of place in the organization—
among other reasons because his sense of property was too deep-
rooted.

The Federation's leading figure was H. M. Hyndman, a literary
man of independent means, who lived, as his American friend
Henry George remarked, "in fine style in a fashionable street."
As late as 1879 Hyndman had been respectable and safe enough
to be invited to address the Manchester Chamber of Commerce on
the importance of Indian prosperity for the trade of Lancashire,
but in the early eighties Hyndman became convinced that Karl
Marx was right. Inspired by the doctrines of scientific socialism—
and by the prospect of being the English Marx—he diverted the
Federation from its original aims and converted it into a frankly
Marxist society. This, to be sure, was no great feat, for the Federation was a tiny group, the control of which was easy to seize.
Besides, it had been a distinctly unsuccessful organization. As
Hyndman told Henry George, the English refused to join it be-
cause of its advanced position on the Irish Question and the Irish
would not cooperate in any case.[4]

Hyndman and his small band of followers saw in the depression
unmistakable evidence of the doom of capitalism and the inevitability of socialism. And they thought that any measures they took
to foment class hatred and class war to end the existing order,
which they regarded as disorder, were more than justified. "Great
Heaven!" Hyndman exploded after a walk in London, "as I go
through the courts and lanes of this city, as I watch the capitalist
class grinding hours on hours of unpaid toil out of half-starved
women and half-starved men I feel no bloodshed, no anarchy, no
horror conceivable to me, could be worse for the mass of the
people than the existing state of things."

SCRAPPING THE OLD 149

In speeches, debates, pamphlets, books, and their newspaper *Justice,* Hyndman and his Social Democrats repeatedly told their compatriots that socialism was imminent and that it would come not because of man's will but as an inevitable result of the workings of the laws of history and economics. Even so, it is revealing that as late as 1904 Hyndman found it necessary to correct a sympathizer who had failed to grasp what he regarded as the essence of scientific socialism:

No doubt Socialism will usher in a period of justice based upon economic and social freedom in the highest sense for the whole human community. We are attaining to that period, however, not by our desire for justice abstract or concrete, but by the material development of society, most of it hitherto unconscious, which brings mankind, whether they like it or not, from Competitive Capitalism, into Trust Monopoly, State Collectivism and Socialism. All we can do is to recognize where the class war is bringing us and try to help to realise the new organisation as soon as possible and with as little of horror as possible.[5]

In short, to oppose the Federation was futile. But to join the Federation was to contribute to the upsetting of the present system and to fall in line with the forces of the future. The Marxian Socialists would come to power soon, Hyndman predicted repeatedly, and he and his followers worked hard to help along what they regarded as historical laws. Socialism, they insisted, was no utopian dream. It could come at any time now—1889, the centenary of the fall of the Bastille, was a favored year—for the economic and social structure of England was ready for revolution. Hence the immediate need was for organization. As Hyndman told a prospective member in Bradford in 1884:

The workers will be able to get something really worth having for themselves and save their children from the slavery they groan under, if only they will definitely make a party of their own and stand aloof from the landlord and capitalist factions which are trying now as ever to pull them by the pretence of political reforms. What reform is worth anything to the man who may be thrown out of work tomorrow by a world-wide industrial crisis, over which his class has no control? What does it matter which faction is in office to the man who is forced each day to sell his power of Labour, or to try to sell it, to a slavedriving class for a mere subsistence wage? You know well and I, a well-to-do middle-class man, know well, that the workers can never hope to gain anything unless they stand together for the interests of their class.[6]

III

Idealistic Edward Carpenter, having read Hyndman's orthodox Marxist analysis of *England for All*, was eager to find out more about the Federation, and he chose well the words he used to describe the committee meeting that he attended: "It was in the basement of one of those big buildings facing the Houses of Parliament that I found a group of conspirators sitting." It was, indeed, this conspiratorial and explicitly revolutionary character of the Federation that helps to explain the difficulty that Hyndman had in both winning and keeping supporters. As a disillusioned Federationist plaintively put it: "I found I could not act with people who seemed to repudiate all practical and legal methods of advancing reforms and appeared *to me* to be desiring, and waiting for, only a Revolution to effect their objects. Now Revolutions, my study of History gives me no love for: they generally end only in bad despotisms." [7]

Still, Hyndman had one inestimable advantage: his congenital optimism. While others were disheartened by the discovery of the extent of working-class apathy, Hyndman insisted that in no time at all indifference would give way to active interest. Convinced in 1883 that the death or retirement of Gladstone was imminent —Gladstone fooled everybody, including himself—Hyndman looked forward to the disruption of the Liberal Party as the event that would open up great opportunities for the Federation. Though even Hyndman felt despondent at times that English workers were so hard to reach, his cheerfulness constantly reasserted itself. Confessing to Henry George in 1883 that he was appalled by working-class prejudices—especially against the Irish —he quickly added that socialist ideas were at least making headway among educated people and that they must shortly yield results. The well-to-do, he said, "begin to see that the whole edifice of capitalist oppression will ere long be shaken to its foundation though they still hope it will last their time." [8]

Other reformers tried to convince Hyndman that he had gone wrong. Henry George, who admired him for his earnestness and his willingness to devote so much energy and money to reform, thought in 1882 that he had succeeded. Hyndman, George remarked, "has been lately a good deal under the mental influence of

Karl Marx; but I think I have already shaken him in this, and will get him out of it before I get through." But while George was attempting to make a single-taxer out of Hyndman, Hyndman was trying to win George to his Federation. He had him and Mrs. George as house guests in London, and after many discussions he thought that he had brought George around to believing that the first thing to do was to replace capitalism with socialism. When neither converted the other, their friendship cooled. What a pity it was, George wrote in 1884, after reading Hyndman's *Historical Basis of Socialism,* that a man of such force should follow so slavishly such a shallow thinker as Karl Marx.[9]

Although Hyndman failed with George, he attracted to his Federation several celebrities who were also indefatigable workers. Most important of all, he won William Morris, who only a few years before had been leading the life of a hermit, refusing to enter, much less join, a club.

Morris's conversion to socialism was above all an emotional matter. He had been outraged by the imperialism first of Disraeli and then of Gladstone; and he had come to despair of the competence of the Liberals to cope with the problem of poverty. No less important, he underwent a series of psychological crises, the main symptoms of which were severe melancholy and an inability to lose himself in his poetry and art. For Morris socialism came to serve as a form of therapy—a medicine to restore his faith in work and art and life. It kept him endlessly busy, and it gave him a sense of purpose. "I live in hopes of being able to cast my capitalist skin and become a harmless proletarian," he wrote characteristically.[10]

Treasurer of the Federation, Morris gave an incredible amount of time to socialist activities. That he wrote incessantly on socialist topics was to be expected; he was, after all, a writer. But he also took on a tremendous number of speaking engagements, and this was quite a feat. Indeed, few of his peers in the literary world would have even dared to face an audience. Algernon Swinburne never gave a lecture in his life, nor would he consent to do so on any terms. George Meredith doubted his ability to hold the attention of a group. And Thomas Hardy considered lecturing both out of his line and beyond his powers of endurance. But not Morris. Despite his lack of preparation for public speaking and despite bad weather and frequently hostile audiences, he traveled through the country and lectured everywhere on socialism as the only possible remedy for the evils that grew out of the private use of capital.[11]

As an agitator Morris spent much of his time trying to refute unjust criticisms of socialism. Of all the unfounded charges made against it, he insisted, the objection that it would crush individuality was the most absurd. For one of the chief aims of a socialist order, he said, was to reassert the dignity of the individual. In a capitalist society most people were condemned to the slavery of dreary, unsatisfying, and exhausting labor; but this would not be so in a socialist society, Morris promised.

Nor did Morris think it reasonable to suppose that cooperative societies and profit-sharing schemes would remedy the injustices in a capitalist community. On the contrary, the very incompleteness of these devices would hurt rather than help the cause of labor, for the big evils, said Morris, were competition, exploitation, and overwork, and they could be wiped out only in a socialist order. "So on all sides," he confessed, "I am driven towards revolution as the only hope, and am growing clearer and clearer on the speedy advent of it in a very obvious form, though of course I can't give a date for it." [12]

IV

The comfort Morris sought in the Federation was disturbed by two unpleasant discoveries. First, he found that the resistance to socialism among workers and other elements of the population was much greater than he had anticipated. While he repeatedly informed his correspondents that the cause was flourishing and that the Federation was making steady progress, he knew that he was engaging in wishful thinking. Impatient though he was for the coming of the new society, he was, nevertheless, forced to acknowledge "the necessary slowness of our movement, and the obvious difficulty of getting 'slaves' to see any possibility of a better state of things than they are used to."

Morris's second discovery was even more painful. He found that although his fellow-members of the Federation talked about fraternity they often acted like brothers of the Cain and Abel tradition. By the end of 1884—the very year that the Federation took the name Social Democratic Federation—the hostilities among the membership became so fierce that Edward Aveling, Karl Marx's daughter Eleanor, Morris, and others seceded and set up their own organization known as the Socialist League. In January, 1885, Morris's Hammersmith Branch of the Social Democratic Federation officially dissolved itself and became the Hammersmith Branch of the Socialist League. The main reason given for this action was that Hyndman and some of his followers were attempting "to substitute arbitrary and personal rule for the principles of Socialism." For the rest Morris refused to say anything against his former associates except that he disapproved of their tactics. But Hyndman insisted that the split was the result of his condemnation of the immoral behavior of Edward Aveling, who, though married, was living with Eleanor Marx.[13]

The slogan of the Socialist League was Agitate, Educate, Organize, and Morris and his group took it seriously. Aveling and Eleanor Marx even went to the United States, where they traveled, spoke, and wrote tirelessly. Morris ran the *Commonweal*, the League's official journal, which supported international revolutionary socialism and attacked parliamentary social democracy and opportunistic party warfare. He attended countless meetings— after a row in the East End in 1885 he was even arrested for assaulting a policeman. He lectured incessantly. And he constantly invited potential new members to his home: George Gissing and William Butler Yeats were among those whom he tried to recruit to socialism.

Morris's literary contemporaries were startled by his behavior. "Why cannot he write poetry in the shade?" George Gissing wondered, and others asked the same question. For Morris, however, the socialist cause was all that mattered. Indeed, if he had had enough money to live and to subsidize socialist propaganda, he would have given up his private art work, which he regarded as worthless, and devoted himself entirely to laboring for the new order. As he bluntly put it: "Society is to my mind wholly corrupt, and I can take no deep seated pleasure in anything it turns out, except the materials for its own destruction in the shape of discontent and aspirations for better things. To keep ourselves alive for revolution, and to gather what influence we can for that purpose are the only aims I can recognise in the daily work of those who consider themselves Socialists." [14]

Morris was sufficiently encouraged at times by the progress of the League to expect that, though middle-aged, he would live to witness the coming of the socialist order, but repeated disappointments broke down his hopes. The reading room run by the Hammersmith Branch, though open to the public, had to be given up; despite efforts made to publicize it, attendance remained insignificant. Outdoor meetings, whether in Hyde Park or on street corners, were frequently wrecked by wet or rough weather. Speakers were hard to secure; young Bernard Shaw was always willing to lecture, but few others were so amenable. Weekly sales of *Commonweal* numbered about twenty-six hundred, Morris reported in July, 1886; but to pay its way sales had to be doubled. Financial troubles were chronic; to raise money the ordinarily dignified Morris even consented to have his photograph sold.[15]

Worst of all, anarchists penetrated the League and introduced new sources of factionalism. As early as 1886 there was serious dissension, but Morris tried to be patient with the anarchists. In 1887 his Hammersmith Branch sent to the Socialist League a reminder that its main function was to educate the masses in the principles of socialism; some enthusiasts even wished to send up balloons loaded with socialist literature to celebrate the Queen's Jubilee. By 1888 the Hammersmith Branch protested angrily that the anarchist members of the council of the Socialist League were trying to restrict the freedom of discussion of local units and to make local criticism of the central authority a basis for expulsion. If, in these circumstances, Morris lost patience with children who played under his study windows and took to dashing out, as Yeats reported in 1888, to chase them away, the explanation is perhaps clear.[16]

In 1890 the Hammersmith Branch ended its connection with the now anarchist-dominated Socialist League and became the Hammersmith Socialist Society. The tragedy, Morris noted, was that time that should have been spent in condemning capitalism was wasted in denouncing comrades. But after years of searching Morris at last had a congenial organization.

The Hammersmith Socialist Society was a small group of people who were held together by their admiration, respect, and love for Morris. Their object was to teach socialism to the uninitiated by means of lectures, street meetings, and publications, and they lived up to their aim. In the last years of the Great Depression— Morris died in 1896—the Hammersmith socialists carried on their war against what they liked to call "the accursed capitalist system." Few feudal overlords in the Middle Ages that Morris loved so much and so irrationally had enjoyed the loyalty that he won from his band of socialist vassals. Even socialists in rival organizations revered him. Bernard Shaw, who rarely had kind things to say about his comrades, was devoted to him. And John Burns, a man not easy to please, respected him for his energy, his unpretentiousness, and his manliness.

Outside socialist circles the feeling was different. Algernon Swinburne could refer affectionately to him as "our dear old Morris," but Edmund Gosse expressed the dominant view when he said, after reading a biography of Morris in 1899, that the socialism did not fit the man: "It did not belong to the carpets and the Kelmscott Press and the tapestry kings and queens." [17]

Morris's last major socialist publication was *News from Nowhere,* which appeared first as a serial in *Commonweal* in 1890 and then was reprinted as a book the following year. It was designed explicitly as a counterblast to Edward Bellamy's recently published *Looking Backward;* but to Morris's great disappointment it failed to become the best seller that the American utopian novel became. Indeed, fair-minded W. T. Stead, always ready to right a wrong, was outraged that Morris's book received so little notice in the English press; and he publicized it in the *Review of Reviews,* arguing courageously that Morris's dreams were often "wiser than other people's waking thoughts." [18]

v

Unlike the Hammersmith Socialists, the Fabians had no figure so inspiring as William Morris. At first it seemed that they might, for their parent organization, the Fellowship of the New Life, was founded by the Scottish philosopher Thomas Davidson, who had extraordinary qualities of leadership—above all an ability to inspire idealism, loyalty, and self-denial. But his Fellowship, which lasted until almost the end of the century, placed more emphasis on the character development of individual members than on social reconstruction. The Fabian Society, founded in 1884 as an offshoot of the Fellowship, aimed above all at social reorganization.

It, too, would have led a calm and philosophic existence but for one fact: it attracted a number of young and restless intellectuals with much energy to consume and many hostilities to release. People, not ideas, made the Society in the early years of its history—and three people in particular: Mrs. Annie Besant, Bernard Shaw, and Sidney Webb. Without them the Society would have languished. With them it enjoyed a spirited and noisy childhood.

The most experienced propagandist among the early Fabians was Mrs. Besant. As Charles Bradlaugh's chief associate in the agitation for atheism and birth control, she had had plenty of opportunity to develop her skills as a reformer as well as to receive expert guidance from one of the masters of the art of influencing working-class people. And she had learned to lose herself in work to fight the melancholy that at times tempted her to go off to the Antipodes to live among kangaroos.

Mrs. Besant's conversion to socialism distressed Bradlaugh. But it delighted her new associates, for she wrote easily, bringing out pamphlets and articles with speed and effortlessness that made her colleagues envious. "I send you four tracts [on socialism] which will show you my position," she wrote to a friend in 1886, but she could have forwarded a much greater number of publications. Even more important, however, Mrs. Besant knew how to capture and hold an audience. Almost everyone who ever heard her lecture came away convinced that he had rarely, if ever, listened to a better orator. The reaction of meticulous John Burns to a speech she delivered in 1888—"the finest exposition of socialism in a lecture I have ever heard"—was typical.

Mrs. Besant's sense of mission was profound and the energy she could rally prodigious. "I am a little overworked and overtired," she wrote characteristically in 1888, "but there are so many things to do, and so few to do them. And I don't care for life if I can't fill it with work." It was unfortunate for the Fabians, therefore, that after a few years Mrs. Besant did not find socialism emotionally satisfying. In 1889 she went to Paris to attend a socialist congress, and later in the year the *Fabian Essays,* which included one of her pieces, appeared. But by then Mrs. Besant had turned theosophist, and from 1890 on she used her ability and energy as a writer and speaker to further the teachings of Madame Blavatsky. In fact, she came to view her whole life as a preparation for her conversion to theosophy. And when she brought out her lively autobiography in 1893—only a few years after her abandonment of the Fabians—she told her publisher that she hoped above all that the story of her life would serve to make theosophists.[19]

VI

Although socialism ceased after a few years to provide Mrs. Besant with an outlet, it served Bernard Shaw much longer and more effectively. Indeed, it is not too much to suggest that socialism was his salvation. It gave him the sense of success in his late twenties and thirties that he secured from nothing else. For the Bernard Shaw of the late Victorian period was, from the standpoint of public recognition, an almost chronic failure; and London was a fortress in which he found it almost impossible to batter a breach. The time was still far off when his fellow-dramatist Henry Arthur Jones would complain angrily that Shaw was taken seriously as a thinker. The time was still further off when Shaw would refuse to permit organizations to use his name as an ornament for fear that otherwise he would be a member of every society in the world. The five novels Shaw wrote in the early eighties even he—probably unjustly—considered "all jejune and rotten," and they convinced him that he should abandon the novel as an art form. The musical criticism that he wrote in the late eighties and early nineties he found gratifying for a while but not for long, although later he would unashamedly proclaim himself as having been the outstanding music critic of his time. And the highly topical plays that he began to write in the early nineties did not promise particularly to relieve what Henry James and many others considered to be the feeble condition of the contemporary English theater. As the critic William Archer pointed out in 1895, after noting that England had neither an older nor a younger generation of dramatists: "All our active playwrights are men between 40 and 50, and at present I really see no one coming on—except perhaps Bernard Shaw and even he is on the verge of 40." Similarly, a reader's report prepared for the publishing house of T. Fisher Unwin recommended that Shaw's Bohemian novel *Love among the Artists* not be reprinted. Despite the author's individuality, it pointed out, his work was not "likely to command much attention." [20]

If Shaw bloomed late as a man of letters, he found himself early as a socialist propagandist. After reading *Progress and Poverty,* he became convinced that socialism was the answer to the difficulties facing England and the world. With plenty of time to spare—and his mother to support him—he attended socialist lectures and meetings and read voraciously in the British Museum, discovering among other works the first volume of the French translation of *Das Kapital.* In 1884 he joined the Fabians, and he could never again complain of unemployment or underemployment. He listened, he argued, he studied, and all the while he learned how to observe and describe the people he met. The Society kept him so busy for the next two decades that he constantly expected to die from overwork. It is even doubtful that the most wretched sweated worker put in the number of hours that he did.

The fact is that Shaw ascribed his originality to his refusal to be simply a man of letters and to his determination to be immersed in the life of his times. As he wrote in 1902: "Instead of belonging to a literary club I belong to a municipal Council. Instead of drinking and discussing authors and reviews, I sit on committees with capable practical greengrocers and bootmakers (including a builder who actually reads Carlyle) and administer the collection of dust, the electric lighting of the streets, and the enforcement of the sanitary laws." In much the same way Shaw came to explain the distinction of his plays: he had to work hard at public speeches and Fabian pamphlets and other such "sordid things between every hundred lines." Small wonder that Shaw was to tell his biographer Frank Harris in 1919 that his portrait was useless. To do his biography properly it was necessary, Shaw pointed out proudly and correctly, not only to read the several millions of words that he had written but to "get up the whole history of the last quarter of the nineteenth century and the first quarter of the twentieth." [21]

Among the many things that Shaw learned during his years as an active Fabian lecturer, committee member, editor, and pamphleteer—and what a pamphleteer!—perhaps the most important was the value of laughter. "Last night at Morris' I met Bernard Shaw, who is certainly very witty," young William Butler Yeats remarked in 1888. Shaw, however, rarely used wit for its own sake. It was a device by which he tried to attract attention to important topics. It was also his way of making life endurable. "You must learn to laugh," he advised an earnest friend in 1902, "or, by Heavens, you will commit suicide when you realize all the infamy of the world as it is." By the early twentieth century Shaw had learned to laugh so well and to make others laugh that he rightly came to fear that people would not take him seriously—that they would view him merely as a comedian. But some of Shaw's Fabian colleagues appreciated the value of his gift. As Beatrice Webb was to write at the time of the founding of the *New Statesman*, "If we fail to make it instructive perhaps Bernard Shaw will make it entertaining!" [22]

During his early years as an active Fabian agitator Shaw also learned how to publicize himself. He went out of his way to invite newspaper attacks, welcoming them as the best possible advertisement. "When you have been ruined as often as I have, you will find your reputation growing with every successive catastrophe," he remarked in 1903. "Never ruin yourself less than twice a year," he advised, "or the public will forget all about you." Shaw's strategy worked so well that he quickly established his reputation as the cockiest of the Fabians. It was typical of him as a joiner and a permeator that he attended the organization meeting of the British Economic Association in 1890. But it was also typical of him that, although Lord Salisbury's Chancellor of the Exchequer was in the chair, Shaw created a furor by suggesting "with all respect to Mr. Goschen, that the head of the Association should not be a gentleman who was identified with any political party in the State." Despite Shaw, Goschen became the first president of the Association.[23]

VII

The drive that Bernard Shaw and Mrs. Besant brought to the Fabian Society was matched by that of Sidney Webb. Happy only when he worked, Webb worked always and at the sort of material that few of his colleagues in the Society could master. For he served as the great gatherer of statistical and factual materials for the Fabian agitation. But Webb was also a man of ideas—although his main theoretical contribution has often been overlooked. It lay neither in the idea of permeation nor in the idea of the inevitability of gradualness. It lay, rather, in the idea of socialism itself, which Webb defined so loosely as to embrace anybody who believed in state help. Since everybody favored government intervention to some extent, Webb made everybody a socialist. England, he insisted, was already a socialist country. The big question, therefore, was the pace at which its further socialization should proceed. And Webb and his colleagues repeatedly stressed that they were gradualists.

Webb's marriage to Beatrice Potter, the earnest social investigator, made him much more available for the Fabian cause. He would no longer have to refuse to run for a seat on the London County Council—as he had been forced to do—because he could not afford to leave his civil service post. "I am probably going to throw up my place presently," he told John Burns in 1891, "but one does not relinquish such a thing in a hurry, and I want first to ensure a livelihood." Marriage to Miss Potter assured Webb of an income: he now could resign his post and devote full time to socialist agitation.

Since Beatrice Webb's capacity for work was as great as his— even greater, perhaps, because she suffered from insomnia and therefore worked while he slept—they formed an extraordinary team. When Webb remarked in 1895 that he and his wife were "really very much driven by work," he was, if anything, understating the facts. Their chief glory was their ability to set deadlines for themselves and then to live up to them. Rejecting a request to review a book, Webb explained in December, 1896: "Our book on Trade Unions (analysis) will take us right up to next October, and even then it will be a squeeze to get it out. Then follows six months of London Elections (School Board and County Council), when we shall be fighting hard against a 'ratepayer' reaction. By that time Mrs. Webb and I will need to lie on our backs in the open air for a time, utterly dead beat." In November, 1897, Webb reported with great relief that the book was done, but he was embarrassed to have to add that its publication was delayed by a strike.[24]

Even when the Webbs entertained—which they did often— they worked. They chose their guests carefully. Trade union leaders, politicians, professors, journalists, and foreign dignitaries were the people they invited to their home; and as they fed them, they tried to indoctrinate them, for dining with the Webbs was invariably accompanied by permeation. It is a testimonial to their industry as hosts—and permeators—that collection after collection of late nineteenth- and early twentieth-century manuscripts contain dinner invitations that the Webbs sent to celebrities whom they sought to win to the Fabian point of view. Typical of many was an invitation Sidney Webb extended to John Burns in 1894: "Shaw is coming in to dinner here at 7.30 next Saturday, the 24th inst., and we have asked Massingham [the journalist] to join us. Will you not come too? We shall be very glad to have the chance of a comfortable chat about things in general." Typical, too, was a letter Webb wrote in 1895 to Professor Edwin Seligman, the American economist and editor of the *Political Science Quarterly:* "I hope you will spare time for a talk, and Mrs Webb joins with me in cordially inviting you and Mrs Seligman to give us an evening next week."

The Webbs permeated not only in their own home but in the homes they visited. And they wrote warm letters about their Fabian colleagues in order to gain access for them to important people. When young H. G. Wells visited the United States, Webb told Professor Seligman to be sure to meet him. "I think his novels interesting and stimulating," Webb wrote enthusiastically, "but his more recent sociological studies—Anticipations, The Making of Man and a Modern Utopia—seem to me even more valuable as original and suggestive contributions to that somewhat-abused branch of knowledge."

The Webbs, after only a few years of marriage, had won a considerable amount of recognition. By 1898 scholarly James Bryce correctly labeled them the chief English authorities on the history of trade unions. W. T. Stead accurately described them as "among the most useful workers in all municipal work in London." And other well-informed contemporaries stood in awe of their achievements as hard-working reformers and tireless authors.[25]

VIII

No other early members rivaled the contributions that the Webbs, Shaw, and Mrs. Besant made to the Fabians. But the Society attracted other people of talent: Edward R. Pease, longtime general secretary of the group, who constantly urged visitors to look in at the Fabian office on the Strand and did his share as a permeator; William Clarke, who became the chief Fabian expert on rings and trusts; Edith Nesbit, soon to achieve fame as a writer of children's stories; Hubert Bland, her husband, who became the most popular editorial writer on the Manchester *Sunday Chronicle;* and Graham Wallas, the thoughtful political scientist and conscientious worker who gave much time to the London School Board.

This is not to suggest that all the early Fabians were intellectual giants. Far from it. A fair number of the early members joined simply for social reasons. As late as the period of the First World War Bernard Shaw discovered at a Fabian summer school that when evening came brains were useless without social gifts, and so at the age of sixty-one he learned to dance. Many early Fabians had made Shaw's discovery long before and had even joined the Society in the hope of making friends. But the commanding position of Shaw and Webb kept the organization from ever becoming a mere club for lonely Londoners. Indeed, as early as 1892 a leading English disciple of Henry George could call the Fabian Society the "most able and effective propagandist body in this country." [26]

Along with Social Democrats, Socialist Leaguers, Christian Socialists, and unaffiliated socialists, the Fabians deluged England with a quantity of socialist literature that staggered contemporaries—and has discouraged scholars ever since. "A good deal of Socialistic dope is exported from this country, and much of it is dumped in America," Ernest Benn was to point out in 1931, but Benn's remark could just as well have been made in the late nineteenth century. Writing and speaking endlessly, late Victorian socialist leaders were always complaining of being tired, and they certainly had reason to complain. But they were driven people, and they clearly needed the reassurance of tiredness to live with themselves and to feel that they were accomplishing something. As zealous John Burns, then a member of Hyndman's Social Democratic Federation, noted in his diary in 1888 at the approach of his thirtieth birthday: "What work I have done under physical difficulties that would have deterred many. What a great deal remains undone. Stick to it Jack." [27]

⁅ XI ⁆

THE FAILURE OF A CAMPAIGN

The main accomplishment of the late Victorian socialists was to alarm the comfortable classes. Insisting endlessly that the depression meant the doom of capitalism, the socialists announced confidently that the future belonged to them. "Ideas are certainly astir," H. M. Hyndman wrote in the early eighties, and he rejoiced that the turn of the socialists must come soon because of the awkward state of the economy almost everywhere in Europe. "Business is all very dull and that must eventually tell," he assured Henry George, adding that every worsening of economic conditions brought the Revolution that much closer.

Nor was Hyndman's an unusual view. Year by year socialism grew in importance. It would soon move from the stage of debate to that of action, an American living in Liverpool predicted in 1886. Daily it was receiving more and more recognition, Sidney Webb pointed out in 1889, noting proudly and snobbishly that it was being dealt with in a series of lectures at one of the "best" Cambridge colleges. By 1890 a Greek socialist in London was sure that he could "distinctly hear socialism knocking at the doors." And a year later the very first number of the *Economic Journal*, published by the British Economic Association and open to writers of all schools of thought, included an article on socialism. During the nineties, moreover, socialist lectures at universities became frequent. H. M. Hyndman, Eleanor Marx, and Wilhelm Liebknecht lectured at Oxford in 1896 at sessions chaired by no less a figure than Frederick York Powell, the Regius Professor of Modern History and an outspoken humanitarian.

Edward Carpenter, remembering in later years the expectations of the late Victorian socialists, was to write, "There seemed a good hope for the realisation of Morris' dream—and we most of us shared in it." But year after year the optimism of the socialists was proven unfounded. The centenary of the fall of the Bastille did not become the signal for the fall of capitalism. The assassination of Sadi Carnot, the president of the Third French Republic, did not mark the beginning of the Revolution. And decrepit Greece was not destined to accelerate the coming of the big change in England. Despite their disappointments, socialists tried to respond in the spirit of Edith Nesbit's song:

> What matter if failure on failure
> Crowd closely upon us and press?
> When a hundred have bravely been beaten,
> The hundred and first wins success! [1]

If the comfortable classes often believed the predictions of the socialists, the main reason was that the hard times gave few signs of ending. "We have been in a state of riots and threatened revolution here of late," George Gissing wrote from London in 1886, "and I see that the same thing is spreading over the country." Finishing *Demos,* a novel that dealt with socialism, Gissing hoped that current events would help the sale of the book—even make his fortune—and strengthen his reputation as a writer, and so he did not regret the social unrest. To many of his comfortable contemporaries, however, it symbolized the end of the old order. When one aged Tory wrote to another in 1887 to wish him well "in spite of agricultural and general depression and of the menacing spectre of fast approaching socialism," he summed up a widespread fear of what awaited the well-to-do. Occasionally, to be sure, a traditionalist linked himself with the past and denounced an opponent as "a loud mouthed Chartist," but far more typically he condemned his new enemies as loathsome socialists. Indeed, Edward Bellamy knew what he was about when he had a character in *Looking Backward* (1888) remark that she would not dare live in Europe, for workers there were even wilder than in the United States, and that Greenland, Patagonia, and China were the only stable societies left in the world.[2]

II

Many members of the respectable public were convinced, of course, that dynamite and daggers formed indispensable parts of the equipment of socialists. Yet while this association of socialism and violence was often unfounded, it did have some basis in fact. "Raise again the blood-red banner, that your masters fear to see" —so went an inflammatory socialist song of the period. And its spirit recurred in the speeches, pamphlets, and newspapers of some of the late Victorian socialists.

Back in the time of George III the king's attorney had given it as his opinion that John Wilkes had tended "to inflame the Minds and alienate the affections of the People from His Majesty, and excite them to traitorous Insurrections against the Government." By the time of the elderly Victoria many of her most respected subjects would have given it as their opinion that that devil Wilkes was angelic compared to those fiendish socialists. For in London as well as other towns socialist street-corner activities sometimes precipitated what Edward Carpenter fondly referred to as "amusing and exciting incidents" with the police and town crowds. But it is doubtful that Carpenter chose one of his adjectives too well. W. T. Stead, present in 1887 when the police broke up a procession to Trafalgar Square, reported to Gladstone that their conduct was marked by a viciousness and a brutality that he had not seen in his entire life.

The truth is that socialists rejoiced in such episodes because of the publicity they won for their cause. When in 1888 John Burns celebrated the second anniversary of his acquittal, along with Hyndman, of a charge of seditious conspiracy, he noted frankly in his diary: "I think it would have done more good if we had all got 12 months but we were not so fortunate. Next time we may get more than what either the movement or we ourselves require. Till that time arrives we must do our work best to deserve it."

In short, contemporaries were not always wrong to link socialist meetings with riots. And this association of socialism with violence was furthered by a number of incidents on the Continent. It was not without cause that when Marie Corelli, laden with royalties from her novels, took a Continental trip in 1886, she made sure to stay away from Brussels until after a big socialist meeting had taken place there.[3]

If some businessmen went out of their way to discharge socialists, it was not simply that they did not wish to employ workers who wanted to do away with the private ownership of the means of production; the reason was also that they thought of socialists as men of violence. It was one thing for aristocratic Theodore Roosevelt to dismiss John Burns as "noisy and underbred, with the rank, aggressive, underbreeding of the satisfied provincial." But Roosevelt's language was tame compared with that used by English employers to characterize a socialist worker like Burns. Indeed, two items that Burns recorded in his diary in 1888 are particularly revealing. He saw some socialist workers playing cricket, but because their managers were present he did not even dare to speak to them. For, if their socialism were found out, they would lose their jobs. Burns, looking for work, noted a few months later: "I am precluded by the fact that I am a Socialist and an 'agitator.' Many men complain that they can't get work through not being known. I have to make the opposite complaint." [4]

III

Like some of the socialists themselves, antisocialists often used the word socialism vaguely, imprecisely, and comprehensively. They thought of it as the triumph of envy, a gospel of grab, and the invention of demagogues. A Tory Member of Parliament, attending some meetings in Trafalgar Square in 1888, reported that he "heard thieves, pickpockets, dynamiters and Socialists talking and praising Mr. Gladstone, who relied upon their support and because he relied upon them he was afraid to condemn their evil work." Gladstone disapproved of socialism as much as any of his Tory contemporaries, but this image of him was not unusual. In fact, some of the people who abandoned the Liberals for the Conservatives in the late nineteenth century did so not only because of the Irish Question but because of the fear of socialism: the Conservative party seemed to them a greater safeguard against the socialist menace. Lord Salisbury's overwhelming victory in the election of 1895, an embattled Tory remarked, did an immense amount of good. The defeat of the Liberals with their socialistic plans, he added unfairly but characteristically, made it possible for people to turn to their work with renewed confidence and enthusiasm.[5]

The great irony is that, although the socialists succeeded in alarming the comfortable classes, they failed to win any appreciable support from labor. It is striking, for instance, that when Friedrich Engels died in England in 1895 Eleanor Marx cautioned John Burns to tell no one of the time and place of the funeral. And it is perhaps not too farfetched to suggest that Engels's repeated insistence on a strictly private burial was due in part to his awareness that the English Marxists, hopelessly and venomously divided among themselves, would be unable to stage a very impressive working-class demonstration for the occasion.

Whatever Engels's reasons, there is no doubt that Edward Carpenter estimated that his branch of William Morris's Socialist League, which sought recruits among the large working-class population of Sheffield, numbered no more than one hundred members, of whom only a dozen or perhaps twenty were active. Nor is there any doubt that as late as the mid-nineties Robert Blatchford belittled the Fabians as "merely a London club." While Blatchford correctly recognized the Social Democratic Federation as the oldest and largest socialist body in Britain, he quickly added that the socialists in the North of England and Scotland—the two regions where they had relatively the greatest success—were attached to neither the Fabian Society nor the Social Democratic Federation. And almost twenty years after the formation of the Fabian Society Bernard Shaw himself acknowledged that socialism had made little headway among English workers; they were simply not interested in it, he told John Burns.

The disillusionment among the middle-class leaders of the socialists was often profound. For one of the saddest features of the socialist movement, as Edward Carpenter perceptively pointed out, was that it encouraged some well-to-do idealists "to try and leave their own ranks and join those of the workers, when—by their very birth and training being unable to bridge the gulf— the result has been that they, belonging neither to one class nor the other, outcasts from one, and more or less pitied or ridiculed by the other, have fallen into a kind of limbo between." [6]

IV

The failure of the socialist campaign to recruit working-class support was due in part to bickering among the socialists themselves. Not that it is hard to understand why this factionalism flourished. To become a convert to socialism a person had to be emotionally a nonconformist; he had to have a need to stand apart. Sir Norman Angell, fondly recalling his late Victorian years, remarked that he took up such heresies as socialism, agnosticism, and republicanism; and if more heresies had been available, he would have adopted them, too. Angell's need to be different was similar to that of many of his fellow socialists. But the vital point is that once a person became a socialist he did not lose this need that made it possible for him to become a convert in the first place.

Socialist groups thus became perfect settings for temperamental outbursts and personality clashes. Mrs. Annie Besant was perhaps the only socialist who used letterheads with the words "Be Strong." But Bernard Shaw was not the only socialist whose dislike of his father helped to make him a rebel against authority in general. And the novelist Olive Schreiner was not the only socialist who quarreled with her family over her views and left home as a result. When a number of such rebellious individuals joined forces, they constantly used one another as releases for their aggressions and infantilisms. On at least one occasion Shaw insisted that the Fabian Society had always been "consciously and purposely intolerant and actually expulsive of cranks and people with eccentric and visibly proclaimed temperaments." But Shaw was wrong. The early Fabians and the other late Victorian socialist groups luxuriated in temperamental people. Edward Carpenter was doubtless a genius, but even his admirers found him unreliable and fickle to the point of eccentricity. And when Robert Blatchford said of himself that he was temperamentally mercurial and naturally belligerent, he would have been just as correct if he had been describing many of his colleagues in the socialist movement. What is remarkable, therefore, is not that the socialists often quarreled but that they did not clash even more than they did. For they enjoyed—and needed—what Mrs. Besant called "the pleasure of the fight." [7]

The antiquarian Daniel Thomson, publishing in 1887 an ecclesiastical history of Dunfermline, went out of his way to caution his readers that the intense religious beliefs of the past were often accompanied by a virulent and boundless hatred of opponents. And he reminded his audience that what by modern standards were trifling religious issues had often in the past excited a fantastic amount of zeal. But Thomson might just as well have been writing about the socialists of his time, for their quarrels often resembled those of the religious sects that he described. And just as in 1743 the religious leader Benjamin Ingham wished that "a hearty Love, a Mutual Correspondence, and a fine Fellowship in Spirit could be brought about amongst all the Labourers, and awakened Souls throughout the World," so late Victorian socialists hoped for fraternity, unity, and harmony in their ranks. But Ingham had an advantage that the socialists by and large lacked. He could call on God to end the controversies and hostilities and to make the disputants love one another.

Already in the eighties it often seemed that the socialists despised each other even more than they hated the capitalists. "We will march side by side"—so went a socialist song. In practice, however, there was little such marching; and when a Positivist critic of the socialists complained of their "mean and envious spirit," he knew what he was saying. Engels and Hyndman disliked each other; Eleanor Marx and Hyndman despised each other; almost everyone except Eleanor Marx detested Edward Aveling. W. T. Stead found John Burns "a very good fellow" and Robert Donald, the able editor of *London,* considered him the outstanding leader of the English labor movement, but Stead and Donald were not socialists. Mrs. Besant, on the other hand, could not stand Burns—and she could stand him even less after he imputed base motives to her old friend Charles Bradlaugh. Burns, in turn, recorded in his diary his hostility to the egotists and cowards who were wrecking the Social Democratic Federation.[8]

And so the frictions went on and on. Yet the point is not only that almost every socialist disapproved of a good number of his colleagues but that he went out of his way to show his feelings. And the personal abuse that comrade after comrade heaped on his cohorts almost invariably made reconciliation at a later time difficult and even impossible. This absence of a gentleman's code had unfortunate results. "What hampers us most," said Hyndman, "is personal jealousy among those who agree in the main."

When young John Stuart Mill found that *The Last Days of Pompeii* was filled with errors in scholarship and even Latin grammar, he refused to review it. Since "no principle requires that we should point out errors of this kind in our friends," Mill said, "it is of no use wounding their *amour-propre* and depriving ourselves of their hearty cooperation." To the late Victorian socialists this attitude of Mill's was largely alien. They rejoiced to damn one another's writings and to expose one another's incompetence. H. M. Hyndman, deploring some scrape precipitated by the imprudence of the anarchist leader Prince Kropotkin, smugly told Henry George that "even revolution must be carried on with some judgment." But a chief difficulty of the socialists was that they rarely thought that any of their comrades had judgment.[9]

v

The frictions and rivalries that hurt the socialist movement in the eighties continued to plague it in the nineties. Beatrice Webb's diaries are filled with her personal feuds and those of her colleagues, and so is the private correspondence of every socialist leader of the time. Robert Blatchford, whose *Merrie England* brimmed over with gentleness, kindness, and love of people, was a different person when he spoke of most of his socialist colleagues. He found Keir Hardie so slippery that he could not stand the sight of him, and he reacted just as strongly to Olive Schreiner. He considered Hyndman a humbug, Shaw a prig who needed a good kicking, and John Burns a master of arrogance and selfishness. And since the workers they sought to lead were often mean, weak, cowardly, and ignorant, according to Blatchford, he often felt despondent about the socialist cause. As he wrote to his close friend Alexander Thompson in 1894: "Are these creatures worth fighting for; are they fit to fight alongside of? By God, Alec, I feel ashamed. I do. I feel degraded. We cannot win battles with such a rabble rant. Neither friends nor enemies are clean enough to spit upon. Grrr!"[10]

Blatchford's feelings were no stronger than those of many of

THE FAILURE OF A CAMPAIGN   171

his cohorts. When Beatrice Webb told John Burns in 1896 that she was sorry that they had drifted so far apart since the years when they had worked together for the socialist cause, she called up an image of past harmony and unity that had never existed. William Campbell, the Australian labor leader, was more in the spirit of things when he cautioned John Burns against a colleague—"the greatest Curse and Traitor that ever stood amongst a body of working men"—and when he urged Burns to see to it that when this colleague returned to England he would receive the treatment he deserved. So, too, was Eleanor Marx more in the spirit of things when she sought information with which to strike back at an English socialist who, while engaged in union activities in New York, was praising Hyndman and denouncing Burns; so, too, the German revisionist socialist, Eduard Bernstein, when he urged his English publisher to bring pressure to bear on the editor of the *Daily Chronicle* to prevent his enemy Ernest Belfort Bax, of the Social Democratic Federation, from reviewing his new book; so, too, Bernard Shaw when he advised Burns to seize an opportunity to put Keir Hardie in his place; so, too, the Fabians Hubert Bland and Edward R. Pease when they complained about Shaw as a mischief-maker and fomenter of antifraternity.[11]

This jungle atmosphere helps to explain the failure of the socialist Independent Labour Party that Keir Hardie founded in 1893. While Bruce Glasier, the Scottish socialist, thought that Hardie's faults were minor compared to his virtues—his earnestness, his prodigious energy, his indignation at the sufferings of the poor, and his faith in a new social order—most of the other socialist leaders disagreed with him. Not only were they unwilling to support Hardie's Party, but they actively opposed it.

Even when in the midst of the Boer War the Labour Party was founded under the name of the Labour Representation Committee—a quite unimportant event when it happened and one that was barely noted by contemporaries—there was every reason to suppose that the old animosities would undermine it. Indeed, as late as 1904—twenty years after the Social Democratic Federation took its name and William Morris seceded from the group to form the Socialist League—Hyndman was still deploring the lack of cooperation among socialists, still asserting the readiness of the Federation to work for unity, and still insisting that without unity the socialist influence would be limited. "I have been writing and speaking for Socialism for just four-and-twenty years, and I shall go on writing and speaking for Socialism," he said. "But my articles and speeches," he added pathetically, "would have much more effect if we were all together." And it impressed Hyndman at the age of sixty-two that it was absurd for socialists to talk about the reorganization of society when they could not even reorganize themselves.[12]

VI

It was not only because of their own disunity that the socialists failed to win the support of the working classes; there were other important reasons as well. The socialists repeatedly found that, however hard they tried, they simply could not overcome the indifference of the masses. So often workers just did not seem to care; they were so absorbed in their private lives that they could not be enticed by schemes of social reorganization. "The apathy of the Trade Unionists is very disheartening," John Burns wrote characteristically in 1888. "It requires a terrific amount of energy to rouse them from their apathy," he remarked of a working-class audience in the same year. Historical evolution worked with painful slowness, Plato E. Draculis wrote in 1892, adding bitterly that those who had most to gain from the socialist revolution seemed to be indifferent to its coming. And Edward Carpenter, after much experience with workers, concluded that far from being volatile they were stolid. They were slow to recognize either the burdens they bore or the sources of their hardships. The socialists found, moreover, that even when workers were not apathetic they simply accepted their poverty as necessary and inevitable. They thought of slums as having existed since the world began.[13]

Those workers who were neither apathetic nor fatalistic were often, to the distress of the socialists, the very people who, imbued with notions of self-help and hard work as ways of getting ahead, wanted to become capitalists themselves. John Burns, after meeting an old fishmonger who had angrily attacked socialism for years, noted in 1888: "After 24 years of severe thrift and temperance he has been unable to save more than would pull him through his last illness and is now absolutely penniless, yet would

rather die than accept relief. Of such is the kingdom of Capital."
It was painful for socialists to discover that workers so often had
the same mentality as capitalists and that their greatest ambition
was to join the possessing classes, for, as George Moore had a
character remark in *Esther Waters,* "the world is so full of ups and
downs, you never can tell who is who." [14]

Working-class apathy and fatalism, on the one hand, and working-class faith in self-help and social mobility, on the other, made
the missionary efforts of socialists difficult. But there were other
complications. Spirited, energetic, and ambitious workers—the
ideal converts to the socialist cause—were often the very people
who emigrated because of the greater opportunities they hoped
to find in the United States or the colonies. "I bring with me
youth, a small family, a few useful literary talents, and that is
all," wrote William Cobbett to Thomas Jefferson in 1792. To be
sure, few late Victorian emigrants were as well equipped as
Cobbett, but Disraeli eloquently expressed their daydreams of
riches and renown when in a speech in 1876 he declared: "A colo-
nist finds a nugget, or he fleeces a thousand flocks. He makes a
fortune, he returns to England, he buys an estate, he becomes a
magistrate, he represents majesty, he becomes high sheriff, he has
a magnificent house near Hyde Park, he goes to court." Variations
on this image of mobility lured away many workers who were
dissatisfied with economic conditions in England and, in the
process, deprived the socialists of the type of recruit they so eagerly
sought.

Emigration also helped those workers who remained in England. For one thing, they often received remittances from relatives who did well in other parts of the world. More important
still, they had fewer workers with whom to compete for job opportunities. At different times and in different places labor
shortages occurred, forcing up wages. In 1895, for instance, George
Gissing complained that for £20 a year he could not find a satisfactory servant for a small house he had in Great Yarmouth and·
that he would have to offer higher wages. Since young girls preferred the greater freedom and higher wages they secured in
factories, Gissing predicted—as did many ladies' magazines of the
time—that the English, like the Americans, would increasingly
have to manage without domestic help. It is ironic that about

twenty years earlier Gissing, then living in Boston, had been so impressed with the American standard of living that he remarked that almost everybody—"even the servants"—traveled to Europe.[15]

VII

Above all, however, it was the pattern of the depression that worked against the socialists. For, while underemployment and unemployment were invaluable aids in their agitation, other features of the late Victorian business cycle were not. The falling prices of the age were a calamity to businessmen, farmers, and landowners; but they were a boon to workers, who year after year could buy more commodities for less money.

At the same time wages declined less than prices. It is true that the type of notice that had so often been posted during hard times still appeared: "In consequence of the depressed state of trade we are reluctantly compelled to announce that a reduction of 10% in the wages of all persons employed in this mill will take place after next week." But because of strikes and unions and the fear of them such notices appeared less often than in the past. Despite the depression, in other words, wages often remained stationary or dropped only slightly. In some instances they even rose, but such increases were unusual, for in an age when employers were constantly complaining of declining profits, workers could not say what the cotton spinners of Ashton had said in a period of prosperity: "that the time has now arrived when you *can* give us an advance." [16]

The result of the price movements and wage trends was that real wages increased during the late Victorian period. But the difficulty is that no one can say precisely by how much. On the one hand, socialists insisted that the poor were getting poorer; on the other hand, ardent defenders of capitalism like Sir Robert Giffen, W. H. Mallock, and Leone Levi, eager to prove that working-class conditions were improving markedly, insisted that real wages were darting ahead. Unfortunately, trustworthy statistics of real wages are hard to come by for most periods of history; for the late Victorian age the figures are distinctly inadequate. Retail prices varied from community to community and within communities; prices in Manchester were different from those in London, prices in one part of London or Manchester were different from those in another, and even in neighboring shops they differed. Besides, some working-class wives were better at comparison shopping and bargain hunting than others. So, too, the wages of the hundreds of different kinds of workers varied from town to town and within towns. And in many families there was more than one wage-earner.

While it is impossible to say to what extent real wages rose, there is no question that they did increase—and more impressively in some cases than in others. No doubt Giffen, Mallock, and Levi were unduly optimistic. But the average worker—that convenient and indispensable myth—was unquestionably better off when the depression ended than when it began. In the main, his improved real wages were due to the price decline. It was this relationship that a shrewd contemporary had in mind when he confessed that he could not make himself believe that a general fall in the prices of consumers' goods was an evil thing—regardless of its effects on businessmen. And it was the benefits that low prices brought to workers that the banker Thomson Hankey had in mind when he noted sarcastically: "To the trading community any action of whatever kind which will raise prices generally must be a wise one!! and low prices must be injurious to the world!!" Certainly no one would have seriously argued by the end of the century—as some Bolton trade unionists had as late as 1860— that English workers were worse off than American slaves. In the moderate words of an aged Manchester businessman, who reminisced toward the end of the century about labor conditions several decades before: "The working classes were much worse off than they are now. They had lower wages; and their wages would purchase far less of necessities and pleasures of life than now." [17]

Other improvements in the condition of the working classes disproved the charges of the socialists that labor was suffering from increasing misery. Free and compulsory elementary education created unprecedented opportunities for economic and social mobility. The constant revision of public health and factory laws helped to make living and working conditions healthier than they had been before. Legislation dealing with artisans' dwellings, child labor, hours of work, and workmen's compensation showed the willingness of politicians of the capitalist parties to use the state to lessen the hardships of working-class life and belied the socialist charge that the Conservative and Liberal parties were tools of the plutocracy and enemies of the workers. "Who turns alone the world's great wheel, / Yet has no right in commonweal?" The answer to this question that socialists asked became more and more dubious in the late Victorian period.[18]

In the agitation for legislative reforms trade unions frequently played an important part. And if socialists were often wary both of the reforms and of the unions, the main reason was that they feared that workers, as their position improved, would become satisfied with their lot. If unions succeeded in reminding employers that they needed further concessions because, as some Wigan strikers once put it, "your 'umble servants 'as wifes and Famileys to Keep," workers might lose interest in any basic reorganization of society. Indeed, the more victories the unions achieved against what some Bolton workers called "the twin-monsters, competition and machinery," the greater the defeats the socialists would suffer. It is no surprise that John Burns felt strongly that the socialists had to try to capture the Trades Union Congress.[19]

VIII

Despite the impressive gains that labor won in the late Victorian period, the socialists still found countless facts of working-class life to exploit in their agitation. Slum conditions, the horrors of illness and old age for workers, the inadequacies of poor relief, and the chronic menace of unemployment and underemployment —all these provided rich material for their campaign. And much more than many Continental socialists, English socialists had the weather as an ally. "What freezing means in England— cold that strikes to your very marrow—I pray you may never know," Rudyard Kipling once told an American. English workers knew it well, and socialists never tired of reminding them of it and of the other hardships that they suffered. "I have hungered in the streets; I have laid my head in the poorest shelter; I know what it is to feel the heart burn with wrath and envy of 'the privileged classes.' " The socialists assumed that like George Gissing's Henry Ryecroft, and like Gissing himself, workers resented the wealth of the respectable public, and they played on this resentment endlessly.

Some of them felt it deeply themselves. John Burns, anxious in 1888 because his wife was ill and winter was coming, noted bitterly in his diary that while idlers could go to the Riviera "a worker must go to Hell or what is worse live and endure the life of one." And when Burns visited Brighton the sight of prosperous Jews made him seethe with antisemitism. So, too, Plato E. Draculis fumed when he was told to leave England for a warmer climate; "as if I were able to do so as Lord Randolph Churchill," he wrote. Indeed, this type of resentment was often expressed in socialist song:

> We know there are some with leisure
> Who roam the world so sweet;
> But we to our factory-prisons
> Are chained by the hands and feet.[20]

At the height of the prosperity of the early seventies the *Economist* had acknowledged that England was a country whose poor were very numerous. By the end of the century the poor were fewer than they had been, but they were still numerous. They were the people who, when they worked, often engaged in dangerous occupations or sweated industries. They were the London girls to whom, as George Moore said, "rest, not to say pleasure, is unknown." They were the people of whom Arthur Morrison wrote in *A Child of the Jago*—women who considered the making of matchboxes highly remunerative work, women who spent sixteen hours a day at sewing shirts and earned ninepence or a shilling, women who in four days made a hundred sacks and received one and sevenpence. Unfortunately for the socialists, however, these "bottom people" were the very ones whose immense apathy and fatalism made them unreachable.

But the comfortable classes were rarely aware of this. They feared that the socialists were rapidly winning labor support, and that they had succeeded in teaching workers to say with them, "Oh what a lot it is to be a prisoner in the bastille of Capitalism." By the end of the century it was widely assumed that almost all workers were socialists, just as back in the forties it had been taken for granted that they were Chartists.

The socialists, to be sure, encouraged the impression that they had won converts on a large scale, and they continued to speak so confidently and optimistically in public about their imminent triumph—"social upheaval may come at any moment"—that even some of the most tough-minded of their opponents believed them to be right. Privately, however, the socialists were disheartened by their failure to achieve even a portion of what they had expected to accomplish among the masses in the late nineteenth century. They made the mistake of underestimating the resistance that they had to overcome. And they forgot that history, as Edward Carpenter wisely remarked, was "a difficult horse to drive." [21]

⟡ XII ⟡

SCHEMES EVERYWHERE

Just as socialists promised workers a much better future, so, too, did hundreds of nonsocialist reformers. Indeed, if ever there was a period up to 1900 when English urban workers had cause not to feel neglected and rejected, it was during the late Victorian age. And when rural spokesmen protested angrily against what they regarded as the overattention given to urban labor, they had reason to complain, for in the age of the Great Depression reformers gave clear priority to the needs of the urban working classes.

It was simple justice that Lord Shaftesbury should have been the best known friend of labor until he died at eighty-four in 1885. For Shaftesbury had an incredibly successful record as the champion of chimney sweeps, destitute children, shoeblacks, needlewomen, railway workers, costermongers, cabmen, prisoners, drunkards, cripples, the blind, and the insane. After Shaftesbury's death, however, workers had so many protectors in the ranks of reformers that no individual could possibly stand out in the way that he had for so many decades. "The ideal of life which Lord Shaftesbury marked out for himself," the Anglican clergyman and humanitarian F. W. Farrar noted without exaggeration, "has become the ideal of life to multitudes of blessed toilers." [1]

How to improve the position of urban labor—this was the central problem for countless reformers during the last third of the nineteenth century, and they advanced an overwhelming variety of solutions. Although what they proposed was often not particularly novel, this fact did not keep them from writing and speaking with a fervor which suggested that they were the first to uncover important truths. But whether their proposals were fresh or stale is not what mattered. What gave their schemes particular urgency was the widespread anxiety over the persistence of hard times.

Help workers to help themselves and to prepare for the future, said Herbert Spencer, Barwick Baker, the witty controversialist W. H. Mallock, and Charles Loch of the Charity Organization Society. It was easy for reformers who doubted the relevance to late Victorian England of Spencer's doctrine of self-help to dismiss him with characterizations ranging from windbag to rubbish man. But the fact remains—even though it has often been overlooked—that Spencer was as much concerned as they with promoting working-class welfare.[2]

Encourage workers to appreciate the importance and value of education, said Matthew Arnold and the eminent chemists Lord Playfair and Sir Henry Roscoe. Persuade workers to give up drinking, said George Cruikshank, William Hoyle, General Booth, Francis W. Newman, and a horde of temperance leaders. Teach workers to change their food habits, said Newman and a small band of vegetarians.[3]

Get rid of free trade and create more jobs for British workers, said tariff reformers. Enlarge the Empire and develop closer colonial ties, said imperial reformers. The expansion of the British Empire under the sympathetic guidance of a Tory Ministry, declared a dedicated and typical imperial reformer in 1895, would make possible the opening of new markets for British goods.

Make it easier for workers and their families to emigrate, said Charles Bradlaugh, General Booth, and John T. Middlemore. "I was glad to hear, whilst in Birmingham last week, so many particulars of your children's Emigration Homes, and of your many sacrifices in connexion with them," John Bright wrote enthusiastically to Middlemore in 1875. But this is not to suggest that advocates of emigration as a remedy for working-class distress failed to recognize its dangers. As Thomas Hughes sadly noted of a skilled artisan whom he knew, "He is one of those whom England can ill spare and America is indeed fortunate to get."

II

The sordid conditions under which workers lived aroused the particular indignation of a host of humanitarians. Years before Charles Booth's epoch-making volumes on the life and labor of Londoners began to appear in 1891, housing reformers had been agitating for slum clearance programs and the erection of model artisans' dwellings. What a special investigating commission accurately observed of Carlton Street in a powerful pamphlet on *Squalid Liverpool* (1883) other humanitarians remarked with equal justice of other slums: "Here resides a population which is a people in itself, ceaselessly ravaged by fever, plagued by the blackest, most appalling poverty, cut off from every grace and comfort of life, born, living, and dying amid squalid surroundings, of which those who have not seen them can form a very inadequate conception." The brutal truth was that it could rarely be said of an English town—as George Gissing remarked of Eastbourne— that it lacked a single street that could be called a slum. But the equally brutal truth was that it could often be said of a slum—as Arthur Morrison had a character say of the Jago—that after this there could be no hell. It was no accident that George Potter, George Mitchell, and other labor leaders placed improvements in housing high in their list of aims. Nor was it an accident that George Peabody, Lord Iveagh, and other philanthropists focused particular attention on the need for better working-class dwellings. For they were convinced that adequate housing would do more to prevent drunkenness, idleness, dissipation, and vice than any number of sermons.[4]

Establish settlement houses in the worst sections of towns and show the poor that they are not a separate nation, said Arnold Toynbee, Canon Barnett, Dr. Elizabeth Blackwell, and the hero of *The Way of All Flesh*. In fact, as early as 1885 W. M. Rossetti noted proudly and accurately that the recently founded Toynbee Hall had already become the headquarters of idealistic young university men who were determined to humanize the conditions of life in the East End of London.

Keep slum children busy and off the streets, said F. W. Farrar, Mrs. Humphry Ward, and Benjamin Waugh, the Congregational minister and co-founder of the London Society for the Prevention of Cruelty to Children. When Farrar first worked in London in 1876 as canon of Westminster, he was impressed—and alarmed— by the almost complete absence of adequate recreational facilities for slum children. By the end of the century Farrar conceded that much remained to be done. But at least the creation of some youth centers had made somewhat less true the old reproach that, although the English provided schools and churches for the masses, they permitted the Devil to supply their amusements.

Establish homes for the reclamation and reeducation of prostitutes, said Mrs. Josephine Butler, Mrs. Gladstone, and Sir William Willis. London streets were a disgrace at night, Willis confessed in 1889, and he was not alone in being shocked by the bigness of the daily parades of fallen women of all shapes, sizes, ages, and classes. As in London, so elsewhere, humanitarians pointed out, homes were desperately needed to restrain and retrain the prostitute population.[5]

Make workers aware of the importance of personal cleanliness and strict public health measures, said Florence Nightingale and Edwin Chadwick, that "thoughtful and contriving administrative mind," as John Stuart Mill had rightly called him. It is true that Miss Nightingale and Chadwick were sometimes overzealous in their insistence on sanitary reform, but the reason is not far to seek. It was one thing, after all, for George Gissing to complain of a servant who lacked the most elementary notions of cleanliness and used his best towels to wipe the floors. But this was nothing compared to what was the real difficulty: that the poor often resented as snobbery anything that smacked even mildly of cleanliness. Indeed, it was no accident that Florence Nightingale found it necessary to emphasize repeatedly that one of the main responsibilities of district nurses was to inform local authorities of sanitary defects which they noticed in the dwellings of the poor.

As in earlier decades, however, sanitary reformers found it hard to get people stirred up about cleanliness—either private or public. The old remark of the prominent population expert and statistician, William Farr, still applied: "I wish you would give us a History of the Plague—in the manner of Defoe—but higher and better—interweaving sanitary schemes—and moralizings. It would do more than almost anything else—to accelerate Reforms. Why not bring it out monthly like Thackeray and Dickens?—and keep the subject alive?" Indeed, W. T. Stead did not go too far when he insisted during the cholera scare of 1892 that the disease was a godsend that saved far more lives than it destroyed. "There is hardly any of the ordinary diseases but kills more than the Cholera does," he wrote discerningly, "but they do not do it in the sensational fashion of our Asiatic friend, and his advent gives an immense stimulus to sanitation everywhere at the smallest possible expenditure of life." [6]

<h2 style="text-align:center">III</h2>

Nor was this the range of the proposals that reformers made to improve the position of labor in late Victorian society. Far from it. Induce workers to practice birth control, said Charles Bradlaugh, Mrs. Annie Besant, Dr. Charles Drysdale, and other Malthusians. Ernest Dowson, faithful to Cynara only in his fashion, was nevertheless astonished by the pride his countrymen took in being prolific; and he once quipped that if they had any imagination they would deify the rabbit. To Malthusians, however, the population problem was not a subject to joke about. No act of morality was more important than adjusting the size of the family to its income, Dr. Drysdale bluntly told Gladstone during the sensational prosecution of Bradlaugh and Mrs. Besant for the republication of an old American work on birth control.

That still unmarried friend of Mrs. Besant, Bernard Shaw, pointed out in 1890 that the population problem faced all parties, whether socialist or antisocialist. But Malthusians complained chronically that insufficient attention was given to their remedy for the ills of society. And they were right. It is revealing that even Sir William Wilson Hunter, the authority on the population problems of India, argued that with railways, irrigation, schools, and land law reform India could manage without birth control and the gospel according to Bradlaugh. It is not strange, therefore, that an ardent member of the Medical Branch of the Malthusian League wrote dispiritedly: "it is to me a by no means edifying spectacle to notice the way in which this movement and this question is persistently and systematically ignored by those who on other questions are not so backward in acting as the world's authorities, teachers and guides."

Impatient for results—the population of England and Wales increased by almost 10 million between 1871 and 1901—Malthusians did not wish to wait for influenza, diphtheria, scarlet fever, typhoid fever, cholera, and bronchitis to solve the problem of overpopulation. It was much more humane, they argued, to make knowledge of birth control universal. Then a Tess would not have to feel "quite a Malthusian towards her mother for thoughtlessly giving her so many little sisters and brothers." And the mother of an Esther Waters would not complain, "I've 'ad a terrible time of it lately, and them babies allus coming. Ah, we poor women have more than our right to bear with!" [7]

IV

Other reformers gave priority to other changes. Encourage workers to join the cooperative moment, said George Jacob Holyoake and such Christian Socialists as Thomas Hughes, J. M. Ludlow, Edward Vansittart Neale, and Elizabeth Blackwell. Indeed, after decades of service to the cause, undaunted Holyoake pointed out hopefully in 1901 that even some eminent businessmen had come to recognize that British industry could hold its own in the world market only by the adoption of the cooperative principle.

Enact social legislation worthy of a civilized society, said Frederic Harrison and other Positivists. Insure workers against accidents and prepare them for old age, said Edward Bellamy, J. A Spender, and any number of proud New Zealanders. At forty-five Bellamy pointed out temptingly in *Looking Backward*, workers would retire and have the rest of their lives to devote to their own improvement.[8]

Guarantee labor a living wage through government action, said Henry W. Macrosty of the Carlyle Society. Reduce the work-week and create more jobs, said trade union leaders. The Government without reducing the wages of workers, should introduce the eight hour day in all its workshops, the Battersea branch of the Amalgamated Society of Engineers urged in 1893—and for two reasons First, it was the duty of the Government to set an example for the rest of the country of how a good employer should behave. Second it was the duty of the Government to help to solve the unemploy

SCHEMES EVERYWHERE

ment problem by enabling the jobless to take on the work that would result from the shortening of the work-week.[9]

Lighten the tax burden of the working classes, said advocates of tax revision. Indeed, it is often forgotten that reformers had frightened the comfortable classes with their clamor for the revamping of the tax structure many years before the introduction of the so-called People's Budget of 1909—"the worst and crudest budget of modern times—worthy of the shallow and rhetorical Henry George, whom our Chancellor, his namesake Lloyd George, much resembles." The prolonged depression inevitably encouraged much talk—and much loose talk—about taxation; it is understandable that professional economists particularly were appalled by what they heard. C. F. Bastable, the Irish political economist, found English ignorance of public finance astonishing; Alfred Marshall deplored the academic neglect of the subject; and L. H. Blunden urged scholars to work tirelessly to counteract the fiscal fallacies of the age.

Henry George and his British followers were, of course, the reformers who helped above all to make public finance a subject of lively public discussion in late Victorian England. Yet, while it is true that single-taxers were disappointed with the results of their agitation, they inspired other reformers to advocate progressive inheritance and income taxes as devices by which to shift the fiscal burden to those who could better afford to bear it. No doubt about it, Sir William Harcourt's budget of 1894, prepared by Arnold Toynbee's pupil, up-and-coming Alfred Milner, was a major victory for tax reformers; and it was correctly viewed as a dangerous measure by traditionalists.[10]

Abandon the gold standard, said Moreton Frewen and other bimetallists. Insisting that the remonetization of silver would restore prosperity and end unemployment, they recalled with pride the silver-using England of Cecil, Cromwell, and Pitt; they lashed out at those—Jewish bankers in particular—who proclaimed their unwavering enthusiasm for monometallism; and they cooperated with American supporters of the free coinage of silver.

Charles Dickens had confessed late in life that the more he read about currency doctrines, the less he understood them; young Arnold Bennett thought of differential calculus and bimetallism as equally dim mysteries; and middle-aged W. T. Stead, considering the silver fever, was grateful that, although he had flirted with many schemes in his time, he had managed to avoid going wild over currency reform. To believers of all ages, however, bimetallism was a certain remedy for a multitude of evils. The distinguished economic historian James E. Thorold Rogers could insist that the history of currency demonstrated the fallacies and sophisms of bimetallism; and the eminent banking authority Thomson Hankey could feel relieved in 1882 that the bimetallists were not gaining ground. But the Bimetallic League carried on its activities with such ardor that a Monometallic Association had to be formed to fight the silver heresy. "The bimetallists in England have become very aggressive," an alarmed contemporary noted in 1895, "and the Monometallists, who treated them with too much contempt, have been at last obliged to carry war into their camp." The truth is that the William Jennings Bryan campaign of 1896 frightened English monometallists almost as much as it did their American counterparts. "Please bury Bryan deep in a political dungeon," Rudyard Kipling wrote to an American. "What Bryan has done is like an inebriate regulating a chronometer with a crowbar," said Winston Churchill, insisting that the silver heretic had to be defeated at any cost.[11]

v

Although urban workers were the chief concern of late Victorian reformers, the agricultural classes also had their advocates. It is true that rural reformers were relatively few in number, but they made up in zeal for what they lacked in statistical strength. It was, for instance, a testimonial to their effectiveness that George Gissing, always on the hunt for literary themes that might sell, encouraged his brother Algernon to write about country life because of the interest that reformers had aroused in the rural plight. And a hard-headed publisher's reader urged the publication of a novel about a tyrannical country gentleman because there was, he thought, a sizable public for books that sided against the squire.[12]

Almost always rural reformers were agricultural fundamentalists; they considered farming the best of all ways of life—the healthiest, the noblest, and the most useful. They deplored the change from an agricultural to what James Russell Lowell called "a proletary population," and they insisted that the greatest danger that faced England was the rural exodus. If it were not halted, the security of the nation as well as its moral fiber would be permanently wrecked. In the words of an advertisement for H. Rider Haggard's moving and unjustly forgotten book, *A Farmer's Year* (1899): "It deals . . . with that gradual depopulation of the country districts which, if not checked, seems likely to bring about national consequences of a character far more grave than are anticipated to-day by those who, dwelling in towns and subsisting on foreign produce, imagine that to them the prosperity or the ruin of British land is a matter of indifference." Like every agricultural fundamentalist, Haggard considered the land question the most important of all the topics of his time, and he devoted the last part of his life to trying to make his countrymen—Joseph Chamberlain, among them—share his view. In fact, Haggard would have preferred to give up novel-writing, which he found wearisome, and devote all his time to fighting for rural England. But he needed the income from his fiction to carry on his work as a reformer.[13]

Ever since antiquity, rural enthusiasts had berated towns as unhealthy and corrupting influences, but with the accelerated urban development of the late eighteenth century rural spokesmen became all the more vocal in their criticisms. "I would give an hundred pound," the great agricultural authority Arthur Young wrote characteristically to Fanny Burney in 1792, "to see you married to a farmer that never saw London, with plenty of poultry, ranging in a few green fields and flowers and shrubs disposed where they should be around a cottage and not a breakfast room in Portman Square fading in eyes that know not to admire them."

With the urban expansion of the nineteenth century Arthur Young's horror of towns was repeatedly expressed by others. Thomas Carlyle proclaimed London unbearable, Rossetti found it hateful, Edward Lear considered it disagreeable, and Yeats described it with such adjectives as dull, dirty, and horrible. To Marie Corelli it was "a den of quarrelsome, fighting, pushing, struggling humankind," and to John Lockwood Kipling it was "the city of Calamity." While London was the town that rural enthusiasts denounced most heartily, Manchester, Birmingham, and Liverpool were also favorite targets. Edwin Waugh could refer to Manchester as "the darling old smoky town" and others could talk affectionately of "dear dirty old Manchester," but to agricultural fundamentalists those who had kind words to say about towns were simply misguided.[14]

For rural reformers it was urgent both to stop the rural exodus and to encourage people to leave the dreadful towns and settle in the countryside. But the difficulties were enormous. Thomas Hardy, widely recognized in the 1890s as *the* literary authority on country life, could write of Angel Clare that "the conventional farm-folk of his imagination—personified by the pitiable dummy known as Hodge—were obliterated after a few days' residence. At close quarters no Hodge was to be seen." Unlike the hero of *Tess*, however, townspeople clung to their stereotype of Hodge; and efforts to get them to settle on the land—and become Hodges—proved fruitless.

So, too, the rural exodus turned out to be harder to check than reformers anticipated. The inescapable fact was that impressive numbers of rural laborers—and their children—wanted to take advantage of the greater economic opportunities that they believed they would find in towns. And they wished to escape from what they considered the monotony of rural life. George Gissing was in harmony with the currents of the age when he had Henry Ryecroft remark that only the feeble-minded would put up any longer with rural life. Tired of tending cows and intent on bettering themselves, farm laborers longed for urban pavements and music-halls.[15]

VI

Even before the Great Depression began witty Colonel William Bromley Davenport singled out British farmers as the longest-suffering people of whom he had ever heard, for they had an interminable case history of being plagued by pests who considered it their duty to give them advice. By 1875 Davenport ridiculed such politicians as Henry Fawcett and Sir William Harcourt because they "knew as much about agriculture as a codfish, and that was putting it in a very unflattering manner for the codfish." Yet if Davenport's complaints were legitimate in the early seventies, they became all the more valid in the age of the Great Depression. The rural classes suffered from a dearth of many things but not of givers of advice.[16]

To improve conditions in the countryside reformers urged a wide variety of changes. Nationalize the land, said Alfred Russel Wallace and his fellow-socialists as well as antisocialist Henry George and his disciples. Private property in land is robbery; the land belongs to the people; landlordism is founded on force and fraud; no man made the land—these were some of their more popular slogans. By 1891 Helen Taylor went so far as to assure George that land nationalization had come to be regarded as a necessity in Britain. But other informed contemporaries were much less sanguine. For land nationalization was widely viewed, in the words of the Coventry *Standard,* as "only the beginning of a persecution by the Communistic Radicals of all people having anything to lose." As Jesse Collings, ardent land reformer and Member of Parliament, wisely told Wallace, "The difficulty you will have to contend with is in convincing your readers of the justice of taking away from the present holders without compensation the raw material of the land which they now own." And as Professor John Stuart Blackie rhetorically asked Wallace: "should we not require a *Bismarck* and a *Von Stein,* and a *battle of Jena* to boot, to bring about so sweeping a change?"[17]

Free the land from feudal fetters and eliminate large farms, for they were only partially cultivated anyhow, said Joseph Arch, the agricultural trade union leader, and other advocates of land tenure reform. If farms were smaller, Arch told Gladstone in 1879, describing himself as one vitally interested in the restoration of agricultural prosperity, capital could be found to cultivate them properly and more work would be found for laborers. There should be a quantitative limit, beyond which no individual should be permitted to own land, said Francis W. Newman, who went so far as to serve as the president of a farm laborers' union. So, too, insisted such outspoken members of the Land Tenure Reform Association as Sir Charles Dilke, Cliffe Leslie, and Edward Lyulph Stanley, all of whom were alarmed that 150 people—among them the Dukes of Devonshire, Richmond, Cleveland, and Sutherland —owned half the land of England and that much acreage was going uncultivated.[18]

Give farm laborers more of a stake in rural society, said Jesse Collings and Edward Lyulph Stanley. Make England a country of proud and secure peasant proprietors, said Collings. To lift farm laborers from their depressed condition and to help them become independent, said Stanley, give them the right to vote, the right to cultivate waste and common land, a reorganized scheme of rural education, and a reform of the law of master and servant.

Following the enfranchisement of rural labor and the enactment of compulsory education laws, reformers intensified their efforts to extend the number of peasant proprietors. As Frederic Impey, honorary secretary of the Allotments and Small Holdings Association, put it in 1886, "I believe all of these questions in which we are interested will come enormously more to the front under the pressure of the political changes which have given power at last to the smaller people in the rural districts who will combine with the intelligent classes of the towns to solve the land question on a satisfactory basis." Impey, to be sure, proved to be unduly optimistic; yet it was a sign of the times that even Liberal leaders of the end of the century explicitly recognized the urgency of a positive rural policy. And Sir Henry Roscoe, the eminent scientist and Liberal Member of Parliament, harped on the importance of revamping rural education so that it would contribute to the stability of country life.[19]

VII

Just as spokesmen for the rural classes had to make up in energy and zeal for what they lacked in numbers, so, too, did another group of reformers: the advocates of women's rights. Unlike agricultural fundamentalists, however, the women's rights people had one special advantage—a profound and irrepressible sense of oppression. Mercilessly ridiculed by many of their contemporaries, they nourished feelings of persecution that produced both extraordinary actions and startling thoughts: one tireless feminist even came to believe that the women of ancient Egypt enjoyed more substantial rights as citizens than their English counterparts of the late nineteenth century. In these circumstances, *Punch* and other antifeminist publications, far from damaging the women's cause, unwittingly helped it along. The more the New Women and the Fast Girls were derided, the more they rallied and asserted themselves—especially since so many of them had income and leisure. They were not people to be moved by the stock jeer that they go home and wash the baby.[20]

The women's rights movement, which became the object of much anxious humor in late Victorian England, owed much to two events of the sixties: the end of slavery in the United States, and the movement for the democratization of the British suffrage. The freeing of the American slaves convinced some reformers that women—both American and British—were the next submerged group to be lifted up. And the agitation that culminated in the Reform Act of 1867 convinced others that women, too, must be enfranchised. Just a year after the publication of John Stuart Mill's *Subjection of Women* (1869) even cautious Charles Dickens spoke of the emancipation of women as "drawing very near." [21]

That the suffrage issue figured so prominently in the women's rights movement is understandable. For reformers were convinced that once women had the right to vote and sit in Parliament they could easily legislate away the other abuses from which they suffered. Aware that women in England and Wales outnumbered men by 600,000 in 1871—the figure was more than a million by 1901—they had confidence that the time would come when women would easily dominate the political life of England. It is a mistake, nevertheless, to think of the women's rights advocates as obsessed simply with the vote, for many of them focused on other injustices and inequalities from which women suffered. When Florence Nightingale explained to John Stuart Mill her reasons for not joining a franchise group, she insisted that there were "evils which press so much more hardly on women than the want of the suffrage." Some reformers urged greater opportunities for the higher education of women. Some pressed for the opening of more occupations to women. Some clamored for the repeal of the Contagious Diseases legislation, the mere existence of which legalized prostitution. And some campaigned to secure the property rights of married women and to improve the conditions of working-class women, often among the worst victims of the Great Depression.[22]

Like other reformers, the champions of the women's cause often had extraordinary powers of self-deception. Emily Davies was right when she reported in 1867 that, although Charles Darwin refused to sign a petition for the enfranchisement of women, she had secured some excellent names. And Leonard Courtney was also right when he reported in 1885 that the number of parliamentary candidates pledged to the enfranchisement of women was im-

THE "MILL"-ENNIUM.
The Honourable Member for Westminster.—"I BEG TO PROPOSE—THE LADIES!"

Fun, May 4, 1867

pressive. But Miss Davies, Courtney, Henry Fawcett, and many other champions of the cause wanted so desperately to achieve their aims that they often engaged in wishful succeeding. They underestimated the determination of their opponents, and they convinced themselves that they had more adherents than they knew. Indeed, Sir Charles Dilke had good reason to belittle the accuracy of their claim in 1884 that they had 250 friends in the House of Commons; they reached this figure, as Dilke assured Gladstone, by some highly dubious arithmetic.

The great truth was, of course, that Gladstone opposed the enfranchisement of women, and so did John Bright. The no less important truth was that there were too many other competing and worrisome questions to deal with in an age of depression to make possible experimentation with so emotion-packed a proposal as the enfranchisement of women.[23]

VIII

Just as socialists fought one another, so, too, did nonsocialist reformers. Labor leaders and champions of the cooperative movement repeatedly insisted that trade unionism and cooperation were not antagonistic to each other, but as late as 1885 J. M. Ludlow conceded that they had not found a satisfactory working relationship. And what was true of them was true of other reformers. Just as nonsocialists fought nonsocialists and socialists fought socialists, so, too, they fought one another. Socialists dismissed as superficial the efforts of nonsocialists to improve the conditions of urban labor, the rural classes, and women. And nonsocialists belittled the plans of socialists as hopelessly impractical and wrongheaded. Plato E. Draculis and other socialists viewed General Booth's scheme of social salvation as foredoomed, and H. M. Hyndman, William Clarke, and Walter Crane, among other socialists, considered Henry George's proposals nothing more than quack remedies. General Booth, Charles Bradlaugh, and Henry George, on the other hand, found the errors of the socialists fundamental.[24]

It is true that George and his British followers tried for a time to work with the socialists, and such Fabians as Sidney Webb and Edward R. Pease tried to cooperate with the single taxers. Webb even begged George to disregard the attacks on him from the wilder socialists. But the pleas for harmony failed—so much so that, as Bernard Shaw pointed out, it became fashionable for British socialists to conceal their historical indebtedness to George. What happened to the projected Webb-George alliance was typical. Schemes of reform were everywhere in late Victorian England, but so were feuding reformers. "How they hate one another," Hyndman once exclaimed of landlords and capitalists. But his exclamation applied equally well to many socialist and nonsocialist reformers.[25]

❧ XIII ❧

SCHOOLS AS WEAPONS

Years before the Great Depression began, individuals and organized groups had urged the English to do something about their educational system—or, rather, their lack of it—but the reformers were able to effect few of the changes they thought desirable. To their endless distress and frustration they found that almost every educational change involved both religion and money. And the bigger the reform they proposed, the more resistance it met on sectarian and financial grounds.

Almost invariably the reformers—whether they were obscure citizens active in local affairs, or such celebrities as Prince Albert, Sir Lyon Playfair, Richard Cobden, George Cruikshank, or Matthew Arnold—warned that other countries were far ahead of England in the provisions they made for education, and that it was dangerous for the English to remain a nation of illiterates and semiliterates. During a visit to the Continent in 1838 young Richard Cobden, for instance, was enormously impressed by the emphasis the Germans gave to popular education. In Prussia especially he found that by the time people were in their twenties almost all of them—whether men or women—could read, write, and do arithmetic. Fifteen years later Cobden rejoiced that a friend who had just visited the United States returned with a conviction that he had long held: that the English would be outdistanced by the Americans unless they raised the educational standards of their working classes. His friend's findings, Cobden hoped, would alarm English businessmen and move them to action.

Nor were Cobden and his friend lone worriers. Quite the contrary. The eminent Shakespearean actor, William Charles Macready, who knew the United States well, similarly feared that the English would act only when it would be too late for them to maintain their position among the nations of the world. "You must perceive," he wrote dispiritedly to an American in 1859, "that we do not move in the way of improvement, until lessons have been given in the examples of the United States and our own Colonies. In this all-important question of Education, we shall go on talking about it, till left far behind in the intelligence of the masses by you and them." So, too, John Bright repeatedly decried the backwardness of English education—the more so when he thought of what the English in America had done to make schools as "universal as air and water." Indeed, when Bright gave advice to an English friend who was about to visit the United States shortly after the end of the Civil War, he urged him to pay particular attention to American educational institutions, especially in the New England States.

As with English schools, so with English libraries. "What a scandalous condition England is in with regard to public libraries," George Gissing exclaimed in 1878. Nor was his outburst unjustified. For years reformers like William Ewart had pointed out that English libraries were designed not to diffuse knowledge but to confine it. In the United States, on the other hand, public libraries were well-established institutions—and free for all to use.[1]

II

Reformers complained not only that the English masses received almost no formal education but that even the small segment of the population that went to school was subjected to the wrong kind of instruction. Technical training was largely ignored. So useful a skill as drawing, for instance, received none of the attention in England that it was given on the Continent. "No country invests a larger amount of Capital in works of Art of all kinds than England," wrote Prince Albert in 1856, "and in none, almost, is so little done for Art Education!" On the elementary school level a leading criticism was the failure of the English to teach the metric system, and as a result children were condemned to years of torture mastering an unduly complicated arithmetic. On the grammar school and university level the chief objection was to the neglect of science and modern languages and the overattention to Greek and Latin.

The worst of it was that those who conducted grammar schools rarely engaged in self-criticism. Their justification for the emphasis they placed on the rules of Greek syntax, for instance, was simple: to master this material was to train the intellect. They granted readily that there would be few occasions in later years when students would be able to apply their knowledge of Greek syntax, but they argued that there would be "few circumstances or stations in life, in which the strength and versatility which such studies impart to the mind will not be found of essential value." But for boys who had no aptitude for classical languages grammar school was a painful and wasteful experience. Thomas Hughes, as an old man, pityingly recalled one of his fags at Rugby who ranked low because he had no talent for Greek or Latin. Indeed, Hughes's youngest son did not take to the classics or mathematics in school. Still, he did learn to ride, shoot, and tell the truth, and since the boy eventually became a Texas cattle rancher, Hughes felt that he could not complain that his education had been wrong. Nevertheless, the amount of waste that the stress on classical languages involved was great, and it was unwittingly acknowledged by no less eminent an educator than Thomas Arnold. Having received a protest about an insufficiently expurgated edition of Horace that was used at Rugby, Dr. Arnold reassured the complainant that his boys were so unaccustomed to reading on their own in Greek and Latin books that not one out of a thousand would be familiar with the offensive passages.[2]

There were, to be sure, some educational institutions that aimed to keep up with the social and scientific developments of the nineteenth-century world. Mr. Bosworth's Academy near Tottenham, according to its prospectus of 1831, gave particular attention to the "application of the Sciences to the Arts of Life, and especially to the improved state of our Machinery and Manufactures, and the results of Chemical Analysis." And London University was formed in the late 1820s for the purpose of providing middle-class Londoners with a "complete scientific and literary education." The annual charges were to be moderate—in contrast with the minimum of £200 or £250 that Oxford and Cambridge required for an academic year with almost five months of vacations. "We hope much from the new University . . . and trust that all your great cities are to supply their crying wants in this particular," wrote an American Anglophile, who was appalled by the backwardness of English higher education.

Although the University was slow to receive a charter and degree-granting authority, its growth was still impressive—especially in view of the public's inertia and the active academic opposition that it had to overcome. Hardly less impressive was the foundation of Owens College, the forerunner of the University of Manchester. The members of the committee which drew up the plan for the institution in 1850 recognized the desirability of classical training, particularly for people who were to devote their lives to trade. At the same time, however, they recommended that, since most of the students would be sons of businessmen, instruction be offered in such subjects as bookkeeping, commercial law and geography, and economic history.[3]

A variety of societies and publications also sought to keep the English in touch with current technological and economic changes. The Society for the Encouragement of Arts, Manufactures and Commerce, founded in 1754, was granted a royal charter in 1847 in recognition of the useful services that it had performed and would continue to contribute in the future. The *Art Journal,* as its editor pointed out with obvious pride in 1852, was conducted so as to promote the interests not only of art but of those manufactures that depended on art. And that tireless Scot, Robert Chambers, spent a lifetime issuing publications intended to further the diffusion of useful knowledge among the British people.[4]

III

The deliverance from educational backwardness that reformers had long been awaiting came in 1867 with the enfranchisement of urban labor. Now that workers could vote, their children—the voters of the future—would have to be taught to read and write, and there would be fewer and fewer Esther Waterses in England—illiterates who trembled for fear that their disability would be found out. Gladstone's Education Act of 1870 went too far for ultra-traditionalists who were sure that the measure meant that the young hereafter would be reared as atheists. On the other hand, the Act did not go nearly far enough for the more ardent reformers. If it had been discussed longer and more carefully, said education-minded John Bright, it would have had fewer inadequacies. It was, however, amended by subsequent measures, and the result was the belated creation of a system of free, compulsory, and national elementary education. "One used to think the authorities of Oxford and Cambridge who educate our future Statesmen and Legislators the most important men," wrote Florence Nightingale in an outburst of enthusiasm, "but now it is the Elementary Schoolmasters who have to educate not only our future fathers and mothers but those who have to elect legislators and statesmen."

Still, it is a mistake to assume that the old English wariness of educating the working classes disappeared. As the keen American consul in Bradford noted in 1878: "I have not unfrequently met the statement that this education is an injury, rather than a blessing to all concerned, To the *laborers* because it makes them discontented with their lot, and leads them to seek easier and more genteel occupations . . . To the *employers* because it makes them the target of the workman's jealousy and envy: the workman looking upon the capitalist as a natural enemy, and upon the employer's profits as more largely his by right." At the same time, however, it is a mistake to assume that workers necessarily appreciated the opportunities that schools opened up for their children. Arthur Morrison, remarking that the elementary education laws were no more enforceable in the Jago than other statutes, explained that working-class parents often believed it best to keep their children out of school, for then there was no record of them and there was less of a possibility of trouble with the authorities.[5]

While the elementary school struggle was being fought and won, reformers intensified their campaign for more technical and scientific studies, compulsory secondary education, greater facilities for university training, and more educational opportunities for women. As a well-known classical scholar summed up the educational situation in 1882: "For primary education in England efficient provision has been made; of secondary and higher education the supply is sparse and capricious, while academic training remains the monopoly of the privileged and the wealthy." The decisive fact was, however, that educational reformers found in the prolonged depression both an invaluable ally and a cue to attention and action that earlier reformers had lacked. Indeed, their faith in education was colossal and moving—even pathetic. Schools were a cure not only for the depression but for any number of other difficulties—intemperance, crime, misery, poverty.

For the first time in English history scientists figured prominently in the ranks of the educational reformers. In fact, some of the most hardworking and successful of the late Victorian agitators were distinguished scientists. Thomas Henry Huxley was the best known of them, but he did not stand alone. Henry Roscoe, German-trained professor of chemistry at Owens College, was particularly important in late Victorian times—even though he has long been forgotten. In 1881 he was appointed a member of the Royal Commission on Technical Education, and it was a sign of the growing respect for science that three years later Gladstone informed Roscoe that he had been proposed to receive a knighthood in recognition of his distinguished service. Anthony John Mundella, a Member of Parliament and social reformer, urged Roscoe to accept the honor for one reason above all: "It will encourage and delight men of science (Huxley especially, who has written an excellent letter on your work, and on the way that such work has hitherto failed to be recognized)."

When Roscoe himself became a Member of Parliament, he promoted the Technical Education Acts of 1889 and 1891, measures that made available funds for instruction in the application of the principles of science and art to industry. He also served as secretary to the National Association for the Promotion of Technical (including Commercial and Agricultural) and Secondary Education, the purpose of which was to develop the scientific talents of the people on whom English industries depended and to encourage the more effective teaching of foreign languages for those who were to engage in foreign trade.[6]

IV

Never before were the English made so aware of the educational systems of other countries as during the late Victorian period. When Matthew Arnold said in 1886 that he was immersed in documents concerning German popular education, he spoke not only

for himself but for a generation of energetic reformers who viewed
it as their mission to awaken their countrymen to the accomplishments of other nations. It is true that they often exaggerated the
advantages and achievements of foreigners in the sphere of education, but their exaggerations were central to their strategy of
frightening their countrymen to such an extent that they would
act quickly and make up for the negligence of decades. "Englishmen must keep abreast in skill and knowledge with continental
workers," said a distinguished Cambridge classicist in the inaugural
address that he delivered in 1882 at the opening of University
College, Liverpool, "else slowly but surely, not to speak of decay
of industries, even in this country wealth following intelligence
will pass into the hand of the foreigner, and English men and
women find themselves made hewers of wood and drawers of
water to capitalists of alien training and extraction." The English
were feeling keenly the effects of economic competition, said Sir
Lyon Playfair in 1888, but they must remember always that in
the modern scientific age this rivalry was based on intellect.
Though science had transformed the character of industry, the
world had not yet adjusted to the change, and it was this, Playfair
suggested ingeniously, that had produced the long period of depression. With the intensified foreign competition, the *Times*
cautioned in 1888, it would be impossible for the English to retain
their markets unless workers, through technical education, put
themselves on a level with the best of their class in Berlin, Paris,
and Philadelphia.[7]

In the nineties English fear of German and American competition reached unprecedented heights, and so, too, did English
interest in German and American education. "Thirty years ago,"
James Bryce pointed out correctly, "the English thought the Teu-
tons of the Continent mere theoretists, and would not have taken
any lessons in practical matters from them. To-day the achievements of Germany in applied science and the expansion of her
export trade have set all the rest of Europe to study her methods."

Although by the end of the century prices and profits started
slowly to rise, German and American competition remained, and
reformers continued their efforts to expose the inadequacies of
English education. If the English were to survive the industrial
competition which raged everywhere and which time was sure to

intensify, they must follow the example of the Belgians and other peoples who had profited greatly by the study of business subjects, said a Member of Parliament and reformer at a conference in Manchester in 1899 on higher commercial education. "The cry that we are being outbid on all sides by Germany and America is no new one," Sir Henry Roscoe declared in 1900, "but it becomes louder and louder every day, and now it is admitted by all those best qualified to judge that, unless some drastic steps are taken to strengthen our educational position in the direction long ago taken up by our competitors, we stand to lose, not merely our industrial supremacy, but the bulk of our foreign trade." Urging the adoption of a national policy that would place England on an educational level with its rivals, Roscoe bluntly added: "No effort, no expenditure, is too great to secure this result, and unless our leaders both in statecraft and in industry are quickly aroused to the critical condition of our national affairs in this respect, and determine at once to set our house in order, our children and grandchildren may see England sink to the level of a third-rate Power, for upon education, the basis of industry and commerce, the greatness of our country depends." [8]

V

The reformers were remarkably adept in stimulating interest in education. More schools, better schools, and schools stressing the proper subjects—these would prevent the decline of England. The lingering depression and the intense foreign competition that remained even after the end of the depression aroused in them a zeal worthy of missionaries, and each success inspired them to further efforts. Matthew Arnold could think of himself as an old recluse, for he rarely went to parties. And he could complain that his work for the Education Department left him no time for joining literary societies: "Life is too short for these things—at least *my* life, as school-inspecting has made it, is." But Arnold and many other reformers rejoiced to have an excuse for avoiding what they regarded as frivolous social functions when they had so much serious work to do.

By far the most impressive triumph of the reformers was the Education Act of 1902, which recognized the obligation of the state to provide secondary education. But the reformers scored

dozens of little victories, the cumulative effect of which was important. In 1882, while the Royal Commission on Technical Education was still gathering evidence, the Manchester Chamber of
Commerce strongly endorsed the efforts being made to further
technical instruction, and it authorized its president to serve as an
ex-officio member of the council of a projected Manchester Technical School. In 1884 the Central Technical College, established
by the City and Guilds of London, was opened to provide facilities
for higher technical education. On a more elementary level classes
were held at the Technical and Recreative Institute of the Goldsmiths' Company, the Regent Street Polytechnic, the People's
Palace, the Lambeth Polytechnic Institute, and dozens of similar
institutions that offered instruction in those branches of applied
science and art with which Englishmen had to be familiar if they
were to keep up with foreigners.[9]

Although James Bryce justly complained in the nineties that
little had yet been done to organize systematic instruction on a
large scale in commercial subjects, the outlook for such training
had never been so promising before. The Manchester Chamber of
Commerce and similar bodies cooperated with local educational
institutions to improve the training of youths planning a commercial career. In 1889 the Chamber congratulated the Manchester School Board for establishing evening classes for the study
of business subjects. And a year later the Chamber went so far as
to appoint an Education Committee. There were many other evidences of the new concern with business training. A Macclesfield
school examiner's report noted in 1896 that questions in commercial geography were particularly well answered. "We are endeavoring to raise the Educational Question here to such a level as the
House of Commons and Her Majesty's government think modern
requirements demand," the headmaster of a Macclesfield school
reported proudly to his Member of Parliament in 1899.

Nor did the administrators of business and technical courses
neglect to warn their students of their responsibilities. In the
plain words of the Technical Instruction Committee of the borough of Congleton: Students "need never expect in these days of
such keen and increasing competition any lasting beneficial results
or to become successful in any business or profession, unless they
are regular attenders and hard and diligent workers at school."

But even for the most gifted the number of scholarships was pitifully small. Sir Lyon Playfair, a great believer in science scholarships, had arranged to have some of the surplus funds left from the Exhibition of 1851 made available for grants to gifted students; and in the nineties science research scholarships totaling between £5,000 and £6,000 annually were granted to promising British students who with further study might make valuable contributions to applied science. But the supply of funds was absurd in relation to the supply of students.

Reformers repeatedly emphasized that in the modern world scientists were key figures. Indeed, by the early twentieth century an eminent naturalist even suggested that they be given special privileges in keeping with their importance to society: Once they demonstrated their competence in some field of research, they should be exempted from taxes and rent, they should be fed and clothed by the government, and they should be free to devote all their time to science. The naturalist who made this suggestion was trying to cheer up a scientist with domestic troubles, but his remark reflected a not unusual sense of the social usefulness of science.[10]

VI

Individual reformers had favorite schemes that they pushed and particular abuses that they decried. William Brewer, Member of Parliament for Colchester, supported industrial training for soldiers. Such training was good not only for morals but for morale, and when soldiers became civilians they would not view their period of service as a waste of time; with industrial skills they would not become paupers and a source of weakness to the community. Aged George Cruikshank urged the extension of compulsory education to encourage temperance and combat poverty, misery, and crime. A contingent of reformers—Wilkie Collins among them—exposed and condemned the sadism that infested English educational institutions. Caroline Herford, conducting a small training college for kindergarten teachers in Fallowfield, Manchester, worked to humanize the education of small children. John Benjamin Smith endlessly pressed for the adoption of the metric system, by means of which children could learn arithmetic in much less time; and since knowledge of the metric system would enable the English to compete better in foreign markets, there was no sense in wasting valuable school time in teaching youngsters to multiply £83. 15s. 31/4d. by 197. Sir Henry Roscoe stressed the importance of technical training for girls, and so did Dr. Elizabeth Blackwell, who maintained that such training would prevent poverty and prostitution. James Bryce emphasized the need for instruction in commercial subjects: "the stress of competition is now so keen that no nation can afford to neglect any expedient which may help to give its citizens a better chance than they would otherwise have." An American Anglophile, Mrs. Dunlap Hopkins, worked to open fresh fields of employment for English women by giving new life to the Royal School of Art Needlework and by publicizing the usefulness of an advanced school of applied design that would encourage manufacturers to seek their new designs in England, instead of spending their money in Paris. Frederic Harrison and other Positivists fought for a multitude of educational changes. And a host of reformers agitated for greater educational opportunities on all levels for women. On the other hand, freedom-loving William Butler Yeats could not understand why women—when they did not have to do so—would want to subject themselves to imagination-destroying examinations.[11]

Educational reformers rejoiced that after years of agitation religious tests were abolished at Oxford and Cambridge during Gladstone's first Ministry. Even so, Dissenters continued to be suspicious of the older universities. As John Bright had rightly told the Oxford political philosopher T. H. Green: "they.are mainly of the middle class, and their general impression of an Oxford education is not a favorable one. They think it costly—leading young men into extravagance and often into profligacy, and not qualifying them for commercial life."

Yet it was not only Dissenters who complained about conditions at the older universities. On the one hand, young William Butler Yeats, visiting Oxford in 1888, found it so attractive that he wondered how anybody could do any work there. On the other, young German-trained Lincoln Steffens, while he also found Oxford and Cambridge centers of unequaled beauty, was appalled by the antiquity of their educational system. Old methods and ideas, he wrote scornfully in 1892, lacked the attractiveness of old towns and buildings. Even bookish Lord Zouche remarked after his son had completed his university work: "So I hope he may now throw those stupid books into the fire, and begin to learn something useful and practical, and better worth knowing, than the mediaeval humbug of a scholastic education."

Though few university men ever looked at a Greek or Latin book after they took their degree, the emphasis on classical training remained dominant. As late as 1903 an Oxford don discouraged a friend from sending his son to Balliol, New College, or Corpus Christi because they required too much work in classics. The don also had his doubts about one other Oxford college: "There *are reading* men at Christ Church and very *good* men: but no doubt the *wealth* of the average Christ Churcher is unfavourable to anything like study." [12]

VII

The strength of the classical tradition in English university life throws light on the enthusiasm with which some reformers greeted the founding of the London School of Economics and Political Science. In December, 1895, when the School was nearing the end of its first term, William A. S. Hewins, its director, wrote to the American economist E. R. A. Seligman: "You will be interested to know that we have been more successful than we anticipated. More than 200 students have joined the School, and of these about 70 are going through the whole or part of a three years' course of training." A year later Hewins told Professor Seligman that, although there were still difficulties to contend with, the School was safe—it could be considered established. So, too, Sidney Webb, who had had much to do with the founding of the School, rejoiced in 1896 that—with more than 300 students—it was a thriving institution. And when, later in the year, the Great Western Railway Company paid the fees for forty of its officers to enroll as students, Webb was ecstatic.

But those who thought that Webb knew nothing of what a university should be—and feared that the new institution would be a socialist propaganda center—were not happy. As H. S. Foxwell bluntly put it in 1902, "The future in London is anything but promising: the new University being largely wirepulled by Sidney Webb, a man whose conception of a University does not rise beyond that of a loosely federated aggregation of technical schools, all under the thumb of the London County Council Technical Education Committee which has scarcely a University man upon it."

While economics was coming into its own at the London School, it fared less well at Oxford. "We work under great disadvantages —for those of us who teach for the Honour School of Modern History have still to struggle for the due recognition of Economic History, and most of the rest of us are still expected by general opinion to teach Fawcett and Mill in a cut and dried fashion easy to be 'got up.' " These words, written by William J. Ashley in 1887, were still largely true at the end of the century. At Cambridge, on the other hand, Professor Alfred Marshall, a meticulous scholar and an ardent humanitarian, was arousing unprecedented interest in the contributions economic studies could make to the betterment of social conditions. But the results of his efforts— perhaps as fine a group of disciples as any contemporary European scholar produced—were not to make themselves felt until the twentieth century.[13]

The prestige of classical training was so great that the provincial universities were constantly under pressure to prove that they were not merely commercial travelers' schools but institutions providing culture of the most intellectual kind. Yet they had at least two great advantages. In the first place, their very newness meant that they lacked the traditions and the vested interests that made innovations so difficult at Oxford and Cambridge. Secondly, they speedily aroused the confidence, sense of pride, and support of the citizens of their community.

As late as 1898, H. S. Foxwell argued that as a result of the English disbelief in intellect academic people were poorly paid and no one cared about them—least of all the leaders of the business community. But for several decades the experiences of the provincial universities had proven Foxwell at least partly wrong. When the administration of Owens College appealed for a university charter, the Manchester Chamber of Commerce memorialized the Government in 1879 to back the appeal. The need for science and modern languages was increasingly felt, the Chamber pointed out, for the vast industries of the North of England were competing

more and more with those of foreigners who had a superior training in science. If the English were to maintain their industrial
position, the Chamber emphasized, it was essential that "the highest teaching of science should be made available for every branch
of our industry." In 1881, one of the most memorable years in
English educational history, a royal charter established the Victoria University with its seats in the great towns of the North of
England. Not that Manchester was the only provincial university
that was able to enlist the support of its community. Indeed, William J. Ashley spoke wisely when he predicted in 1901 that the
newly founded University of Birmingham would succeed if it
managed to arouse local pride and patriotism.[14]

The campaign to make the late Victorians conscious of the
glories of science was not confined to formal educational institutions. It was also carried on by such old organizations and publications as the British Association, the Royal Institution of Great
Britain, and *Nature*. Nor was there any dearth of new publications and organizations that aimed at spreading science-conscious-
ness. The Society for the Promotion of Scientific Industry, for
example, had as its aims "the increase of the technical knowledge
and skill of those engaged in the various Industries; the Improvement and advancement of Manufactures and the Industrial Arts
and Sciences; and the general progress, extension, and well-being
of Industry and Trade." To accomplish its objectives the Society
encouraged scientific research, gave prizes for inventions, and arranged to have agents stationed in foreign industrial centers with
a view to keeping the English informed as to what was taking
place abroad. When the Society held its first exhibition in 1874,
it was barely known to the public, but with Lord Derby as president and Lord Salisbury and John Bright as vice-presidents the
Society was guaranteed publicity for its activities. Similar organizations were founded in the next decades, culminating in the establishment in 1904 of the British Science Guild. Formed as a
result of a suggestion that the astronomer Sir Joseph Norman
Lockyer made when he served as president of the British Association, the Guild aimed to encourage in the English that faith in
science that other nations had and to popularize the contributions
that science made and could make to national affairs.[15]

VIII

The glory of the educational reformers was their insatiability. Sir Henry Roscoe, marveling in 1899 at the educational changes that had taken place since mid-century, could glory in what the schools had done to improve the condition of the masses, to raise standards of living, to spread knowledge, and to advance civilization in all classes of society. But that did not mean that Roscoe and dozens of other reformers considered their work done. Although they were often accused of wanting to Germanize or Americanize or in some other way impose foreign practices on English schools, they were courageous and patriotic enough to recognize the ways in which English education still needed to be changed. The hard times had given point to their arguments and the momentum they gathered during the late Victorian period survived into the early twentieth century. They continued to complain, to agitate for change, and to exhort their fellow-citizens to wake up.

They still had much to do. Scores of reformers had been calling for more attention to the study of modern languages; but as late as 1908 an Oxford phoneticist was still lamenting the neglect in England of so useful a language as German. In 1887 Alfred Marshall had referred to the Massachusetts Institute of Technology as perhaps the best center of its kind in the world; but years later the English still had nothing comparable to it. In 1889 Gladstone had noted that higher education was more expensive in England than perhaps in any other country; but it continued to be out of the reach of many talented but poor young people. In the last decades of the century Gladstone and many others had pointed out the serious financial needs of the older universities; but in 1907 Lord Curzon, the new chancellor, still deplored Oxford's lack of the resources that would enable her to meet modern requirements.

One insuperable difficulty remained to perplex the reformers. For, while the English were trying—and often successfully—to catch up educationally with other countries, the foreigners did not stand still. As General Francis Walker, the president of the Massachusetts Institute of Technology, reported in 1888, "Our students have increased from 302, in 1882, in which year I took charge, to 720 this year." A great number of changes would have to be made, he added, to satisfy the growing demands for scientific and technical training. And as Professor William J. Ashley of the University of Birmingham wrote in 1909 to an American: "Things are progressing satisfactorily here in Birmingham, tho' the scale of what we are doing is tragically small compared with what you are accustomed to in America." [16]

⁂ XIV ⁂

A FAITH IN DOUBT

After God, romantic love, and the beauties of nature, the subject that inspired perhaps the most abundant and popular poetry in early Victorian times was free trade. Judged by even the loosest standards, most of this poetry left much to be desired—it clearly fell into the category of what the young H. G. Wells was to call "unnecessary blethering." Yet this is beside the point. For, while the fervor that free trade aroused in its supporters seems incredible now, it was a formidable reality then. Indeed, free trade was not only an economic doctrine but a Philosophy, a Religion, and a Cause of Causes. Free traders not infrequently gave the most vigorous years of their lives to preaching the faith, and in the process they often impoverished themselves. But no sacrifices they made were too great, for they believed that they had found the answers to some of the greatest questions that man had to deal with. "Our cause is just and we are all determined to persevere until we triumph," John Benjamin Smith wrote characteristically in 1839. "Had I not been cursed with the knowledge of what was just and true, I might have lived in peace like other men," wrote dedicated T. Perronet Thompson in a no less representative statement.

Adam Smith could well be proud. In 1780, four years after the appearance of *The Wealth of Nations,* he had told his publisher of his fear that he was just about the only customer left for his book. But even Adam Smith could be wrong. It was not the demand for and supply of *The Wealth of Nations* that mattered nearly so much as the quality of the demand. Two generations after the publication of Smith's masterpiece England was swarming with tiny bands of busy Smithians. And if they exercised an influence out of all proportion to their numbers, the reason is that they were unshakable in their faith and indefatigable in spreading it. "I was then living at Leeds, and in the midst of the agitation," Samuel Smiles, the great exponent of self-help, was to recall. "I spoke at many meetings—from platforms and even from pulpits—on behalf of the cause; and was in constant communication with Mr. Cobden." As with Smiles, so with dozens of other free traders. Once converted, they became tireless crusaders.[1]

II

Free traders denounced corn laws and other protective tariffs with a passion usually reserved historically for religious heresies. Using adjectives that ranged from abominable, odious, accursed, and base to immoral, detestable, cruel, and iniquitous, they argued that the restrictions and prohibitions of the commercial code of the British Empire were in the highest degree harmful to British interests, for they encouraged people to depend on artificial aids instead of on themselves. Let England and all other countries concentrate on what they were best suited to produce, and consumers would benefit from this international division of labor in the form of superior goods at lower cost, good-will would be encouraged among nations, and international peace would follow. "Tariffs gone, armies would go, and the better time for mankind would have come," as John Bright pithily put it.

The stress that free traders placed on peace was of central importance in their agitation. They were seeking support from a generation that remembered the French Revolutionary and Napoleonic conflicts as well as the host of eighteenth-century wars. Free traders viewed these struggles as disgusting economic contests between groups of selfish and greedy protectionists, and they considered it a main part of their task to prevent such conflicts in the future. They must convince people of the stupidity and wickedness of maintaining large military establishments which made not only for high taxes, and therefore poverty, but for international discord as well.[2]

As early as 1835 Richard Cobden was impressed with the strides that the cause was making: "There is a general belief now that we are approaching the end. Free-trade is looked upon as an inevitable necessity even by the landlords and farmers." But Cobden was unduly optimistic, and in the next decade he and other free traders often doubted that they would succeed in their attack on protective tariffs. It was one thing for alert Richard Monckton Milnes, immersed in public questions, to be convinced by 1841 of the need to get rid of import duties. "I see nothing but Sir Peel (as the French call him) between us and Chartism," he anxiously told Thomas Carlyle. But what was clear to Monckton Milnes was not at all clear to those with whom he trafficked socially—the landowners whom free traders called monopolists. These people had many theoretical as well as practical reasons— including strong military arguments—for defending protective tariffs. And they were powerful politically. Cobden, in fact, after examining a list of towns wholly or in part represented by monopolists, exclaimed in disgust: "It is indeed lamentable how little independence or public virtue is to be found in many of the *English* constituencies. *We* are worse than in Scotland or Ireland."

Skillful propagandists, free traders went out of their way to make their appeals as emotional as they could:

> Monopolists! your grasp relax
> And let the starving poor be fed;
> Ye Senators, repeal the Tax,
> The odious, impious, tax on Bread.
> Oh! hearken to a nation's cry—
> Let not the famished millions die.

But despite busy and trying years of agitation, the reformers had little to show for their efforts. Cobden was insulted even from the pulpit of the church to which he belonged in Manchester; his curate denounced him publicly for inciting the working classes. And T. Perronet Thompson wrote dispiritedly to a colleague in 1844: "Has it ever occurred to you to consider, how completely we have outlived what used to go by the name of the *Reform Cause*. I should suppose a man would be laughed at, who should mention it now in public." Attending a torpid free trade meeting shortly afterwards, Thompson was despondent: "What a flash in the pan has all this Reform struggle come to! I confess I do not see what is to give it life again, or where the life is to come from." Thompson was particularly furious with the Chartists for luring workers away from free trade and enticing them with promises that he regarded as deceptive, and he was convinced that, if the Chartists had been hired to sabotage the free trade cause, they could not have done their work better. So, too, Richard Cobden wrote revealingly to a wealthy and sympathetic landowner: "You are one of the very few of your order who can see through the mirage of stagnant self-interest, and discover the true path of patriotism in the removal of those absurd restrictions which obstruct trade, and remotely peril the interests of the landed proprietors themselves."

The Irish poet and reformer, Thomas Moore, described accurately the view that free traders took of the motivations of landowners:

> There were lords and squires of high degree,
> Who in bread-fruit held large property—
> And of all afflictions, ills, and vices,
> Thought none so dreadful as low prices;
> Wherefore they held it just and meet
> That the world should not too cheaply eat;
> Nay, deemed it radical insolence
> To wish to dine at a small expense,
> And swore, for the sake of themselves and heirs,
> That, happen what might with *other* wares,
> *No bread* should be less dear than theirs.

At the same time, however, "The Hymn of the Wiltshire Labourers" expressed the faith that many free traders held that divine intervention would help to win the lords and gentry to their side:

> Oh God, remind them of His sweet
> Compassion for the poor,
> And how He gave them Bread to eat,
> And went from door to door.[3]

III

At last came the news for which free traders had been waiting from what seemed like time immemorial. As Thomas Carlyle expressed it on December 5, 1845: "All hands here are rejoicing since yesternight that Peel has decided to Abolish the Corn-

Laws. . . ." Carlyle admired the courage and the manliness that Peel's action required. And John Bright hoped that the efforts of the free traders would save the landlords despite themselves and that the time would come when they would even thank the free traders for exposing their ignorance.

But landowners were outraged by Peel's behavior—and understandably so. In the plaintive words of one demoralized monopolist: "The sudden conversion of the two great parties—Whig and Tory—to the Repeal of the Corn Laws which they have hitherto equally resisted—apparently with no motive for their change of sentiment—but the increased violence of Demagogic agitation —and the substitution of a naked question of class interests for one of party traditions (which were at least clothed under the garb of *Principles*)—is very like the commencement de la fin." What landowners thought of as ruin free traders regarded as the most beneficial revolution in the history of man—the greatest act in any age for the improvement of the condition of the people and the increase of the wealth of the nation.

" 'The Bill is through, and I shall be home to tea.' So went a message from Richard Cobden, my father, to my mother in Manchester just one hundred years ago," Mrs. Cobden Unwin pointed out during the centennial celebration of the repeal of the corn laws. But Cobden himself never underestimated the difficulty of the victory—despite the generous support that the Anti-Corn Law League had received from the millowners of Lancashire. Manchester, as he discerningly wrote to J. B. Smith,

was a good cradle for the League, for there were strong *purses,* and their owners thought they would be replenished with Free Trade. It was one aristocracy pitted against another and with a good moral right on their side too.—But you know we had but little sympathy from the 'workers' till the work was done. The fact is there is an unhealthy disparity of condition in the factory towns, with its millowner employing his thousand hands, which will always militate against a hearty and fearless cooperation on ordinary political questions.

Nor did Cobden ever forget the fierce resistance that the free traders met in that mighty but unreliable engine—the press. He often resented being so much at the mercy of the Manchester *Guardian,* which was "always ready at a pinch to throw us over, and play into the hands of the Tories." [4]

IV

It is wrong to view the aftermath of the repeal of the corn laws as the age of Cobden. Historians have often made this mistake, but Cobden never did. Admittedly, some further steps were taken toward commercial freedom. But at home the landowning classes continued to dominate the scene; and developments abroad were disappointing. "And gladsome commotions / Of Laughing old oceans, / Proclaim,—that *Free Trade* wins the World to its notions!" Such had been the vision; but the reality was that commercial freedom failed, with a few exceptions, to attract support in foreign countries. And starting with what free traders deemed the unspeakable Crimean blunder of 1854–56—the "muffy war," as Charles Kingsley called it—wars came into fashion again.

It is true that Cobden had long been critical of the two aristocratic parties that dominated English politics, and he had long insisted that modern English history would have to be rewritten before justice could be meted out to them for their relentless efforts to wreck a country that had been so blessed by nature.

Apart from their stand on free trade, Cobden had as little use for the Whigs as for the Tories, but he had hoped that, once both Whigs and Tories came to accept free trade, they would then curry public favor by bidding against each other about other things and, in the process, reformers and the population in general would benefit. By 1857, however, Cobden was so fed up with Whig and Tory politics and politicians that he confided to a friend that he preferred not to sit in the House of Commons, for he had little hope of agreeing with any party or constituency on the big issues of his time. And this was a man who ordinarily was at his best when there were staggering difficulties and powerful interests to overcome! In short, Cobden considered suffering and even disaster inevitable owing to the ignorance in both England and the world of sound economics.[5]

Of course, free traders found the Anglo-French Commercial Treaty of 1860 encouraging, especially because they had feared the aversion of the French to imitating anything English. But the Treaty had marked limitations, and soon after it went into effect attempts were made in France to modify and undo it. And from the United States, then engaged in the Civil War, so well-informed an authority as George Bancroft told John Bright that he could not hold out much hope for the spread of free trade principles. Cobden, too, was alarmed and depressed by the reports that he received from American friends. He rejoiced in 1865—the year of his death—that the North seemed sure to win. But he feared that the development of American resources would suffer from a false political economy, for the fallacies that he had devoted a lifetime to exposing were rife again. Cobden had never doubted that free traders would ultimately triumph in the United States. "The protectionists may mystify the people for a time," he had once said, "but in a country where the press is free, and the population generally educated, I have no fear that monopoly in any form can be perpetrated." By the end of his life Cobden was much less confident, and young Henry Adams, son of the American minister to Britain during the Civil War, confirmed Cobden's doubts. Back in Washington, Adams reported to John Bright in 1869 that free trade was distinctly out of favor.[6]

For one other important reason free traders were disheartened by the course of events during the aftermath of the repeal of the corn laws. They believed that just as England should lead the world in the direction of freer trade, so, too, she should assume leadership in promoting an international system of weights, measures, and money. John Benjamin Smith was especially vigorous in urging such a role on successive ministries and parliaments. Uniform weights, measures, and money would not only be convenient for business, he pointed out, but they would form ties between peoples that would make for greater mutual respect and therefore encourage world peace. Smith knew of nothing, he told the House of Commons in 1855, that could contribute more to good will among nations.

A dozen years later Smith was calling the attention of Disraeli to the advantages of "the same yard measure, the same pound weight and the same gallon all the world over," for in an environment of railroads, steam navigation, and the electric telegraph, people were ready for still further changes that would simplify their relations. Disraeli acknowledged that the subject was important, and he told Smith that he would "like to have an opportunity, some day, of talking it over." A commission was even formed with Smith a member. But by May, 1868, Smith anxiously cautioned Disraeli that at any moment he might be out of office, and that at least he could make his administration memorable by the adoption of a common measure and a common money. Disraeli, however, did not choose to have his ministry remembered for such an achievement. Free traders consoled Smith that the efforts of the friends of international weights, measures, and money would eventually triumph. But they underestimated the combined force of apathy, tradition, and nationalism in the affairs of their world.[7]

V

It was bad enough that in the quarter-century after the repeal of the corn laws free trade made only slight progress in foreign countries. Worse still, the last decades of the century saw protectionism on the offensive almost everywhere. "What a pity that our friend Cobden is no longer with us!" the devoted French free trader Michel Chevalier told John Bright in 1868. Indeed, every free trader felt Cobden's loss as tariffs became more and more protective and as interested groups tried to make them go still higher. For country after country, building up its domestic industries, sought to ensure native producers against underselling by foreigners. Young Alfred Marshall, working on his first book, visited the United States in 1875 in order to study protection at first hand. But he could just as well have stayed at home, for even in England new-style protectionists were appearing, and such survivors from corn law days as John Benjamin Smith, Thomas Bazley, John Bright, and Charles Pelham Villiers spent their old age repeating the arguments—and fighting the enemies—of their youth. A few months before Bright died in 1889 even the Manchester Chamber of Commerce, of which he had been a member for fifty years, passed a protectionist resolution.[8]

Toward the end of Gladstone's first Ministry the resolute free trader Sir Louis Mallet resigned from the Board of Trade. Explaining to John Bright the reasons for his action, he wrote angrily in 1872, "All attempts at international cooperation in removing restrictions on trade, and strengthening the agencies of peace and Economy—are systematically and cynically suppressed—and my office at last became a sham and a sinecure, and I have therefore insisted on its suppression also." Impatient Mallet,

serving under a Liberal Government headed by free trader Gladstone, complained that the administration was insufficiently active
in furthering the free trade movement abroad. And Mallet's
criticism was similar to that of all vigorous free traders in the
seventies: first Gladstone—who should have known better—was
not doing enough to further commercial freedom in the world;
then Disraeli was lax in advancing the cause. All the while higher
import duties were being imposed by a host of countries.

The process was under way before the world economic crisis
began in 1873; but as the depression deepened protectionism
mounted. In these circumstances the Cobden Club—formed to
advance commercial freedom, peace, and goodwill among nations
—had much to do. It invited important foreigners to official and
unofficial functions and tried to spread the faith among them;
James A. Garfield, for instance, was an honorary member. But
the age of the Great Depression provided an uncongenial setting
for its activities or those of free traders in general. In fact, after
years of agitation, disheartened Michel Chevalier complained to
John Bright in 1876 of the great number of Frenchmen under
the insecure Third Republic who seemed to care only about
politics: "Of industrial and commercial interests they take little
heed of [sic]. They do not care a fig about it." The Manchester
Chamber of Commerce, addressing the chambers of commerce of
France, expressed concern that there were still highly placed
Frenchmen eager to see the old restrictive policy restored—and
this in 1876, the centenary of the publication of *The Wealth of
Nations*. It was only small comfort that Cobden Prizes were at
last to be awarded at Oxford and Cambridge for suitable essays
on political economy.[9]

VI

As economic conditions worsened during Disraeli's Ministry,
free traders brought increasing pressure to bear on the administration to negotiate more favorable commercial treaties. In 1877 the
Manchester Chamber of Commerce urged that the Government
use its influence to further the adoption of free trade principles,
and that special efforts be made to reduce and abrogate hostile
tariffs in foreign countries and the protective duties levied in India and the colonies. The Chamber reminded the Government

that in negotiating a new commercial treaty with France the interests of both countries would be served best by the fullest application of commercial freedom. So, too, Anglo-Spanish relations would improve if high duties were removed, and the Chamber requested the support of the Government to extend trade with Spain. In 1877 the Chamber went so far as to hold an open meeting in order to impress both the Ministry and Parliament with the need to grant to the commercial classes more effective recognition than they were receiving.[10]

The economic crisis struck a new low in 1879, and foreign tariffs reached a new high. The Manchester Chamber—and many others—reminded Lord Salisbury, the Foreign Secretary, and other officials of their plight and urged state intervention in behalf of freer trade: "At the present time, when the industries of this district, and indeed the whole country, are suffering from great and perhaps unparalleled depression, we consider that the attention of the Government should be specially directed towards the development of our trade with Foreign countries." Still, the Chamber recognized that there were instances when direct and official intervention might be harmful rather than beneficial. In the United States, for example, the Chamber suggested that it was desirable to encourage American importers to bring pressure to bear on members of Congress in behalf of commercial freedom.

Free traders were repeatedly startled by the strength of the economic fallacies that ruled the world. Thomas Hughes, reporting to an American admirer in 1879 that the English were suffering severely from bad harvests and tariffs which kept out British goods, wrote sharply: "You at any rate ought to show a better example, being merely old and strong enough now not to want handicapping in your favour against any producers in the world. Your *people* (meaning thereby the poor majority) can't after all be either so sensible or so powerful as one is told they are, or they would be tired of paying so heavily to build up fortunes for the small minority." In much the same spirit John Bright, a loyal and outspoken friend of the United States, wrote to Cyrus Field in 1879:

I do not think anything an Englishman could say would have any effect upon an American Protectionist—the man who possesses a monopoly by which he thinks he gains is not open to argument. It was so in this Country 40 years ago—and it is so with you now. It is strange that a people who put down slavery at an immense sacrifice, are not able to suppress monopoly which is but a milder form of the same evil. Under Slavery the *man* was seized—and his labor was stolen from him, and the profit of it enjoyed by his master and owner. Under Protection the *man* is apparently free, but he is denied the right to exchange the produce of his labor, except with his Countrymen who offer him much less for it than the foreigner would give. Some portion of his labor is thus confiscated.

In our Protection days—our weavers and artisans could not exchange with American flour—they exchanged with an English farmer who gave him sometimes only half the quantity the American would have given him. Now your farmer is forbidden to trade with the Englishman, and must give to an American double the quantity of grain or flour, for many articles he is constantly requiring, that he would give if your laws did not forbid his trade *with England.*

A country may have democratic Institutions—its government may be republican and based on a wide suffrage, and yet there may be no freedom even for that which is the source of life and comfort. If a man's labor is not free—if its exchange is not free—the man is not free. And whether the law which enacts this restriction be the offspring of republican or autocratic government and power, it is equally evil, and to be condemned and withstood by all who love Freedom and understand what it is.

Nations learn slowly—but they do learn—and therefore I do not doubt that the time will come when Trade will be as free as the winds—and when Freedom of Industry will do much to put down great armies and the peril and suffering of war.[11]

Like Bright, other free traders continued to hope that the wisdom of commercial freedom would defeat protectionist folly. The Manchester Chamber of Commerce, for example, reasserted in 1879 its full confidence in free trade, economy, and peace as the means by which to keep England great and make her greater. For free traders were sure that their economic ideas were not only sound but just; protectionism, on the other hand, was an unjust and indefensible policy by which producers who could not meet foreign competition were supported at the expense of their own countrymen. Free traders remembered the suddenness with which the English had repudiated the old retrograde policy, and while it was taking foreign countries a long time to learn, their conversion might occur with equal suddenness. Small wonder that free traders kept looking hopefully to the United States—and to an American Cobden—to take the lead.

Within England itself, however, there were disturbing signs by the late seventies. "There is an attempt to raise the cry of protection," wrote Joseph Smith, a perceptive Essex farmer. But Smith thought that those who called for the revival of tariffs were wild and deluded men: it was only a question of looking at population statistics, and then any reflective person would realize that the swelling urban communities would never permit their food to be taxed for the benefit of the agricultural interest. So, too, John Bright assured the American free trader David Wells that English opinion was more convinced than ever of the wisdom of the modern policy. And another veteran of the anti-corn law crusade told Wells that free trade was so much a part of the thinking of the English that the restoration of import duties was out of the question; but he noted ominously that the depression was inducing some people to clamor for reciprocity. Similarly, the ever-watchful American consul in Bradford reported that especially in manufacturing centers the idea of retaliation was winning backers even among people who formerly were free traders.[12]

In the eighties protective tariffs continued, with few exceptions, to hold sway in the world, and in England reformers undertook a vigorous campaign for tariff revision. "Protection," an English disciple of Henry George remarked, "is very plausible to a man who finds himself being pushed out." Appealing to landowners, farmers, merchants, manufacturers, and workers, protectionists insisted that it was unfair that foreigners, who used hostile tariffs to shut out English goods, should be permitted to send their own products freely to England. Tariff reformers called themselves fair traders, and the policy they favored was reciprocity. If foreigners permitted free entry to English goods, the English should do the same; if foreigners levied high imposts on English goods, the English should retaliate. Fair traders concentrated on unemployment and the fear of further unemployment in their appeals to workers. And they deplored the low prices and profits that manufacturers, merchants, farmers, and landowners were receiving in the age of the Great Depression. That highly intellectual and consistent free trader, Auberon Herbert, could deem it desirable that England be the cheapest country in the world for people to live in; but even devout free traders were alarmed by the depths to which prices were sinking and welcomed a price rise as a sign of the return of good times. "What is becoming of political economy anyhow?" asked a shrewd American journalist.[13]

With their doctrines being challenged, free traders were forced to reexamine their philosophy and restate its validity. For a long time they had tended to take it for granted as something self-evident. But with what Gladstone called "the mischievous imposture . . . now stalking abroad under the name of Fair Trade," such self-complacency was no longer possible.

As early as 1878 Sir Louis Mallet had strongly encouraged Richard Cobden's family to permit John Morley, a young and able free trader, to write a biography of Cobden. It would be important not only for Cobden's reputation, said Mallet, but for the influence of his doctrines. In 1881 the work appeared in two volumes, and Gladstone and Bright, among a host of others, rightly found cause for high praise. "My estimate of your Father's noble qualities and splendid services hardly admits of being raised above the point at which it has long stood," Gladstone wrote. "If any thing had been lacking, such a work as Mr. Morley's would certainly have supplied the deficiency." John Bright was eager for everyone to read the volumes: "What a mine of wisdom and of teaching there is in them!" There was, but in a setting of falling prices and profits and mounting German and American competition the work could hardly accomplish what free traders hoped from it.

In the same year that Morley published his exposure of the fallacies of protectionism a young government official, writer, and literary critic caused a minor rift in Anglo-German relations. On the basis of statements issued by German chambers of commerce, Edmund Gosse compiled an unflattering report on the working of protection in Bismarckian Germany. Joseph Chamberlain, then Gladstone's president of the Board of Trade, was so pleased with Gosse's indictment that he had it brought out as a parliamentary paper. As a result Bismarck imposed limits on the expression of criticism of governmental economic policy by both German officials and chambers of commerce. And he complained to the British ambassador and urged Lord Granville, Gladstone's Foreign Minister, to punish the English official responsible for the report. "All this," Gosse remarked exuberantly, "has greatly improved my status here." [14]

Free traders could draw comfort from the biography of Cobden —"a life which is in some sort a poem," as Bright put it; they could draw comfort from Gosse's exposure of German protective tariffs; and Bright could assure Gladstone and other free traders that the fair trade movement would not "need much killing." Nevertheless, there was much to dishearten the friends of commercial freedom. Sir Charles Dilke, participating in the negotiation of a new commercial treaty in Paris, discovered the power and persistence of French protectionists and reported to Gladstone what a major effort it was for him to control his temper. Lord Derby insisted in 1881 that most of the Conservative Party was still loyal to commercial freedom, but already a few politicians in his party were boldly agitating for a revival of protection. And the American consul in Bradford, impressed by the resolute and powerful men who led the Fair Trade League, warned the State Department that the Conservative Party was moving toward protection. By 1884 groups of farmers and landowners were strenuously advocating a tax on corn, and Liberal leaders feared that the Tories would make a big campaign issue of protection. In these circumstances it is no surprise that the Cobden Club moved swiftly into action, raised money—even the Archbishop of Canterbury was asked to subscribe—and issued pamphlets attacking protectionism.[15]

In an electoral address of 1885 a Yorkshire politician announced unmistakably: "I am, from conviction, and from long experience, a thorough Free Trader, and have no sympathy with the so-called Fair Trade Movement, which is only Protection in disguise." But the number of politicians who defended commercial freedom so openly and straightforwardly was shrinking. Only a dozen years before a Cobden Club member had rejoiced that free trade in England was above party. By the mid-eighties, however, Tory leaders—Lord Randolph Churchill among them— were increasingly making vague public statements concerning their position. And privately even so cautious a politician as Lord Iddesleigh, the former Sir Stafford Northcote, was inquiring of an ardent tariff reformer how reciprocity was to be achieved. In short, there is no question that John Bright was overconfident when he assured an American in 1886 that it was just as improbable that England would return to protection as it was that the United States would restore slavery.

Particularly disturbing was the growth of protectionist sentiment within the membership of so stalwart a group as the Manchester Chamber of Commerce. It is true that in May, 1886, the Chamber asserted its unchanging faith in free trade and condemned the principle of retaliation as reactionary; but some members opposed the resolution. In the fall, a startling motion was proposed, seconded, discussed, and defeated—but only by a very narrow margin: "Having waited in vain more than forty years for other nations to follow England's Free Trade example, this Chamber thinks the time has now arrived to reconsider its position." [16]

VIII

In the political campaigns of 1886 there was much discussion of the tariff question and of its connection with the Great Depression. Free trade had impoverished both industry and agriculture, said protectionist politicians, and until this fatal doctrine was repudiated the English economy would continue to suffer. In the words of the Tory Sir William Bromley Davenport, one of the most outspoken of the protectionist Members of Parliament:

It is evident—forty years of experience has shown—that personal effort and enterprise is unable to give us a remedy—(hear, hear)—and something must be done by legislation in that direction—(cheers),—and that is to bring in a measure which will have for its object some sort of duty on foreign goods. (Renewed cheers.) That can be done, and will be done. (Loud and continued cheering.) This new Parliament which is being elected has amongst its ranks a larger number of Fair Traders than any Parliament that had ever been before.

Election oratory, art, and literature overflowed with references to foreigners who were taking advantage of English stupidity, and posters showed—among dozens of other depressed figures—an unemployed English worker weeping at the feet of Britannia, while American, German, Belgian, and Swedish vessels sailed towards the English shore.

Free traders, on the other hand, insisted that tariffs, far from being cures of the depression, were among its main causes. Indeed, it was fortunate for them that workers, both urban and rural, continued to think of free trade and cheap bread as inseparable. And to make them continue to think that way such diverse reformers as Joseph Arch, Charles Bradlaugh, and Henry George pleaded with them to ignore the siren-calls of protectionists, cautioning them that to repudiate free trade was to abandon the cheap loaf. Even so, when resolute free traders contemplated the growth of protectionist sentiment in both England and the world, they could only despair of human progress and of the part that reason played in the lives of men. For they remained convinced that anyone who had a mind would readily recognize that protectionism was both foolish and foredoomed.[17]

During Salisbury's Conservative Ministry of 1886–92 free traders found additional reasons for concern. A group of Members of Parliament constantly called for tariff reform to meet ruinous foreign competition. Fair traders in the Manchester Chamber of Commerce and in similar bodies in other towns tried to pass resolutions in favor of reciprocity and retaliation, and sometimes they succeeded. Fair traders also sought constantly to win labor support; the secretary of the Fair Trade League went so far as to send a contribution to the collection that was raised when John Burns was imprisoned.

From abroad the news was also disquieting for free traders. John Bright received upsetting reports that Australian and American trade unionists were becoming more and more protectionist in their outlook. Canada enacted a new protective tariff. The United States, long exposed to what free traders called "the protection craze," went McKinleyite. Foreign tourists in Britain found that they had to restrict their purchases; like many other travelers, young Lincoln Steffens discovered that the United States limited the number of suits—so inexpensive in London— that he could take home. And William J. Ashley, the economic historian with protectionist sympathies, cautioned an American scholar to be wary of a prospective book reviewer's strong free trade bias. In short, much to the alarm of the friends of commercial freedom, the number of people in the world who shared their outlook seemed to be shrinking rapidly. Rudyard Kipling, living in the United States, emphatically told W. E. Henley in 1893 to get rid of the idea that the Democrats under Cleveland would demolish the McKinley tariff wall: "They will at the most pull out a few bricks with vast clamour. Free trade won't come." [18]

If free trade would not come elsewhere, it must go in England, said fair traders; and the long-continuing depression inspired them to greater efforts. They filled the newspapers of the time with distressing accounts of the hardships to which English workers were exposed because of foreign tariffs and the failure of the English to retaliate. Typical of thousands was a disturbing report that appeared in the *Northern Whig* in 1894: "An English lady who designs and paints fans beautifully, and to one of whose fans a first-class prize was awarded at the Chicago Exhibition, in competition with fan painters of all other nations, was so unable to hold her own in England owing to foreign competition that she has accompanied her brother to the colonies, not to practice art, but to help him in farming and household duties."

Fair traders could count on widespread support from farmers and landowners. Silk manufacturers, hurt by heavy French competition, were also more than ready to abandon free trade. And the cotton people were protesting more and more. James Edgcome, the secretary of the Fair-Trade Club, informed Sir William Bromley Davenport in 1895 that he was encouraged by the interest the tariff question was attracting, and in particular he found some of Joseph Chamberlain's recent remarks very heartening. With a general election impending, Edgcome called Davenport's attention to the importance of using the political situation to further the cause of tariff reform. It is true that Edgcome had long been conscious of the danger of "the growing tendency among our home agriculturists to fight for their own hand, and make a fiscal change impossible by demanding for themselves what the towns won't grant." He was also aware that the Irish Question, the issue of the reform of the House of Lords, and the rift within the Liberal Party after Gladstone's retirement in 1894 would complicate the election. But he correctly anticipated that there would be many opportunities to discuss the preservation of the British domestic market for home industries. And the Club therefore arranged for large printings of pamphlets and leaflets for distribution to voters. Even George Moore acknowledged the agitation for tariff reform. In *Esther Waters* he had a character report a conversation with a stranger who opposed having the Government tax corn "to 'elp the British farmer." [19]

IX

The Liberals were beaten in 1895, and Lord Salisbury headed a coalition of Conservatives and Liberal Unionists that governed England for the next decade. Although Sir Charles Dilke thought it safe to predict that there would be no return to protection, even the most sanguine free traders would have considered this an over-optimistic view. In 1896 they celebrated the fiftieth anniversary of the repeal of the corn laws, and the Cobden Club held a special dinner to honor Charles Villiers, the sole survivor of the major anti-corn law agitators. The next year the Manchester Chamber of Commerce celebrated its centenary, and Lord Rosebery, according to contemporary reports, brilliantly vindicated the policy of free trade. But even on these momentous occasions the friends of commercial freedom were on the defensive. A long depression, marked by falling prices and profits and resentment of foreign competition, had caused great doubts to be cast on the validity of their doctrines. And what they regarded as a vicious combination of selfish interests and abysmal ignorance was vigorously defending protectionism everywhere. To their endless distress and dismay, there were in the world few leaders of whom they could say, as they did when the French economist Léon Say died in 1896, that he had labored for the free interchange of the products of labor without reference to national boundaries. And it was hard for them to understand how people could resist so long the wisdom of Richard Cobden.[20]

All the while tariff reformers looked to Lord Salisbury's Government for help. Among many others, a delegation from the Association of English Hop-Growers called attention to their depressed condition and the severe foreign competition to which they were exposed—the prices they received were less than the cost of hop production. Poultry farmers pointed to the invasion of foreign produce from which they were suffering. And in *"Made in Germany,"* the book that quickly became a classic of popular economic literature, Ernest E. Williams gave a poignant description of the inroads that foreigners were making into the English economy and called for tariff reform as one way to stop the invasion.[21]

In 1896 the protectionist president of the Silk Association wrote

to Sir William Bromley Davenport about Lord Salisbury's Colonial Secretary: "I am glad to see that Mr. Chamberlain has given
a hint that he is not a fanatic on Free Trade. I was told a few
months ago at the Board of Trade that we might get him to help
us, as he was not sound on Free Trade! Whenever you decide to
move I shall be ready to work amongst the working men or serve
on any Committee." But what wrecked the plans of the protectionists was something that they had despaired of ever happening
again: prices and profits started to rise in the very last years of
the century, and for most segments of the economy the depression
lifted. A long period of distress had revived protectionism, and the
return of prosperity undermined it. While free traders exulted,
fair traders insisted that the good times could not last. Foreigners,
with high tariffs that assured them of their home markets, would
continue to dump their goods in England and undersell English
producers.

Even in an uncongenial setting of rising prices and profits the
protectionists continued their efforts. Although the depression was
over, the memory of it was still alive, and they exploited it as
much as they could. By 1899 a free trader, who had left the Liberal
Party because of his belief in maintaining the union with Ireland,
wrote to the new head of the Liberal Party, Campbell-Bannerman,
and urged him to work to bring back the Unionist Liberals: "The
recent legislative efforts of the present government have been well
fitted to bring home to the minds of Unionists who are sincerely
liberal a sense of the heavy price they and the nation at large have
to pay for the ruptured state of the Liberal party, and the introduction of protectionist arrangements in India with the avowed
object of preparing for such arrangements at home cannot fail to
startle and even horrify many who believed that free trade had
been secured as a permanent benefit." [22]

Both protectionists and free traders made constant appeals to
the working classes. Protectionists argued that a vote for free trade
was a vote for unemployment and for continued foreign competition. And during and after the Boer War, when it became clear
that England had so many enemies in Europe, they emphasized
the dangers of English dependence on foreign sources of food
supply. Free traders, on the other hand, exploited memories of
corn law days and the hungry forties, and they argued that a vote

for protection was a vote for the end of the cheap loaf. Harold Cox, appointed secretary of the Cobden Club because of his talent as a publicist, paid particular attention to the labor vote. In 1900 he encouraged T. Fisher Unwin, the publisher and son-in-law of Richard Cobden, to reprint the late Henry George's *Protection or Free Trade* because it was just the kind of book that would appeal to workers both in Britain and the Empire. Indeed, George himself had been aware that no one could accuse him of being an agent of English industrialists—a charge that was often made against free traders.[23]

X

The protectionists had one inestimable advantage: they won Joseph Chamberlain to their side. But Chamberlain, astute politician that he was, did not confine himself simply to tariff reform. On the contrary, he proceeded to link imperial and social reform —old age pensions in particular—with protectionism. Small wonder that W. T. Stead reported in 1903 that politics was arousing more interest in England than it had for years. "The whole country here is convulsed by Chamberlain's proposal to abandon Free Trade," Bernard Shaw wrote excitedly. In fact, when Prime Minister Arthur J. Balfour refused to make predictions about the future of his Government, he knew what he was doing.

The friends of commercial freedom were roused, and the energy and ingenuity that they showed were remarkable. The prominent journalist Justin McCarthy, working on his *Portraits of the Sixties,* used his discussion of Richard Cobden as a weapon against Chamberlain; and as a frontispiece he chose a picture of Cobden, Bright, and Villiers because he thought that it would be particularly effective and relevant. James Bryce, the outraged Gladstonian, made many speeches and reminded his listeners of how much they had already suffered from "J. C.'s influence." Bernard Shaw, immersed in statistics and blue books, spent so much time writing and speaking against Chamberlain that he even had to cut down on his correspondence: "I must break off now, and go back to Free Trade, and preferential duties and exports and Chamberlain etc. etc. etc." [24]

Nor was this all. A leading member of the Cobden Club, preparing a statement for the public, found a title that would attract attention, *A Great Apostacy*, and he used pronouncements of the young Chamberlain to embarrass the old Chamberlain. Young Winston Churchill, developing his oratorical gifts in the attack on "Chamberlain and his Merrie Men," told an American free trader how inspiring he found it that on both sides of the Atlantic so many were "fighting in a common cause—you to attack protection, we to defend Free Trade"; a double victory, he was sure, would mean much for the wealth and welfare of the world. T. Fisher Unwin reprinted Ebenezer Elliott's *Corn-Law Rhymes*, and free traders assured him that the work would be of great service at this critical time. Even the Royal Economic Society did not remain aloof from the controversy. Professor F. Y. Edgeworth specifically requested Professor Seligman, as American correspondent of the Society, to report on the reactions of American economists to Chamberlain's proposals.

One central point that free traders emphasized repeatedly was the effect that protection in England would have elsewhere. If England introduced hostile tariffs, other countries would raise theirs even more. If, on the other hand, England continued free trade, other countries might still follow the English example. Shortly before the American presidential election of 1904 Winston Churchill even suggested that a Democratic—and free trade—victory in the United States would serve to crush the protectionist movement in England.[25]

Like the free traders, the tariff reformers had outstanding talent on which to draw: William J. Ashley, the economic historian who prided himself on never having wanted to be a medievalist for the sake of medievalism and who had translated Gustav Schmoller, that idol of protectionists; William Cunningham, the economic historian and authority on mercantilism; and William Knight, the energetic literary scholar and publicist. Indeed, such was the productivity of tariff reformers that Chamberlain told Knight in 1903 that he thought that the public already had as many books and pamphlets on fair trade as it could digest. But the protectionists had other advantages. Winston Churchill described them as "a great faction possessing all the resources of wealth and influence, with absolute confidence in itself and supreme contempt for

its opponents, backed by a gigantic press and a powerful organisation." Churchill's description was accurate but unfair, for his
words applied almost equally well to the free traders.[26]

Both in the cabinet and the country Chamberlain split the coalition of Conservatives and Liberal Unionists, and by the fears
that he aroused he helped not only to reunite the Liberals but to
drive some Conservatives back to free trade Unionism. And then,
in the election of 1906, the voters overwhelmingly repudiated protection. Free traders were more jubilant than they had been in
decades. Churchill, who had abandoned his father's party and
turned Liberal because of his opposition to protection, wrote discerningly to an American free trader:

> Thinking it all over, I am prepared to claim the Manchester election as a
> great event. Manchester was the home of Free Trade, Free Trade was assailed.
> I left my party and went to Manchester to contest its great commercial di-
> vision, and the division which contains the historic Free Trade Hall. When
> I went, Manchester and Salford were represented by nine Conservative mem-
> bers—all of more or less pronounced Protectionist views—including the Prime
> Minister. The result of the Poll dispossessed all these nine gentlemen from
> seats which many of them had held for twenty years, and installed in their
> place—by immense majorities—nine Liberal or Labour members all definitely
> pledged to Free Trade. . . . Could anything be a plainer tribute to the
> wisdom of an instructed democracy than this emphatic asseveration of the
> economic doctrines of Mr. Bright and Mr. Cobden, after the successful prac-
> tice and matured consideration of fifty [sixty] years. I think it will be a
> long time before Protection is ever raised in the same form in England.[27]

XI

Chamberlain repeatedly insisted that his policy of fair trade
with the foreigner would not increase in the least the cost of food
and other necessities. On the contrary, he argued that the growth
of trade—especially within the Empire—that his policy was designed to encourage would serve to lower prices. His opponents
believed otherwise, however, and so did the mass of workers, who
showed by their votes that they continued to subscribe to the words
that one of their number had once written to John Bright: "The
condition of us working men is hard, but heaven only knows what
it would have been now, but for you, and your good friend Mr.
Cobden." As the octogenarian sage and free trader Goldwin Smith
pointed out, commenting on the election results, the manufacturing districts were still filled with painful recollections of the corn

laws. While Smith remembered the forties, most of the voters of
1906 knew them only by oral tradition, but this was enough.

Joseph Chamberlain came too late. He remembered the Great
Depression, and he reminded the English of it. Voters, however,
wished to forget it, and the upswing of the business cycle made it
possible for them to do so. In short, the time was still distant when
Philip Bright, son of the great free trader, would report mournfully, "Today we revert to protection." And even then—on March
1, 1932—Bright could not believe that the change would be permanent. The time was even more distant when—in 1938—a discouraged free trader, convinced that "Protectionist arrogance and
folly" might go to any lengths, feared that the statue of Richard
Cobden near Mornington Crescent had been permanently removed—although it had been taken down simply to be cleaned and
repaired.[28]

❧ XV ❧

OTHER ENGLANDS

For Richard Cobden, John Bright, John Benjamin Smith, and other leaders of the free trade movement, the repeal of the corn laws was only a starting-point, not a climax. And among the other big changes to which they wished it to lead was the dissolution of the British Empire. It is certainly true that they did not succeed in putting their anti-imperialist philosophy into practice; but this hardly lessens the historical importance of their outlook. For, while their successors in time know that they failed, their contemporaries did not have this knowledge. Quite the contrary. The fact that free traders had been able to bring about the repeal of the corn laws made it seem possible that they might succeed with some of their other plans to revamp British institutions.

Cobdenites were blunt about their anti-imperialism. They believed that England should eventually abandon those territories in which native populations predominated. And they thought of the Americans as having set the right example for other colonies inhabited by English-speaking peoples. Looking eagerly to the independence of Canada, Australia, and New Zealand, they considered political freedom both desirable and inevitable; and they hoped that the American experience would teach the British to grant independence without the hardship of revolution.

The anti-imperialism of the Cobdenites rested on their conviction that empire was inseparable from both militarism and war. Colonies necessitated high taxes and heavy and unproductive expenditures to support large military and naval establishments and they led to unavoidable conflicts with competing powers. Better, therefore, to repudiate colonies and not become a nation of soldiers and sailors. "Surely at some future day," John Bright wrote hopefully in 1846, "our race may find it possible to live in peace and security without making one part of the human family skilful in the destruction of the rest." Colonies were a burden, and as long as England had them they would serve as a constant invitation to struggles with other powers. "Surely the phrenologists ought to be able to discover another organ in our brain, corresponding with the propensity for taking possession of the territory of our neighbors!" Cobden impatiently told an American in 1850. Indeed, Cobdenites had the same opinion of the consequences of the British imperial status as that expressed by Thomas Paine during the age of the French Revolution:

> Look round the Globe from East to West,
>   Or cast a glance from Pole to Pole
> 'Tis Britain bars the world from Rest,
>   'Tis Britain harrows up the Soul.[1]

II

The Crimean War—the first struggle involving the major powers since Napoleonic times—made the Cobdenites surer than ever that they were right. Decrying the British and French attempt to stop Russian expansion into the Turkish Empire, they expressed their feelings both publicly and privately with a courage, even a recklessness, that had few parallels in the nineteenth-century world. As the war approached Cobden bitterly told C. P. Villiers, his friend in the House of Commons, that the work of Parliament was being seriously neglected: "This is one of the great evils of war—that it distracts the public attention, and gives scope for the demoralization which necessarily ensues when there is no longer a vigilant eye directed towards our domestic affairs. But how much greater will be this distraction when our own fleets and armies begin to take a part in the fray!"

Cobden was right. The war atmosphere proved to be all-encompassing. Charles Dickens, caught up in it, wrote feelingly as he awaited news of the taking of Sebastopol: "When a church clock strikes, we think it is the Joy-Bell, and fly out of the house in a burst of nationality—to sneak in again. If they practice firing at the Camp, we are sure it is the artillery celebrating the Fall of the Russian, and we become enthusiastic in a moment. I live in constant readiness to illuminate the whole house. Whatever anybody says, I believe." The war, he confessed, made him "a mere driveller—a moon struck, babbling, staring, credulous, imbecile, greedy, gaping, wooden-headed, addle-brained, wool-gathering, dreary, vacant, obstinate civilian."

But not so Richard Cobden and his friends. While they could feel no enthusiasm for England's ally Turkey, they felt deeply about the sufferings of the populations of all the belligerent powers. And in the midst of the conflict Bright dared to accept election as an honorary vice-president of the American Peace Society. "What a shocking business this war is!" he wrote to J. B. Smith in 1854. "How would you like to be a Cabinet Minister with so much blood on your head and conscience? Tho' I suspect statesmen are not troubled much with conscience—and their heads seem of little use for any good purpose." Alarmed by the war spirit that seized the country, Bright could not find words to describe his "feeling towards the Government—absolute hatred of *them*, and contempt of the people whom they have deceived, and whose passions they now obey." Cobden, for his part, was amazed by the brutality and ignorance that appeared in wartime England; and the triumph of unreason he found appalling. Cows and pigs, he decided, were "far more logical and reliable animals than the two-legged creatures you generally herd with." If only the English would stop trying to settle the affairs of the world! But the trouble, he told J. B. Smith, was that old vicious cycle:

> Peace makes riches flow,
> Riches make pride to grow,
> Pride brings war;
> War brings poverty,
> Poverty brings peace:
> Peace makes riches flow, etc. etc.

Indeed, the only cure for English meddling in other countries' affairs that Cobden could envisage was American competition; but he feared that the United States, too, would commit follies of its own.[2]

The searing experience of the Crimean War was hardly over when the Indian Mutiny began, and it, too, was a great trial for the Cobdenites. "I have no faith in England's destiny in the East. I don't believe it is our mission to civilize or Christianize the population of India. *That* has never been our honest object in going there," Cobden wrote indignantly to J. B. Smith in 1857. Although he was pessimistic to the point of despair about England's Indian policy and feared the legacy of resentment and hatred that the atrocities committed by both sides made inevitable, he was reassured at least that the laws of nature would ultimately assert their supremacy: "Climate and geography will teach us that we have no business, with our white faces, so far from home, and we shall throw up India." In the meantime, however, he had no hope for the success of any scheme of reform. Even if the English devoted their full attention to Indian affairs, it would still be impossible for them to provide good government for a massive population thousands of miles away in a country whose climate so little suited Europeans. For the rest Cobden condemned the notion of keeping India for the sake of the Indians as the worst sort of cant.

John Bright—with what Cobden called his "ardent temperament"—reacted no less strongly to the implications of the Mutiny. As he told a friend in 1857:

I dare scarcely write on the India question. A century of aggression, with all its folly and crime, is now yielding its natural fruit. We are a nation professing Christianity, and sanctimonious beyond the pretensions of our neighbors—yet we are probably more boastful and arrogant than any other people. But three years ago we were affecting to defend civilization and freedom throughout Europe—we were attempting to bully every nation that would not join in our folly—and now we exhibit ourselves as unable to govern the territories we have conquered—and a portion of the subjects of the British Crown, equal in number to the population of many European kingdoms, is in a state of anarchy! Surely we may learn something from the great reverse—if blindness has not settled down irrevocably upon us! I believe morality to be as necessary for a nation as for an individual, and that it is the only true Conservatism.[3]

The Mutiny ended, and then came more troubles. The Austro-Sardinian War (1859), the American Civil War, the Danish War (1864), and the Austro-Prussian War (1866) showed that peace was scarcely a favorite instrument of national policy. It was one thing for Cobdenites to insist that there could be no more noble mission than the attempt to teach people the stupidity and wickedness of wasting their resources on armament races that fomented inter-

national hatreds and conflict. But converts to this view were hard
to find among the leaders who had the power to determine the
policies of their countries in the age of Palmerston, Napoleon III,
and Bismarck. "The adventurer on that Throne has no chance but
in the distraction of his peoples' minds, and in the jingle and
glitter of theatrical glory," Charles Dickens wrote shrewdly in
1863, expressing the widespread fear that Napoleon III would in-
volve England in a general conflict. Even that conservative of conservatives, Robert Curzon, who despised almost everything about
the nineteenth century, found himself wondering that there should
be wars in his supposedly enlightened age.[4]

III

At last Palmerston, that fierce exponent of an aggressive and
meddling foreign policy, died; urban workers received the right
to vote; and Gladstone, the friend of Bright and the recently dead
Cobden, headed a Ministry. With good cause the Cobdenites permitted their hopes to run high, for Gladstone believed in a pacific
foreign policy that rested chiefly on the exercise of English moral
influence; and he opposed the use of threats except when they were
seriously intended. His view of the Empire was also "sound," for
he worked on the assumption that the English-speaking colonies
were already well on the way to independence, and he regarded
the other parts of the Empire as a burden.

The extent to which Gladstone was influenced by the Cobdenites became clear in one of his first acts as Prime Minister: he
offered to John Bright the India secretaryship. Bright rejected the
office, but he consented, after much pressure, to serve as President
of the Board of Trade. He refused the India Office because of ill
health as well as an unwillingness to face the difficulties that the
post inevitably would present. But the offer—not its refusal—was
what mattered.[5]

In some ways Gladstone lived up to the expectations of the
Cobdenites. Often they would have preferred that he act more
quickly, that he economize more, and that he retrench more on
military appropriations; and they were outraged toward the end
of his Ministry that he—and Bright—permitted England to be
drawn into the Ashanti War. "What can be more lamentable than
to see Bright, instead of denouncing it, as he or Cobden would as-

suredly have done ten years ago, actually sharing the responsibility of this criminal blunder?" unbending Sir Louis Mallet wrote in 1873. Nevertheless, Gladstone did push through a remarkable number of domestic reforms, and his foreign and colonial policies were, on the whole, satisfactory to the anti-imperialists. He kept England out of the Franco-German War; and despite the exasperating demands of Senator Charles Sumner and others, he settled the dispute with the United States over the Alabama claims— even at the risk of offending English ultra-patriots who charged that he yielded too much. He treated the English-speaking colonies as mature societies that were soon to strike out on their own. In 1870, with the end of the Maori War, he recalled British troops from New Zealand. For the rest, Gladstone resisted the pressures to have his Government add to the size of the Empire. Charles T. Beke, agitating for the annexation of Ethiopia, made no progress.[6]

What mattered to Gladstone's enemies, however, was not so much what he did in the colonial sphere as what he might do. The fear that the Empire was in danger was expressed early in his Ministry, but it was not until 1872 that Disraeli made that fear politically important. Disraeli's motives were many: to find an issue by which to defeat Gladstone and secure power for the Conservative Party; to enhance the popularity of the monarchy; to work up patriotic feelings that would smother the annoying republican movement. Whatever his motives, Disraeli made the Empire a living issue in British politics, and many contemporaries believed that it played an important part in the Tory electoral triumph of 1874. Indeed, at a victory banquet an outspoken imperialist drew loud applause when he told the assembled Conservatives that they were celebrating "the increased prospect of the safety, happiness, and prosperity of the whole empire."[7]

If before becoming Prime Minister Disraeli made people Empire-conscious, six years of his Government made it seem that there was only the Empire, the whole Empire, and nothing but the Empire. "No one honors more than myself the Colonial Empire of England; no one is more anxious to defend it," Disraeli declared, and despite the abundant evidence to the contrary he refused to believe that any Member of Parliament would seriously contemplate the loss of India or of any other part of the Empire. In 1875 he purchased the Suez Canal shares of the Khedive of

Egypt. In 1876 he sponsored the Royal Titles Bill proclaiming the Queen Empress of India. With a view to preventing Russian expansion into the Turkish Empire, he embroiled England for years in the Eastern Question, and in the process he acquired Cyprus. And he involved England in the Afghan and the Zulu wars.

As early as 1876 Gladstone, just man that he was, confessed to W. T. Stead, "I have been too much in personal conflict on political matters with Lord Beaconsfield to be altogether a fair judge of incidents connected with his utterances." By 1878, however, Gladstone lost all control. "Dizzy has surpassed all my expectations, all my fears," he told John Bright, and he spoke for all outraged Cobdenites, to whom militarism, jingoism, imperialism, and war were the greatest sins that man could commit against man. The wife of an American diplomat, breakfasting with the Gladstones in 1878, noted in her diary that a "delightful" conversation about the Eastern Question took place; but the way Gladstone felt about the subject made it impossible for any discussion of it to be delightful.[8]

IV

Imperialists denounced Gladstone as both mischievous and dangerous. "He was always pandering to the mob, ignoring the pit and boxes, and speaking only to the gallery," as one of them put it. Anti-imperialists, on the other hand, never again admired Gladstone so much as they did in the years when he condemned Disraelian imperialism. They thought of him as the greatest Briton of the modern age, and it would have seemed impossible to them that a time would ever come when his autograph would have no market value. "The people know no other name," the hearty anti-imperialist Goldwin Smith assured him. Oscar Wilde, then a student at Magdalen College, Oxford, sent Gladstone a sonnet inspired by his noble protests against the Turkish massacres in Bulgaria. Even Herbert Spencer, who viewed letters as a waste of his time and energy, wrote to Gladstone to thank him for having aroused public opinion against Disraeli's pro-Turkish policy and for having kept England out of a war that would have been both a disaster and a disgrace. And the historian Edward A. Freeman, writing from Greece, informed Gladstone that he was as popular there as at home.[9]

Anti-imperialists raged at Disraeli and his "Rule Britannia non-sense." Francis W. Newman, eager for the British to decolonize peacefully and with good-will, was so ashamed of Dizzyism that he even hesitated to correspond with his foreign friends. What he regarded as the worst ministry of the century convinced him that it was imperative to place restrictions on the powers of the executive in the determination of foreign policy. "You have had a wholesome lesson on the latent resources of an undefined prerogative, and another on the uses to which a female sovereign may be put by a political sharper," Goldwin Smith told Gladstone. Dr. Elizabeth Blackwell denounced the crude ambition that was responsible for so much demoralization and horror. And George Jacob Holyoake gave vent to the vicious antisemitism that Disraeli so often provoked: "We are betrayed by a man who has 'no drop of English blood in his veins.' If we go into a war it will be a Jewish war—for Jewish pride and passion—not for any English interests." At least one person would have smiled at these words—Disraeli's grandfather who changed his name from Lara to D'Israeli in order to make clear his Hebrew origins.[10]

From the time of Disraeli's Ministry through the Boer War of 1899–1902 the jingo—noisy, aggressive, condescending, arrogant—figured prominently in English life. It is wrong, however, to assume that the jingo was the only kind of imperialist. Far from it. There was also the sort typified by George Eliot, who could think of nothing she would care more to do than to awaken in her countrymen an awareness of the human claims of those peoples who differed most from the British in their beliefs and traditions; by the Foreign Office official, who, when placed in charge of the department to administer Cyprus, proceeded to study modern Greek and found it far from being the degenerate jargon that some British professors of Greek said that it was; by John Lockwood Kipling, who would have taken great pride in Indian progress except for the fact that there was "always something that tends to keep one humble in India"; by the elderly humanitarian, who recalled among the chief experiences of his life the time he spent with inspiring people who had carried the Gospel to the cannibals of the South Seas; by the members of the Aborigines Protection Society, who saw it as the mission of the English "to penetrate into every part of the world and to help in the great work of civilization," but who also insisted on alerting their countrymen to a sense of their duties towards the native races so that they would avoid the retribution that befell the Spaniards; and by the unrecorded English in scattered parts of the world whose efforts caused even an American anti-imperialist to report during a visit to Egypt in 1902 that they did not "seem to be ambitious of exploiting the country in order to despoil it, but only to build it up." [11]

Disraeli's vigorous—and expensive—policies convinced anti-imperialists all the more that colonies were a burden. Even General Charles George Gordon—and he was no anti-imperialist—wrote to a member of the House of Lords in 1877:

if England took Lower Egypt, she must take the Soudan which would be a White Elephant to her, it would cost her at least £250,000 a year, and never would benefit her. I do not think the acquisition of Egypt (Lower) would be worth the sacrifice, and again, these people would need much looking after, for they are bigots and Mecca is close. I quite authorize Your Lordship to say this is my opinion, should you ever hear the subject discussed. I say it would be downright madness to go and incur obligations of such a nature as the capture or annexation of Egypt would bring on us.

At the same time, however, it is striking that an important change took place in the thinking of some anti-imperialists during the course of Disraeli's Ministry. It is true that they blamed the depression on his policies, and that they continued to consider the colonies a strain and a drain. Yet as the depression deepened they suggested increasingly that the English try to make the colonies less of a burden by developing greater economic ties with them. Since so many of England's traditionally best customers were setting up protective tariffs to keep out English goods, it was desirable to further economic relations with the colonies and, in the process, make them pay their way. As late as 1861, for example, there had been loud complaints about the apathy of English cotton traders and merchants towards investments in India. By 1876, however, the Manchester Chamber of Commerce memorialized Disraeli about the India Museum in London and commended its value for "promoting more intimate commercial relations between this country and India and opening new outlets for the employment of English enterprise and capital." And during that grim year 1879 the Chamber urged Foreign Secretary Lord Salisbury to try to counteract the depression by extending commercial relations with the colonies.[12]

V

The voters repudiated Disraelian imperialism in the election of 1880, and Gladstone reverted to a pacific foreign policy based on moral suasion. He withdrew from Afghanistan. When the Boers inflicted a humiliating defeat on the British at Majuba Hill (1881), he resisted the demands of ultra-patriots for revenge. As a staunch anti-imperialist reported after an interview with Gladstone: "Personally, I have no doubt he abhors the war as cordially as any of us and would willingly go on with negotiations for peace in spite of the reverse we have suffered." Indeed, in the face of heavy criticism from imperialists, Gladstone did arrange a settlement with the Boers.

In Egypt, however, everything went wrong. The outbreak of riots in Alexandria in 1882 resulted in the British bombardment of the town, and Gladstone was faced with a war against Egyptian nationalists. The situation was alarming for anti-imperialists. John Bright resigned from the Government to protest against the bombardment of Alexandria, but he said almost nothing publicly. His reasoning was that it was pointless to overthrow Gladstone's Government, for the Conservative Ministry that would follow would be infinitely worse and would probably bring on a war with France.

The grief of anti-imperialists over the Egyptian war was unspeakable. Thomson Hankey told an American: "I wish we were well out of it. I do not see what good we shall derive by insisting on the introduction of a better state of finances in Egypt and I am by no means satisfied that the large masses of the people are not entirely antagonistic to all our *sound principles* of good government." Herbert Spencer, though suffering from a nervous disorder that compelled him to avoid public commitments, helped to form an Anti-Aggression League, and he insisted that as a result of his efforts in the anti-imperialist cause he wrecked his health permanently. And Wilfrid Blunt, the pro-Egyptian and anti-imperialist poet, expressed his fury in *The Wind and the Whirlwind:*

The Empire thou didst build shall be divided.
Thou shalt be weighed in thine own balances
Of usury to peoples and to princes,
And be found wanting by the world and these.[13]

The British victory at Tel el-Kebir in 1882 was a welcome relief
to Gladstone and his supporters, for they were embarrassed by
their imperialistic involvements. "We are as you may suppose in
great spirits here at the glorious news from Egypt," wrote Sir William Harcourt, Gladstone's Home Secretary. But Britain's most
famous war correspondent, Sir William Howard Russell, found
the English celebration of their victory absurd. Writing from
Egypt, he told Sir John Millais: "Surely you are all stark staring
mad . . . but in the range of my reading there never has been
such an exhibition of enthusiasm over any military success in the
world and I can only suppose it was a relief to find we could beat
the Egyptians after all, and do it very cheaply." For his part, Russell protested consistently and courageously against England's
Egyptian policy as wicked, unprincipled, and disastrous.[14]

Gladstone's involvement in the Egyptian Question was not
ended, for the decision to require the Egyptians to evacuate and
abandon the Sudan had an unexpected result: General Gordon,
supervising the operation, was massacred with his garrison at
Khartoum. For the English people the experience was traumatic.
In Tennyson's words:

Warrior of God, man's friend—not here below,
But somewhere dead far in the waste Soudan,
Thou livest in all hearts, for all men know
This earth has borne no simpler, nobler man.

Imperialists as well as anti-imperialists raged—imperialists because Gladstone's policy had been far too weak, anti-imperialists
because it had been far too meddlesome. Swinburne denounced
Gladstone as "Judas of Hawarden," and Andrew Lang, a great
admirer of Gordon, exploded: "What a waste. How long are we
to endure our infernal squabbling politicians, like cats on a roof.
I wish I were an American, a German, even an Australian almost,
to be out of this world of political quacks, and cowards, and liars."
Anti-imperialists were no less furious. Mrs. Annie Besant busied
herself at meetings to protest against the conflict in the Sudan. Disheartened to the point of illness that a supposedly Liberal Ministry

was engaged in a war that she found both pointless and unjustifiable, she wondered about the morality of Victorian politics.[15]

Gordon's fate was still on people's minds when an acute Anglo-Russian crisis developed over Afghanistan. "It is a melancholy thing," Joseph Chamberlain wrote to John Bright, "that these complications should embitter the close of Mr. Gladstone's career. No man could ever have been more sincerely anxious for Peace." But Bright was hardly sympathetic. He found Gladstone's conscience unduly flexible, and he had no doubt that, if Disraeli and Salisbury had pursued the policies that Gladstone was pursuing, the whole Liberal Party would have condemned them. Shamed and saddened by the "other blunders and other crimes" that followed the bombardment of Alexandria, he told an American in 1885:

We have troubles all the world over, for we are everywhere—and our people are not wise enough to see that the greater the Empire the greater the dangers and the more the future is dark and full of peril. This is a lesson the people can not learn—with so large a military expenditure and with so many families living upon it, and with so many of our people connected with the Colonies, there seems little chance of our national policy being improved and corrected. We are giving power to our population. I wish we could give them wisdom with it.

Even more despairingly, Bright told another American in 1885: "We want a thorough change in our notions of foreign policy—when it will come I know not—perhaps some great catastrophe is approaching. I sometimes suspect it. Earthquakes come without noise. . . . Europe is nearly ready for one, and its nations, we amongst them, may need a lesson." Like his Quaker friend John Greenleaf Whittier, Bright wished that he could call any country Christian. But at least Whittier reassured Bright that one of the finest acts of his life was his resignation from the Ministry.[16]

VI

The imperialism of Gladstone, like that of Disraeli, was chiefly political and psychological in origin. A search for power and prestige, it was largely shaped by suspicions and fears of the intentions of other countries—most notably France and Russia. As Ouida aptly expressed it in a poem published in the *Times* in 1882:

Great England put her armour by, and stretch'd
Her stately limbs to slumber in the sun.
The nations, seeing then how long she slept,
Commun'd together, and in whispers said:
"Lo! She is old and tired; let us steal
"The crown from off her brow. She will not know!"

Yet the fact remains that, owing to the lingering depression and the further growth of foreign competition and hostile tariffs, interest in the economic possibilities of colonies became more and more pronounced in the eighties. Publicists, businessmen, and politicians increasingly recommended imperialism as a sure cure for falling prices, declining profits, and unemployment. It is true, for example, that the renowned explorer Joseph Thomson saw no reason in 1881 to expect a commercial future for Africa; but Henry M. Stanley, on the other hand, told the Manchester Chamber of Commerce and dozens of similar groups that there were staggering prospects for the extension of civilization and commerce in Africa, and he reveled in statistics as to how many tons of railway traffic each white man in Africa would require each year. It was symptomatic that in 1883 the president of the Manchester Chamber of Commerce urged Parliament to oppose Portuguese annexation of the Lower Congo, for, if the Portuguese were not stopped, there would be native uprisings and English trade would suffer. When troubles with the natives interfered with trade in Sierra Leone in 1885, the Manchester Chamber again called on the Government to take action. And in subsequent years the Chamber pressed for government intervention in behalf of the trading interests in Gambia, Uganda, and the Sudan.[17]

Among politicians, too, the eighties saw a marked growth of interest in the possibilities of empire. Lord Rosebery became perhaps the best known imperial enthusiast, but he had an impressive number of parliamentary colleagues. Nor did these politicians hesitate to link their imperialism with vulgar economics. While twentieth-century historians may feel embarrassed to acknowledge this link, late Victorian politicians felt no such embarrassment. Indeed, those who championed schemes of imperial federation were particularly outspoken about their economic aims and hopes. Charles Gould, in an electoral address to his Derbyshire constituents in 1885, praised imperial federation because it would have "most beneficial results in regard to our languishing industries." And Sir William Bromley Davenport favored giving every possible inducement to the colonies to federate, for then they would remove their tariffs on English goods, and a vast market would be opened to English industries in every part of the world.

For his part, Lord Rosebery doubted that the colonies would enter a federation without the stimulus of a great war that would awaken their loyalty to England. And others found the idea of federation hopeless from the start. Herbert Spencer, for example, thought that geography made it impossible. "In the normal order of things," he wrote, "federation results primarily from the needs for combined defence, and is only likely to prove stable under the stress of such needs. But it is obvious that combined defence of the scattered parts of the British Empire can have no such reason or advantage as the combined defence of states in juxtaposition." [18]

VII

In May, 1885, John Greenleaf Whittier congratulated John Bright on the improved state of international affairs—on the prospect of peace between England and Russia and on the evacuation of the Sudan. In June Gladstone resigned, Salisbury headed a Conservative Ministry, and what John Bright had feared—a bigger dose of imperialism—ensued. In a confidential letter in October, Lord Ripon warned Bright of the serious danger that Burma was to be annexed. Ripon opposed such a step for the good old anti-imperialist reasons: it would be a burden; it would increase military expenditures; and it would multiply the chances of war. But Ripon added gloomily that the annexationists, led by Lord Randolph Churchill, were powerful: "The *Times* advocates it; there is a strong party in India in favor of it; and the English Jingos are sure to back it up." Lord Ripon was proven right very soon.

It was no accident that imperialists rejoiced during Salisbury's long second Ministry (1886–92). That man Gladstone, with his plans to sever colonial ties and even to disrupt the union with Ireland, was defeated. At last the Empire was safe; at last the anti-imperialists were on the defensive. Imperialists, to be sure, distorted Gladstone's ideas and conveniently overlooked his approval of the decline of imperial separatism and his endorsement of the flexible relations that were developing within the British Empire.

For all that, it was surely appropriate that the fiftieth anniversary of the Queen's accession occurred while Salisbury was Prime Minister. For it was Disraeli, his predecessor as head of the Conservative Party, who had worked so hard to increase the prestige of the monarchy by stressing the imperial issue.[19]

In the year of the Jubilee—1887—even the strictest advocates of economy could not justifiably complain about the cost of ceremonials, for since the time of the Queen's coronation public funds had been used for only three state occasions of any magnitude: the funeral of the Duke of Wellington in 1852; the marriage of the Prince of Wales in 1863; and the thanksgiving service for the recovery of the Prince in 1872. The concern for economy was, nevertheless, pronounced. The firm that examined the coronation chair found it shaky, decayed, worn, and covered with names and dates inscribed with knives by mischief-makers; still, it recommended that the chair could be safely used. Unlike the Government, however, private citizens and businessmen ignored the demands of economy. They splurged with decorations and illuminations—especially in those places of residence or business that were located along the route of the procession in London, and the Queen received so many presents that she had to set the rule that she would accept gifts only from individuals whom she knew personally.[20]

The British Empire figured prominently in the celebrations of 1887. The manager of the oldest and largest circus and managerie in Britain had proposed a cavalcade of triumphal cars, with particular attention to be "drawn to the Colonial Car, entitled the 'Congress of Nations'—representative of our Colonial possessions, this magnificent Car being drawn by 10 Elephants." The manager's proposal was rejected, but even without his cavalcade the Empire was omnipresent—in sermons, speeches, newspapers, books, and in the hordes of visitors who spoke English with various Colonial accents. For imperial reformers 1887 was a year never to be forgotten; for anti-imperialist reformers it was a year to forget as soon as possible.[21]

The period after the Jubilee saw a further growth of interest in the economic possibilities of the Empire. In 1888 the Manchester Chamber of Commerce sent to the Government a copy of a revealing resolution that its members had passed:

As foreign nations, which were formerly our best customers, are rapidly extending their own manufacturing industries, besides greatly restricting the sale of our goods by ever-increasing tariffs, this Chamber would urge upon her Majesty's Government to foster by every possible means the systematic creation of New Markets by enabling such part of our annual surplus population of over 350,000 souls, for whom our industries fail to find employment, to be drafted into Canada, Australia, and South Africa on rational, self-supporting principles, thereby doubling the present purchasing power of these colonies every five or ten years, and drawing them into much closer union with the mother country.

Nor was this all. Protectionists in the Manchester Chamber insisted that the time had come to achieve commercial union with the colonies through a scheme of preferential import duties and to replace universal free trade by free trade within the Empire. Free traders, on the other hand, insisted that this proposal would have disastrous results. Yet the decisive point is that all members of the Chamber, whether protectionists or free traders, urged the Government to take "a stronger and more active interest" in the development of economic ties with the colonies.

The United Empire Trade League reflected, perhaps best of all, the changes that had occurred since Gladstone's first Ministry. Formed in 1891, it had two main objects: to further trade relations among the Queen's subjects, and to advance the interests of British enterprise throughout the world. As the League's honorary secretary, the Tory politician C. E. Howard Vincent, bluntly put it, "The importance of developing by all possible means the Commercial relations between the Mother Country and the Colonies, and between the Colonies themselves, has now become paramount." No doubt about it, areas that so many English had previously ignored or scorned were attracting unprecedented attention in an age of prolonged depression.[22]

$\{$ XVI $\}$

IN THE TIME OF THE
IMPERIALISTS

Even in the early nineties, imperial enthusiasts continued to be-
rate their countrymen for being insufficiently empire-conscious.
Despite ministries headed by such resolute imperialists as Disraeli
and Salisbury, despite years of agitation by members of colonial-
minded organizations like the Tory Primrose League, and despite
Sir John Seeley's inspiring *Expansion of England* and scores of
other publications extolling the idea of empire, imperialists continued to deplore the persistence of mass indifference.

Just as in the early eighties an English Sanskrit scholar protested that everything connected with India made people sleepy,
so in the early nineties imperialists complained that anything concerning any part of the Empire had the same effect. Florence
Nightingale, obsessed with England's colonial obligations and responsibilities, fumed in 1891 that the publishers of Sir William
Hunter's *Indian Empire* had permitted it to go out of print, and
she sent them indignant letters. "Now is the time for books," she
told them, insisting that Hunter's work be reprinted in a month.
So, too, Cecil Rhodes longed to make his compatriots more
colonial-minded. Like Nicholas Forsyte in *The Man of Property*,
Rhodes was willing to make almost any sacrifice as long as he
could benefit the Empire; but he was repeatedly distressed to find
that few Britons had his sense of dedication. W. T. Stead aptly

described Rhodes to Gladstone in 1891: "He is a young man, not
yet forty, who has spent most of his life on the confines of civilization, but his ambition, his capacity, and his wealth render it probable that he will take a prominent part before long in Imperial
affairs at home as well as abroad." By 1892 Rhodes had no doubt
that the great hope for the British Empire lay in the still further
growth in the world of McKinleyism. For the more foreign countries enacted hostile tariffs, the more the English would be forced
to develop their commercial and other relations with the colonies.[1]

But Rhodes's friend and booster, W. T. Stead, saw the trouble
as even more basic. Looking forward to a union of the English-
speaking peoples, he complained repeatedly that the initial difficulty was that England did not exist as a community for many
Englishmen, and that patriotism, as a religious impulse, had little
hold on the English masses. To inspire loyalty to England and the
Empire was for Stead a preliminary step toward wider loyalties,
and to prepare the way for them he used his position as a journalist and editor to play up the glories of the English naval tradition
and the activities of modern empire builders. "State your impressions of Mr. Cecil Rhodes. Why is his personality so important?"
This was a question that Stead included in a typical contemporary
history scholarship examination given in his *Review of Reviews*.
It is no surprise that Rhodes considered the *Review* a valuable
medium for the propagation of colonial-consciousness. Nor is it
surprising that Stead was resented for booming Rhodes.[2]

II

Imperialists had another great scare in 1892 when Gladstone
returned to power. As twenty-seven-year-old Rudyard Kipling,
living in Vermont, expressed it to his fellow-imperialist W. E.
Henley: "It's a funny thing when you're out of England to watch
an Empire between ministries flapping about like a ship taken
aback and to hear the groans of despair among the fellows in the
outer ports when she lies over on the other tack and all the colonies begin to say:—'Now, what particular brand of dirt are *we*
going to eat.' I saw it and it made me sick, sick, sick." It is ironic
that Kipling's first child had the poor grace to be born on Gladstone's birthday; but fortunately the child was a girl. "If she had
been a boy," Kipling told Henley, " 'twould have been my duty

to stand her on her head in a drift lest she also should disgrace the Empire."

Gladstone's attempt to introduce home rule for Ireland failed in 1893, he resigned the next year, and his successor was Lord Rosebery, the leader of the Liberal Imperialists and an eloquent spokesman for imperial federation. By 1895 Lord Salisbury again headed a Ministry, Joseph Chamberlain became his Colonial Secretary, and imperialists had a government that gave them the vigorous foreign and colonial policy that they sought. "I was perfectly sure that Chamberlain could not be in the colonial office many weeks or months without making things hum in about sixteen different corners of the universe," wrote a perceptive American editor. Indeed, Salisbury's third Ministry (1895–1902) was occupied largely with events abroad: the Venezuelan boundary dispute that almost brought war with the United States; involvements in the Near and Far East that risked war with Russia; the reconquest of the Sudan that almost led to war with France; and difficulties with the Boers that produced a deterioration of relations with Germany, France, and Russia.[3]

Such resolute spokesmen of empire as Alfred Austin, W. E. Henley, and Rudyard Kipling found new sources of inspiration in current events. Austin, named poet laureate by Salisbury's Government, outdid even his old gushy self in his ultra-patriotic outpourings. Indeed, he could have easily held his own with any chauvinist in the Germany of William II. Queen Victoria, who often had word sent to him that she admired his ideas and his style, was particularly moved by the poem he wrote to commemorate in 1897 the sixtieth anniversary of her accession.

Cynics, to be sure, abhorred the diamond jubilee as a pointless and wasteful celebration—just an excuse for making wine and whiskey flow. But not Austin. He worshiped manliness and power in both poetry and life, and he had only scorn for the "babes of this Castaly-and-water-suckled generation." A very short man, he wanted an incredibly big empire; and preferring a sepulcher to disgrace, he considered war a small price to pay for power. It was only natural that anti-imperialists should ridicule him as a nonentity, but imperialists had no doubt that he would rank high in the annals of English poetry. For his works dealt with the subject that—next to God—meant most to them.[4]

W. E. Henley also found during the age of Salisbury and Chamberlain the recognition that he had long been seeking. The Government awarded him—and later his widow—a pension. And high-ranking army and navy officers thanked him profusely for his efforts to publicize defense needs. "It must gratify you," Lord Roberts wrote to Henley in 1897, "to see how well the country has responded to the call for increasing the Navy."

As a writer, Henley could do almost anything—except praise Gladstone and the anti-Homeric age that he represented. Editor first of the aptly named *Scots Observer, an Imperial Review* and then of the *New Review,* he kept the Empire, the navy, and the army constantly before his readers. Crippled, chronically ill, restless, and subject to severe depressions, he looked to the British Empire for the strength and good health that he personally lacked. Edmund Gosse properly called him the poet of "strenuous vitality." [5]

Yet the wonder was that as a twenty-one-year-old Henley confessed to Swinburne that he was in a worse position than Thomas Chatterton and that he was "as trouble-scarred and as unfit to struggle with life as a soldier after a Beresina and a new Russian retreat." And Henley was the man for whom Henry James had hoped in 1879 that he would soon come to terms with life. In short, despite "Invictus," Henley's soul was not unconquerable; he himself conquered it, and his love of the Empire helped him in his triumph over personal tragedy.

Oscar Wilde thought of Henley as a captive of the vilest kinds of philistines, and it is true that Henley worked hard to forward the careers of writers who were staunch imperialists. The extraordinary thing about him was that he also went out of his way to help writers whose politics differed sharply from his Tory imperialism. Indeed, it would be hard to find any other figure in the history of nineteenth-century literature who did so much for unlikeminded colleagues. Prince Kropotkin, Thomas Hardy, George Meredith, H. G. Wells, Arthur Morrison, William Butler Yeats, and Joseph Conrad, among hordes of others, testified to the aid and comfort he gave them. "Such literary reputation as is mine owes its most to you." These words of George Meredith were words that Henley heard often—and from writers who, like Meredith, despised Tory imperialism. [6]

Of all the imperialist publicists of the end of the century, Henley's friend Rudyard Kipling achieved—and rightly so—the greatest contemporary fame. His fellow-writers, especially among the anti-imperialists, often belittled his efforts as sentimental, superficial, contrived, and suffering from haste. While Sir Arthur Sullivan felt honored to do the music for the "Recessional," Kipling's jubilee hymn, W. S. Gilbert found Kipling "either cryptically too high or Music Hally too low."

Often, however, criticisms of Kipling were inspired by politics: people who disapproved of his imperialism dismissed his writings as worthless. Often, too, the belittling of Kipling was the result of nothing more than sour grapes. In an age when so many writers struggled long and unsuccessfully to reach the public, Kipling won an audience early in his career. In 1890 he joked with a Scottish friend about the horrors of the young author who was praised: "It's no the speeritual exaltation that I'm protestin' against ye'll understand, for suchlike is good for us all. It's the perneecious consequences o' Butter an' the chances of its meelitatin' against the Higher Arit." Kipling wrote more seriously to Henley: "Yes, men tell me I am young in this country but I have put seven years of India behind me and they do not make a man younger or more cheerful." Kipling's success was, in fact, impressive. He received large numbers of requests for autographs, advice, and dedications. And the magic of his name enabled even his mother and sister to find a publisher for a volume of their poetry.[7]

Kipling attributed his success to the simplicity and directness of his language; he made a religion of using the shortest and fewest possible words. "Wordiness," he told a literary critic, "is all seven of literature's cardinal sins." The best training for an author, he argued, was the writing of telegrams. It is true that Kipling recognized Edgar Allan Poe as the master of all writers of short stories, but he insisted that he was "not in debt for style to anything or anybody but the telegraph system." Kipling's language doubtless had much to do with the fame he won, but it was perhaps mainly important because it suited his glorification of endurance, courage, restraint, self-sacrifice, and the other qualities on which his idea of empire depended.[8]

TIME OF THE IMPERIALISTS 255

It was not only men of letters who exalted the Empire; scholars, too, attempted to cultivate colonial-mindedness. It is undeniable that none of them produced a work comparable with James Mill's *History of India* or Seeley's *Expansion of England,* but what matters is that they spurred on the systematic study of Empire history. In 1896 M. A. S. Hume, the authority on Imperial Spain, suggested to T. Fisher Unwin, the publisher and son-in-law of Richard Cobden, a series on the makers of the British Empire. H. F. Wilson, private secretary to Joseph Chamberlain, consented to serve as editor, and the Queen accepted the dedication. Wilson described the series with enthusiasm. It was to be scholarship with a purpose, history with a point.

At the present time [1898], when the strange apathy of the middle of the century has been happily dispelled, and the colonies and dependencies of the Crown occupy an increasingly large space in popular estimation, a condition of things to which the stirring spectacle presented by the Colonial and Indian detachments at the Jubilee celebrations of last year in no small measure contributed, a series such as this needs no apology from those who have designed it. Among the schoolboys of today are the statesmen of tomorrow: and it is surely fitting that they should learn before they are called upon to play their part in the maintenance and development of their imperial heritage upon what a sure foundation of patient and self-sacrificing effort this country's greatness has been reared.

IV

The morale of anti-imperialists was probably never lower than in the age of Salisbury and Chamberlain. "If only there had been a Cobden in these latter days, how different would be our foreign policy," wrote one dispirited anti-imperialist. Herbert Spencer was so despondent that he even refused to join an anti-imperialist organization: aggressiveness was so universal that the result could only be military despotism. As he put it in 1898:

Now that the white savages of Europe are overrunning the dark savages everywhere; now that the European nations are vying with one another in political burglaries; now that we have entered upon an era of social cannibalism in which the strong nations are devouring the weaker; now that national interests, national prestige, pluck and so forth are alone thought of and equity has utterly dropped out of thought, while rectitude is scorned as "unctuous"; it is useless to resist the wave of barbarism. There is a bad time coming, and civilized mankind will (morally) be uncivilized before civilization can again advance.

Michael Davitt, the Irish social reformer, home ruler, and Member of Parliament, agreed with Herbert Spencer on few subjects. But at the merest mention of imperialism and jingoism Davitt worked up Spencerian passion. At least once he joked that Ireland, like other countries, should demand its share in the partition of Africa. Ordinarily, however, imperialism was not a subject to release Davitt's humor. In India, Africa, and Ireland, he declared repeatedly, the English stood for neither liberty nor humanity; quite the contrary. Indeed, the chief curse of the world of the late nineteenth century, he insisted, was the imperialism which the English had taught other peoples to imitate.[9]

Even some American Anglophiles were alarmed by the Salisbury Government's imperialism—especially in the period of the Venezuelan boundary dispute. Albert Shaw, the editor of the American *Review of Reviews,* deluged his English journalist-friends with pleas to use their connections to bring pressure to bear on their Government. Under Tory leadership, Shaw wrote to Percy Bunting, the editor of the *Contemporary Review,* "almost the whole of English public opinion has become infected with a new sort of craze for imperial dominion that quite subordinates old-fashioned scruples of conscience. . . ." The present gospel of empire, Shaw protested, was based on the assumption that "the continents of this planet exist simply as possible additions to the British empire, while the waters of the planet exist in order to make easy access for British merchantmen and British men-of-war between the home island and all the outlying parts."

Shaw was more blunt with W. T. Stead. Calling Salisbury an even worse trouble-maker than Disraeli, he expressed the hope that the return to power of the Liberals would end the imperialism that was blinding the English to considerations of right and wrong in their foreign relations. But Shaw was not too hopeful: the Liberals, he thought, were better than the Tories, but they, too, had to a shocking extent gone imperialist. They, too, were out for conquest; they, too, disregarded the rights of small powers. No question about it, Shaw told Stead, the peace and happiness of the world required the dissolution of the British Empire. Damning the British colonial system as the most unjust and objectionable of all the major political developments of the modern age, Shaw wrote:

There is nothing I long for more than to see Australia attain her independence, to see Canada adopt a flag of her own, and to see South Africa set up housekeeping as another United States. When this happens English trade will be more flourishing than ever, and all four of England's great offshoots can enter into the closest ties of offensive and defensive alliance with the mother country and with each other, and wars can be banished from the earth. The one great fact today that makes for war and discord in the world, far more than the Russian empire, is the British empire.

These words were written by an Anglophile and the editor of a journal dedicated to the promotion of more harmonious Anglo-American relations!

For their part, however, English anti-imperialists were alarmed by developments in the United States. The readiness with which Americans talked about going to war over the Venezuelan boundary dispute came as a blow to almost everybody. "As regards my countrymen," Henry James confessed to Sir John Millais, "I am mainly struck with their having grown, in my many years of absence, out of my knowledge. Still, I do know them well enough, I think, to say that the madness will evaporate." And the political economist William Smart, soon to hold the chair at Edinburgh of the father of anti-imperialism, Adam Smith, bitterly protested to an American economist, "I never heard of such nonsense as some of your newspapers have been talking."

After the Venezuelan affair came the Spanish-American War and the further growth of American jingoism—sure signs that the United States was far from immune to the imperialism of the late nineteenth-century world. To English and American anti-imperialists this new America—expansionist, aggressive, and arrogant—was a shocking departure from the country that they regarded as the hope of mankind. "What a change in the spirit of the U.S.A. within twelve months," James Bryce, the leading British authority on the United States, remarked in 1898. "They are entering a troublous period," he added sorrowfully.[10]

v

By 1899, however, English anti-imperialists had more troubles of their own to worry about. Olive Schreiner's solution for the problems of the people of South Africa—that they learn to love one another—did not work. British fears that the Boers planned to expel them and Boer fears that the British intended to drive them out precipitated a war that had long been anticipated. "It is very interesting to be in London these days and read the war news," Mark Twain wrote in October. But the disgust, the shame, the grief of the anti-imperialists—Mark Twain among them—was unspeakable. "We underestimated Chamberlain's power for mischief," James Bryce confessed. "This war is a vile business," said J. M. Robertson, the anti-imperialist journalist; and what disheartened him especially was the tone of the newspapers. It appalled him that people believed the imbecilities they read; that they did believe them was evidence of the childishness and stupidity that dominated human affairs. "My politics," Robertson confessed, "grow steadily more pessimistic: the breed seems incapable of social science for centuries yet."

But the fiery anti-imperialist poet, Robert Buchanan, reacted very differently. Despising the hooliganism that went with jingoism, he thought it imperative for writers to speak up. "My experience," he remarked, "is that there are far more people than is generally imagined whose souls are revolting against the present relapse into Barbarism, and that these people are multiplying every day." So, too, James Bryce assured an anti-imperialist editor that Scotland seemed to be opposed to the war.[11]

The war did not end so fast as the imperialists had hoped, and it went worse before it went better. "What terrible news from South Africa," a Tory newspaper proprietor rightly noted in December, 1899. But each day that passed and each setback that occurred made the anti-imperialists more righteous in their indignation. "It is turning out a far more serious matter than our people commonly supposed," the socialist artist Walter Crane wrote to an anti-imperialist friend in 1899, "and perhaps the fire-eaters will have cause to regret that they did not listen to the other side to begin with." Crane found Christmas a mockery in a country involved in such an unjust, inhumane, and immoral struggle. When some of his Fabian colleagues—led by Bernard Shaw—in effect took the side of the Salisbury Government by remaining neutral and refusing to denounce the war, Crane's fury was boundless. Even Shaw at his wiliest could not calm him down. "They tell me you are going to resign your Fabianship on account of the Imperial High Toryism of myself and others," Shaw wrote. "But don't resign from the Fabians—at least not at this moment."[12]

Anti-imperialists were overwhelmed by the casualty lists but even more by the moral and ethical losses that the war brought, and they thought of the destruction of the Transvaal Republic as the most scandalous act in English history since the burning of Joan of Arc. "Behold the beauty of a war when the work of a Chamberlain," wrote an anti-imperialist editor; but at least he consoled himself with the thought that even the defeat of the Boers would not piece the Colonial Secretary together again. Even when victory came in South Africa, declared that angry old man Goldwin Smith, military government and a standing army would also come—capital illustrations of the value of colonies to the mother country. Anti-imperialists constantly asserted their patriotism, but they acknowledged no allegiance to the predatory empire of which the imperialists wished to make England the center. They could not say of the Boer War what Henry James was to say of the First World War—that England never entered any struggle "with cleaner hands and a cleaner mind and slate." [13]

Even some imperialists had deep misgivings about the war. W. T. Stead, in particular, was outraged that the dispute had not been peacefully settled. A convert to the cause of arbitration and a leading figure at the Hague Conference that took place a few months before the Boer War began, Stead denounced the conflict as wicked and Chamberlain as the perpetrator of a heinous crime. The important thing now, he insisted, was to agitate against the war; and he expected to be jailed before he was done. "We are in great hopes that we are going to be beaten in South Africa," he told an American journalist, "and if so it will be the most splendid demonstration in favour of arbitration that could be imagined. What we have got to get into the people's mind is that God's curse will rest upon any nation that refuses arbitration."

However much Stead condemned English treatment of the Boers, anti-imperialists did not forget his jingoistic activities. As John Burns savagely but not too unjustly put it: "the tragedy of it all is that you and Rhodes are the real authors of this bad business. Your 'Big Navy,' your 'Anglo-Saxon Imperialism,' your 'Federation of the British People,' all these shibboleths, cries and catchwords have been exploited and diverted to criminal ends by the thieving murderous crew of mine owners and Peers who dominate Africa and run this Cabinet."

Unlike Stead, however, most imperialists found the war an uplifting experience. They rejoiced to think of the gentlemen of England leading farmers, clerks, and workers to victory over the cowardly, hypocritical, and dirty Boers. They were stirred, as the Tory politician and writer George Wyndham expressed it to Henley, "to see this Empire wake from sleep, and yawn and stretch its limbs to the earth's end." And they felt privileged to be able to participate. In Wyndham's words: "None of us can be the Empire. But it is much to be one of the midwives: to see the labour, but to have certitude that there will be joy in the morning." [14]

VI

Military blunders and Boer resistance delayed victory, and it slowly became plain that this would not be the short war that the Americans had just waged against the Spaniards. It was painful to discover that once fighting began there was no telling what would happen. "I have many British friends in Rome; but when we meet we talk of the antiquities and the weather," an American scholar remarked embarrassedly. In February, 1900—four months after the conflict started—Kipling turned for consolation to a military expert who was said to have predicted the end of the struggle in another two months. "If this is so," Kipling wrote, "I feel like Pepys mightily cheered." But thirteen months later the war was still on, and Henley complained indignantly that he had no idea of how it was really going; but he hoped that the English would not weaken and become overly generous to the Boers. Indeed, the imperialists were too humiliated to be able to afford to be too magnanimous, for the war lasted more than thirty-one months.[15]

The imperialists had some consolations, to be sure. They were comforted by the results of the election of 1900: although the newspapers expected them to do better, they certainly more than held their own. They were also reassured by the enthusiasm and the sense of brotherhood and solidarity that the war evoked in different parts of the Empire. Goldwin Smith scoffed at the contingent that the Canadians sent to join in the war—it was simply the result of pressures that Chamberlain brought to bear on the Canadian sycophants of English Tory imperialists. But psychologically the contingent was, as Balfour correctly said when a book on it appeared in 1901, "a most important Imperial movement." During the First World War Sir Arthur Conan Doyle rightly complimented a friend for having been among the few who, years before, had anticipated the importance of colonial troops.

The delayed victory confirmed imperialists in their belief that in the future England must be better prepared. As Kipling expressed it in a typical piece:

> So the more we work and the less we talk the better results we
> shall get—
> We have had an Imperial Licking—it will make us an Empire yet!

Continental and American Anglophiles also considered the war a useful lesson for England. Maffeo Pantaleoni, the distinguished liberal economist, insisted that the experience would require the English to modernize their fighting forces, and this he favored. For it would be fortunate for Europe, he said, if England—its only truly liberal country—were powerful. So, too, Mark Twain, although he considered the war a disgrace and a crime, felt strongly that England must not fail; otherwise the world would be dominated by Russia and Germany. "Even wrong—and she is wrong—England must be upheld. He is an enemy of the human race who shall speak against her now," Twain told a fellow antiimperialist.[16]

Both imperialists and anti-imperialists were concerned about foreign responses to their troubles with the Boers, but reactions abroad were rarely reassuring to the imperialists. Almost everywhere foreigners sided emotionally with the Boers—the more so when, after the annexation of the Transvaal and the flight of President Kruger, the Boers turned to guerrilla warfare and the British to the burning of farms and formation of concentration camps.

James Bryce and others urged that accounts of British atrocities in South Africa be received with the greatest caution; but all of Europe, as a German socialist said with only slight exaggeration, united to favor the Boers. "I am getting so sick of the constant, stupid abuse of England in all the papers here," wrote John Lockwood Kipling during a trip to France. It was bad enough that French newspapers were filled with pro-Boerism, but it was even more distressing to Kipling that walls and blank spaces everywhere were filled not only with dirty words but with "Long Live the Boers" and "Down with the English." Young Gwen Raverat, of the Darwin family—sent to Hanover to study German—was chased and stoned by street boys crying, "Watch out, you English, the Boers are coming." Indeed, pro-Boerism was so great in Germany that Professor Max Müller, the distinguished Oxford scholar, had difficulty in finding a German journal in which to publish an article defending the English position in the South African dispute.[17]

In the United States, too, the pro-Boers were outspoken. "It is wholly illogical, but nevertheless in accordance with the observed workings of human nature, that the less the Boers need sympathy, the more they get," Secretary of State John Hay wrote to Joseph Choate, the American Ambassador to Britain. Organizations raised money for the relief of Boer sufferers. Irish-American groups actively circulated accounts of English atrocities in South Africa. The American Anti-Imperialist League, the membership of which included such celebrities as Andrew Carnegie, Mark Twain, Carl Schurz, Samuel Gompers, and William Dean Howells, denounced English as well as American colonialism. And congressmen, senators, and other politicians catered to the anti-English vote. The American Anglophile Frederick William Holls was so infuriated by the widespread stereotype of the Boers as heroic underdogs that he wrote angrily to a British historian: "The fact that the so-called Republics are shams, being only oligarchies of corrupt and narrow-minded men, seems to have entirely escaped attention."

Holls could have added that pro-Boerism both in the United States and Europe was often only a disguise for hatred of England. As one American Anglophobe put it, English history now recorded not only a Bloody Mary but a Bloody Victoria. And in the savage words of another Anglophobe:

> Hurrah for the Boers! for the downfall of Monarchs,
> The Neroes of nations, the curse of the world;
> May the Twentieth century see their destruction
> And their blood-reeking flags all tattered and furled! [18]

VII

Foreign criticisms of English policy in South Africa were no more devastating than those advanced by English anti-imperialists

As Frederic Harrison reported in 1901, "I am pegging away . . . week by week against the atrocities and follies into which our insane government are dragging our poor country." Wildly cheered at the meetings he addressed, Harrison was consoled that there were others who hoped that the Boers would win. And so there were. Ouida despised the Government so much that despite the poverty and ill health of her later years she refused to accept a pension from the men who so maltreated the Boers. The poet William Watson, hating the war and the national temper from which it arose, abandoned his literary activities and wrote only to express his loathing and horror of current events. And George Gissing, convinced that England was being both morally and materially ruined, wondered that people had the courage to go on writing books.[19]

But Goldwin Smith, that worshiper of the memory of Cobden and Bright, had no self-doubts. He raged at jingoism, imperialism, and avarice as the causes of the war. He denounced Cecil Rhodes, Joseph Chamberlain, and Alfred Milner as conspirators who forced war on the Transvaal in order to gain possession of the mines. "What shame these villains have brought upon my country," he wrote to an American anti-imperialist. "An Englishman who understood the real honour and greatness of his country might well put on mourning," he added. Nor was Smith alone in impugning the personal integrity of officials in high places. Even Lord Ripon was convinced that Chamberlain was engaging in private speculations of a dubious character.[20]

Yet, if ever there was evidence that England was a free country, it was during the Boer War. Anti-imperialists protested that the press was being gagged and freedom repressed, but the fact that they could complain openly and loudly showed how little their liberty was restricted. When at the invitation of English anti-imperialists a leading Boer intellectual went to England to present the Boer case, some riots occurred at meetings that he addressed and he met with some intolerance. But he was invited, and he was permitted to enter the country that was fighting his country. And he found an English publisher who brought out his account of his experiences.

It was no surprise that the anti-Boers flooded the market with their publications, but the pro-Boers were certainly not shy. They published a staggering number of pro-Boer articles and volumes even as the war went on. Michael Davitt, working on a South African book, told T. Fisher Unwin that before publishing it he wished to make sure that he had something special to say. But few of his contemporaries, whether imperialists or anti-imperialists, had his high standards. Pro-Boers much less famous than Davitt found publishers without difficulty. In fact, Unwin was repeatedly reproached by imperialists for his pro-Boer and anti-English publications. The Countess of Jersey protested to him about one of the books that he brought out because it was a "dangerous one to be placed in Working men's and other Public Libraries, or to be given as Prizes to young people." When shortly after the end of the war Unwin published Kruger's memoirs, George Moore fittingly congratulated him: "Well, I am glad your pro-Boerism came to more than mine did." [21]

Early in the war Goldwin Smith predicted that the anti-imperialists would show their strength when peace returned. Events proved Smith to be right. The generous treatment granted to the Boers in the post-war period owed much to the efforts of anti-imperialists. But it was also due to a general revulsion to imperialism that grew up in the period after the war. Unfortunately for Joseph Chamberlain it was at this very time that he tried to link tariff reform with a strengthening of the ties of empire. And the failure of his program was partly the result of the resurgence of fears of the burdens and dangers that went with imperialism. Chamberlain had made his people too empire-conscious.

It is edifying that the war was hardly over when complaints about mass indifference to the Empire grew once more. A dedicated publicist, who wished his countrymen to wake up to the extraordinary possibilities of West Africa, had difficulty in interesting even a publisher, much less the English people. "As for the colonies," Edmund Gosse wrote bluntly, "they simply bore me." And Gosse did not speak for himself only.[22]

XVII

THE OTHER ISLAND

Nineteenth-century Irish reformers spent much of their time raging at the lethargy and apathy of their countrymen, and they had every reason to rage. For it is a mistake to suppose that many Irish were seriously concerned with the Irish Question. Even those who did show a lively interest in it could rarely agree with other reform-minded Irish. John Butler Yeats, the gifted artist and father of the poet, took pride in the contentiousness of his countrymen, comparing them favorably with the ancient Athenians. Yet the fact remains that their delight in disputation often degenerated into that curse of quarreling about which William Morris complained in the ranks of the socialists; and it was most unusual when two Irishmen, as George Moore happily phrased an unhappy truth, "set out 'to strike a blow for Ireland' without coming to blows."

Sir Robert Peel, when denounced unfairly by some of his opponents, refused to follow the example they set of harsh and abusive language. But this kind of verbal restraint was rare in the ranks of Irish reformers, whose talent for starting and prolonging venomous quarrels was extraordinary. Daniel O'Connell, the hero of the Catholic emancipation movement, was only one of many reformers who wondered why the Irish should excel in feuding.[1]

Just as Irish concern over the Irish Question has been exaggerated, so, too, English unconcern over the Irish Question has been exaggerated. Disraeli went too far when he reported in 1843 that Ireland was the only subject about which the English thought and spoke; but both before and after the Great Famine of the late forties an impressive number of English reformers agitated actively to redress Irish grievances and make Ireland less of a Pandora's box—"full of doubt and terror and difficulty." Daniel O'Connell, to be sure, rarely had kind words to speak of the English; he was, in fact, capable of delivering against them the most savage kind of tirade. Yet even O'Connell wrote of one English Member of Parliament in 1837, "As an Irishman I feel the deepest debt of gratitude for his support of every measure calculated to procure justice for Ireland." And a few years later O'Connell wrote to another sturdy English defender of Ireland, "I do not and never did forget the steady support Ireland received from you when you had it in your power to give her cause an effectual support in parliament."

It comes as no surprise that already as a young man Richard Cobden proclaimed himself willing to do almost anything to placate the justly aggrieved Irish. But even young William E. Gladstone, overflowing with Tory prejudices and fed up with priests and agitators, prayed at the time of the agitation for Catholic emancipation that the measure would be passed and that "English injustice may be removed and forgotten, that we may not expiate it by the blood of poor England." [2]

II

Long before the Famine, lawlessness had been a feature of Irish life that appalled the English, who often conveniently overlooked the lawlessness in their own society. Young Gladstone could be understanding about Irish violence and insist that it was "more excusable in them to be intemperate in their method of recovering their rights, than in the English to be intemperate in withholding and refusing them." But few of Gladstone's contemporaries could be so broadminded about the outbreaks of violence in Ireland. As an English officer stationed in Kilkenny wrote disgustedly in 1833, "There is no society—people are afraid of going out of a night; and even in the day time the officers generally carry pistols in their pockets."

During the Famine years the English stereotype of the Irish became increasingly that of a race of violent people. "London has been uneasy today with a rumor that the South of Ireland was in rebellion," Gladstone reported in 1848. For his part, Gladstone was not easily taken in, but many of his contemporaries were, for they thought of the Irish as a people who shared the sentiments that Thomas Francis Meagher expressed in a courthouse speech in 1848. In the light of Irish history, Meagher declared characteristically, "I am no criminal—I deserve no punishment. Judged by that history, the treason of which I stand convicted, loses all its guilt—has been sanctified as a duty—will be ennobled as a sacrifice." [3]

The years of the Great Famine were a traumatic experience for the Irish people; even traumatic is too mild a word to convey the severity of the impact on them of funerals, funerals, funerals, to say nothing of the hunger and disease that preceded death. Thomas Carlyle, visiting Ireland after the prolonged disaster, found the crops excellent, but he could barely look at the vast quantities of healthy potatoes; they were "too tragical to behold," he wrote, adding significantly that they were "not blighted yet." The fear that the blight would return persisted for a long time among the Irish. Even more important, the explanations of the Famine that were set forth in the late forties had tremendous staying power, and they shaped Anglo-Irish relations for the rest of the Victorian age. "It seems to me that an adequate realisation of the magnitude of this disaster is very necessary for any one who wishes to understand the Irish peasant of to-day," an Irish writer commented in 1894. The truth about the Famine quickly came to matter less than the mythology that gathered about it, and the essence of this was that the other island was responsible for Ireland's greatest misfortune. The English emerged as monsters who preached and acted on the inhuman doctrine that the best thing for Ireland was to permit the Famine to wipe out a large section of its population. The steps that the English took to deal with the unprecedented and baffling disaster were ignored. And the efforts of the dedicated English friends of Ireland were overlooked.

John Bright, returning from a visit to Ireland in 1849, was particularly outspoken about the necessity for measures to improve the condition of the country. Critical of Lord John Russell's Government because it had no systematic Irish policy and trusted too much to accident, he insisted on the urgency of healthy changes.

Land reform was the most pressing need, Bright declared, arguing that it was both insane and criminal to sacrifice a whole people to maintain a small number of landlords. Bright's central idea was that land reform would make Ireland a peaceful country, and this in turn would encourage capital investments, new settlements, the further growth of wealth, and the improvement of the standard of living of the Irish people.[4]

Emigration—despite the dangers that it involved—was the main English answer to the Irish Question. "It will solve a very painful political problem," as a contemporary typically put it, "and there will after all be plenty of inhabitants left for the requirements of a pastoral country which Ireland ought in a great measure to be." But it was hard for Irish patriots to take this view. Constantly exposed to the shrieks of their people as they emigrated, they witnessed the personal tragedies that occurred each time a boat left for the United States. If Ireland was worth fighting for, they reasoned, it must certainly be worth living in.

Long before the Famine, some Irish had discovered that they could manage better in the United States than in the best house in Ireland. But during and after the Famine large numbers of Irish made this discovery, and as they made it they nursed their wrath against England. Nor was this all. Already in pre-Famine times Irish reformers had been able to secure aid from American sympathizers, who, as a committee from Philadelphia wrote to Daniel O'Connell in 1838, had a deep interest in "the land which gave them birth, where abide the tombs of their fathers, and where still live hundreds of thousands of people who are their near and dear relations." But in post-Famine times Irish reformers had unprecedented American resources on which to draw. "The aspect of the streets," wrote a British consular official in New York on St. Patrick's Day in 1867, "might lead a stranger to suppose that the population consisted entirely of that happy nationality.'

Often, to be sure, Irish-Americans raised more of a clamor about the Irish Question than the Irish themselves, and as early as 1848 the English had reason to express anxiety over what an eminent aristocrat called without exaggeration "the very extensive plan of the Irish leaders connected with American sympathizers." Twenty years later, however, the ties were much closer. All well informed English, Charles Dickens wrote, recognized "a gather ing cloud in the west considerably bigger than a man's hand, under which a powerful Irish-American body, rich and active, is always drawing Ireland in that direction." No doubt about it, there was truth in the remark that no country had less ability to hold its people than Ireland, but that no people were more emotional about their homeland once they left it.[5]

III

Despite occasional outbreaks of violence, Ireland was more tranquil during the early fifties than it had been for years. John Bright, visiting the country, was rightly impressed by the bitterness that divided the Irish sects and parties. And this limited their effectiveness. It was one thing for the editors of the *Irish Quarterly Review* to announce that they would continue to give their earnest attention to questions of reform; but these questions invariably became entangled in ruinous personality clashes and savage outbursts of personal abuse. It was no accident that when James Stephens, that most uncivil of civil engineers, organized the Fenians in 1858 he stressed above all the need for unity and obedience. "I believe it essential to success," he wrote, "that the *centre* of this, or any similar organisation, should be perfectly unshackled—in other words, a provisional dictator. On this point I can, conscientiously, concede nothing." [6]

Even the Fenians—although they have sometimes been treated as a well-knit group—were speedily beset by dissensions. Irish freedom was their goal, and they were eager to work and suffer and sacrifice for its achievement, insisting with James Stephens that they could no more be diverted from their aims than stars could be wrested from their orbits. Already by 1860, however, some of Stephens's colleagues had such serious misgivings about him that they tried to depose him. Some deplored "the degrading serfdom imposed on us by this man." Others, while they were sure that the work of the Fenians could be accomplished, doubted that Stephens was the man to do it, for he was too radical in his social views, and he went about needlessly intruding them in private society.

Stephens's supporters insisted that "the confidence of our shareholders in James" could not be upset, but it constantly was. As a result, they were endlessly in the position of trying to rescue

him and themselves from "the vile calumny of the base, and un-
scrupulous men, who have been endeavoring, through motives of
ambition and emulation, wilfully and malevolently to asperse the
characters and blast the justly earned popularity of the purest,
the noblest, the most self-sacrificing—and . . . the most trusted
Irish patriots of the present day." This rhetoric was important
because it recurred so often. One reform movement after another
was stricken—and buried—with it.[7]

Stephens rejoiced in the reputation that the Fenians early acquired as firebrands who would plunge Ireland into a bloody
civil war, but this reputation seriously restricted their ability to
raise money with which to carry on their activities. Stephens and
other Fenian leaders complained chronically that they were without means and that the men of property were against them. And
the American Civil War made fund-raising difficult in the United
States. "The want of money has been a far greater injury than
all our enemies could have done us," Stephens repeatedly told
American Fenians in the early sixties; but despite his persistent
appeals he often had to acknowledge that he had received nothing
worth mentioning from the United States. So little money was
coming in by late 1863 that Stephens resorted to the dubious
device of founding a paper as an income-producer. This did not
help, and frustrated Fenians damned those who did not sell "all
but the clothes on their backs for dear old Ireland!" Although
by 1867 the Fenians in the United States had formed 374 circles,
their financial troubles were immense. Their exchequer, the
Governor-General of Canada cheerfully yet accurately reported,
was at a low point. Even more important, he added, "the failures
of their warlike operations in Ireland and Canada have so discredited the efficiency of the organisation as an instrument of of-
fense against England that they find it impossible to raise funds!"[8]

The combination of internal dissensions and restricted financial
resources had hampered the Fenians during the early years of their
existence. By the late sixties their situation was as precarious as
ever. Fenians both privately and publicly denounced other Fenians, and efforts to achieve harmony and unity failed. So, too,
did attempts to raise money; and agents for the Irish Republic,
seeking to sell bonds that were to be redeemed six months after

Irish independence was achieved, had a hard time disposing of them. Dedicated Jeremiah O'Donovan Rossa, alarmed by the growth of disaffection among Fenians, reported their "determination to skedoodle shortly if there is not some appearance of Fight." Even Stephens thought it a miracle that "we have been able to hold out." If the critical state of Fenian affairs were known, he confessed, "I should either consent to move at once and as we are or dissolve the organisation." In short, the outbreaks of Fenian violence that occurred in the late sixties were measures undertaken by disappointed and desperate members of a group that was a group in name only. They reflected the weakness of the Fenians, not their strength.[9]

IV

The fears that the Fenians inspired in the English were both well founded and imaginary. It is true that the newspapers of the time played an important part in creating and sustaining a sense of panic; but they could do so because there was a sufficient basis in fact to make all kinds of fictions concerning the Fenians seem credible. No government building, according to the popular view, was secure as long as Fenians were about. And the life expectancy of every official—from the Queen and the Archbishop of Canterbury to the most minor bureaucrat—was decidedly limited. Fenians, after all, were pledged "to wage war in the name of the Irish Republic on the troops or other forces of Queen Victoria wherever they may be found."

The panic created by Fenianism was not confined to nannies and hysterics who needed a bogey. Robert Curzon spoke for many of his sober-minded contemporaries when he wrote in 1867, "I hope the government will take some decisive steps to protect old fogies like me from all these Fenian outrages, for really people are safer in Turkey than they are here." And Charles Dickens, staying at the Shelburne Hotel in Dublin, was rightly impressed by the alarm of the English in Ireland: "The Hotel is constantly filling and emptying, as families leave the country, set in a current to steamers." Indeed, the strain of life in Dublin was so great that the American consul petitioned Congress for compensation for special services. The imprisonment of Americans who were charged with participation in Fenian insurrections, he explained to the Secretary of State, entailed "the most fatiguing labor, often continued far into the night, which was so severe and protracted that it resulted in my complete physical prostration." [10]

In the years of Fenian atrocities it was impossible for the English to believe that the conspirators acted for only a tiny segment of the population. It was easier to suppose that all the Irish— whether they lived in Ireland, England, or the United States— were Fenians. The Home Office, to be sure, kept in close touch with the chief constables in those English towns which had a large Irish population, and it was remarkably well informed as to the meetings, plans, and membership of the Fenians. The Secretary of State for War distributed arms in counties and towns where threats were thought to exist, and during the election of 1868 extra precautions were taken against possible Fenian outbreaks. Special constables were appointed and, as in the period of the Chartist scare of 1848, town authorities were warned of the possibility that those who consented to serve might "not be of a class on which much reliance can be placed." At the same time the Home Office cautioned local officials not to use government-lent arms in mere election riots; there had to be clear evidence that the riots were inspired by the Fenians.[11]

It is no surprise that anti-Irish sentiment in England reached a new high in the late sixties. But it is surprising that despite this hostile setting a number of English politicians pressed hard for Irish reforms. Often, to be sure, such Members of Parliament as John Bright, John Stuart Mill, and Gladstone were damned as traitors for their efforts to pacify Ireland in any way other than military. But they had the integrity and the courage to urge moderation and reform at a time when the memory of Fenian outrages was fresh and the fear of further atrocities was widespread— at a time when the English people, as one highly placed official put it, were "awakening to the necessity of these reckless desperadoes being put down."

· To Bright, Mill, and Gladstone, the Irish Question was mainly a moral question, and it aroused in them deep feelings of shame and guilt. It is revealing, for instance, that when in 1868 a Frenchman proposed a translation of *England and Ireland,* Mill gave his consent only on condition that he should receive no royalties: he was repelled by the thought of earning money from a book on that painful subject.[12]

Since John Bright was a central figure on the English political scene in the late sixties, his view of the Irish Question—which he discussed repeatedly with Gladstone—was particularly important. Long and outspokenly critical of English treatment—or what he regarded as nontreatment—of the Irish, Bright rightly enjoyed the respect of many Irish reformers. The widow of an Irish revolutionist, sending him a copy of her husband's memoirs, told him that she ventured to do so because of the generous interest he took in the cause of her unhappy country. It was this kind of reputation that helps to explain why Bright was one of the few prominent English politicians of the late sixties who dared not only to visit Dublin, but to speak there at an open meeting in defense of the Union and even to hope that he had done some good.

Bright was aware that the Government had the resources to suppress insurrections in Ireland, but his argument was that until the English learned to rule wisely and justly there would be a long series of outbreaks. "Ireland is our humiliation," he wrote in 1866 to Horace Greeley, the friend of many an Irish political refugee, "and our ruling class prefer occasional riot and civil war to remedial legislation." Although Bright deplored Fenianism, he interpreted it as a response to English misgovernment of Ireland. It was absurd to wait for insurrections and then to act, he insisted. The English should meet the ungenerous deeds of the Fenians with unprecedented measures of kindness. "For twenty years," Bright told a Dubliner in 1868, "I have always said that the only way to remedy the evils of Ireland is by legislation on the Church and the Land." Indeed, a letter that Bright wrote to an American abolitionist during the Civil War throws a great deal of light on his own attitude towards the Irish: "You will derive much satisfaction from your labors on behalf of the Negro. To have lifted from his back only a portion of the burden under which he has groaned, will be a blessing to you in a day to come, more than can be derived from the results of successful ambition. I wish you every success, and all the consolation and recompense which God gives to those who act justly by the suffering ones of his creatures." What Negro slaves were to the abolitionist the Irish were to Bright.[13]

V

Historians and publicists have often viewed the Irish laws passed during Gladstone's Ministry of 1868–74 as concessions that did too little and came too late, but they have underestimated the difficulties of the setting in which the legislation was enacted. The reformers found it hard to overcome what John Bright called "the prejudices and ignorance of the English ruling class." And Fenianism convinced many people that they must make no concessions to the Irish because to yield was to encourage still more bullying. Furthermore—and this point has often been forgotten— Gladstone did not have the stature in pre-Ministry days that he acquired after he became Prime Minister. Nor were the Liberals of that period of the same stature as those who assumed power in December, 1868. Gladstone did not know how far he could go, and his political position compelled him to speak with reserve and caution about Irish matters, for many Whigs were wary of tampering with the Church and the land. As John Bright revealingly remarked as late as January, 1868: "The Liberal Party is not in a good position for undertaking any great measure of Statesmanship. Some Whigs distrust Mr. Gladstone, and some who call themselves Radicals dislike him. He does not feel himself very secure as leader of a powerful and compact force. The Whig Peers are generally feeble and timid, and shrink from anything out of the usual course. We want a strong man—with strong brain and convictions for a work of this kind, and I do not see him among our public men." In these circumstances, the reforms of the Gladstonians, far from being of the too little and too late variety, did much and came early. For their time they were extraordinary achievements.

The statute for the disestablishment and partial disendowment of the (Anglican) Church of Ireland was especially notable. Passed at a time when Darwinism, higher criticism, agnosticism, and atheism were on the ascendant, it was bitterly resisted by Anglicans; Connop Thirlwall, Bishop of St. David's, stood out as one of the very few Anglican clergyman who supported it. The great

Anglican fear was that once disestablishment began it would not stop. "It is a difficult and dangerous question," wrote the unbending Anglican Robert Curzon, "as of course the Welsh church will go next, and then the English. Which will be capital sport for the Pope, the dissenters, and the devil." Curzon hoped that the Queen, as defender of the faith, would remember her coronation oath and resume the use of the royal veto. His disgust with the House of Commons was overpowering. He even came to suspect that Guy Fawkes was perhaps right after all.

Curzon's reaction was much more extreme than that of most of his fellow-Anglicans, many of whom counted on public indifference to defeat the measure. They argued that the Irish would not be grateful for the destruction of the Established Church, and that the masses of new voters did not care about the issue. "I doubt whether, in England, there is any very strong feeling in favor of the bill," an Anglican clergyman remarked characteristically, adding that it was simply the reformist press that was stirring up trouble. Disestablishment, an old acquaintance of Gladstone similarly noted, "seems to create little more interest than the disfranchisement of a corrupt Borough would have done ten years ago." [14]

It is revealing that both enemies and friends of disestablishment engaged in anti-Catholic outbursts. Opponents of the measure, arguing that Romanism was the principal source of Irish miseries, predicted that disestablishment would worsen the plight of Ireland. And they pointed with pride to the long tradition of Anglican missions to the Irish Roman Catholics and to the need for more such missions. Friends of the measure insisted that the strength of Roman Catholicism was due to the privileges of the hated Church of Ireland. Remove these privileges of the Anglicans, and Roman Catholicism, which had long flourished because of persecution, would lose much of its appeal. This belief was held by Charles Dickens, among many others. In language reminiscent of his friend Carlyle, Dickens raged at the "hundreds of thousands of pestilent boobies (pandered to by politicians)" who supposed that the Church of Ireland was a bulwark against Roman Catholicism; "as a crying grievance," he told Anthony Trollope in 1868, "it has been Popery's trump card!"

That the measure was carried was due to the conviction of the

Gladstonians that harmony between England and Ireland required the removal of religion as a source of friction. And John Bright and other dissenters could rejoice that they had adhered fearlessly and uncompromisingly to their opposition to the very idea of a state church.

Gladstone, to be sure, was widely and viciously denounced. Indeed, it is understandable that he refused to become involved in other conflicts—the dispute, for instance, over the marriage of a man and his deceased wife's sister—for, as he said in a masterpiece of understatement, he was "involved in a greater controversy." On the one hand, Gladstone was accused of being another Charles II—a secret Roman Catholic—a charge that plagued him for years. On the other, he was condemned as an opportunist who would wreck his own church for the sake of personal ambition and power. The truth is, however, that Gladstone had long deplored "the sickening extent and miserable effects of that worship of idols and deification of impostures which still forms so large a part of Statecraft as regards its ecclesiastical relations." And even as a very old man—in 1897—he derived "much satisfaction from every fresh effort to withstand and baffle the incessant efforts of the Papacy to establish absolutism in the Church of Christ." [15]

A resolution seconded by Ernest Jones and adopted at a meeting in Salford in 1868 admirably summed up the arguments advanced by the Gladstonians: "the claims of justice, the peace of Ireland, and the welfare of the United Kingdom," the resolution stated, required that the Church of Ireland should cease as a state establishment. To Gladstone and to some of his advisers, moreover, a vital consideration was the international disrepute that the Church of Ireland had brought to England. As Goldwin Smith counseled Gladstone, "In speaking about the Irish Church I hope you will not forget to point out how such a proof (as it is inevitably taken to be) of the injustice of our Government excites the foreign sympathy which makes Irish disaffection really dangerous." Gladstone acted on Smith's advice.[16]

VI

If church reform in a setting of Fenian outrages and anti-Irish feeling was difficult, so, too, was land reform; but, as John Bright hopefully pointed out, "not being a *religious* difficulty perhaps men may regard it with more of practical common sense." Like church reform, land reform threatened powerful vested interests, and it inspired fears that dangerous precedents were being set. "I wish one knew what Mr. Gladstone's land bill is to be and if it is one which a grand Irish Landlord can accept," one panicky contemporary said. To be sure, the Land Act that was passed in 1870 went too far for some people and not far enough for others; some were convinced that it would benefit only Irish lawyers. But what mattered was that any land law was passed at all—that Parliament had legislated, however hesitantly and inadequately, concerning landlord-tenant relations in Ireland.[17]

The Gladstonians were not smug about their Irish reforms; they did not suppose that they had solved the Irish problem. For it was, after all, no easy task, as John Bright rightly remarked, to remove abuses that had developed in the course of many generations of unsalutary neglect. Yet the decisive point was that despite strong opposition the Gladstonians had acted to eliminate certain glaring evils, and that they would not hesitate to act again.

The Gladstonians had met Fenian violence with kindness and generosity, and Irish reformers could no longer doubt that they had powerful friends in England. Irish Catholics, Gladstone was assured frequently, appreciated the church and land reforms with which his name was identified. It is significant that when Disraeli became Prime Minister in 1874 one of his first important actions was to plan a visit to Ireland. Although the trip was called off because he was stricken with a severe attack of gout, the intention— not its consummation—was what counted. It is edifying, nevertheless, that for many years afterwards Irish reformers insisted that the illness that prevented Disraeli from keeping his engagement was diplomatic. Such was the distrust that warped Irish views of English intentions.[18]

⸘XVIII⸘

THE HEYDAY OF THE
LAND AGITATION

Ten years after the passage of the Land Act—when Gladstone began his second Ministry—Irish reformers were in a much stronger position than before. They had outspoken and powerful English supporters in Parliament and the press; voters in English towns included increasing numbers of workers of Irish origin; and the continued growth of the Irish-American population meant that there were more and more people to whom reformers could appeal for funds. Above all, however, the improved position of Irish reformers was due to two events: the adoption in 1872 of the secret ballot, which helped to end the domination by landlords of Irish seats in the House of Commons; and the coming of the Great Depression, which served to overcome that lethargy of the peasantry that had so long hindered the Irish cause.

II

"I am not at all satisfied with the position or working of the Home Rule Association," Isaac Butt wrote candidly in 1872 to a parliamentary colleague. Butt, an Irish Protestant lawyer and economist, had made his reputation by defending Fenian prisoners; and he had written an important book on the Land Act of 1870. He was, in a word, a natural choice for the leadership of the Irish home rule movement. The difficulty was, however, that he had few people to lead—so widespread was Irish apathy. Butt recognized that the Home Rule Association, formed in 1870, required wider support and a more efficient organization, but a conference held in Dublin in 1873 to meet these needs had disappointing results. While Butt was sure that it had helped to make the public more aware of the home rule cause, he conceded readily that it did little to improve the financial position or to increase the membership of his group.[1]

When after the election of 1874 Disraeli's Tories controlled the Government, Irish prospects seemed unpromising. Irish Members of Parliament, as John Bright rightly told Gladstone, "have no cohesion and no respect for each other—and no faith in their leader, and they are utterly helpless separated from the English and Scotch Liberals." That very year, however, twenty-nine-year-old Charles Stewart Parnell took his seat in the House of Commons. By 1877 the battle between Butt and Parnell was well under way, and the old leader wrote to his colleagues: "You have seen no doubt the correspondence between me and Mr. Parnell which has been published in the papers. It is of the greatest importance that the opinion of a full meeting of our party should with as little delay as possible be expressed upon the questions raised in that correspondence." Butt's defeat signified the end of the method of gentle persuasion; Parnell's victory meant a "get-tough" policy. Butt died soon after his defeat, and in a short while he was virtually forgotten. Indeed, his small group of loyal admirers had every reason to complain that his contributions to the struggle for home rule were not simply belittled but ignored.

If English politicians were appalled by the change from Butt to Parnell, they had good cause. As one Tory Member of Parliament accurately said of Parnell in 1879: "Here was a man, who, without eloquence, without wit, without humour, and without anything but sheer, stolid, determined obstinacy and obstruction in him, had contrived to block the business of Parliament and bring the national representation into discredit and dishonour." Parnell's methods upset the English—so much so, that Queen Victoria offered to intervene to help bring about an agreement on the measures to be taken to prevent further Parnellite obstruction. In fact, when the author of a standard *Handbook of Parliamentary Procedure* reported that it needed thorough revision because of the recent revolution in parliamentary procedure, he did not have to explain that Parnell had had much to do with the changes that were made. Yet while it is true that Irish obstructionist methods disturbed the English, it is no less true that these tactics delighted Irish-Americans. The upshot was that badly needed contributions grew impressively.[2]

III

In the very years that Parnell and his followers in Parliament were making nuisances of themselves, the position of the agricultural classes in Ireland deteriorated sharply. The depression was serious enough in its own right, what with bad harvests and falling prices making tenant farmers less and less able to pay their rents. Yet what made the depression even worse was that it revived memories of past disasters, most notably of the Great Famine. Furthermore—and this has often been overlooked—rural distress soon affected conditions in Irish towns. By early 1880 the Lord Mayor of Dublin was justly alarmed by the increase in the number of people receiving relief. He had not even had time to prepare a summary statement of the plight of his town, he reported, "for in truth we are so overwhelmed with work and the situation is daily becoming so much more grave, that we are, in the first place, scarcely able to overtake our work, and in the next what would be only literally true one day would be less than true in a week hence." [3]

Parnell and his parliamentary followers were suspicious of the social radicalism that the agricultural distress was encouraging. For all that, Parnell consented in 1879 to become president of Michael Davitt's newly founded Land League. He hoped that by playing an active role in the League he could win more converts to home rule as well as increased support from overseas. He would make use of the Fenians in the League but at the same time maintain his own independence.

Shortly after his election, Parnell visited the United States for a purpose of which there was no doubt; and such visits by other Irish leaders took place increasingly. In the United States they found the Irish National Land League and other Irish-American groups busily at work reminding American citizens—both native and adopted—of "poor down-trodden Ireland," and the Irish-Irish added their pleas to those of the Irish-Americans. As early as 188

Parnell reported to Henry George that two of his parliamentary colleagues were so adept as money-raisers that they were accomplishing more for the cause in the United States than they could possibly do in Parliament. Yet it is not strange that Irish visitors found their missions to America a strain: they had arduous itineraries with endless speaking engagements. As Michael Davitt, that veteran of many a money-raising campaign in the United States, was to remark towards the end of his life: "Nothing will induce me to undergo again the torture of that kind of work. I have done it once or twice too often when a dozen years younger than I am now."

In *The Land-Leaguers* (1882), his grim posthumously published novel, Anthony Trollope raged at Americans for underwriting Irish violence. And some Americans—John Bright's friend John Greenleaf Whittier among them—considered it improper for their countrymen to meddle in Anglo-Irish affairs. But Irish-Americans did not think so, and Irish reformers urged them on, calling for more and more meddling—and more and more money.[4]

From the start Land Leaguers differed widely among themselves. Some supported far-reaching changes, and some favored only mild reforms. Henry George, eager for converts to his scheme of land nationalization, was alarmed by the amount of moderation that he found among Leaguers as well as by what he regarded as their mismanagement of their resources and opportunities: "Sometimes it seems to me as if a lot of small men had found themselves in the lead of a tremendous movement and finding themselves being lifted into importance and power they never dreamed of are jealous of anybody else sharing the honor." But what the members of the Land League really thought mattered much less than the popular impression of them that speedily emerged. According to the public image, they were revolutionaries with a taste for violence; they had no respect for life or property; and they would stop at nothing. Michael Davitt, the chief figure in the League, had been an active Fenian agent who before his imprisonment had engaged in the surreptitious transmission of arms from England to Ireland. To be a Leaguer was to be a Michael Davitt.

This, of course, was nonsense. The Fenians in the League were, as a well-informed Member of Parliament told Joseph Chamberlain, "more noisy and energetic than numerous." And Davitt stood much to the left of his colleagues, who were constantly alarmed—even before his conversion to Henry George's doctrines—by his denunciations of landlordism. It is true that even moderate Leaguers were critical of the preponderance of large landed estates in Ireland, and they were even more critical of absentee landlords who drew off large sums each year from a small and poor country. For the rest, the changes that they sought were slight compared to those favored by Davitt and the ultra-Leaguers. Indeed, it is revealing that already in 1880 some English Members of Parliament were remarking that Davitt's influence on Parnell was having desirable effects from the English point of view. Their reasoning was that Parnell's followers in Parliament would withdraw from the League if their leader continued to act under Davitt's dictation. Gladstone's Government had a grand opportunity to win over many of the Leaguers who regarded Davitt as a wild man.[5]

IV

The fears that the Land League aroused in England were enormous, and many English thanked God that they were not Irish landlords. At the same time, however, whether they were Tories or Liberals, they were increasingly determined to meet Irish violence with superior English force. Jingos, as Gladstone noted in 1880, were having a grand time clamoring for every conceivable kind of repression in Ireland. To Joseph Chamberlain and John Bright, however—and they were both important figures in Parliament—the policy of coercion was shortsighted. Chamberlain even threatened to resign over the question.

To pacify Ireland, Chamberlain told Gladstone, it would not suffice, as in earlier times, to remove from the scene a small band of conspirators and members of secret societies: even if half the country were arrested the position of landlords would still be intolerable. Chamberlain accurately argued that agrarian discontent was responsible for only a tiny number of serious disturbances; and despite the activities of Land Leaguers, he pointed out, rents were being paid throughout most of Ireland. Nevertheless, disaffection was both widespread and justified, and the only way to deal with it, he insisted, was through remedial legislation. If the Government made clear its intentions concerning land reform, the agitation in Ireland would collapse and die. Sympathetic towards tenants who had been abused for so long, Chamberlain favored guaranteeing to them the three F's (fair rent, fixity of tenure, and free sale). A bill incorporating these concessions, he shrewdly told Gladstone, "will be accepted by all but the few extreme men who

"BRAVO, WILLIAM!"

Sensation Scene from Melodrama " The Land Bill," Act II.

WILLIAM STRIKES AN ATTITUDE, DEFIES HIS ENEMIES, AND DEFENDS HIS BILL.

Fun, May 25, 1881

are not Land reformers at all, but Fenians and rebels using the Land question for their own purposes." [6]

John Bright also insisted that land reform was the only way out of the difficulties of Anglo-Irish relations. To break the strength of

Parnell and Company, he argued, the English had to show their good will and good intentions in parliamentary action. Bright, for his part, had no doubt that the aims of the Parnellites went far beyond the reform of the Irish land system: they were simply using the agrarian distress for their own ends. Even so, Bright believed that the campaign against rent and landlordism would wear itself out if the Government legislated wisely. He correctly anticipated that there would be strong English opposition to new laws "on the ground of the violation of 'free contract' and of the received rules of political Economy." But the vast majority of Irish tenants would be satisfied, he assured Gladstone in 1880, and Land Leaguers would no longer be in a position to carry on their vile activities.[7]

The policy of land reform, according to the Gladstonians, was justified by the enlightened self-interest of England. If fresh coercive measures were adopted before concessions were made, they argued, the result would be that moderate and ultra Leaguers would unite against the English. But the Gladstonians' conception of what was good for their country differed widely from that of many of their contemporaries, who clamored for bigger and better displays of force against Land Leaguers. The abuse that was heaped on Gladstone because of his conciliatory policy reached unexampled heights. Edward Carpenter's father spent the last years of his life vilifying the Liberal leader. "Has any one, I wonder, even of his own family, ventured to wish Mr. Gladstone a happy new year today?" Colonel William Bromley Davenport, Tory landlord and Member of Parliament, asked in 1881 in a letter to a newspaper editor. "I entirely agree with you," wrote a likeminded Tory advocate of coercion, "that another Oliver Cromwell is needed to Pacify Ireland and that it would have been a good thing for the country generally if W. E. Gladstone had been finally placed in Westminster Abbey before he made his electioneering tour in Scotland."

There was, in fact, no base motive of which Gladstone was not accused. As Davenport savagely put it in one of the poems—"The Premier's Soliloquy"—that he wrote to make his life in Parliament endurable:

> Though sweet to my colleagues and me
> 'Twixt landlords and tenants the strife,
> 'Tis sweeter, far sweeter, to see
> The Landowner run for his life.

Davenport concluded with these lines:

> Half the land thus besprinkled with gore
> Shall belong to the tenant that delves;
> Then shoot me a few owners more,
> And I'll give you the whole for yourselves.[8]

In the light of the vilifications to which he was subjected in the early eighties—"Gladstone! Worse and Worse!"—it is perhaps understandable that he did not adhere strictly to his old rule of refusing the requests of correspondents for his autograph: it was doubtless pleasant to hear that some people still approved of him. The fact that Gladstone went ahead, despite the hostility he met, was due to several things. He was fresh from a great electoral victory; most of his party stood solidly behind him; and he was bolstered by expressions of confidence from people like the labor leader Henry Broadhurst, who actively favored Irish land law reform.

But Gladstone's character also had much to do with his conduct, for his self-image required him to act according to what he considered the standard of proper Christian behavior. And, as he himself was aware, his good health and his advanced age gave him enormous advantages. Charles Darwin, born like Gladstone in 1809, complained repeatedly that old age was telling on him and that he found it hard to deal with difficult topics or even with more than one topic at a time. Gladstone, on the contrary, functioned best when the subjects piled up—and even then he found time for a little relaxation with his beloved Homer. When Gladstone warmed to his work, as many contemporaries noted, his years dropped away and he was young again. Furthermore, as he himself well knew, his age gave him a certain freedom of action and immunity from criticism. As he phrased it to John Bright, that other grand old man of Victorian politics: "It is I think one of the advantages of the last stage of public life that one may use it to say things which, though true and needful in themselves, could not properly be said by any man with twenty or even ten years of his career before him." [9]

V

Gladstone introduced his Irish land legislation in April, 1881, and young Arthur J. Balfour was not the only Member of Parliament to grumble that with land bills and the like he had little time left to himself. The Tory opposition was strong; and, to the disgust of Gladstone and Bright, the Irish group in Parliament, filled with hostility and rebelliousness, caused innumerable difficulties, for they did not want the measure to pass. As Bright wrote: "they are against anything that will tend to pacify the Country, and are working in league with the American Irish Fenian conspiracy—from which come the large funds subscribed weekly, and the outrages which disgrace and alarm the Country." For the rest of his life it rankled Bright—and understandably so—that the Parnellites were so hostile to those English reformers who, long before Parnell had ever been heard of, had been fighting for justice for Ireland.

The Land Act that was finally passed in 1881 went too far for some critics and not far enough for others; but in the light of contemporary conditions it was a remarkable measure. It was passed at a time when anti-Irish feeling ran high because of the atrocities of some Land Leaguers—at a time when landlords were convinced that Gladstone, Bright, and Chamberlain were intent on their extermination—at a time when it was widely believed that with the three F's the Irish peasant would be more than ever at the mercy of moneylenders. To the distress of the William Bromley Davenports of England, the Gladstonian conviction that "Something Must Be Done" triumphed. As Davenport expressed it:

> Though Irish landlords, as a rule,
> Have done their duty well
> Perchance some impecunious fool
> Has tried his rent to swell;
> But yet 'tis wrong, convinced I am,
> For Pat to take his gun
> And shoot him through the diaphragm;
> Still—"Something must be done." [10]

Along with land reform went the abundant use of repression, for Gladstone's Ministry, as Chamberlain correctly told Henry George, was "driven by public opinion." Parnell was arrested for inciting his countrymen to intimidate tenants who took advantage of the provisions of the Land Act; the Land League was suppressed by proclamation; and freedom of speech, press, and assembly were severely restricted. Further arrests occurred, and jokes about jails circulated on a large scale. There was no point in sending an artist to Ireland, a writer told an American editor, for by the time he arrived the whole population of the South of Ireland would be in jail. Indeed, kindhearted Arnold Toynbee returned from a visit to Ireland in such a state of nervous excitement that when a friend called on him Mrs. Toynbee begged him not to talk to her husband about what he had seen.

Henry George, coming to Ireland for the first time, was similarly outraged. "Surely the masses of the English people," he wrote to an American, "cannot understand the sort of government that they are maintaining here, and how the first principles of human liberty are being trodden under foot by an irresponsible dictatorship wielded in the interests of a panic stricken and maddened class." Except for Russia, George considered the British Government in Ireland the worst in Europe. "Don't be uneasy about anything you hear of us here," he told his son. "The worst that could happen would be to go to jail, and that is an honor in this country." So, too, Mrs. George, planning to attend a meeting of the Ladies' Land League, warned her children that she might be arrested. "If I am so honored don't get alarmed," she wrote spiritedly, "it will sell Papa's books like hot cakes and I will live in grand style."

But neither George nor his wife understood the extent to which the English had been stirred up not only by Irish outrages against landlords and livestock but by the reluctance of the Irish Members of Parliament to denounce these outrages. "God grant that our just indignation may not degenerate into the weakness of vengeance or panic," wrote the Bishop of Salford in 1882 following the cold-blooded murder of two British officials in Phoenix Park, Dublin. But after years of reports of heinous crimes against men as well as cattle in Ireland it was hard for many English to be forgiving.[11]

VI

Henry George's private letters written from Ireland in 1882 make clear the extent to which Irish land reformers were (to his disgust and despair) moderate in their plans and hopes for the future. George himself, thoroughly fed up with Gladstone's Government, looked forward to the collapse of the Liberal Party and to the formation of a truly progressive party that would see in land reform the beginning of a genuine revolution. But few Irish leaders agreed with him. It was bad enough, George complained, that those who managed the Land League were very far from radical. Worse still, they viewed him with suscipion and fear; "from the very first," he confessed, "I could feel the distrust of the Parnellites." Parnell himself, George found after a lengthy conversation, was "no more radical on the land question than the rest of them." He as well as that other important Irish leader, John Dillon, would have nothing to do with schemes that went beyond the encouragement of peasant proprietorship. Although the facts were unpleasant, George faced up to them: "that the conservative influences in the management of the League have come out in full force, and that they want to settle the land question before it goes too far." In a word, George recognized that his work had to be done not only without the help of the moderate Leaguers but with their active opposition.[12]

George had pinned his hopes mainly on Davitt, who favored land nationalization and the single-tax program, and he tried to reassure himself that, if nothing else, his presence in Ireland had served to encourage and fortify his disciple. At times George was jubilant: "Michael Davitt is full of the idea of popularizing 'Progress and Poverty.' That was the first thing he said to me. He had read it twice before, and he read it twice again . . . and as you may see from his speeches and letters he believes in it entirely. He says if a copy of that book can be put in every workman's club and Land League and library in the three kingdoms the revolution will be made." George's family was no less excited about the implications of Davitt's active support of the doctrine that the land should belong to the people. For such a man to proclaim boldly his support of the nationalization of the Irish land, remarked Henry George, Jr., was the realization of his father's dream.

Time and again, however, George was disappointed. "Davitt is all right," George assured an American friend. "He believes just as we do, but he is very much afraid of breaking up the movement, and is sensitive to the taunt that he has been 'captured by Henry George and the *Irish World.*'" The upshot was that Davitt went so far as to avoid being seen in the presence of George. Indeed, even when Davitt came out for nationalization with compensation,

George, though he strongly opposed the proposal, tried to be understanding about it. For he appreciated the strength of the opposition that Davitt had to face. The main trouble, George concluded, was that the Irish masses were insufficiently informed on the land question. Even so, he continued to hope that they were ahead of their leaders and that the course of events would prepare the way for land nationalization and the single tax.

A letter of apology that Davitt wrote in 1886 when George ran for mayor of New York admirably sums up the plight of the ultra Leaguers: "Your telegram says you were deeply grieved at my silence. A moment's reflection will convince you that I could not speak during your canvass without being guilty of an unwarranted interference in an American Election on the one hand, and running an almost certain risk of bringing out Parnell or some other powerful opponent of your principles among the Parliamentary Party who would be induced to attack you in retaliation for my support." [13]

VII

The combination of land reform and coercion did not work as effectively and as speedily as the Gladstonians had wished, but at first their hopes ran high. As early as December, 1881, Joseph Chamberlain optimistically told Gladstone that the power of the Land League was broken—that the League had lost the backing of the farmers and retained the support only of the Fenians and the rabble. Six months later, however, Chamberlain was more restrained in his analysis of the Irish situation. He did not despair because the centuries-old Question had not vanished as if by magic because a Liberal Ministry was in office. Chamberlain's well-taken point was that agrarian outrages were fewer owing to the operation of the Land Act of 1881. For the rest, he insisted that the English had to continue to work to remove those remaining irritations that caused Irish disaffection.

Gladstone, for his part, tried not to be overoptimistic. "The face of Ireland is like the harvest in England, singularly various," he told Chamberlain in his best scholarly manner. "From some parts come good and sanguine accounts, from others the accents of despair." In short, Gladstone had no notion that he had ended the

Irish Question, and he remained alive to the difficulties that remained.[14]

The main trouble was that the Irish economy, like the English economy, continued to suffer from the Great Depression. Hardly less important, however, the fact as well as the anticipation of violence hampered the Irish economy. As John Bright rightly noted in a letter to Gladstone, "Irish Capital comes to England for investment—English Capital shuns Ireland, as it fears certain loss." And as Lady Wilde wrote in January, 1882, with the exaggeration that befitted the mother of the poet: "The gentry are *ruined*, and the People are not a bit better off. The shopkeepers of Dublin are nearly Bankrupt—the Householders are broken up." Lady Wilde considered her own plight desperate because for three years she had received no rent from her Irish properties. But she granted that hers was a small loss compared to that sustained by some of the Irish she knew. Impressed and appalled by the downward mobility that was taking place, she deplored the fate that compelled a lord to sell his plate to stay alive and several ladies to go to the workhouse.[15]

Despite the adverse conditions under which the Land Act went into operation, it produced results, especially after the enactment of legislation dealing generously with arrears of rent. It is true that the failure of the League's no-rent campaign owed something to the intervention of the clergy, but it owed much to the Land Act—and the willingness of many Irish tenants to give it a chance. Indeed, what mattered most was the psychological impact of the Act.

Year by year, the Irish situation improved. By the summer of 1882 Gladstonians rejoiced in their hero's successful handling of the Irish land problem. By 1883 even some Irish leaders acknowledged that the Land Act was doing an immense amount of good. "The security it has given against capricious evictions," as one of them cogently put it, "has made the people feel they are no longer exactly *slaves*. It has given them a 'foothold' to struggle for more." By 1884 even cautious John Bright was impressed by the remarkable tranquility of Ireland. Tenants, he noted cheerfully, were taking advantage of the security given them by the Land Act to make improvements that had not been possible in earlier times— all of which redounded to the benefit of laborers, for whom there was more demand, as well as the community at large. "If this continues and grows," Bright wrote, "we may hope for the subsidence of animosity even in the political field." Despite years of involvement in Anglo-Irish relations, Bright could still dream of peace and harmony and good will.[16]

{XIX}

NO PARLIAMENT IN DUBLIN

Home rulers began their agitation a few years before the Great Depression began, but the distress of the late seventies and early eighties made available to them possibilities that they had not envisaged. By championing land reform in a time of acute agricultural crisis, they won more and more friends for the political reorganization that they favored. In the words of William O'Brien, the perceptive Irish journalist and Member of Parliament: "the famine of 1879–80 and Mr. Davitt's miracle-working Land League gave Mr. Parnell the opportunity of a people's uprising for their very lives."

Always, however, home rulers feared that economic concessions and victories—and the return of prosperity—would encourage a resurgence of the political apathy against which they had so long struggled unsuccessfully. As an Irish landowner shrewdly remarked in 1888: "Prices are rising. There is the prospect of a splendid harvest. Nationalists very low about it." Indeed, when Yeats wrote of Maud Gonne, that bewitcher of bewitchers, that he heartily endorsed her devotion to the national idea rather than to any secondary land reform movement, he acknowledged that many of his countrymen did not share his view.

II

Goldwin Smith, pondering the accumulation of Irish reform legislation, told Gladstone in 1881 of his hope that Ireland would now be satisfied to remain in the Union. At that time, however,

John Bright had a better grasp of conditions. Parnell's main object, he wrote to Gladstone, was "a break-up of the United Kingdom, for he hates us and England even more than he loves Ireland."

Bright recognized that Parnell's importance stemmed in large part from his monomania, his refusal to be diverted from his political goal. When contemporaries used the word "terror" to characterize Parnell, they chose their language well. It is true that Henry George found Parnell weak, and he eagerly looked for signs that confidence in him was waning. But the reason for this is not far to seek: George deplored Parnell's social and economic conservatism and his unhesitating subordination of economic to political aims.[1]

In 1883 the American businessman and economist Edward Atkinson wrote discerningly of the English Liberals: "Their only conception of their work is to make good laws for Ireland in *London*—they do not yet see that *good* laws must be made and can be made only where they are to be applied. Even Bright and Potter [the labor leader] are blind to this but I think Gladstone sees further but is powerless." In the early eighties, too, a number of English reformers accepted—and welcomed—the inevitability of Irish home rule. This was particularly true of socialists. A. R. Wallace, for example, predicted that the English would soon recognize that the forcible rule of one people by another was inimical to all ideas of good government and only evil could result from it. And H. M. Hyndman was certain that, if Parnell had properly exploited Gladstone's difficulties during the Egyptian crisis, Ireland would already be on its way to autonomy.

Irish reformers, on the other hand, expected a hard struggle. Michael Davitt, taking his usual broad view of things, was convinced in 1884 that the thing for Irish reformers to do was to reach the English and Scottish agricultural laborers who would be enfranchised by the impending Reform Act. By championing their social rights and exposing the abuses to which they were subjected, Irish reformers might be able to persuade them in turn to stand up for justice to Ireland. Nor did Davitt change his mind about the desirable strategy. For years he told English and Scottish working-class audiences that their hardships enabled them to sympathize with the plight of the Irish: "Those who oppose *us* here constitute the same minority which in your country reap which they do not sow, eat and do not work and live in joy and pleasure at the expense and labour of those who are exposed to every misery and suffering." [2]

III

In February, 1885, Mrs. Gladstone, that model of the loyal wife, trembled for the future of her country and her husband. "Perhaps when you receive this letter," she wrote to Mrs. Carnegie, "we shall have been put out of office." Mrs. Gladstone proved to be wrong— but only by a few months. Gladstone resigned in June, bringing to an end a Ministry that had lasted for more than five years. Even out of power, however, his influence was pervasive. In the caustic words of that sturdy champion of coercion Alfred Austin, "As regards politics, we shall have to wait for Gladstone's death or retirement for us to know where we are."

Salisbury's Government of 1885–86 depended in large measure on the votes of the Parnellites, and Gladstone hoped that this dependence would encourage Lord Salisbury to deal with the home rule problem. "My object has been all along to press Lord Salisbury on," Gladstone reported to a journalist years later. But while Gladstone was disappointed by Salisbury's reluctance to cope with home rule, he was not let down in another respect. The Salisbury Ministry did sponsor the important land purchase measure known as the Ashbourne Act, by which funds were provided for Irish tenants to buy their holdings on very generous terms. Michael Davitt and Henry George disapproved of the measure because it did not go far enough and because it would delay the more fundamental land reforms that they favored. But Parnell and his parliamentary followers, alarmed by the economic heresies that had spread in Ireland, supported it.[3]

In December, 1885, word leaked out that Gladstone had been converted to home rule. The news shocked his contemporaries— even those who thought him capable of the worst kind of mischief. "What times we are in! and God grant that much worse may not be coming!" said the widow of an Irish landlord, whose Tory son had stood for Church and Queen in Ireland and been beaten in the election of December, 1885. "You wisely say nothing of politics—and I follow your good example," wrote one embittered Tory to another in January, 1886. But such restraint was rare.

For years Gladstone had excelled in inspiring diatribes that do not at all fit in with the decorum that allegedly goes with Victorianism:

> No church, no property, no throne,
> No lie that logic can't condone,
> No ruling power but his alone,
> This seemed his plan!

During the home rule crisis, however, Gladstone surpassed all his previous records. Even Algernon Swinburne, though he took pride in holding the same opinions as Shelley, Landor, and Byron, joined in the attack on Gladstone:

> No; the lust of life, the thirst for work and days with work to do in,
> Drove and drives him down the road of splendid shame;
> All is well, if o'er the monument recording England's ruin
> Time shall read, inscribed in triumph, Gladstone's name.[4]

It is striking that already in 1886 Tories denounced home rule for all the reasons that were to figure a generation later in Ulster's famous Solemn League and Covenant of 1912. Home rule would be an economic disaster; it would subvert civil and religious freedom; it would destroy Irish civilization; and it would imperil the Empire. It is true that some of the fears of Tories had little basis in fact. It is also true that some Tory leaders—most notably Lord Randolph Churchill—yielded to demagogic outbursts that alarmed even those who agreed with them. Yet the fact remains that no nineteenth-century controversy revealed so clearly the irrationalities that marked Anglo-Irish relations as the struggle over the home rule bill that Gladstone introduced during his third Ministry (February–July, 1886).

IV

In the best of circumstances there would have been intense opposition to the repeal of the Act of Union that had created the United Kingdom of Great Britain and Ireland. But Gladstone's bill "to make all the world happy by installing Mr. Parnell in Dublin" came after thousands of lurid accounts of Irish violence. In these circumstances it did not stand a chance. It was one thing for a high-spirited landlord on his way back to Ireland to joke that his address would be such and such unless the Moonlighters got him; and once back he could still joke that he was trying to figure out how "to make hay in spite of weather and of Land League." But Sir William Bromley Davenport, the determined Tory son of the by now deceased Tory father, angrily declared: "Long years of lawlessness, outrage, and murder in Ireland should warn us against granting to that country the power to work us still greater, perhaps unlimited, evil." Indeed, while Davenport recognized home rule as the leading question before the country, it infuriated him that it was diverting attention from another that struck more closely to home. Alarmed by bad trade, foreign competition, and unemployment, he told his constituents that it was time to stop complaining about the depression and praying that heaven work a miracle in England's behalf. The attention that Ireland was receiving should be devoted to a reexamination of England's absurd free trade policy.[5]

It was no surprise that the Tory opposition to home rule was vigorous, intense, and even hysterical; but it was a surprise that some of Gladstone's own followers reacted as strongly against home rule as the Tories. "The sudden movements of our Politicians on the Political Chess board exceed, I fancy, the worst you have to complain of in the United States," Helen Taylor aptly wrote to Mrs. Henry George.

Joseph Chamberlain and John Bright—two of the best friends the Irish ever had in England—were outraged by Gladstone's proposal. It is true that as early as April, 1885, Chamberlain had submitted to Cardinal Manning a private memorandum on Irish local government. Yet it is also true that by December he had cautioned Gladstone that the English working classes were definitely opposed to home rule if it meant the creation of a separate parliament in Dublin. Certainly, however, the salient fact is that Chamberlain believed that the land question was at the bottom of Irish difficulties and that Anglo-Irish harmony could be achieved only by the large-scale adoption of John Bright's plan of converting Irish tenants into peasant proprietors. "I greatly fear," Chamberlain wrote to Bright in February, 1886, "that Mr. Gladstone is on another tack—if so I shall not be able to sail with him for long." A month later Chamberlain had no doubt that Gladstone's home rule plan was the equivalent of a proposal for separation, and that it would endanger imperial security as well as all further Liberal reforms. But Chamberlain's entreaties did not deter

Gladstone, who accepted his resignation from the cabinet: "Your great powers could ill be dispensed with even in easy times. I shall rejoice during what remains to me of life to see them turned to the honour and advantage of the country." [6]

John Bright's opposition was much more distressing to Gladstone than Chamberlain's. Nothing, in fact, pained Gladstone more during the whole home rule controversy than Bright's hostility. Like Lord Hartington and other members of Gladstone's party, however, Bright could not consent to a measure that offended the entire Protestant population of Ireland. No less important, Bright simply did not trust the Parnellites, and he repeatedly warned Gladstone not to trust them. "If I could believe them loyal —if they were honorable and truthful men I could yield much— but I suspect that your policy of surrender to them will only place more power in their hands to war with greater effect against the unity of the three Kingdoms with no increase of good to the Irish people."

Bright was the sort of person who would speak on a subject only when he felt that he could do so with authority, and he thought that he knew the Parnellites well. His years of experience with them in the House of Commons had made him unbending. They were people who had insulted the Queen, torn down the flag, and made a travesty of parliamentary government. To entrust to their rule the population of Ireland was both unwise and unjust—and Bright spoke proudly as one who for decades had been preaching justice for Ireland.[7]

Pressures were brought to bear on Bright to relent. One old friend, reminding him of his mighty contributions to such causes as free trade, a cheap press, the extension of the franchise, and disestablishment, urged him to crown his career by using his influence and power to establish an Irish Parliament in Dublin. But Bright remained adamant. As he bluntly told the electors of the Central Division of Birmingham: "I cannot trust the peace and interests of Ireland, north and south, to the Irish Parliamentary party, to whom the Government now propose to make a general surrender. My six years' experience of them, of their language in the House of Commons, and of their deeds in Ireland, makes it impossible for me to consent to hand over to them the property and the rights of five millions of the Queen's subjects, our countrymen, in Ireland." Thus Bright ended his career as he had begun it—in controversy. And he showed the same earnestness, courage, and eloquence for which Richard Cobden had admired him decades before.[8]

The irony was, however, that for many years Bright had planned to give up politics. At the time of his breakdown in 1856 it had seemed that his career was at an end, and many times in the next three decades he doubted that he could go on with his work in Parliament, for he recognized that official life was not natural to him as it was to Gladstone. Indeed, he wanted to stop being an actor and start becoming a spectator, for the excitement and work that politics entailed were too much for him. "I feel often a wish to rush into obscurity, and to leave to others the labours and perils which are before us," he had confided to Gladstone in 1880. It is, then, a measure of the depths of his feelings about the Parnellites that he rallied as he did during the home rule crisis.[9]

Even after the defeat of Gladstone's bill in July Bright was unable to discuss the subject of a Parliament in Dublin without becoming highly emotional. He could not see subjecting the loyal Irish to a group of conspirators who were sustained by money from England's enemies in the United States. And he was amazed that any thoughtful Liberal could envisage doing so. Bright found it tragic that Gladstone had wrecked a great political party, but if he persisted in his pro-ruffian policy he would also bring disaster to Ireland. Bright readily gave Gladstone credit for the great things that he had done during the course of his career, but he had no doubts about his fallibility. Gladstone's blunders in Egypt and on the Afghan frontiers were bad enough, but they were minor compared to his mistaken Irish policy. What distressed Bright particularly was his conviction that without Gladstone's support there would not have been twenty English Members of Parliament who would have favored the home rule bill.

Gladstone, for his part, believed that if reason operated the distance between Bright and him could be greatly narrowed. Invariably, however, the mere suggestion of a Parliament in Dublin inflamed Bright: "I will not give up one of the three Kingdoms to men who sit in our Parliament with American dollars in their pockets, contributed by the avowed enemies of England in the States, who would rejoice to see war between their Country and

NO PARLIAMENT IN DUBLIN

ours." Throughout the crisis, to be sure, Bright was convinced that if the English had acted sooner they could have averted their present troubles. But Bright had lived long enough to recognize that foresight was a rare quality in the ranks of politicians.[10]

V

The implications for the Liberal Party of the home rule controversy were not lost on contemporaries. In fact, when staunch Gladstonians denounced Bright, Chamberlain, Hartington, and other Liberal Unionists as deserters and traitors, they were often expressing not so much their love for Ireland as their fear for the future of their party. Even William Butler Yeats, who resented English home rulers for their patronizing attitude towards the Irish—"some new sort of deserving poor for whom bazaars and such like should be got up"—recognized their earnestness and the high cost of their Irish policy. Indeed, the words that an obscure Tory wrote to a friend in 1886 are especially revealing: "I trust Gladstone's last 'manoeuvres' have made you, like so many old Whigs, quite conservative. I think nothing will save our country now but a common stand made by those two Parties as against the Radicals."

Nor were the Liberal Unionists unaware of the implications of Gladstone's conversion to home rule. Chamberlain early recognized that Gladstone's policy had wrecked the Liberal Party as a controlling influence in politics. And John Bright, who barely a decade before had rejoiced that it was not easy to break up the Liberals, now conceded that a single individual could lead his party to ruin. To be sure, that vigorous and articulate anti-home ruler, Matthew Arnold, was wary of Lord Salisbury and the Tories, but he expected much of Lord Hartington. "His Liberalism is limited, but sound; and he has no political tricks," Arnold assured Andrew Carnegie. But few Liberal Unionists shared Arnold's enthusiasm.

Socialists were delighted with the mix-up. As early as December, 1885, Mrs. Annie Besant had noted cheerfully that the breaking up of political parties that she had long hoped for was starting. A year later she was jubilant over the muddle that Gladstone's policy had produced. All this would redound to the benefit of the socialists.[11]

The general election of July produced a House of Commons in which the Tories were not so numerous as they would have liked to be. But, as long as they had the backing of the Liberal Unionists, their position was safe. And so it was during Lord Salisbury's long second Ministry (1886–92). On the one hand, the coalition of Tories and Liberal Unionists pressed for further land purchase acts and other measures in line with their policy of trying to kill home rule with economic kindnesses. On the other hand, they used repression on a large scale to maintain public order, believing that Ireland should be ruled rather than administered. As the patriotic historian and authority on Ireland, James Anthony Froude, expressed this coercionist outlook: "You can govern the Irish more easily than any people in the world under a military or quasi-military authority. The police are uniformly faithful and loyal. You have never yet succeeded in governing them constitutionally and I think you never will."

It was Arthur J. Balfour, Chief Secretary for Ireland, Salisbury's nephew and a philosopher of stature, who speedily came to symbolize the policy of coercion. The Irish as well as the Gladstonians viewed him as a master of truculence, high-handedness, and brutality; but when people met him in person they were understandably shocked that he did not live up to what they expected from the "Bloody" Balfour who figured so prominently in the newspapers. Far from being hungry for power, he spent much of his time being sick of politics and aching for the life of intellect. And he was the kind of fair-minded intellectual who, though well qualified to do so, refused to write a biography of John Stuart Mill because he was out of sympathy with the philosophical, religious, and political views of the author of *On Liberty*.

As an ardent Unionist, Balfour was prepared to anticipate the worst from the Irish. In the revealing words that he wrote at the time of the Jubilee of 1887: "I am inclined to think that there can be no doubt that the Irish Mayors must be asked—just as if they were loyal subjects of Her Majesty! Some may return insolent answers; but I see no harm in them; rather the reverse." And as he confided to a friend:

I am not of a sanguine temperament, and am certainly not sanguine about the future of Ireland. But there can be no doubt whatever, in my opinion, as to what is the course we ought to pursue; and if the people of this Country can only realise the true character of the problem with which we have to deal, and have patience and persistence to deal with it, in the only spirit in which it can be dealt with successfully, I have good hope of the result; but a condition of things which is the result of causes that have been at work for hundreds of years, cannot be cured in a single session or by a single ministry.[12]

VI

The position of the Gladstonians was desperate in the period after the defeat of the home rule bill and the election of 1886. Francis Schnadhorst, Chamberlain's old colleague from Birmingham, could rejoice in Gladstone's perpetual youth, and he could insist that the Liberals would soon be fine. But despite Schnadhorst's cheerfulness the outlook was gloomy. "The bitterness between Hartingtonians and Gladstonians increases," James Bryce reported accurately in 1887. "The rift has become a chasm," Chamberlain told Carnegie, and he predicted that it would take years to undo the damage caused by Gladstone's home rule policy. Chamberlain was even certain that Gladstone's personal popularity was waning, but this, he added, gave him no satisfaction, for if another General Election were held, the result would be a large Tory majority. So, too, Bright could not forgive Gladstone for the troubles that he had brought on: "He thought a big scheme and his great authority would carry him through—and he has fallen in the attempt. I doubt much if any reconstruction or reunion of the Party will ever take place so long as he is dominant in the majority of it—to have him with his policy is not possible, and he can hardly shake off his policy." [13]

Gladstone, rich in self-righteousness, had no misgivings about the course he had taken. Although he still hoped in 1887 to write a large-scale study of ancient Greek religion, he was so obsessed with the need to win converts to home rule that he had little time to give to his book. Until the Irish Question was out of the way, he insisted, the English could not go on to the other problems with which they had to deal. "I have worked hard, for an old man very hard, this year," he proudly told Carnegie.

One difficulty Gladstone had not anticipated, and it caused him much embarrassment. As he confided to Carnegie in 1887: "It is no part of the duty of the leader of a party to provide for its finance. It is twenty-one years since I first began to lead the Lib-

erals, and I never till this year heard of the calls upon the purse."
The trouble, Gladstone explained, was that, while most Liberals
had stood behind him, nine-tenths of the wealthy members had
seceded. To convince Carnegie that the financial distress of the
Liberal Party was a suitable case for the exercise of the philanthropist's generosity—and Gladstone succeeded—he sent him a
private and confidential memorandum signed by John Morley,
among others, pointing out the urgency of a special appeal for
funds. Not only had nearly all the contributors to the central
funds left the Liberals, but many of the moneyed men had with-
drawn from the local associations as well. The consequences, the
memorandum emphasized, were alarming. Local agents had to be
dismissed, many associations were virtually disbanded, and new
ones could not be formed. Furthermore, while the Tories were
flooding the country with publications and lectures, the Liberals
had to restrict their educational efforts because of limited funds.
And this was dangerous in a society based on virtually universal
manhood suffrage.[14]

Anti-home rulers continued to outdo each other in their attacks
on Gladstone. The usual occupation of W. E. Henley's *Scots Observer* was to revile Gladstone, but this was a widely shared activity. "I call him Lucifer," an English woman told an American visitor. "Do you think he is destined to live till he has broken up the
British Empire?" John Temple Leader, the spirited Tory and a
contemporary of Gladstone's at Christ Church, asked a friend.
Gladstone, to be sure, could joke that Sir John Millais, whom he
had not seen for a long time, must have forgotten even his face.
Anti-home rulers, however, had no such good fortune: everywhere
they saw Gladstone's face with its determined and confident look.
Poor John Temple Leader, wintering in Italy in 1888, was even
called on by Gladstone; and as a gentleman who respected the old
school tie, he returned the call and took Gladstone and his family
sight-seeing. "I found him a most entertaining companion," he
grudgingly confessed, "but not a word on politics passed between
us."

There was nothing new in the arguments that anti-home rulers
used to justify their passions. The Irish were an inferior people—
fickle, impulsive, unstable, unreliable, violent; and they could not
be trusted to govern themselves, much less the Protestants in Ire-

land. Besides, if they were granted home rule, the Scots would also demand it, and so would the Welsh. By 1887 even James Anthony Froude complained that he had written so much on the Irish Question, which he had long regarded as an unpleasant subject, that he felt no inclination to join the current clamor. In a private letter, however, he restated his position, which was that of the mass of anti-home rulers:

The Celtic Irish are and always have been hostile to this country. While this country cannot for its own safety's sake allow them to be independent. Any form of self government which is conceded to them whether in the shape of a national Parliament or of local councils they will use I suppose as they have always done every liberty which we have hitherto extended to them to increase our difficulties in keeping the Island attached to us. That has been the history of the past. I have no reason to suppose that there will be any difference in the future.[15]

VII

If the aftermath of the failure of the home rule bill was a trying time for Gladstonians, it was even worse for Irish reformers. As a Killarney landowner and Unionist cheerfully described their plight: "The defeat of the Home Rule Bill has produced a strangely sobering effect on the mass of the people here. The police and every one notice it. They have become extraordinarily civil. Probably they are watching with some anxiety to see what a new Government will do. Many of our friends have uneasy consciences and wish to stand well just at present in the eyes of magistrates, police and the party of order."

From 1886 to 1890 Irish reformers spent about £4000 a year trying to "educate" voters in English constituencies—and with very good cause. For, although the vicious articles in the *Times* implicating Parnell in Irish atrocities proved to be based on the work of a forger, the inescapable truth was that many English were willing to believe the worst of Parnell and his followers. And hardly was Parnell cleared of encouraging crimes of violence than he was named corespondent in the O'Shea divorce case.

Gladstone, convinced that Parnell's private life had offended the moral sensibilities of English supporters of home rule, repudiated him. But the Irish leader refused to fade away. Parnell's behavior, Gladstone insisted, would neither frighten nor break up his Liberal phalanx. But other party spokesmen were much less confident.

Sir William Harcourt, deploring Parnell's conduct as the height of selfishness, feared that the worst of the mischief was that the Irish leader had undermined the kindly feelings between the English and the Irish peoples that the Liberals had worked so hard to build up.[16]

Irish reformers, for their part, reverted with fervor to their old tradition of feuding, dividing into savage Parnellites and no less savage anti-Parnellites. Indeed, it was hard to believe that these were the people who only a few years before had served as an example for single-taxers, socialists, and other reformers of what a determined and well-organized group could accomplish. "We have come to a very critical pass in the history of our Home Rule movement in Ireland," a leading anti-Parnellite Member of Parliament reported without exaggeration.

Anti-Parnellites swamped Irish-Americans with appeals for funds with which to defeat the Parnellites. Parnellites begged for money with which to crush the anti-Parnellites. And both groups continued to plead for contributions to help evicted tenants. But the revival of factionalism in Ireland made money-raising difficult in the United States.

It is true that Yeats and other Parnellites searched eagerly for signs that their hero's behavior had not appreciably damaged the home rule cause, but the evidence was hard to find. To support Parnell, as one irate Irish-American put it, "would be an affront to the virtuous women of Ireland; nor could we expect them to maintain their preeminence for virtue among all the nations of the earth, or to continue to have the same abhorrence of impurity, if we condoned such conduct before their very eyes."

That Parnell died in 1891 made little difference—so intense had the hostilities become between Parnellites and anti-Parnellites both in Ireland and the United States. On the day of Parnell's death Yeats wrote a poem "Mourn—and Then Onward," published in *United Ireland;* but Yeats's appeal for unity was futile. Parnellites were especially bitter towards the clergy for the part that they had played in the downfall of their leader. And anti-Parnellites remembered only the end of Parnell's career, not its beginning and its middle. "Away, away! You're safer in the tomb!" Yeats wrote, but even in the tomb Parnell did not find safety.

Factionalism in Ireland flourished as perhaps never before. I reached such a point by the spring of 1892 that Gladstone hoped that a few Irish-Americans would visit their old country "and get an end put to this nonsense." And the secretary of the anti-Parnellite party, Arthur O'Connor, with a dozen years of parliamentary service behind him, wrote apologetically to a generous American supporter: "It must be a sickening thing for men like yourself, who for so long and with such earnestness and unselfishness have striven to help us, to witness the painful and humiliating situation into which we have drifted over here—and that at a time when harmony and cordial cooperation is most indispensable." [17]

The imminence of a general election made the quarrels of the anti-Parnellites, led by Justin McCarthy, and the Parnellites, headed by John Redmond, particularly alarming. Without help from America, McCarthy told Dr. Thomas Addis Emmet, the president of the anti-Parnellite Irish National Federation of America, many seats in the House of Commons would go by default. But the difficulty was that, although the Federation received much help from parish priests, its fund-raising activities were repeatedly hampered by some fresh outburst of scandalous bickering in Ireland. An Irish-American inmate at Sing Sing Prison, sending along his five dollars, wondered why some of his compatriots were so timid in contributing. But an Irish-American businessman bluntly explained to the secretary of the Federation that people were unwilling to give because they considered the Irish cause hopelessly lost. The Irish-Irish lacked both statesmanship and patriotism.[18]

VIII

As the election approached, insiders among the home rulers were concerned about Gladstone's health. In 1890 Harcourt had rejoiced that the Grand Old Man was still leading the Liberal Party with undiminished vigor. But by June, 1892, W. T. Stead was worried because Gladstone had aged considerably and because those who knew him well doubted that he would be in a condition to work even if he remained alive another year. As so often in the past, however, Gladstone fooled even those who knew him best. Home rule was the big issue in the campaign, and Gladstone's sense of England's duty to Ireland was so profound that it made him capable of superhuman feats.

The election gave Gladstone enough votes—with the help of the

Irish Members of Parliament—to carry home rule. And John Morley, worshiper of Mill and critic of coercion, became Chief Secretary for Ireland. McCarthy's anti-Parnellites were jubilant. Powerful John Dillon, thanking an American supporter for financial aid, pointed glowingly to the seventy-two seats his party had won contrasted with the nine secured by Redmond's Parnellites. This verdict, he hoped, would make clear to all Irish reformers the stupidity of maintaining two parties. So, too, Arthur O'Connor, though he would have preferred to have had even fewer Redmondites returned, reveled in the election results: "We hold the balance of power in the House of Commons between the Liberal and Conservative parties."

Even so, the feuds among Irish home rulers continued, and when they described one another they used adjectives like infamous and treacherous. Michael Davitt thought that the behavior of some of his colleagues, especially those from "dirty Dublin," was enough to make the Gladstonians abandon the Irish in despair. And Justin McCarthy, as leader of the anti-Parnellites, spent much of his time apologizing to American backers: "I can quite understand and appreciate the increased difficulties which certain troubles among ourselves may and must have imposed upon you and put in your way quite lately." [19]

While Irish home rulers denounced one another, Irish anti-home rulers publicized their hostility to Gladstone's plans. Both before and after the election of 1892 they proclaimed their ardent support of the Act of Union, emphasizing that events since the introduction of the first home rule bill had strengthened them in their convictions. "I share your hope," Joseph Chamberlain wrote to the Moderator of the General Assembly of the Presbyterian Church in Ireland, "that the effect of this and other representations from the Non-episcopalian churches in Ireland will be to bring home to the majority of the electors in this country the strong objections entertained by Protestants in Ireland to Mr. Gladstone's separatist policy."

After the elections, Irish anti-home rulers continued their campaign. However much they might complain of the unfair tax load that they had to bear under the old system, they did not wish to abandon that system. The Dublin Chamber of Commerce insisted that the maintenance of the Union was essential to the health of the Irish economy. And the General Assembly of the Presbyterian

Church in Ireland warned that home rule would endanger the
spiritual health of Ireland.[20]

IX

On February 13, 1893, the London correspondent of the New
York *Times* laconically wrote in his diary: "Gladstone's introduction Home Rule. 1200 words." But for years those were the words
that home rulers had been longing for and that anti-home
rulers had been dreading. Through the spring and summer the
battle over the bill raged. In fact, a well-known Irish-Australian
politician and reformer, planning to bring out a book, urged his
English publisher to delay its publication until the fall: "Ireland
is in a ferment at present and will read nothing but newspapers
till the Home Rule Bill leaves the Commons."

Since it was not until September 1 that the lower house passed
the measure, the financial pressures on the Irish Members were
tremendous. Justin McCarthy could live on the income from his
newspaper work, but most of the Irish Members were young men
without means, and because they received no salaries as Members
of Parliament they could be active and in full attendance only if
they—and their families—were subsidized. "Our great trouble is
the ancient one of want of Funds to keep the party here in London," as one of them put it. Like Michael Davitt, the typical Irish
Member could accurately, if ungrammatically, say that "neither
the Party or myself have a copper between us." And McCarthy,
Dillon, and others were not simply engaging in flattery when they
cabled Emmet's National Federation of America: "In the struggle
of the last fourteen years, almost the dominant factor, next to the
courage and tenacity of our people at home, has been financial
assistance from our kindred and friends beyond the seas." [21]

In addition to money, the Federation tried to supply Irish Members of Parliament with favorable publicity. They secured statements from distinguished Americans in support of Gladstone's
bill. Governor John B. Altgeld of Illinois was one of many who
wrote to Dr. Emmet, "The time has come for Ireland to have
Home Rule, and I am heartily in favor of every measure that will
tend to bring it about." The Federation also saw to it that Gladstone was deluged with letters and telegrams commending his
effort to win justice for Ireland.

Like Irish-Americans, people of Irish origin in countries like

Canada and Australia joined in the clamor. In fact, when an energetic Canadian advocate of Irish home rule was about to return home, Davitt thought it important to arrange a public testimonial for him. "It would please the Canadians *very much* and would be sure to be a good investment in the way of procuring continued help from Canada," he wrote cannily.[22]

In the course of the controversy home rulers often reported their opponents demoralized, but Lord Salisbury spoke for all on his side when he called the passage of the bill an impossibility. By its rejection of the measure in September the House of Lords saved anti-home rulers from what they regarded as the worst threat to national security since the time of Napoleon.

The fury of home rulers was unspeakable, and some of them were willing to take immediate steps to limit the powers of what they had often referred to scathingly as "the landowners' House." Indeed, an American political scientist, finishing a book on the English constitution, feared that the House of Lords would be in limbo before his work was published. And the author of a number of articles on the corrupt origins of some Irish peerages urged a publisher to reprint them in book form because they would do much to further the agitation against the upper house.[23]

But it was not until August, 1911, that ardent Liberals could rejoice that the crisis over the House of Lords had ended. In the meantime, what saved the Lords as well as the Act of Union were Gladstone's advanced age—eighty-four—and the discouragement even of ardent Gladstonians over the mess in which the home rule issue had embroiled their party. "He will be a bold man who will rush in where Mr. Gladstone failed," the young Unionist Winston Churchill aptly told an Irish-American home ruler.[24]

X

If ever a Victorian had reason to agree with Lewis Carroll's complaint about what a short time even a long life lasted, it was Gladstone. When he was about to leave Eton in 1827, he wrote with adolescent precocity and pomposity, "I shall depart with sincere regret: and I have long ago persuaded myself that I never can expect another period of my life to be so full of joys and so free from sorrows as that which I have passed here." Two generations later

Gladstone was a sad old man, but despite his frustration over the failure of his greatest crusade, he had his consolations. An Irish newspaper did not exaggerate when it said of him: "He unquestionably devoted the last ten years of his splendid career to the Irish cause and its generous advocacy. Through many years of opposition he held to his allegiance to Home Rule, when he might by a declaration against it have re-united his party, and enjoyed the place and power of the Premiership almost ever since."

It is true that there were still some old-style Fenians like Jeremiah O'Donovan Rossa who saw little difference between a Balfour and a Gladstone and would trust no British politician. But even O'Donovan Rossa noted mournfully in his diary in 1895 that he met an O'Neill in England who told him: "I know England will have to give this measure of Home Rule; she cannot help doing it; she must do it; there is a great change in the people of England; the people now want to see justice done to Ireland."

Gladstone, with his formidable inner resources, had much to do with that change in the English people. No wonder James Bryce remarked of the glowing tribute that he paid to him when he died in 1898, "It was but a small part of what we would like to have said about so extraordinary and inspiring a personality." [25]

❧ XX ❧

CONTENTIOUS MEN

Even after the defeat of the home rule bill the financial requirements of Irish reformers remained great. There were always
evicted tenants to care for; educational work among the English
had to go on; and Irish Members of Parliament, if they were to
play their part, had to receive help in order to stay at Westminster.
Although the need for aid was real, money became increasingly
hard to secure, for the world economic crisis of 1893 made fund-
raising difficult in the United States, Canada, Australia, and New
Zealand.

Joseph P. Ryan, hard-working secretary of the National Federation, received pathetic reports from members in all sections of the
United States. "A dollar is as hard to get as an oyster in mid-
summer," a Baltimorean noted. "It would seem cruel to encourage
the sending of a dollar anywhere out of town," wrote a member
from New Britain, Connecticut. "The industrial interests of the
Country are in a very bad condition at present and immense
numbers of our people are idle with no immediate prospects of
going to work," Ryan reported in turn to Justin McCarthy.[1]

Yet it was not only the business cycle that hindered the raising
of money for the Irish cause; exasperation with the clashes of Irish
reformers also had much to do with it. "No more American dollars for the men who seem to have forgotten Ireland in the fever
of ignoble ambition," declared one outraged Federationist. "Oh!
the Damn Scoundrels, factionists, renegades and traitors called
Redmondites or Parnellites. I wish I had the power as I have the

will to cast them into the Irish Sea never again to curse the land
with their loathsome presence," an American Southerner exploded. In short, it was not strange that Emmet and other officials
of the Federation complained that they could not go on waiting
for the intervals between Irish scandals to do their work. Disgust
and apathy, they warned, were spreading fast among Irish-
Americans.[2]

The feuds among Irish leaders flourished until the end of the
century. At the outset anti-Parnellites fought Parnellites (Redmondites), but then the anti-Parnellites broke up into factions.
"I saw both Dillon and Healy today and I think there is no fear
of any open rupture for the present," Michael Davitt reported in
October, 1892; but the break came soon enough. The group that
included McCarthy, Davitt, Dillon, and William O'Brien wanted
to make it possible for the Parnellites to return to a united and
strengthened party, and so they urged a policy of forgiveness. The
group headed by Timothy Healy favored a policy of no quarter
to the Parnellites; they wished to eject them from public life.

Along with the clashes of opinion went sharp personal animosities. It was one thing for a newcomer, who prided himself on not
being involved in the dissensions and jealousies of his colleagues,
to argue that, since neither side could drive out the other, to try
to do so would wreck the party altogether. But this kind of appeal to reason presupposed reasonable men, and they were a
rare breed at the time. The fact is that the hostility between Dillon and Healy became particularly intense; and though by the
end of 1893 Dillon's supporters among the Irish Members of
Parliament numbered about forty and Healy's about thirty,
Healy had powerful ecclesiastical backing and, therefore, considerable strength among the people at home.[3]

It was bad enough that Irish reformers quarreled; worse still,
they did so openly. People heard and read their denunciations of
one another, and as the reports spread, so did the inaccuracies
and exaggerations. Davitt, with years of experience behind him,
could say of a Healyite publication that he never read the vicious
sheet and that its lies and blackguardism did not disturb him. But
few of the leaders in any of the Irish camps could be so restrained.
It is true that in August, 1894, McCarthy appealed to Irish
leaders to end the public outbursts that had done them so much

harm, and he was gratified by the results. But the effects of Mc-Carthy's appeal wore off quickly, and in any case the private tensions remained. Davitt, for example, was convinced that Healy and his ecclesiastical supporters lacked charity and respect for truth, and he despised them for making a living issue of the dead Parnell. They would have to be fought and defeated, he predicted, but the present was not the right time for the battle.[4]

II

Gladstone resigned in March, 1894, and for a year Lord Rosebery headed a Ministry. In June, 1895, Salisbury formed his third Government, giving cabinet posts to such Liberal Unionists as Chamberlain and Lord Hartington (by then the Duke of Devonshire). For a decade the Unionists—first under Salisbury (1895–1902) and then under Balfour (1902–5)—were entrenched. "The English seem to like a landlord government. May they have their rents doubled for their partiality!" exclaimed Michael Davitt, convinced that land reformers would be unable to extract any valuable measures from Parliament. But Davitt was wrong. The most impressive achievement of the Unionists in the Irish sphere was the enactment of further land purchase legislation in 1896 and 1903; but they passed other laws designed to give the Irish a stake in the Union.

At the end of Salisbury's Ministry of 1886–92, Alice Balfour, the sister of the politician, had acutely remarked that "everything that makes people know about the work done for Ireland during the last few years is of great importance." So, too, during their later period in power Unionists kept the public informed about their many efforts in behalf of Ireland. Always their hope was that the removal of economic grievances would isolate home rulers and deprive them of the support of the Irish people. The kind but firm government of Ireland, as Winston Churchill told an Irish-American leader in 1896, would give the Irish people material benefits that would undermine the attempts of agitators to keep them in a state of indignation. "Everything that can be done to alleviate distress and heal the wounds of the past is done," he pointed out, "and done in spite of rhetorical attempts to keep them open." Churchill did not deny that through the centuries the English had maltreated the Irish; but in words that can only delight historians reared in the tradition of Frederic William Maitland, he declared it "unjust to arraign the deeds of earlier times before modern tribunals and to judge by modern standards." Furthermore, Churchill's contention was that the English were by now so disgusted with the home rule issue that it would take twenty years before another bill could pass, and by then the need for it would have disappeared. Even Churchill could be wrong.[5]

George Wyndham, the authority on Plutarch and Shakespeare and the literary critic who had helped to spread the fame in England of Stephen Crane's *Red Badge of Courage,* served as Chief Secretary for Ireland from 1900 to 1905, and his administration showed both the weaknesses and the strengths of the Unionist outlook. On the one hand, Wyndham had no guilt feelings about being where he was not wanted. "The Government of Ireland," he proudly told his close friend W. E. Henley, "is a cross between the modern Government of India and the Government of an Italian State in the XIIIth Century. I am there as a sort of Ghibelline Duke, holding an outpost recalcitrant to the idea of Empire and populated by Guelphs." .

At the same time, however, Wyndham was constantly on the alert for opportunities to improve the economic position of the Irish. He was especially impressed with the potentialities of that beautiful but desolate area, the West of Ireland, where he thought that work of the kind the Romans used to do needed to be accomplished. "If one could turn the river of Imperialism into this back-water spawned over by obscure reptiles; if one could change these anaemic children into full-blooded men! They are part of the Aryan race," he wrote revealingly to Henley. "The problem," he noted specifically, "is can you make the men fish; can you make the women work at lace, hand-made curtains and tapestry? If you can, you may some day build up life." [6]

Wyndham pursued economic policies that he knew extremists on both sides would condemn, but he was secure enough to enjoy being called every conceivable name. Wary of abstractions, he prided himself on basing his course on careful observation of the Irish scene; and he thought that he saw results. As he told Henley in 1903: "I am absorbed in my work here. Politically we have halcyon days and I am trying to launch as many crafts as I can on the smiling, but treacherous, seas. All the talk is of agreement, regeneration, revival." Wyndham could hardly wait to get to London to tell Henley about the great fuel revolution that was to occur in Ireland as a result of the substitution of oil for coal. "I mean to let old Ireland have a chance at last," he wrote in his typical paternalistic style. "But—and here is the miracle—they are all beginning to believe in the future," he added hopefully.[7]

III

Like English Unionists, a number of Irish leaders also gave priority to economic changes—but for different reasons. By far the most notable of them at the turn of the century was Sir Horace Plunkett, a reformer of great energy as well as insight. Plunkett believed that the home rule agitation had had the unfortunate result of diverting attention from the fundamental defect of the Irish economy: its stark poverty. As he put it in 1898, "If only we could get the real sympathisers with Ireland in America to take the view that by improving the economic and social status of the people of Ireland the political question will be most surely, and perhaps more rapidly, settled, our troubles would be near their end." Plunkett's conviction was that government intervention and private charity together were insufficient to relieve suffering in Ireland, for, except for a small part of Ulster, the condition of the country varied between depression on the one hand and famine on the other. The great hope, therefore, lay in the growth of industry and the spread of agricultural cooperation. And since Plunkett took a rural view of Irish progress, he worked for years —with remarkable success—to win converts to his belief in the importance of educating Irish farmers in the ways of modern scientific agriculture so that they could compete against the state-aided producers of foreign countries.[8]

Unlike most Irish reformers, Plunkett looked to the possibilities of the future, not to the grievances of the past; and, unlike many of his colleagues, he was peaceloving. With his strong views, however, he inevitably became involved in clashes—most notably with political leaders. Plunkett was particularly exasperated by Irish fund-raising missions to the United States; "they must only cause me to work a little harder in order to offset the inevitable disturbance to economic and social development from political unrest," as he perceptively put it. Not only that, however, for he believed that the money would be far better used if it were employed for the development of the Irish economy. "If only we could get some of those gifted political leaders who for some reason or other have been given a marvellous power of influencing the thought and action of our people, to abandon the easy path of political agitation and turn their attention to industrial and commercial progress, it is hard to say with what leaps and bounds the country might advance to that goal of prosperity to which these men would lead them by another road." [9]

Obsessed with the economic backwardness of Ireland and with the menace of Irish dependence on a single and declining industry, Plunkett clamored for the more efficient use of resources and for the cultivation through education of industrial habits and attitudes as well as a lively spirit of self-help. He proselytized endlessly. "I do wish you would close your political eye and ear for a brief period, and infuse new life into Irish economics," he told the wealthy American politician Bourke Cockran, who was one of John Redmond's chief financial backers. "You have no idea what a force you would be in that arena."

Although Plunkett saw Ireland as a country on the eve of industrial expansion, he did not underestimate the difficulties ahead. As he courageously reported to Cockran: "I fear I take a less optimistic view than you would of the time which will be required, firstly, to get the Irish people to realise certain industrial defects, which may or may not have been due wholly to circumstances over which they had no control in the past, but which the evidence pouring into this Department of Agriculture and Technical Instruction week by week shows us are more real than is generally imagined." [10]

When in 1904 Plunkett brought out his *Ireland in the New Century,* a powerful plea for the modernization of Irish economic life and a book based not on other books but on his daily experiences with Irish difficulties, he anticipated that it would arouse violent protests. At first, however, he found that reviewers dealt generously with it and that public figures wrote him kind letters about it; but soon it raised just the kind of battle that he had expected. "One thing is quite certain: the Book has stirred thought upon Irish problems in a manner quite unprecedented," he accurately noted. Fairminded AE agreed that Plunkett's book had caused more of an uproar in Ireland than any other volume that he could remember. As a conscientious worker for the regeneration of Ireland, AE knew from his own experience how hard it was to try to make farmers efficient; and he thought that Plunkett's book would do good and force people to think about serious questions.

Always, however, the complicated relations of past, present, and future intervened. Plunkett wished to let bygones be bygones; he was interested in what lay ahead. For many of his countrymen this was impossible: what made them Irish was their long-nourished sense of grievance against the English.[11]

It is true that home rulers also deplored economic conditions in Ireland, but they contended that these conditions were primarily due to the mismanagement of Irish affairs in England. When in 1897 a series of disasters wrecked the crops in the West of Ireland, home rulers lost no time in blaming the Salisbury Government for bringing on starvation there. And this tendency to use England as a scapegoat continued for years. In 1904 John Redmond went so far as to urge Cockran to use his influence to prevent a famine relief fund from being organized: "The acute distress," Redmond wrote bluntly, "may be a blessing in disguise —as it may enable us to force the hands of the Government in the proper administration of the Land Act in the West."

In these circumstances it is not strange that English Unionists often grew bitter. Trying to be conciliatory and to make up for ancient injustices, they voted millions of pounds for Ireland. The Irish accepted the money, but instead of letting the past be buried, they tried to keep it more alive than ever. Even Joseph Conrad, himself the offspring of an oppressed nationality, fumed at Irish ingratitude at the same time that he marveled at English generosity.[12]

IV

While Unionists pursued their paternalistic policies in Ireland after 1895, Irish reformers continued to luxuriate in strife. An English publisher's reader, after examining a manuscript by an Irish reformer, singled out as the author's leading traits—and those of his colleagues—"brag, bluster, over-confidence." The publisher's reader doubtless overgeneralized, but the fact is that these traits were widespread enough to make harmony and fraternity rare among Irish reformers. Indeed, one of John Bright's sons thought that the English Liberals should use Irish animosity as a basis for repudiating their commitment to home rule.

In 1896 John Dillon was elected head of the Irish Parliamentary Party, but it was not, as he justly confessed, "a position which any intelligent man who understood all the circumstances of the situation in Ireland would be anxious to occupy." The Party was so disorganized as a result of the wrecking tactics of Timothy Healy and his cohorts, Dillon charged, that it would require a great deal of effort to build it up again. And it would take much time for the country to overcome the apathy produced by recent scandals and fights.

For years Dillon had insisted that the great opportunity of the Irish would come when Joseph Chamberlain and his followers definitely joined the Tories. Now that this had happened Dillon was certain that if the Irish were united they could win home rule within five years. Of the seventy-one Irish Members of Parliament who were home rulers he thought that he could count on the loyalty of all but fifteen or sixteen; and he considered only about ten of the minority active trouble-makers. "Faction in Ireland has 99 lives," he noted, and his strategy, therefore, was to allow time for the fragments to fragment. As he told the secretary of the National Federation of America:

That process is already going on. Redmondism in Dublin is split into two fiercely contending factions. And I find the best policy is to let them fight it out—without intervening actively. Healyism is gradually dying out. All we have got to do is to occupy the ground and stick doggedly to the fight— maintaining discipline at any cost—and strong in the confidence that if we can hold our Party together we shall in the course of time in three years be the only Constitutional Party in the field. But we must not expect anything very wonderful for a year or two. The people must have time to recover from all the disillusion and disappointment of the last five years.[13]

The comments that Irish reformers made about those in other factions continued to be devastating. Davitt scorned John Redmond for what he regarded as his cheap heroics. Of the Healyites, whom he considered a bunch of traitors, Davitt wrote to O'Brien: "Their ingratitude towards Dillon, their openly-avowed indifference to the fate of the Party, their general rottenness of character and disposition are such that it ought, in my humble judgment, to be a patriotic duty to relieve Ireland of the shame of having them in Westminster as her representatives." Yet the low opinion that Davitt and other Dillonites held of Redmondites and Healyites was precisely the opinion that these groups held of them. Davitt, for his part, had no doubts about how objectionable the members of the other factions found him. Indeed, the very qualities that endeared him to a humanist like AE—his fearlessness in the face of both secular and ecclesiastical authority, his lack of parochialism, his sympathy with the oppressed everywhere—made him suspect to many of his contemporaries.[14]

There was, to be sure, plenty of awareness of the need for harmony, and attempts were made to use the important anniversaries that occurred in the late nineties to restore unity. Queen Victoria's Jubilee in 1897 and the centenary of the rising of 1798 were admirable occasions for pleas for fraternity among Irish reformers. But the appeals failed. John Dillon made a famous speech in which he pointed out that when Victoria came to the throne the Irish population numbered more than eight million; after sixty years of her reign it was down to four and a half million. The Jubilee, therefore, he declared, was an occasion not for rejoicing but for grief. As Davitt ashamedly and angrily remarked, however, Healyites, Redmondites, as well as his own Dillonites were "tumbling over each other after tickets entitling them to Jubilate in the House of Commons Gallery and to lunch in Westminster Hall!"

So, too, the memory of the stamping out of the insurrection of the United Irishmen at Vinegar Hill failed to promote harmony. Maud Gonne, who went to the United States in 1897 to prepare Irish-Americans for the coming event—and to work to restore unity among them—did not succeed in her mission. It was one thing for Yeats to insist that he would be a member of Miss Gonne's group even if she declared the world flat or the moon an old Irish hat. But Miss Gonne did not always have the effect on others that she had on Yeats. In spite of her efforts it was disunited Irishmen who celebrated the deeds of the United Irishmen. Dublin, "the centre of faction-mongering and all Irish treachery against Ireland's cause," Davitt wrote angrily, needed "much more than a monument to Wolfe Tone to purge it free from the

virus which has poisoned every movement that has arisen from
Tone's time to our own."

It is true that Dillon and some of his supporters looked repeatedly for signs that factionalism was fading. But even Dillon,
despite his watchful waiting and wishful looking, reported in
1898 to the secretary of the American Federation that Irish-Irish
apathy matched Irish-American apathy. For, while the cliques
carried on their feuds, the masses had lost interest. Prospects were
so deeply discouraging that Davitt expected Dillon to resign at
any moment from the leadership of the party.[15]

V

The dangers of disunity among both Irish and Irish-Americans
became particularly clear in the period of the Spanish-American
War. There was much talk of an Anglo-American alliance; President McKinley and Joseph Chamberlain both favored it; and Irish
groups everywhere were alarmed. Davitt went to the United States
to agitate against the projected alliance, and by June he and his
colleagues rejoiced that they had provoked Chamberlain to such
an extent that he made a savage attack on Irish-Americans.

But others—astute Moreton Frewen among them—reasoned
that it was to Ireland's interest to help bring about an Anglo-
American alliance. "Would not the United States, a community
friendly on philosophic grounds to Irish aspirations, as also driven
that way by local pressure from politicos—would not the United
States find the means from time to time to intervene very usefully
in order to get what is right done here by Great Britain?" Frewen
was convinced that an alliance was imminent, but he underestimated the passions it aroused and the extent to which it moved
Irish-Americans into action.[16]

The example of cooperation among Irish-American groups in
the face of the threat of an Anglo-American alliance stimulated
renewed efforts for unity among the Irish cliques. A meeting
scheduled to take place in Limerick in January, 1899, made even
Davitt, who suffered chronically from insomnia and attacks of
what he called "the political blues," feel cheerful. As he wrote
to Emmet, "I am very hopeful of the outcome of this conference
as almost all the public bodies of Ireland have already openly
supported the efforts of the Limerick Board of Guardians to put an

end to the disastrous dissensions of the past nine years." Indeed, Davitt urged Emmet to send a message to the conference promising generous aid from Irish-Americans to a United Irish reform movement.

Once again the effort failed. Davitt was convinced of the need to organize a new Land League movement and a genuinely nationalist and democratic Irish party, but the old obstacles remained. "Redmond and Healy are I regret to say still working hard to prevent the refoundation of a united Party," Dillon told Emmet. Nevertheless, Dillon, like Davitt, hoped that the factions would be forced by public support of reunion to submerge their differences before the next general election. Then, however, when relations between Dillon and O'Brien deteriorated, Davitt became desperate, and the letter that he sent to O'Brien is one of the saddest documents in the history of Irish reform: "For my part a quarrel or the semblance of a quarrel between yourself and Dillon would compel me not alone to leave the movement but to leave Ireland. To continue on forever with no prospect but endless wranglings would be an act of insanity which I am resolved not to commit." [17]

At last the factions joined forces in 1900 and created a united party, but even this happened under unfortunate circumstances. Dillon's understanding was that Redmond, Healy, and he would step down. But Redmond and Healy came to an agreement that Redmond should assume the leadership. And they secured the support of William O'Brien. Dillon consented to the arrangement but with the feeling that he had been betrayed by O'Brien.

In the same letter in which Dillon told Emmet of his views on the reunion he noted that a big demonstration was taking place in Dublin backing the war effort against the Boers. Unionists from all parts of Ireland were participating; and many workers had been given the day off at full pay to go to Dublin to swell the crowds. No wonder Dillon found the spectacle revolting.

It is understandable that both Irish-Irish and Irish-Americans figured prominently in pro-Boer organizations. For the interest in empire, of which the Boer War was a symptom, had much to do also with the English resistance to Irish home rule. It was one thing for William Butler Yeats, when asked to contribute to an anthology that a staunch imperialist and Unionist was editing, to answer with obvious satisfaction, "But considering that I am nothing of an Imperialist and very much of an Irish 'extremist' I am afraid that in any case I could not take part in your venture." In the venture of the United Kingdom, however, the Irish had no choice except to participate. Indeed, it was one of the tragedies of the home rule movement that it came in an age of growing concern over Britain's imperial status.[18]

VI

For several reasons the outlook for the reunited Irish Parliamentary Party seemed poor in the early part of the twentieth century. In the first place, years of contention had encouraged widespread indifference, and this in turn meant limited financial resources. One of Redmond's main tasks was money-raising, and he constantly had to write begging letters to potential contributors, reminding them that he and his colleagues were poor men. Secondly, there was little reason to believe that the reunited party would stay together; "most unfortunately," as Redmond correctly noted, "there is still much enmity between some of our leading men." Nor did the business cycle make the prospects of the party seem favorable, for rising prices and profits served to make Irish farmers, the backbone of the country, less concerned with political change. And the cluster of land acts and land purchase acts—and the promise of more legislation—gave them a stake in the preservation of the United Kingdom.

It is edifying that as late as 1915 a thoughtful Irish journalist observed that the ironic result of Davitt's efforts was that England rooted the farmers of Ireland in the land and in the process riveted them to the English connection. It is no less edifying that even Douglas Hyde, the scholarly and patriotic president of the Gaelic League, was convinced in 1915 that Irish farmers, owing their farms to English land legislation, were opposed to political change. Almost on the eve of the Easter Rebellion, in other words, it seemed that the Unionist policy of economic kindness was working to prevent the United Kingdom from becoming a disunited kingdom.[19]

⟨XXI⟩

AFTER THE VICTORIANS

It has long been a tradition to deride Macaulay for his pride in the progress of early Victorian England. Often, however, those who have fostered the tradition have been unfair: they have forgotten that Macaulay, having spent years doing historical research of a sort that puts most modern scholars to shame, based his view of his own time on what he had found out about the past. The point is not that he considered early Victorian England merry; it is that he found the England of earlier ages harsh. As he aptly put it in 1844, "the ignorance of the populace of our time is knowledge and their vice virtue when compared with the ignorance and vice of their great grandfathers." But Macaulay did not deny the ignorance and vice of his own period. Far from it. And he was right to insist on the humanitarian advances that the early Victorian generation had made over its predecessors. By the same token, however, the reformers of the late Victorian age had reason to dwell on the advances that their generation had made over Macaulay's.

In 1867 at least one humanitarian wondered whether reform would "do us all any good," but generally the late Victorian reformers did not admit such a doubt. Bolstered by the conviction that problems had solutions, they compiled an impressive record of achievement. Judged by any valid historical standard—whether in relation to their predecessors in England or their contemporaries on the Continent and in the United States—they stand out as a remarkably successful lot.[1]

In a famous lecture of 1869 on "The Future of England," John Ruskin protested against words, words, words, arguing that what people thought, believed, or knew did not matter. The only thing that mattered, he insisted, was what they did. On the basis of Ruskin's standards, the late Victorian reformers easily held their own, for they helped to bring about the passage of laws relating to such a host of subjects as education, trade unions, public health, artisans' dwellings, dangerous occupations, factories, workmen's compensation, local government, small holdings, tenants' rights, land purchase, public finance, and women's rights. No less important, they made it a good old English habit to expose abuses and agitate for change. As late as 1892, to be sure, Gladstone insisted that the English, more than any other people, needed the discipline that came from "criticism vigorously directed to canvassing their character and claims." But in this instance Gladstone, preoccupied with the English maltreatment of Ireland, maltreated the English. For, if ever a people received criticism from within—and with a startling amount of openmindedness and good humor—it was the English of Gladstone's last three decades.[2]

The late Victorian reformers had much to their credit, and they knew it. The ardent trade unionist George Howell used a triumphal tone in his remarkable review of *Labour Legislation, Labour Movements, and Labour Leaders* (1902). Michael Davitt proudly placed a long list of legislative victories in the preface to his analysis of *The Fall of Feudalism in Ireland* (1904). And Florence Nightingale saw the time coming when England would be strewn with libraries that bulged with books recounting the results of reform. Even George Gissing's caustic and unsentimental Henry Ryecroft acknowledged the contributions of the late Victorian generation of reformers. The English, he sagely remarked at the time of the Jubilee of 1897, have often been "at loggerheads among themselves, but they have never flown at each other's throats, and from every grave dispute has resulted some substantial gain. They are a cleaner people and a more sober; in every class there is a diminution of brutality; education—stand for what it may—has notably extended; certain forms of tyranny have been abolished; certain forms of suffering, due to heedlessness or ignorance, have been abated."

II

Yet the specific successes of the late Victorian reformers should not obscure what was perhaps their most important achievement, which may be called linguistic. They redefined as removable evils all kinds of practices that people in Macaulay's time had accepted as natural and inescapable parts of the human condition. And by permeating their society with their broadened definitions of abuses that could be wiped out—it was not only the Fabians who permeated—they helped to enlarge their countrymen's expectations of what was desirable and possible for man in this life. Between the death of Lord Palmerston in 1865 and the death of Lord Salisbury in 1903, the late Victorian reformers effected a major transformation in social thought—and without recourse to war or a French Revolution.[3]

Evidence of the change was widespread. It appeared in a moving letter that an Oxford philologist sent in 1882 to Henry George: "I do not know what may be the right remedy, but I feel as strongly as you do that the present state of things is wrong, and ought not to last. My constant wonder is that it has lasted so long." And the change was reflected in a touching letter that a professor of political economy wrote in 1884 to A. R. Wallace: "I feel it to be a tremendous problem—this one of poverty and how to cure it and I am sometimes despondent about each and every cure. However we must try what we can." [4]

The best evidence of the change appeared in the kinds of promises that politicians by the early twentieth century made to their constituents. Virtually all politicians—whether Tories, Liberals, or the newly organized and much feared Labourites—insisted that if voters wanted a better and a more humane society, they should support their respective party. What an English Tory told an American conservative as late as 1931 he could have told him several decades before: that Americans would be startled to discover how liberal and even radical in an American sense the Tories were. W. T. Stead said as much in 1894 when he pointed out that he found less Toryism in England than among educated Chicagoans.

Winston Churchill, with the brilliance that was already his hallmark, summed up in 1906 the shift that had taken place in social thought: "Man is an individualist for some purposes, and a collectivist for others; and it is in the harmonious combination of these opposite philosophies that future statecraft is comprised. Whatever people may say, society is practically agreed upon an infinite number of varying compromises and these will multiply with every additional complication which science and civilisation add to our life." [5]

But perhaps the most convincing testimonial to the achievements of the late Victorian generation of reformers is negative. By the early twentieth century they had made it almost impossible to say all kinds of things that decades before could have been said easily. No one now could legitimately complain, as one of Carlyle's aristocratic friends did in 1854, about the stark irresponsibility of the comfortable classes and their forgetfulness of their obligations to the downtrodden. And no one could complain any longer, as some Bolton workers did in 1860, about the overwhelming public indifference to labor's plight. [6]

III

The special irony was that the Queen who gave her name to one of the greatest periods of peaceful change in world history was out of sympathy with most of the reform movements that distinguished her age. Victoria's glory, however, consisted in perhaps one thing above all: that at a time when more and more of her subjects would not accept their place she as a rule knew hers. And what was true of the Queen was true also by and large of her aristocracy. Sir Horace Plunkett did not exaggerate when he told an American politician in 1899 that the British aristocracy of birth, despite its titles and privileged political position, had less influence on legislation than the American aristocracy of wealth. [7]

The death of Victoria was expected for years before it occurred. Like Elizabeth I, however, Victoria fooled her contemporaries in no way more than by living so long. With a few notable exceptions—Herbert Spencer and Florence Nightingale—all the "big Victorians," as Arnold Bennett liked to call them, predeceased Victoria. Carlyle and Disraeli died in 1881; Darwin in 1882; Lord Shaftesbury in 1885; Bright and Browning in 1889; William Morris and Thomas Hughes in 1896; Gladstone in 1898;

and Ruskin in 1900. Even as late as July, 1900, the private secretary to the Queen reported her health to be excellent. But six months later news of "the very gravest description" came from Osborne, and that "great, noble, active life went from us." [8]

Victoria's death had a great variety of repercussions, both foreign and domestic and both trivial and important. In the United States, Germany, and Ireland it stimulated an outburst of pro-English sentiment which, in the setting of the Boer War, was much needed. In England it occasioned grief worthy of a Queen who knew the meaning of grieving. Victoria would doubtless have been pleased that her death reduced theater attendance. And she would have been delighted that her death was taken to mark the conclusion of the era to which she had long since lent her name.[9]

The age did end in the first month of the first year of the new century. It ended then for the best of all possible historical reasons—because people at the time thought so. The combination of Victoria's death, the beginning of a new century, and the hope that the Boer War would soon be over convinced contemporaries that they were off to a fresh start. But though the Edwardians viewed themselves as a new generation, they were really late Victorians. For they inherited the host of reform movements that the late Victorians had fostered. Joseph Chamberlain, W. T. Stead, H. Rider Haggard, John Burns, Keir Hardie, Sir Horace Plunkett, and John Redmond were only a few of many veteran reformers who greeted the new century with the feeling that there were still many important changes to be made.

A few years before Victoria's death reformers lost their most powerful ally—the Great Depression. It had ended for most sections of the economy in the last years of the century, and the rising prices and profits, to which businessmen had looked forward for so long, returned at last. An economy based on gloom turned into an economy based on high hopes. "Everyone in these days is looking out for hints how to get rich," a contemporary remarked in 1900, making the kind of overstatement that had been impossible for years and years.

But though the depression lifted, the reform movements which it had encouraged remained. Reformers did not stop agitating simply because the business cycle had changed. Many of them, in fact, expected a relapse to occur, and they were eventually proven right. Especially in the years after the Panic of 1907 the business cycle again came strongly to their aid. For three hard years, as W. T. Stead noted in 1910, voters had been feeling the effects of a severe depression.[10]

All the major issues with which the Edwardians dealt—education, the tariff, tax revision, social welfare legislation, women's rights, the revamping of the House of Lords, home rule, imperial reorganization—were subjects that late Victorian reformers had brought to public notice. And all the great legislative victories of the Edwardians were rooted in late Victorian agitation and experience. But this is not to say that Edwardian reformers had an easy time of it. Quite the contrary. They felt keenly the lack of outstanding political and intellectual leaders. They continued to suffer from feuds. And they had to fight their oldest enemy—and probably the greatest force in history—indifference.

IV

Reformers were particularly concerned about the absence from the Edwardian scene of distinguished political and intellectual leaders. W. T. Stead and Percy W. Bunting looked in vain for an English public figure so impressive as the new American President Theodore Roosevelt. Herbert Burrows, the ardent humanitarian, could see no coming men to fill the places of the great dead of recent years. A. H. D. Acland, the dedicated educational reformer, deplored the absence of an Edwardian social critic of the stature of John Stuart Mill or Goldwin Smith. And Winston Churchill confessed his anxiety over the mediocrity of the leaders of the British democracy. Stead, Bunting, Burrows, Acland, and Churchill were doubtless right to complain. For there was no Edwardian Gladstone, Bright, or Disraeli to whom reformers could turn; there were only Rosebery, Campbell-Bannerman, Balfour, and the much distrusted Chamberlain. But the Edwardians, filled with late Victorian memories, could set high standards for themselves. Just as Elizabeth I made her successors seem less gifted than they were, so Gladstone, Bright, and Disraeli made their successors seem less able than they were.[11]

If inspiring leaders were hard to find, quarrelsome leaders were not; and Edwardian reformers, like their predecessors, continued to luxuriate in feuds. John Redmond, having by and large re-

united the Irish home rulers, proceeded to alienate such important
Gladstonian Liberals as Herbert Asquith and Richard Haldane.
And the Liberals themselves were demoralized. The eminent
journalist J. A. Spender and other Liberals worked hard to rid
their party of the personal squabbles that had afflicted it since
before the time of Gladstone's retirement, but the difficulties were
staggering. Lord Rosebery, on whom Matthew Arnold and others
had counted for years, turned out to be a great disappointment
and in no small measure because of his pettiness and self-
centeredness. Campbell-Bannerman aroused enthusiasm for a
time, but he, too, quickly proved himself no worthy successor to
Gladstone.[12]

The personal animosities that beset the Liberals also plagued
the socialists. Even after the formation of the Labour Representation Committee in 1900 Keir Hardie and other Independent
Labour Party leaders continued to feud with Fabians, Social
Democrats, and Robert Blatchford's Clarion group. "I do not
care to have any part in the squabbles and intrigues of such a
group of twopenny pirates as the leaders of the I.L.P.," Blatchford
wrote in 1905. "Masculine persons with brains cannot work with
them," he added condescendingly. Nor was Blatchford's reaction
unrepresentative; it was only too representative. Indeed, Edward
Carpenter spoke wisely when as late as 1914 he explained why
he found the position of Labour Members of Parliament unen-
viable: "They have a great deal to put up with, nagged at on all
sides both by those who blame them from below, and those who
flout them from above." [13]

Personal hostilities were bad enough, but Edwardian reformers
also had to contend with public indifference. The end of the
Great Depression had hurt the reform cause. And then the Boer
War hindered it by diverting public attention from most domestic
questions; reform, as George Jacob Holyoake justifiably complained, was "just now in abeyance." But even after the Boer
War reformers found public indifference appalling. During the
tariff reform campaign Joseph Chamberlain urged publicists to
prepare extremely short leaflets that presented the case against
free trade. For workers, he insisted—and he knew them well—
could not be gotten to read anything more than a very brief statement; even pamphlets were much too long for them. Indeed, the

recourse to violence on the part of a small number of Edwardian reformers, especially the militant suffragettes, was little more than a bid for attention, an attempt to fight against the frustrating effects of public apathy.[14]

V

There was no meaningful division between the late Victorians and the Edwardians. But there was a sharp break between both late Victorians and Edwardians on the one hand and on the other the English who survived the First World War. For the memory of casualty lists made what Rudyard Kipling called "pre-war perspectives" impossible to recapture. The process of alienation had worked rapidly. As early as September, 1914, everyone Kipling knew had lost a relative in action. "We live under a constant sense of gloom, for every day brings news of the death of the son or brother of one of our friends," James Bryce wrote without exaggeration in 1915. And for three more years the dominant theme of English history was the same: "What casualty lists!" [15]

In these circumstances the wonder is not that the English of the twenties felt hostile to the Victorians; the wonder is that they did not feel even more hostile to them than they did. For the Victorians seemed much more remote in time than they really were, and their age was viewed—and resented—as an untroubled and serene period. Even their wars, their cold wars, and the many war scares that afflicted them came to be forgotten in the context of the shattering experiences of the First World War.

The post-war revolt against the Victorians was based on a misreading of English history. But neither the revolt nor the misreading lasted long. A more sympathetic—and truer—image of the Victorians emerged during the Great Depression of the thirties, and it has continued to hold sway in the welfare society of recent years. Now, in fact, the trouble often is that the Victorians are viewed too sympathetically. But this kind of bias is unavoidable. For, as long as humanity stays in fashion, the Victorians are sure to attract admirers. Giants, they had massive shoulders on which subsequent generations of English—and other people—have been able not only to stand but to stand comfortably.

NOTES

AIHS American Irish Historical Society
BERG Berg Collection, New York Public Library
BM British Museum Additional Manuscripts
BPL Boston Public Library
CUL Columbia University Library
HCL Harvard College Library
HSP Historical Society of Pennsylvania
JRL John Rylands Library
LC Library of Congress
MCCP Manchester Chamber of Commerce Papers
MCL Manchester Central Library
NA National Archives
NLI National Library of Ireland
NLS National Library of Scotland
NYPL New York Public Library
PML Pierpont Morgan Library
PRO Public Record Office
PUL Princeton University Library

NOTES

The manuscript sources on which this book is based are cited in full in the following notes. With few exceptions, published materials are identified only in the text, in order that the reader may not be faced with an impossibly large number of notes.

I. 1688–1788–1888

1. Adam Smith to Lt.-Col. Ross, June 13, 1787, Adam Smith Letters, BERG. Henry Gladwin to the Duke of Leeds, Sept. 27, 1788, Great Britain, Autographs, NYPL.

2. Chetham's Library: Papers of the Association for Preserving Liberty and Property, Dec. 12, 1792; Dec. 17, 1792; Jan. 24, 1793.

3. Chetham's Library: Pitt Club Papers, May 28, 1813; May 29, 1815; May 27, 1817; May 29, 1820; May 28, 1822.

4. Harriet Davenport to Edward Davies Davenport, July 21, 1815, Edward Davies Davenport Papers, JRL. Cobden to Charles Villiers, March 30, 1853, Anthony Autograph Collection, NYPL.

5. Mrs. Annie Besant to Mrs. Moncure Conway, Dec. 3, 1885, Moncure Conway Papers, CUL. George Santayana to Henry Ward Abbot, March 23, 1887, Santayana Papers, CUL. Ouida to Andrew Chatto, Jan. 30, 1889, Ouida Letters, BERG. MS poem on Matthew Arnold by Ouida in Sir John Millais Papers, PML. George Gissing to Margaret Gissing, Aug. 27, 1887, Gissing Letters, BERG. Ralph Sneyd to Henry Vincent, Jan. 20, 1846, Ralph Sneyd Papers, JRL.

6. "Wide Awake" to Cobden, postmarked April 13, 1848, Anthony Autograph Collection, NYPL. Lord John Russell to Davenport, April 5, 1822, Edward Davies Davenport Papers, JRL. MS address from the Democrats of England to the Democrats of the United States, undated, NYPL.

7. James Buchanan to C. L. Ward, Dec. 6, 1853, Buchanan Letters, New-York Historical Society. Cobden to unnamed correspondent, March 20, 1857, Anthony Autograph Collection, NYPL. Cobden to Walmsley, Dec. 12, 1857, and July 18, 1857, Misc. Papers, NYPL. Dickens to Emile de la Rue, Feb. 29, 1848, Dickens Letters, BERG.

8. John Bright to John Benjamin Smith, May 23, 1859, Smith Papers, MCL. Lord Crawford to Ernest Jones, Sept. 4, 1863, Ernest Jones Papers, MCL. Jones Papers, Chetham's Library: John Snowden to Ernest Jones, Oct. 16, 1859; Thomas Hunter to Jones, Oct. 19, 1859. Ernest Jones, MS diary, MCL: March 24, 1847; April 4, 1847; May 7, 1847.

9. Palmerston to Henslow, March 24, 1831, Dreer Collection, HSP. Bright to J. B. Smith, Dec. 24, 1853, Smith Papers, MCL. Bright to Bradford R. Wood, April 10, 1862, American Academy of Arts and Letters Collection, LC. Bright to J. B. Smith, Oct. 28, 1865, Smith Papers, MCL. J. B. Smith to Bright, Nov. 4, 1865, Bright Papers, BM43388.

10. Bright to Horace Greeley, Nov. 28, 1866, Greeley Papers, NYPL. Jones Papers, Chetham's Library: William Pyne to Ernest Jones, April 20, 1867; W. Banks to Jones, Jan. 18, no year; Joseph Shepherd to Jones, Jan. 10, 1867; B. Taylor to Jones, Jan. 14, 1867. Ernest Jones papers, CUL: Yorkshire Reform Demonstration at Leeds, April 23, 1867 (printed circular); Peterboro' Reform Demonstration (printed circular). W. E. Rice to Jones, Feb. 11, 1867, Jones Papers, Chetham's Library.

11. Bright to John Oxford, Aug. 8, 1866, Bright Letters, PUL. Bright to Greeley, Dec. 28, 1866, Bright Letters, PML. Bright to C. Edward Lester, Jan. 9, 1867, Misc. Papers, LC. Bright to W. H. Northy, Dec. 25, 1866, Bright Papers, BM44877.

12. Francis W. Newman to Epes Sargent, Sept. 17, 1866, Newman Letters, BPL. Ernest Jones Papers, CUL: Thomas Nicholson to Ernest Jones, April 5, 1867; James Paton to Jones, Jan. 21, 1867; B. Taylor to Jones, Jan. 11, 1867; Reform Fete and Banquet at the Crystal Palace on Monday, Sept. 30, 1867 (printed circular); Resolutions passed at mass meeting in St. George's Square, July 21, 1866 (printed circular); printed notice concerning the organization of a demonstration on Feb. 11, 1867.

13. Robert Curzon to Walter Sneyd, April 30, 1867, and July 10, 1867, Walter Sneyd Papers, JRL. Walt Whitman to W. C. and F. P. Church, Sept. 7, 1867, Church Papers, NYPL.

14. Lady Grey to Ralph Sneyd, no date, Ralph Sneyd Papers, JRL. Bright to Cobden, May 7, 1841, Bright Papers, BM43383. J. B. Smith to Gosling, May 28, 1867, Smith Papers, MCL. Edward Cheney to Ralph Sneyd, March 4, 1869, Ralph Sneyd Papers, JRL.

15. Robert Curzon to Walter Sneyd, May 26, 1868, Walter Sneyd Papers, JRL. Francis W. Newman to Epes Sargent, May 2, 1881, Newman Letters, BPL. J. H. Howell to Moreton Frewen, Jan. 12, 1887, Frewen Papers, LC. Cf. A. Lawrence Lowell to Richard Welling, July 6, 1931, Richard Welling Papers, NYPL.

16. Edward Cheney to Ralph Sneyd, July 28, 1869, Ralph Sneyd Papers, JRL. Trollope to Millais, June 30, 1875, Millais Papers, PML. Mark Twain to Howells, Feb. 23, 1897, Twain Letters, BERG.

17. Lord Lytton to Mrs. Schüster, Nov. 10, 1868, DeCoursey Fales Collection, NYPL. T. Perronet Thompson to H. B. Peacock, Jan. 1, 1869, Thompson Letters, JRL1180. Justin McCarthy to Church, Nov. 18, 1868, Church Papers, NYPL. Lord Zouche to Walter Sneyd, March 9, 1872 and July 24, 1871, Walter Sneyd Papers, JRL.

18. John Bright to Edward L. Pierce, Nov. 16, 1853, Bright Letters, PUL. John Cartwright to George Lamb, March 2, 1819, Dreer Collection, HSP.

19. Cobden to E. Alexander, Dec. 20, 1864 (typewritten copy), Cobden

Papers, BM43676. Florence Nightingale to A. Bourne, Nightingale Letters, Teachers College, CUL.

20. Mill to Nightingale, Dec. 31, 1867, Mill Letters, BERG. Lord Lytton to Mrs. Schüster, Nov. 10, 1868, DeCoursey Fales Collection, NYPL. Ralph Sneyd to Walter Sneyd, Feb. 10, 1870, Walter Sneyd Papers, JRL.

21. J. P. Gledstone to Mrs. S. H. Gay, Oct. 11, 1897, Gay Papers, CUL. *Economist*, XXIX (July 22, 1871), 871. W. M. Rossetti to Cook, July 9, 1871, Rossetti Letters, BERG. Frederic Harrison to E. L. Stanley, Nov. 29, no year, Stanley Papers, JRL1095. Dilke to Kate Field, Nov. 22, 1871, Kate Field Papers, BPL. Dilke to Gladstone, Jan. 3, 1883, Gladstone Papers, BM44149. Cf. John Camden Hotten to Horace Greeley, March 2, 1869, Hotten Letters, PML.

22. *Economist*, XXIX (April 15, 1871), 440. Sir Robert Samuel Wright to E. L. Stanley, Dec. 12, 1871, Stanley Papers, JRL1095. Thomas W. Cook to Francis P. Corbin, Dec. 23, 1871, Corbin Papers, NYPL. Joseph Thompson to E. L. Stanley, Dec. 15, 1871, Stanley Papers, JRL1095.

23. Gladstone to Ponsonby, Dec. 22, 1871, Ponsonby Papers, BM45724. W. T. Stead to Albert Shaw, June 24, 1891, and July 1, 1891, Albert Shaw Papers, NYPL.

24. Disraeli to Sa, April 18, 1850, Lee Kohns Collection, NYPL. Walter Sneyd Papers, JRL: Robert Curzon to Walter Sneyd, Feb. 8, 1869; April 22, 1868; Sept. 4, 1868. Ralph Sneyd Papers, JRL: Charles Bertie Percy to Ralph Sneyd, May 27, no year; Edward Cheney to Ralph Sneyd, July 28, 1869. Southey to William Shepherd, April 30, 1837, Southey Letters, JRL384.

25. Ernest Jones, newspaper clipping, MCL; R. J. Muir to T. Fisher Unwin, Halloween, 1900, Unwin Papers, BERG.

26. Thomas F. Walker to Henry George, Oct. 8, 1885, Henry George Papers, NYPL.

II. THE LONG TRIAL

1. Wells Papers, LC: Francis Lawley to David A. Wells, July 25, 1871; E. W. Watkins to Wells, March 15, 1878. George Burgess to Herbert Burgess, June 11, 1878 (letterpress copy book), Burgess Papers, NYPL.

2. Hugh McCulloch to Wells, July 15, 1871, Wells Papers, NYPL. *Guide to Manchester and Salford* (Edinburgh, 1873), p. 3. *The Cotton Supply Association: Its Origin and Progress* (Manchester, 1871), p. 12. J. B. Smith to Robert Lowe, Jan. 2, 1873 (copy), Smith Papers, MCL. Lord Delamere to Walter Sneyd, no date, Walter Sneyd Papers, JRL.

3. George Burgess to his cousin, Nov. 2, 1875, Burgess Papers, NYPL. Sir Louis Mallet to Wells, July 26, 1875, Wells Papers, LC. John Hopkinson to I. W. Hollis, April 16, 1877, Walter Sneyd Papers, JRL. Henry Ashworth to Edward Smith, June 7, 1877, Edward Smith Papers, NYPL.

4. Bright to Cyrus Field, Aug. 9, 1877, Field Papers, PML. Bright to Smith, Sept. 7, 1877, J. B. Smith Papers, MCL. Agent's Report for Jan., 1878, Hollis to Walter Sneyd, Walter Sneyd Papers, JRL. J. B. Gould to F. W. Seward, May 20, 1878, Consular Letters from Birmingham, NA. C. O. Shepard to F. W. Seward, June 14, 1878, Consular Letters from Bradford, NA. Elizabeth Blackwell to Barbara Bodichon, Nov. 12, 1878, Blackwell Letters, CUL. Bright to Cyrus Field, June 5, 1879, Field Papers, PML. Bright to W. H. Worthy, July 1, 1879, Oct. 30, 1879, Bright Papers, BM44877. Thomas Hughes

to unnamed American correspondent, Sept. 19, 1879, Anthony Autograph Collection, NYPL.

5. Scottish Provident Institute, *Forty-second Annual Report* (Edinburgh, 1880), p. 3. MCCP, Feb. 3, 1879, MCL. A. V. Dockery to F. W. Seward, June 16, 1879, Consular Letters from Leeds, NA.

6. Wilson King to Assistant Secretary of State, Oct. 12, 1880, Consular Letters from Birmingham, NA. Lord Somers to Walter Sneyd, March 4, 1881, Walter Sneyd Papers, JRL. David Seligman to Edwin Seligman, March 3, 1882, Seligman Papers, CUL. Charles Fitzwilliam, electoral address, Nov. 7, 1885, Bagshawe Papers, JRL. MCCP, March 22, 1886, MCL. Thomson Hankey to Wells, June 11, 1884, and July 11, 1885, Wells Papers, LC.

7. Albert Shaw Papers, NYPL: W. T. Stead to Albert Shaw, Sept. 9, 1892; Sept. 14, 1892; July 7, 1894. MCCP, April 13, 1892, and July 8, 1895, MCL. W. H. L. Cameron to Sir William Bromley Davenport, Dec. 29, 1896, Sir William Bromley Davenport Papers, JRL. Henry Adams Letters, NYPL: Henry Adams to W. C. Ford, March 10, 1897; Dec. 19, 1898; Feb. 28, 1899; Nov. 26, 1898.

8. John Stuart Mill to Carlyle, Oct. 17, 1835, Carlyle Papers, NLS. Smith Papers, MCL: Cobden to J. B. Smith, Sept. 6, 1859; J. B. Smith to unnamed correspondent, Dec. 31, 1857. C. O. Shepard to Assistant Secretary of State, Feb. 13, 1879, Consular Letters from Bradford, NA. Bright Papers, BM44877: Bright to Northy, April 30, 1877; Aug. 1, 1877; Dec. 27, 1877; Dec. 29, 1878. George Burgess to John Black, Nov. 29, 1879 (letterpress copy book), Burgess Papers, NYPL. Cf. W. Oulton, *Business and Literature* (Liverpool, 1868), pp. 9, 12–13.

9. T. Foljambe to George Burgess, Aug. 24, 1875, Burgess Papers, NYPL. Lord Granville to Walter Sneyd, Oct. 5, 1878, Walter Sneyd Papers, JRL. Chatto and Windus to Kate Field, April 23, 1878, Stedman Papers, CUL. Wilkie Collins to George Bentley, July 27, 1879, Collins Letters, BERG. E. C. Stedman to R. H. Stoddard, Sept. 2, 1879, Anthony Autograph Collection, NYPL.

10. C. O. Shepard to Robert R. Hitt, Dec. 13, 1881, Consular Letters from Bradford, NA. MCCP, Feb. 20, 1886, MCL. BERG: George Gissing to Ellen Gissing, May 21, 1886, Gissing Letters; Ouida to Chatto, April 15, 1883, June 3, 1886, Sept. 27, 1886 (?), Ouida Letters; Thomas Hughes to Mrs. Carpenter, March 24, 1887, Hughes Letters. James Allen to unnamed correspondent, Dec. 21, 1886, Ecclesiastical Autograph Letters, JRL843.

11. Stead to Shaw, March 11, 1893, Albert Shaw Papers, NYPL. George David Boyle to William Knight, April 15, 1893, William Knight Papers, PML. Henry Lunn to Shaw, Oct. 10, 1894, Albert Shaw Papers, NYPL. Augustus Hare to unnamed correspondent, Dec. 28, 1896, DeCoursey Fales Collection, NYPL. Andrew C. Bradley to Unwin, May 18, 1896, Unwin Papers, BERG.

12. MCCP, Nov. 2, 1885, MCL. Michael Davitt to Henry George, Nov. 1 1885; NYPL: Philip H. Wicksteed to Henry George, Oct. 29, 1882, George Papers; W. Stanley Jevons to J. M. Libbey, Dec. 22, 1878, Misc. Papers. Thomson Hankey to Wells, Feb. 4, 1885, Wells Papers, LC. C. O. Shepard to F. W. Seward, Feb. 13, 1879, Consular Letters from Bradford, NA.

13. *Economic Journal*, I (1891), 12, 6. H. W. Hollis to Walter Sneyd, May 5 1873, April 19, 1873, Letterbooks, Walter Sneyd Papers, JRL.

14. Press clipping, Leamington Spa *Courier*, Nov. 30, 1878, William Bromley Davenport Papers, JRL. Bright to Gladstone, Dec. 24, 1877, and Nov. 15

1878, Gladstone Papers, BM44113. Joseph Smith to George Burgess, July 19, 1879, Burgess Papers, NYPL.

15. Hely Smith, *Thoughts for Electors*, election circular dated Sept. 26, 1885, Bagshawe Papers, JRL. Press clippings, Macclesfield *Courier and Herald*, June 6, 1885, and Sept. 5, 1885, Sir William Bromley Davenport Papers, JRL.

16. Conservative Publication Department, *The Two Records*, circular dated April, 1892, Bagshawe Papers, JRL.

17. Cobden to William Neild, Sept. 30, 1838, William Neild Papers, JRL868. MCC Petition to the House of Commons, Jan. 20, 1838, copy, MCL. Smith to Robert Lowe, Jan. 2, 1873 (copy), Smith Papers, MCL.

18. Coleridge to C. Aders, Aug. 4, 1823, General MSS Collection, CUL. Cf. Mary Howett to Mrs. Lydia H. Sigourney, July 7, 1841, DeCoursey Fales Autograph Collection, NYPL. Curzon to Sneyd, Sept. 5, 1869, Walter Sneyd Papers, JRL. MCCP, July 9, 1875, MCL. Consular Letters from Bradford, NA: C. O. Shepard to F. W. Seward, June 14, 1878; C. O. Shepard to John Hay, Feb. 2, 1880.

19. Newspaper clipping, Salford *Chronicle*, Dec. 17, 1892, Manchester Ship Canal Papers, Chetham's Library. MCL: MCCP, May 26, 1886; Oct. 26, 1887; Dec. 28, 1887; Oct. 31, 1887; April 23, 1888; March 26, 1890. Alfred Waterhouse Papers, MCL: Waterhouse to Joseph Thompson, May 5, 1876, and May 22, 1876. James Dredge to William Eleroy Curtis, Nov. 20, 1891, Curtis Papers, CUL. Alfred Marshall to F. C. Harrison, May 18, 1905, Seligman Collection, CUL.

20. NA: J. Nunn to Assistant Secretary of State, Dec. 22, 1880, Consular Letters from London; Wilson King to Assistant Secretary of State, Oct. 12, 1880, Consular Letters from Birmingham. NYPL: Shaw to Stead, Oct. 23, 1894, and Nov. 20, 1894 (letter books), Albert Shaw Papers; consular statement signed by Bret Harte, Oct. 18, 1884, Misc. Papers; Edward Atkinson to Nordhoff, June 10, 1883, Atkinson Papers. Cf. Elihu Burritt, *Walks in the Black Country and Its Green Border-Land* (London, 1868), p. 358. Peter Ainsworth to Lord John Russell, undated, Autograph Collection, MCL. Bessemer to Carnegie, July 4, 1894, Carnegie Papers, NYPL.

21. Edwin A. Abbey to Millais, Feb. 14, 1895, Millais Papers, PML. George Gissing to Algernon Gissing, Nov. 13, 1876, Gissing Letters, BERG. Lord Beaconsfield to Kate Field, Jan. 19, 1878, Kate Field Papers, BPL. Cyrus Field to Gladstone, April 27, 1877, Gladstone Papers, BM44454. Gilbert to Marion Johnson, Feb. 12, 1880, Gilbert & Sullivan Collection, PML. Albert Shaw Papers, NYPL: Stead to Shaw, Dec. 31, 1892; Edwin H. Stout to Shaw, Aug. 6, 1892; Secretary of Goldsmiths' Company Technical and Recreative Institute to Shaw, Oct. 16, 1891. *Hints to Carriage Buyers* (London, 1893), p. 27. Charles Gide to J. B. Clark, Dec. 26, 1889, J. B. Clark Papers, CUL. Robert Donald to Shaw, Oct. 12, 1896, Albert Shaw Papers, NYPL.

22. Newspaper clipping, W. Farrer Ecroyd to the editor of the Bradford *Observer*, Feb. 28, 1879, Consular Papers from Bradford, NA. NYPL: R. R. Bowker, MS journal, Oct. 8, 1880; Edward A. Freeman to J. M. Libbey, Feb. 27, 1881, Misc. Papers; Walter Besant to Charles Todd, Jan. 22, 1892, Lee Kohns Collection. C. O. Shepard to F. W. Seward, May 13, 1879, Consular Letters from Bradford, NA. NYPL: George Burgess to George Burgess Company, June 21, 1878 (letterpress copy book), Burgess Papers; Bowker, MS journal, Aug. 22, 1880, and Oct. 1, 1880.

23. NYPL: R. M. Gilchrist to K. Parkes, undated, Gilchrist Letters; Shaw

to Henry S. Lunn, March 26, 1894 (letter book), Albert Shaw Papers; Bowker, MS journal, April 3, 1881.

24. NYPL: Eizak Pitman to Mrs. Chivers, Jan. 4, 1883, Misc. Papers; Laura Jean Libbey, MS journal, IV, 509. George Gissing to Margaret Gissing, Sept. 29, 1889, Gissing Letters, BERG. Foxwell to Seligman, July 7, 1917, March 5, 1928, Seligman Papers, CUL.

25. Julian Hawthorne, MS on London environs, p. 36, NYPL. Lincoln Steffens to F. M. Willis, Jan. 29, 1891, and one undated, Steffens Papers, CUL. Walter Crane to Charles Rowley, July 25, 1892, Autograph Collection, MCL. Mrs. Craigie to Unwin, May 19, 1892, Unwin Papers, BERG. Kipling to Henley, Jan. 19, 1893, Henley Papers, PML. Arthur Jordan to Rand School, Nov. 8, 1925, Algernon Lee Papers, Tamiment Institute Library. Bernard Shaw to Lord Dunsany, Oct. 11, 1916, Bernard Shaw Letters, BERG.

26. E. Perry to Sir John Millais, Feb. 19, 1881, Millais Papers, PML. Sullivan to Escott, Dec. 14, 1896, Gilbert & Sullivan Collection, PML. Wolverhampton Art and Industrial Exhibit, 1902, *Catalogue of the Exhibits in the Fine Art Section*, p. 10.

27. John Bowring, *The Influence of Knowledge on Domestic and Social Happiness* (London, n.d.), pp. 3–4. Horace Greeley, *The Crystal Palace and Its Lessons: A Lecture* (New York, 1852), p. 18.

28. Henry Adams to W. C. Ford, Nov. 26, 1898, Adams Letters, NYPL. Joseph Schumpeter to J. B. Clark, June 6, 1907, Clark Papers, CUL. Cf. Max Beer to Algernon Lee, June 12, 1929, Algernon Lee Papers, Tamiment Institute Library.

29. Ruskin to Blanche Atkinson, April 19, 1875, Ruskin Letters, JRL1162. BERG: George Gissing to Margaret Gissing, April 15, 1886, Gissing Letters; Arnold Bennett to George Sturt, May 8, 1897, Bennett Letters. Advertisement on cover of pamphlet by the Wharfedale Poet, *Yorkshire Poems, No. 4* (Leeds, 1876); italics added.

III. THE NEW MASTERS

1. W. J. Ashley to Seligman, April 5, 1906, Seligman Papers, CUL. F. W. Newman to Epes Sargent, Nov. 2, 1878, Newman Letters, BPL. Home Office 45 (79559), PRO: Home Office summary prepared at Mr. Cross's request, Feb., 1879; circular letter from A. F. O. Liddell, Dec. 27, 1878; Jesse Collings to Liddell, Dec. 29, 1878; John W. Robinson to Liddell, Dec. 31, 1878; William Robinson to Cross, Dec. 30, 1878; H. Underhill to Liddell, Dec. 30, 1878; A. H. Webster to Cross, Dec. 31, 1878; Charles S. Grundy to Liddell, Dec. 28, 1878; Henry Morgan to Cross, Jan. 6, 1879; memorandum concerning towns where special measures of relief have been taken; David Ward to Cross, Dec. 27, 1878.

2. Home Office 45 (79559), PRO: William Robinson to Cross, Jan. 24, 1879; John T. Arlidge to Cross, Dec. 30, 1878.

3. Carnegie Papers, NYPL: Mrs. Gladstone to Mrs. Carnegie, Feb. 27, 1885; Mrs. Gladstone to Carnegie, Dec. 1, 1885. Ouida to Chatto, n.d., Ouida Letters, BERG. W. Sharman to George, Dec. 17, 1885, Henry George Papers, NYPL. Macclesfield election address, June 26, 1886, Sir William Bromley Davenport Papers, JRL. Helen M. Gould, MS diary, Nov. 6, 1887, and Nov. 8, 1887, New-York Historical Society. George Gissing to Ellen Gissing, Nov. 13, 1887, Gissing Letters, BERG. John Burns, MS diary, BM46310: June 30, 1888; July 27, 1888; March 18, 1888; June 25, 1888.

4. Plato E. Draculis to William Shaw, Jan. 16, 1891, William Shaw Papers, CUL. S. R. Crockett to Unwin, Nov. 16, 1893, Unwin Papers, BERG. John Burns to Knowles, Jan. 9, 1893, Seligman Collection, CUL. Sir William Bromley Davenport Papers, JRL: James Barber to Davenport, Feb. 13, 1895; James Buckley to Davenport, Jan. 31, 1895. Shaw to Stead, June 1, 1894 (letter book), Albert Shaw Papers, NYPL.

5. *Church Reformer,* July, 1889, J. B. Clark Papers, CUL. MCCP, MCL: June 28, 1873; April 30, 1888; Nov. 4, 1895.

6. Spectator to Editor of Manchester *Chronicle,* Nov. 11, 1833, clipping, J. B. Smith Papers, MCL. Printed circulars of National Association, and Mortimer Grimshaw to Rylands & Sons, Aug. 19, 1864, JRL1185.

7. William Lovett to Moncure Conway, Feb. 3, 1877, Conway Papers, CUL. Baker Letters, NYPL: Baker to Mrs. Lowell, Aug. 31, 1877; Feb. 11, 1878; Aug. 27, 1879.

8. Charles Brocklehurst to Liddell, Jan. 8, 1879, Home Office 45 (79559), PRO. Lord Delamere to Walter Sneyd, undated, Walter Sneyd Papers, JRL. Charles Dickens to F. O. Ward, Jan. 20, 1852, Autograph Collection, JRL341. John Bright to William Fogg, Sept. 23, 1878, Autograph Collection, MCL. C. O. Shepard to F. W. Seward, June 14, 1878, Consular Letters from Bradford, NA.

9. Ruskin to Blanche Atkinson, March 21, 1875, Ruskin Letters, JRL1162. Gissing, MS diary, July 8, 1888, BERG. J. M. Ludlow to Seligman, July 24, 1886, Seligman Papers, CUL. Draculis to William Shaw, Jan. 13, 1897, William Shaw Papers, CUL. Circular reprinted from the *Labour Leader,* Aug. 8, 1896, Unwin Papers, BERG. Joseph Marshall Pickles to G. N. Barnes, April 29, 1899, John Burns Papers, BM46288. Parrish Collection, PUL: Thomas Hughes to unnamed correspondent, Oct. 3, 1893; Hughes to Solly, Oct. 4, 1891.

10. George Potter to Lord Latham, April 30, 1887, LC2(100), PRO. Stead to Burns, Dec. 12, 1892, Burns Papers, BM46288. Hobhouse to Unwin, Feb. 10, 1893, Unwin Papers, BERG. MCCP, July 25, 1887, MCL. George Kidson to Burns, July 23, 1892, Burns Papers, BM46288.

11. James Nugent to Raffles, April 12, 1873, Raffles Autograph Collection, JRL381.

12. MCCP, March 28, 1877, MCL. Wilkie Collins to William Winter, May 16, 1888, Collins Letters, Folger Shakespeare Library. Wilkie Collins to T. Dixon-Spain, June 23, 1887, BM45918. Stead to Shaw, Sept. 21, 1892, Albert Shaw Papers, NYPL.

13. Leone Levi to A. Arthur Reade, March 9, 1882, Arents Collection, NYPL. Levi to Raffles, Dec. 23, 1871, Raffles Collection, JRL380.

14. NYPL: Stanton, MS London journal, Feb. 16, 1879, and Feb. 21, 1879; Bowker, MS journal, Aug. 30, 1880. P. T. Barnum to T. Dixon-Spain, Nov. 20, 1882, BM45918.

15. Temperance Collection, JRL863: Thomas Hardy to T. H. Hildred, Oct. 7, 1882; William Dunn to unnamed correspondent, Oct., 1882. Lord Jersey to R. V. French, Jan. 8, 1881, Great Britain, Autographs, LC.

16. Ruskin to F. O. Ward, undated, Autograph Collection, JRL341. George Gissing to Katie Gissing, Jan. 21, 1889, Gissing Letters, BERG. Ernest Dowson to Moore, Sept. 9, 1889, and one undated, Dowson Letters, PML. Nightingale to All Our Nurses, May 28, 1900, Nightingale Letters, Teachers College Library, Columbia University.

17. Wharfedale Poet, *Yorkshire Poems, No. 4* (Leeds, 1876). Earl of Durham to T. Ellaby, June 10, 1890, Autograph Collection, JRL340. *The New Il-*

lustrated Guide to Southport and the Neighbourhood (Southport, 1878),
p. 3. George Gissing to Margaret Gissing, May 29, 1882, Gissing Letters, BERG.
Draculis to William Shaw, May 18, 1891, William Shaw Papers, CUL.

IV. THE UNPEACEFUL COUNTRYSIDE

1. Robert Burns to Robert Cleghorn, March 31, 1788, Misc. Papers, NYPL.
2. Curzon to Sneyd, June 1, 1870, and Nov. 19, 1872, Walter Sneyd Papers,
JRL. Stafford Northcote to Sir R. W. Rawson, Dec. 3, 1875, BM45918.
3. R. Cowley Powles to Walter Sneyd, July 3, 1877, Walter Sneyd Papers,
JRL. Lord Stratford de Redcliffe to J. M. Libbey, Dec. 21, 1878, Misc. Papers,
NYPL. F. W. Newman to Epes Sargent, Sept. 8, 1879, Newman Letters, BPL.
Cash and account book for 1879, MS volume, Walter Sneyd Papers, JRL.
Blackmore Letters, BERG: Blackmore to Mrs. T. R. Macquoid, Aug. 8,
1879; Blackmore to T. R. Macquoid, April 30, 1880. Lord Somers to Walter
Sneyd, March 4, 1881, Walter Sneyd Papers, JRL.
4. Newspaper clipping, *Times*, Oct. 31, 1879, William Bromley Davenport
Papers. J. R. Lowell, *On Democracy: An Address Delivered in the Town Hall,
Birmingham, on the 6th of October, 1884,* p. 5. Newspaper clipping, *Daily
Gazette*, Feb. 1, 1883, William Bromley Davenport Papers, JRL. Memorandum
from Bright to Gladstone, May 14, 1880, Gladstone Papers, BM44113.
5. Anthony Collection, NYPL: Bowker, MS journal, Aug. 6, 1880; John
Bigelow, MS diary, May 16, 1870, and June 18, 1877; George Burgess to his
cousin, April 3, 1878 (letterpress copy book), Burgess Papers; E. C. Stedman
to R. H. Stoddard, Sept. 2, 1879. Bright to Smith, June 17, 1879, J. B. Smith
Papers, MCL.
6. George Burgess to his cousin, Sept. 4, 1876, Burgess Papers, NYPL. Elizabeth Blackwell to Barbara Bodichon, Oct. 29, 1877, Blackwell Letters, CUL.
Newspaper clipping, *Times,* March 25, 1898, Cockran Papers, NYPL.
7. Burgess Papers, NYPL: George Burgess to Edwin Ransom, June 14,
1880; Burgess to his son, Oct. 18, 1880; Burgess to his cousin, Sept. 4, 1876
(letterpress copy book). JRL: Lord Somers to Sneyd, March 4, 1881, Walter
Sneyd Papers; E. G. Wheler to Henry Martin Cornwall Legh, Feb. 4, 1882,
Henry Martin Cornwall Legh Papers. NYPL: Thomson Hankey to David
Wells, April 12, 1882, Wells Papers; Edward Atkinson to Robert B. Porter,
Feb. 16, 1882, Edward Atkinson Papers. Electoral address of Charles Fitz-
william, Nov. 7, 1885, Bagshawe Papers, JRL. NYPL: William E. Bear to
Thomas F. Bayard, Sept. 23, 1887, Misc. Papers; Edward Thornton to W. G.
Le Duc, Jan. 14, 1878, W. G. Le Duc Papers; Henry Howard to Ezra A.
Carman, Feb. 2, 1883, Ezra A. Carman Papers.
8. John Fiske to wife, Feb. 27, 1883, Fiske Papers, LC. BERG: Gissing,
MS diary, Jan. 5, 1888; George Gissing to Algernon Gissing, Feb. 16, 1892,
Gissing Letters. Cf. H. Rider Haggard to Ella, Sept. 14, 1893, M. F. Hale:
Autograph Collection, LC.
9. CUL: H. S. Foxwell to Seligman, Nov. 24, 1895, Seligman Papers; circular
for *A Farmer's Year,* H. Rider Haggard Papers. Electoral address, July 8
1895, Sir William Bromley Davenport Papers, JRL. Gladstone to Carnegie
June 8, 1897, Jan. 4, 1897, photostats, Misc. Papers, NYPL.
10. Halifax Wyatt to Lord Egerton of Talton, Feb. 23, 1886 (copy), Corn
wall Legh Papers, JRL. Cf. Lord Elgin to General Ross, April 18, 1809
Elgin Letters, PML. JRL: F. W. Bagshawe to W. H. Bagshawe, March 1

1877, Bagshawe Papers; Joseph Ball to H. W. Hollis, Aug. 1, 1877, Walter Sneyd Papers; cottage agreements between Alfred Johnson and Col. Cornwall Legh, Oct. 29, 1887, Cornwall Legh Papers; H. W. Hollis to Samuel Orme, Aug. 14, 1873, and H. W. Hollis to Walter Sneyd, Sept. 29, 1873 (letter books), Walter Sneyd Papers. John Nichol to William Knight, Oct. 16, 1879, Knight Papers, PML.

11. JRL: Lord Somers to Walter Sneyd, March 4, 1881; Edward Hussey to Sneyd, Dec. 24, 1887; Henry W. Bertie to Sneyd, March 29, 1888; rental books, Walter Sneyd Papers. Newspaper clipping, Coventry *Standard*, Dec. 12, 1879, William Bromley Davenport Papers. W. H. Bourne to Robert Gill, Jan. 13, 1887, Walter Sneyd Papers.

12. JRL: E. G. Wheler to Cornwall Legh, Feb. 4, 1882, Cornwall Legh Papers; George Kent to H. W. Hollis, July 26, 1876, Walter Sneyd Papers. Lord Campendown to Knight, Feb. 4, 1882; Knight Papers, PML. Ralph Sneyd to Mrs. Walter Sneyd, Feb. 22, 1880, Walter Sneyd Papers, JRL. NYPL: Mary Gladstone to Carnegie, Aug. 16, 1882, Carnegie Collection; Baker to Mrs. Josephine Shaw Lowell, Nov. 6, 1879, and Dec. 23, 1879, Thomas Barwick Lloyd Baker Letters.

13. JRL: Lord Somers to Sneyd, Oct., 1882, Walter Sneyd Papers; agent to Bagshawe, March 1, 1894, Bagshawe Papers.

14. John Temple Leader to Sneyd, Dec. 21, 1887, Walter Sneyd Papers, JRL. Albert Shaw Papers, NYPL: Stead to Shaw, Aug. 25, 1894; Shaw to Stead, Oct. 23, 1894 (letter book).

15. JRL: Newspaper clipping, *Times*, Oct. 31, 1879; electoral address, April 5, 1880, William Bromley Davenport Papers. Lord Verulam to Sneyd, Dec. 11, 1884, Walter Sneyd Papers. Newspaper clipping, *Times*, July 31, 1880, William Bromley Davenport Papers.

16. Joseph Smith to George Burgess, July 19, 1879, Burgess Papers, NYPL. Wilson King to Assistant Secretary of State, Oct. 12, 1880, Consular Letters from Birmingham, NA. Gladstone to Mrs. Ward, April 16, 1888, Mrs. Humphry Ward Papers, PML.

17. Hughes to Octavius R. Wilkinson, Dec. 19, 1878, Thomas Hughes Letters, Parrish Collection, PUL. J. L. Kipling to A. M. Poynter, July 25, no year, Anthony Autograph Collection, NYPL.

18. Joseph Chamberlain to Haggard, Aug. 1, 1903, H. Rider Haggard Papers, CUL.

19. Louisa Dorothea Stanley to Edward Lyulph Stanley, Oct. 17, 1871, Stanley Papers, JRL1093. Blackmore Letters, BERG: Blackmore to Mrs. T. R. Macquoid, July 18, 1883; Blackmore to C. J. Down, April 19, 1884.

20. MCCP, July 8, 1895, MCL. Newspaper clipping, Coventry *Independent Journal*, Oct. 29, 1879, William Bromley Davenport Papers, JRL. *Hints to Carriage Buyers* (London, 1893), pp. 24–25.

21. George Burgess to Joseph Smith, May 19, 1880, Burgess Papers, NYPL. J. H. Howell to Moreton Frewen, Jan. 12, 1887, Moreton Frewen Papers, LC. Cf. J. W. Martin to Campbell-Bannerman, March 23, 1899, Campbell-Bannerman Papers, BM41234.

V. DOING GOOD

1. John Stuart Mill to G. C. Lewis, Nov. 24, 1837, Mill Letters, CUL. Cobden to Walmsley, Dec. 18, 1858, Misc. Papers, NYPL. C. O. Shepard to

F. W. Seward, May 13, 1879, Consular Letters from Bradford, NA. Elizabeth Blackwell to Barbara Bodichon, Feb. 4, 1884, Blackwell Letters, CUL. Henry George Papers, NYPL: J. C. Durant to George, Feb. 24, 1886, March 22, 1886, March 30, 1886; Helen Taylor to Mrs. George, July 8, 1890.

2. George Gissing to Herbert H. Sturmer, Oct. 4, 1896, Gissing Letters, BERG. Newspaper clipping of 1897 quoting Sir Walter Besant, Henry George, Jr., Papers, NYPL.

3. CUL: J. P. Gledstone to Mrs. Sidney Howard Gay, Oct. 11, 1897, Gay Papers; J. M. Robertson to Moncure Conway, Feb. 13, 1902, Conway Papers.

4. Bright to Smith, Oct. 11, 1852, J. B. Smith Papers, MCL. BERG: Matthew Arnold to Frederic M. Bird, March 18, 1878, Arnold Letters; John Stuart Mill to Florence Nightingale, Dec. 31, 1867 (draft), Mill Letters. Samuel Pearson to T. S. Raffles, June 21, 1876, Raffles Collection, JRL382. William Cobbett materials in Edward Smith Collection, NYPL.

5. NYPL: Wicksteed to George, April 21, 1883, Henry George Papers; W. P. Byles, typescript article, Henry George, Jr., Papers. William Cobbett to Asbury Dickins, Jan. 20, 1818, Cobbett Letters, New-York Historical Society. Campbell-Bannerman to Stead, Oct. 11, 1892 (copy), Campbell-Bannerman Papers, BM41233.

6. Maude Valery White to Millais, Jan. 13, 1887, Millais Papers, PML. Elizabeth Blackwell to Barbara Bodichon, March 10, 1884, Blackwell Letters, CUL. NYPL: R. Murray Gilchrist to Kineton Parkes, Aug. 17, 1891, Gilchrist Letters; Frances Hodgson Burnett to Annie Russell, Sept. 1, 1899, Annie Russell Papers. Florence Nightingale to Trelawney Saunders, Dec. 30, 1885, Nightingale Letters, New-York Historical Society.

7. Thomas Clarkson to Joseph Crossfield, Aug. 26, 1808, Thomas Raffles Collection, JRL374. W. Morrison to Conway, March 9, 1875, Conway Papers, CUL. Holyoake to T. Fisher Unwin, Oct. 13, 1904, Unwin Papers, BERG. Bright to Edward West, Dec. 19, 1877, Bright Letters, PUL. Cruikshank Letters, BERG: Cruikshank to Dickens, April 3, 1841; Cruikshank to Horace Mayhew, June 12, 1867; newspaper clipping, Standard, Feb. 2, 1878. Thomas Hughes to Seligman, Oct. 7, 1883, Seligman Papers, CUL. Baker to Mrs. Lowell, Dec. 10, 1877, Baker Letters, NYPL.

8. William Wilberforce to Black, April 9, no year, Wilberforce Letters, PML. Josephine Butler to William Lloyd Garrison, May, 1874, Garrison Papers, BPL. Florence Nightingale to All Our Nurses, May 28, 1900, Nightingale Letters, Teachers College Library, Columbia University. Harriet Beecher Stowe to Charles Kingsley, March 20, 1852, Stowe Letters, BERG. NYPL: Baker to Mrs. Lowell, Aug. 6, 1881, Baker Letters; Wicksteed to George, Feb. 4, 1883, and George to Father Dawson, Feb. 1, 1883, George Papers; Stead to Shaw, Jan. 14, 1893, Albert Shaw Papers. Stead to Mrs. John Burns, Jan. 18, 1888, John Burns Papers, BM46288. Gladstone to Mrs. Humphry Ward, April 16, 1888, Gladstone Letters, PML. Gladstone to E. T. Cook, Dec. 25, 1889, Misc. Papers, NYPL.

9. Josephine Butler to William Lloyd Garrison, June 10, 1877, Garrison Papers, BPL. NYPL: Baker to Mrs. Lowell, Nov. 6, 1879, Baker Letters; George to Ford, Dec. 28, 1881 (letter book), and George to Francis G. Shaw, Feb. 11, 1882, George Papers. Dowson to Moore, undated, Ernest Dowson Letters, PML.

10. BERG: George Gissing to Margaret and Ellen Gissing, May 9, 1880, Gissing Letters. Matthew Arnold to John Cropper, Nov. 11, 1874, Thomas

Raffles Collection, JRL372. Ruskin Letters, PML: Ruskin to Oddie, April 10, 1875, and Ruskin to Lucy Tuck, April 27, 1876.

11. Thomas Hughes to unnamed correspondent, March 16, 1885, Lee Kohns Collection, NYPL. Cardinal Manning to Conway, March 26, 1889, Conway Papers, CUL. Frederic Harrison to George Eliot, June 5, 1869, Harrison Letters, BERG. Helen Taylor to George, April 12, 1889, Henry George Papers, NYPL. Andrew Reid to A. R. Wallace, March 6, 1894, Wallace Papers, BM6440.

12. Nathaniel Hawthorne to Elizabeth Peabody, Aug. 13, 1857, Hawthorne Letters, BERG. Albert Shaw Papers, NYPL: Stead to Shaw, Jan. 28, 1893; March 31, 1894; March 22, 1893.

13. Josephine E. Butler to Aaron Powell, Feb. 17, 1880, S. H. Gay Papers, CUL. Cf. William Smart to Seligman, June 23, 1895, Seligman Papers, CUL. Baker to Mrs. Josephine Lowell, Dec. 28, 1880, Baker Letters, NYPL. Stead to Burns, April 24, 1894, Burns Papers, BM46288. H. R. Grenfell to Moreton Frewen, Feb. 18, 1887, Frewen Papers, LC. William Frey Papers, NYPL: Percival Chubb to William Frey, Jan. 18, 1887; Thomas Sulman to Frey, undated; E. Beesly to Frey, July 6, 1888; J. H. Bridges to Frey, Oct. 4, 1886; Henry Crompton to Frey, June 27, 1888; Frederic Harrison to Frey, July 20, 1888.

14. Gladstone to Hendriks, June 27, 1867, Gladstone Letters, PML. Josephine E. Butler to Mrs. McCormick, Feb. 17, 1879, National Union of Women's Suffrage Societies Papers, MCL. George Papers, NYPL: George to Walker, June 26, 1884; George to Taylor, June 29, 1882; Walker to George, Feb. 13, 1889; Hyndman to George, March 14, no year. F. W. Newman to Epes Sargent, Aug. 20, 1871, Newman Letters, BPL. Sir Charles Dilke to Joseph Chamberlain, Feb. 3, 1883 (copy), Dilke Papers, BM43953. George Burgess to Joseph Smith, March 11, 1881 (letter book), Burgess Papers, NYPL. John Burns, MS diary, Aug. 1, 1888, BM46310.

15. Florence Nightingale to William Acraman, Sept. 26, 1877, American Academy of Arts and Letters Collection, LC. Nightingale to Miss M. J. Loane, Sept. 9, 1895, Nightingale Letters, Teachers College Library, Columbia University. Dr. Barnardo to Mrs. William H. G. Bagshawe, July 12, 1871, Bagshawe Papers, JRL. Thomas Hughes to unnamed correspondent, Jan. 12, 1877, Hughes Letters, BERG. Thomas Hughes to unnamed correspondent, March 20, 1874, Parrish Collection, PUL. Emily Faithfull to Miss Graves, Oct. 4, 1877, Emily Faithfull Letters, PML. Frederic Harrison to Stanley Withers, March 10, 1885, Stanley Withers Collection, MCL. Richard Congreve to William Knight, June 8, 1885, Knight Papers, PML. Edwin H. Stout to Shaw, Jan. 4, 1893, Albert Shaw Papers, NYPL.

16. Cf. William A. Dunning to Seligman, July 8, 1909, Seligman Papers, CUL. NYPL: George to Austie, June 7, 1882 (letter book), Henry George Papers; Baker to Mrs. Lowell, Dec. 10, 1877, Baker Letters; Darwin to Fritz Müller, Aug. 10, 1865 (photostat), Darwin Letters.

17. Dowson to Moore, June, 1896, and two undated, Ernest Dowson Letters, PML. Cf. Lincoln Steffens to Joseph Steffens, Jan. 8, 1891, Steffens Papers, CUL. Thomas Hardy to Sidney G. Trist, May 18, 1910, Hardy Letters, BERG. Stead to Shaw, Dec. 28, 1893, Albert Shaw Papers, NYPL.

18. Cf. Francis Burdett to Edward Davies Davenport, March 14, 1831, Edward Davies Davenport Papers, JRL. Louis Blanc to Thornton Hunt, Nov. 12, 1863, DeCoursey Fales Collection, NYPL. Thomas Berry to the

Mayor of Chicago, Oct. 31, 1871, S. H. Gay Papers. W. T. Stead to F. W. Holls, July 13, 1900, Frederick William Holls Papers, CUL. NYPL: Stead to Shaw, Dec. 23, 1893, Albert Shaw Papers; George to Nordhoff, Jan. 31, 1880, George Papers.

19. BERG: Carlyle to James Hutchinson Stirling, May 20, 1840, Carlyle Letters; John Stuart Mill to Nightingale, Dec. 31, 1867 (draft), Mill Letters. Leslie Stephen to Moncure Conway, June 14, 1878, Conway Papers, CUL. Thomas Hughes to D. Gourley, March 3, 1868, Thomas Raffles Collection, JRL378. Cf. W. H. Harris to William Frey, Feb. 5, 1884, Frey Papers, NYPL.

20. E. H. K. H. to the Clerk of the Vestry, Vestry Hall, St. Martin-in-the-Fields, Oct. 23, 1869, Home Office 41(23), PRO. Cf. Israel Zangwill to Anthony, Dec. 9, 1924, Anthony Autograph Collection. NYPL: Winston Churchill to Bourke Cockran, April 12, 1896, Nov. 5, 1896, Cockran Papers; Edwin H. Stout to Shaw, Feb. 15, 1893, Albert Shaw Papers. Bret Harte to C. O. Shepard, April 19, 1879, Thomas Raffles Collection, JRL377.

21. Carlyle to Browning, April 25, 1856, Carlyle Letters, BERG. NYPL: George to Walker, June 13, 1884, Henry George Papers; Baker to Mrs. Lowell, Aug. 31, 1877, Dec. 9, 1881, Baker Letters.

22. C. F. Adams to Freeman H. Morse, Nov. 26, 1861, American Autographs, PML. Cobden to Smith, Dec. 28, 1852, J. B. Smith Papers, MCL. Bright to Conway, Sept. 27, 1866, Conway Papers, CUL. Kingsley to Lord Chester, 1872, Kingsley Letters, Parrish Collection, PUL.

23. Nightingale to Count Strzelecki, July 30, 1863, Nightingale Letters, Teachers College Library, Columbia University. Nightingale to Thomas Worthington, April 26, 1867, Nightingale Letters, JRL1154. NYPL: Baker to Mrs. Lowell, July 7, 1880, Baker Letters; Henry George, Jr., to Francis G. Shaw, April 17, 1882, Henry George, Jr., Papers; E. H. Stout to Albert Shaw, July 15, 1893, Albert Shaw Papers. Frewen Papers, LC: George H. Murray to Moreton Frewen, May 5, 1886; Lord Jersey to Frewen, April 21, 1889. Cf. W. J. Ashley to Albert Shaw, Jan. 11, 1895, Albert Shaw Papers, NYPL.

24. Elizabeth Blackwell to Barbara Bodichon, Feb. 4, 1883, Blackwell Letters, CUL. BPL: Charles Bradlaugh to Kate Field, March 26, 1873, Kate Field Papers; F. W. Newman to Epes Sargent, June 10, 1876, Newman Letters. Thomas Hughes to Lord Brassey, Nov. 27, 1877, Hughes Letters, BERG. Albert Shaw Papers, NYPL: Stead to Carnegie, June 16, 1893; Stead to Shaw, Dec. 3, 1892, Jan. 21, 1893, June 17, 1893. Stead to Holls, Dec. 18, 1899, Holls Papers, CUL. H. G. Wells to Carnegie, Oct. 12, 1902, Misc. Papers, NYPL.

25. Benjamin Jowett to George Eliot, May 21, 1880, Jowett Letters, BERG. Benjamin Jowett to Cobden-Sanderson, May 21, 1866, Cobden-Sanderson Papers, PML. Benjamin Jowett to Sir William Bromley Davenport, Sept. 19, 1891, Sir William Bromley Davenport Papers, JRL. Laura A. Whitworth, "Rich and Poor; or, a Christmas Angel," *Manchester Christmas Annual,* 1883, p. 100. Frey Papers, NYPL: Vernon Lushington to William Frey, July 8, no year; Henry Ellis to Frey, July 20, 1888.

26. Newspaper clipping, *Daily News,* Feb. 3, 1883, William Bromley Davenport Papers, JRL. Misc. Papers, NYPL: Gladstone to Carnegie, Sept. 19, 1892, and Feb. 22, 1897 (photostats); Gladstone to E. T. Cook, Dec. 25, 1889. Carnegie Collection, NYPL: Gladstone to Carnegie, April 29, 1890; Frederic Harrison to Carnegie, Sept. 10, 1902.

27. Carlyle to W. D. Christie, undated, Carlyle Letters, PML.

VI. ABIDING INFLUENCES

1. Charles Kingsley to unnamed correspondent, Nov. 26, 1855, Kingsley Letters, PML. Carlyle to unnamed correspondent, April 17, 1850, Anthony Autograph Collection, NYPL. Ruskin to Selwyn Image, March 16, 1871, Ruskin Letters, PML. Alfred Marshall to Seligman, July 10, 1896, Seligman Papers, CUL.
2. Carlyle to Dr. Allen, May 19, 1820, Carlyle Letters, JRL336. Carlyle to unnamed correspondent, July 24, 1855, Carlyle Letters, BERG. Carlyle to unnamed correspondent, Feb. 5, 1838, Carlyle Letters, Folger Shakespeare Library.
3. Carlyle to Dr. Allen, June 7, 1820, Carlyle Letters, JRL336. Emerson to Carlyle, Oct. 7, 1835, Emerson Letters, BERG. Carlyle to "Dear Miss," Nov. 5, 1842 (facsimile), Carlyle Letters, New-York Historical Society. Carlyle to unnamed correspondent, Feb. 16, 1873, Carlyle Letters, BERG.
4. PML: Longfellow to William Knight, May 22, 1881, Longfellow Letters; Matthew Arnold to his brother Tom, Dec. 28, 1858, Arnold Letters. Carlyle to A. J. Scott, May 30, 1844, Carlyle Letters, BERG. Carlyle to Leigh Hunt, undated, Coykendall Collection, CUL. Carlyle to F. O. Ward, Dec. 16, 1845; Autograph Collection, JRL341. Carlyle to Hunt, June 17, 1850, Carlyle Letters, HCL. Ruskin to Blanche Atkinson, Aug. 3, 1873, Ruskin Letters, JRL1162. Bowker, MS journal, March 6, 1881, NYPL. Carlyle to De Quincey, Dec. 11, 1828, Carlyle Letters, BERG. Carlyle to John Harland, Feb. 13, 1845, Harland Collection, MCL. Carlyle to John Carlyle, April 19, 1869, Carlyle Letters, HCL. Carlyle Letters, NLS: Carlyle to John Carlyle, Nov. 9, 1878; Oct. 11, 1878; Dec. 21, 1878; Dec. 14, 1878; March 15, 1879; March 1, 1879; March 22, 1879.
5. PML: Carlyle to Jenny, Nov. 24, 1841, Carlyle Letters; Carlyle MS on laissez-faire. Carlyle to Peel, June 18, 1856 (draft), Carlyle Letters, HCL. Carlyle to A. J. Scott, Dec. 5, 1845, May 30, 1844, Carlyle Letters, BERG.
6. Carlyle to Macvey Napier, Feb. 6, 1832 (facsimile), Carlyle Letters, NYPL. BERG: Dickens to Carlyle, Oct. 26, 1842, and Georgina Hogarth to Carlyle, June 27, 1870, Dickens Letters; Carlyle to Browning, June 21, 1841, and Carlyle to Bridges Adams, March 7, 1848, Carlyle Letters. Carlyle MS on laissez-faire, PML.
7. John Forster to Carlyle, Feb. 18, 1874, Forster Letters, BERG. Carlyle to Miss Wedgwood, April 26, 1849, Gaskell Collection, JRL732. Carlyle to John Carlyle, Oct. 11, 1878, and Oct. 18, 1878, Carlyle Letters, NLS. Beaconsfield to Carlyle, Carlyle Letters, Cheyne House, London. Carlyle Letters, NLS: Carlyle to John Carlyle, Jan. 18, 1879; Nov. 30, 1878; Feb. 22, 1879.
8. Mary Carlyle to Conway, Feb. 6, 1881, Conway Papers, CUL. Carlyle to unnamed correspondent, Oct. 27, 1842, Dreer Collection, HSP. Carlyle to Bridges Adams, March 7, 1848, Carlyle Letters, BERG. William H. Wylie to Conway, April 11, 1881, Conway Papers, CUL. Samuel R. Crockett to unnamed correspondent, March 24, 1896, DeCoursey Fales Collection, NYPL. Sir Charles Gavan Duffy to Unwin, Feb. 14, 1896, Unwin Papers, BERG.
9. Froude to Carlyle, July 10, 1874, Froude Letters, Folger Shakespeare Library. Blatchford to Thompson, Aug. 8, 1885, Blatchford Letters, MCL. Stead to Shaw, May 23, 1894, Albert Shaw Papers. AE to John Quinn, Jan. 1, 1913, Quinn Transcripts, NYPL.

10. Ruskin to George Allen, Dec. 24, 1872, Ruskin Letters, CUL. Ruskin to Henry Stacy Marks, Dec. 27, 1878, and June 5, 1881, Mary S. Harkness Collection, NYPL. Ruskin to Mrs. Browning, March 4, 1855, Ruskin Letters, BERG. Ruskin to Blanche Atkinson, Dec., 1873, Ruskin Letters, JRL1162.

11. Ruskin to Mrs. Frances Talbot, Feb. 21, 1876, Ruskin Letters, JRL1162. Ruskin to Dr. Brown, March 9, 1879, Ruskin Letters, Folger Shakespeare Library. Ruskin to Blanche Atkinson, Nov., 1884, Ruskin Letters, JRL1162. Ruskin to Allen, Sept. 1, 1885, Ruskin Letters, CUL. Ruskin to Lucy Drewitt Tuck, Feb. 8, 1886, Ruskin Letters, PML. Ruskin to Henry Stacy Marks, March 20, 1886, Harkness Collection, NYPL. Ruskin Letters, CUL: Ruskin to George Allen, July 2, 1887; Jan. 1, 1888; Feb. 12, 1888; April 24, 1888.

12. Ruskin to Walter Lucas Brown, Jan. 9, 1858, Autograph Collection, MCL. Ruskin to Mrs. Browning, Nov. 5, 1860, Ruskin Letters, BERG. Ruskin to Dora Thomas, Feb. 5, 1877, Harkness Collection, NYPL. Ruskin to Cowper-Temple, Feb. 8, 1870, Ruskin Letters, PML.

13. Robert Curzon to Sneyd, Jan. 2, 1854, Walter Sneyd Papers, JRL. Ruskin to Mrs. Browning, 1855, Ruskin Letters, BERG.

14. Ruskin to Mrs. Browning, Jan. 15, 1859, Ruskin Letters, BERG. Ruskin to Octavia Blewitt, Jan. 19, 1871, Coykendall Collection, CUL. Ruskin to Dickinson, Jan. 22, 1861, Lowes Dickinson Papers, PUL. Ruskin to Blanche Atkinson, March 5, 1874, Ruskin Letters, JRL1162.

15. Ruskin to Margaret A. Bell, June 2, 1868, Ruskin Letters, PML. Ruskin to Edward Coleridge, Feb. 14, 1868, Misc. Papers, NYPL. Ruskin to Mrs. Gaskell, Oct. 27, 1860, Gaskell Papers, JRL731. Ruskin to Henry Stacy Marks, Feb. 4, 1880, Harkness Collection, NYPL.

16. Ruskin to Lucy Drewitt Tuck, Dec. 3, 1876, Ruskin Letters, PML. Ruskin to C. J. Scofield, Sept. 6, 1871 (photostat), R. H. Stoddard Collection, NYPL. Ruskin to Stanley Withers, Oct. 20, 1884, Withers Collection, MCL. Ruskin to Cowper-Temple, Aug. 4, 1871, Ruskin Letters, PML. Ruskin to Blanche Atkinson, April 22, 1873, and May, 1873, Ruskin Letters, JRL1162.

17. Ruskin Letters, JRL1162: Ruskin to Blanche Atkinson, Oct. 20, 1873; July 14, 1874; July 30, 1874. Ruskin to Lucy Drewitt Tuck, April 27, 1876, Ruskin Letters, PML. George Gissing to Margaret Gissing, May 12, 1883, Gissing Letters, BERG.

18. Ruskin to Quarry Talbot, Jan. 4, 1878, Ruskin Letters, JRL1163. Ruskin to Mrs. Talbot, Dec. 15, 1874, and May 4, 1876, Ruskin Letters, JRL1161. R. M. Dove to George Allen, Feb. 22, 1879, Ruskin Letters, CUL. Harkness Collection, NYPL: Ruskin to Dora Thomas, March 9, 1879, and July 19, 1879; Ruskin to Henry Stacy Marks, Feb. 4, 1880. Carlyle to John Carlyle, March 1, 1879, Carlyle Letters, NLS.

19. Ruskin to Blanche Atkinson, July 13, 1879, Ruskin Letters, JRL1162. Ruskin Papers, JRL1164: mimeographed letter, Oct. 19, 1901; MS notes of meeting of Trustees of St. George's Guild on Oct. 28, 1901, and Dec. 5, 1901.

20. Lawrence Hilliard to A. A. Reade, Feb. 12, 1882, Arents Tobacco Collection, NYPL. Ruskin to George Allen, postmarked April 11, 1873, Ruskin Letters, CUL. Ruskin to Margaret A. Bell, March 18, 1869, Ruskin Letters, PML.

21. Ruskin to Blanche Atkinson, Nov. 21, 1873, and Oct. 28, 1877, Ruskin Letters, JRL1162. Ruskin to Lucy Drewitt Tuck, Dec. 28, 1878, Ruskin Letters, PML. Ruskin to Blanche Atkinson, March 5, 1874, Ruskin Letters, JRL1162. Ruskin to Oddie, March 22, 1875, Ruskin Letters, PML.

22. Ruskin to Blanche Atkinson, Aug. 10, 1874, Ruskin Letters, JRL1162. Carlyle to John Carlyle, Oct. 14, 1877, Carlyle Letters, NLS. Ruskin to Oddie, Sept. 17, 1875, and Sept. 24, 1875, Ruskin Letters, PML.

23. PML: Leslie Stephen to Henley, July 12, 1877, Henley Papers; Ruskin to Mrs. Cowper-Temple, March 26, 1867, Ruskin Letters. Ruskin to the editor of the *Pall Mall Gazette*, May 28, 1889, Ruskin Letters, BERG. Ruskin Letters, CUL: Caroline Gray to Ruskin, Nov. 19, 1884; Ruskin to George Allen, June 19, 1887. Ruskin to Mrs. Cowper-Temple, Oct. 4, 1872, Ruskin Letters, PML. Ruskin to George Oswald, Feb. 20, 1887, Anthony Autograph Collection, NYPL. Oscar Wilde to Ruskin, undated, Wilde Letters, BERG. Gissing Letters, BERG: George Gissing to Margaret Gissing, May 12, 1883; Gissing to Algernon Gissing, Dec. 8, 1884; Gissing to Margaret Gissing, May 12, 1883.

24. PML: Herbert Fisher to Cobden-Sanderson, Jan. 20, 1906, Cobden-Sanderson Papers; Henley to Lord Windsor, Jan. 16, 1900, Henley Papers. Henley to Cosmo, undated, DeCoursey Fales Collection, NYPL.

25. Josephine Butler to William Lloyd Garrison, June 10, 1877, Garrison Papers, BPL. Josephine Butler to Aaron Powell, Feb. 17, 1880, S. H. Gay Papers, CUL. Sir Norman Angell, Typescript Reminiscences 11, Oral History Project, CUL.

26. BERG: Carlyle to Georgina Hogarth, July 4, 1870, Carlyle Letters; Ouida to Chatto, Dec. 31, 1882, Ouida Letters; Longfellow to Georgina Hogarth, June 13, 1870, Dickens Papers. John Bigelow, MS diary, July 3, 1870, NYPL. Bishop Wilberforce to Charles Aspinall, March 20, 1869, Thomas Raffles Collection, JRL386. Dickens to the editor of the *Times*, Nov. 13, no year (photostat), Dickens Letters, NYPL. Dickens to Mrs. Cropper, Dec. 20, 1852, Dickens Letters, Free Library of Philadelphia. Dickens to Mrs. D. C. Colden, Aug. 4, 1854 (photostat), Dickens Letters, NYPL.

27. Dickens to George Holme, March 14, 1870, Dickens Letters, Victoria and Albert Museum, London. Dickens to Mrs. Gaskell, Jan. 31, 1850, Gaskell Papers, JRL729. Dickens to Mrs. Cropper, Dec. 20, 1852, Dickens Letters, Free Library of Philadelphia.

VII. WRITERS PROTEST

1. NYPL: Thomas F. Walker to George, Sept. 12, 1882, Henry George Papers; W. P. Byles, typescript article; Bernard Shaw to Hamlin Garland, Dec. 29, 1904, Henry George, Jr., Papers.

2. Edward Carpenter to Richard Hawkin, Sept. 18, 1908, Hawkin Papers, JRL1040. Charles Sixsmith, MS address, JRL. Tolstoy to Maude, Jan. 31, 1905, Tolstoy Letters, CUL. Edward Carpenter Papers, Sheffield Central Library.

3. Ingram Bywater to Buller, Jan. 27, 1885, Bywater Letters, PML. Blatchford to Thompson, May 14, 1908, Blatchford Papers, MCL.

4. T. G. Hake to Henley, June 20, 1887, PML. H. Rider Haggard to unnamed correspondent, May 5, 1915, Haggard Letters, BERG. William Cobbett to Thomas Smith, June 4, 1830, Raffles Collection, JRL375. Charles Greville to Ralph Sneyd, Oct. 11, 1831, Ralph Sneyd Papers, JRL.

5. John Bright to H. G. Reed, June 23, 1883, Carnegie Autograph Collection, NYPL. Charles A. Cooper to William Knight, Sept. 14, 1892, Knight Papers, PML. Blatchford to Thompson, Aug., 1886, Blatchford Papers, MCL.

6. Louis Blanc to Moncure Conway, Oct. 2, 1872, DeCoursey Fales Collection, NYPL. William Blackwood to Owen, June 29, 1885, Sir R. Owen Papers, BM39554. Spender Papers, BM46391: Bernard Shaw to J. A. Spender, Nov. 24, 1907; Spender to Gould, Sept. 16, 1899.

7. Robert Southey to unnamed correspondent, Aug. 26, 1826, Raffles Autograph Collection, JRL346. BERG: Arnold Bennett to George Sturt, Dec. 15, 1896, Arnold Bennett Letters; Benjamin Disraeli to Isaac Disraeli, Good Friday, 1835, Disraeli Letters. Ouida to J. A. Spender, Jan. 21, 1897, Spender Papers, BM46391. Dilke to Gladstone, Oct. 2, 1884, Gladstone Papers, BM44149. W. S. Gilbert to Salaman, May 16, 1890, Gilbert & Sullivan Collection, PML. Ouida to Chatto, Dec. 3, 1883 (?), Ouida Letter, BERG.

8. Unwin Papers, BERG: Edward Garnett, reader's report, Feb. 23, 1897; H. G. Wells to T. Fisher Unwin, Nov. 25, 1892. Stephen Crane Papers, CUL: H. G. Wells to Mrs. Crane, July 29, 1900; Gissing to Mrs. Crane, Jan. 2, 1899. Gissing Papers, BERG: George Gissing to Margaret Gissing, Jan. 22, 1890; Gissing to Morley Roberts, Nov. 1, 1903, and Feb. 10, 1895.

9. CUL: Baron Corvo to Stedman, Dec. 13, 1899, Stedman Papers; Gosse to Brander Matthews, Oct. 6, 1887, Brander Matthews Papers. Leslie Stephen to Henley, June 17, 1876, and March 7, 1877, Henley Papers, PML. William Barnes to Lucy, Nov. 23, 1880, Misc. Papers, NYPL. BERG: Wilkie Collins to George Bentley, July 3, 1874, Collins Letters; Edith Nesbit to J. B. Pinker, undated, Nesbit Letters.

10. George Gissing to Ellen Gissing, May 8, 1886, Gissing Letters, BERG. Henry James to unnamed correspondent, Jan. 21, 1886, E. T. Cook Papers, BM39927. W. T. Stead to Gladstone, Dec. 9, 1889, Gladstone Papers, BM44303. J. Oswald Dykes to W. L. Watkinson, Dec. 29, 1900, Autograph Collection, JRL862.

11. David Livingstone to James Gordon Bennett, Jr., Nov., 1871 (copy), Misc. Papers, NYPL. Gladstone to Burne-Jones, Nov. 6, 1879, in Alexander William Armour, Notables and Autographs (New York, 1939). Misc. Papers, NYPL: Francis W. Newman to Alexander Strahan, Oct. 3, 1877; Mary Carpenter to unidentified correspondent, Oct. 24, no year. William Holman Hunt to Sir John Millais, June 15, 1883, Millais Papers, PML. J. C. Durant to Henry George, Feb. 24, 1886, George Papers, NYPL.

12. Florence Nightingale to Count Strzelecki, Aug. 19, 1864, and July 30, 1863, Nightingale Letters, Teachers College Library, CUL. Cf. William Ewart to Edward Edwards, Sept. 7, 1849, Edwards Papers, MCL. Herbert Spencer to Moncure Conway, Jan. 10, 1894, Conway Papers, CUL. W. H. Houldsworth to Moreton Frewen, Nov. 9. 1889, Frewen Papers, LC. Gov. Eyre to Shirley Brooks, June 5, 1868, Shirley Brooks Papers, NYPL. Michael Davitt to T. Fisher Unwin, Jan. 3, 1901, Unwin Papers, BERG.

13. William Wordsworth to Mrs. M. A. Rawson, undated, Rawson Papers, JRL415. George Meredith to H. W. Nevinson, June 7, 1904, Meredith Letters, BERG. John Bright to W. R. W. Thorn, Feb. 23, 1869, Bright Letters, Folger Shakespeare Library. John Redmond to Bourke Cockran, Sept. 2, 1903, Cockran Papers, NYPL.

14. BERG: W. Lynd to Andrew Chatto, June 14, 1882, Lynd Letters; Tennyson to H. Buxton Forman, April 29, 1879, Tennyson Letters; Mrs. Craigie to T. Fisher Unwin, April 28, 1897, Unwin Papers. NYPL: Thomas Hardy to G. E. Dixon, April 14, 1899, Lee Kohns Autograph Collection; Lewis Carroll to Mrs. Hargreaves, July 15, 1885 (photostat), Misc. Papers.

W. S. Gilbert to A. Bateman, Jan. 2, 1878, and W. S. Gilbert to B. P. Lascelles, Oct. 24, 1909, Gilbert & Sullivan Collection, PML.

15. Gladstone Papers, BM44303: Stead to Gladstone, Sept. 14, 1880; March 26, 1887; Aug. 17, 1891.

16. Albert Shaw Papers, NYPL: Stead to Shaw, June 22, 1892; Sir Henry Lunn, memorandum on Stead; Journalists' Memorial to the Memory of Stead. Stead to Frewen, Nov. 22, 1885, Frewen Papers, LC. Stead to Shaw, May 6, 1898, and May 4, 1892, Albert Shaw Papers, NYPL. Stead to Frewen, April 20, 1889, Frewen Papers, LC. H. W. Lee to Mrs. John Burns, Jan. 21, 1888, John Burns Papers, BM46288.

17. Stead to Frewen, March 4, 1890, Frewen Papers, LC. Albert Shaw Papers, NYPL: Stead to Shaw, Oct. 17, 1891; March 4, 1893; June 17, 1891; April 21, 1894; July 14, 1897; April 21, 1894; Sept. 24, 1892; March 18, 1893.

18. Stead to James Russell Lowell, Dec. 19, 1890, James Russell Lowell Papers, HCL. Albert Shaw Papers, NYPL: Stead to Shaw, Jan. 28, 1893, and Sept. 9, 1892; Edwin Stout to Shaw, Nov. 29, 1893. Stead to Holls, Aug. 7, 1900, Holls Papers, CUL.

19. Albert Shaw Papers, NYPL: Stead to Shaw, Jan. 14, 1893, and May 21, 1892; Shaw to Davis R. Dewey, Jan. 8, 1897 (Shaw letter book).

20. Percy William Bunting to Shaw, Nov. 5, 1901, Albert Shaw Papers, NYPL. Charles Bradlaugh to Kate Field, Aug. 10, 1872, Kate Field Papers, BPL. Michael Davitt to Thomas Higgins, Feb. 28, 1903 (photostat), NLI. NYPL: Walter Crane to the editor of "The Humanitarian," April 6, 1910, DeCoursey Fales Collection; Robert Donald to Shaw, June 21, 1894, Albert Shaw Papers.

21. BERG: Ouida to Mackenzie Bell, June 12, 1890, Ouida Letters; Charles Reade to Richard Bentley, April 29, 1868 (?), Reade Letters. Marie Corelli to Harris, April 12, 1896, Dreer Collection, HSP. Ouida to Andrew Chatto, June 12, 1885, Ouida Letters, BERG. St. Clair Baddeley to Raffles, Oct. 22, 1883, Raffles Collection, JRL351.

22. Wells to Unwin, Feb. 2, 1902, Unwin Papers, BERG. Plato Draculis to William Shaw, April 3, 1893, William Shaw Papers, CUL. Unwin Papers, BERG: G. J. Holyoake to Unwin, undated; Samuel A. Barnett to Unwin, June 26, 1900. Albert Shaw to Edwin H. Stout, Jan. 27, 1894 (Shaw letter book), Albert Shaw Papers, NYPL.

23. Wilkie Collins Letters, BERG: Collins to George Smith, Oct. 23, 1871, and Collins to George Bentley, March 18, 1873; May, 1873; Sept. 10, 1873. George Du Maurier to Sir John Millais, Sept. 10, 1891, Millais Papers, PML. Gilchrist to Parkes, Oct. 23, 1893, and Aug. 19, 1891, Gilchrist Papers, NYPL.

24. Arthur W. Pinero to S. B. Bancroft, Oct. 29, 1884, DeCoursey Fales Collection, NYPL. PML: Pearl Craigie to Pinero, March 15, 1895, Myra Hamilton Autograph Album; Ernest Dowson to A. C. Moore, Feb. 6, 1889, Dowson Letters. BERG: Leslie Stephen to Thomas Hardy, Jan. 10, 1888, Stephen Letters; W. S. Maugham to W. W. Colles, Nov. 10, 1898, Maugham Letters. George Gissing Letters, BERG: George Gissing to Algernon Gissing, June 29, 1884, and Sept. 7, 1884; Gissing to Margaret Gissing, July 31, 1886; Gissing to Ellen Gissing, Oct. 16, 1887; Gissing to Unwin, Jan. 12, 1895; Gissing to Algernon Gissing, Nov. 25, 1894. Arnold Bennett to George Sturt, Jan. 31, 1897, Bennett Letters, BERG.

25. Robert James Muir to Unwin, Nov. 24, 1899, Unwin Papers, BERG. Francis Turner Palgrave to unnamed correspondent, June 23, 1871, Misc.

Papers, NYPL. BERG: Henry James to Unwin, Dec. 14, 1895, Unwin Papers; George Moore to Thomas Werner Laurie, Dec. 14, 1910, Moore Letters. Ella S. Armitage to Raffles, March 5, 1877, Raffles Collection, JRL372.

26. Ruskin Letters, CUL: John Roberts to John Ruskin, Nov. 3, 1874; Chatham Librarian to Ruskin, Jan. 25, 1883. Keir Hardie to Unwin, May 10, 1899, Unwin Papers, BERG. P. Walsh to A. R. Wallace, May 18, 1911, Wallace Papers, BM46440.

27. Mrs. Craigie to Unwin, Jan. 9, 1894, Unwin Papers, BERG. Matthew Arnold to Stanley Withers, Oct. 3, 1884, Withers Collection, MCL. F. W. Newman to Epes Sargent, Nov. 11, 1869, Newman Letters, BPL.

28. Henry George Papers, NYPL: George to his father, Sept. 15, 1879; George to Charles Nordhoff, Jan. 31, 1880; Blackie to George, Jan. 8, 1880; George to Sir George Grey, July 3, 1880 (copy).

29. Henry George Papers, NYPL: George to E. R. Taylor, Dec. 14, 1880; George to Francis G. Shaw, Feb. 11, 1882; George to Taylor, Jan. 4, 1881; George to Shaw, Oct. 4, 1881; George to Taylor, Sept. 7, 1881.

30. Henry George Papers, NYPL: George to Shaw, Sept. 19, 1882, and April 28, 1882; George to Mrs. George, May 23, 1882. George to Arthur Spencer, March 16, no year, Autograph Collection, MCL. Helen Taylor to Mrs. George, Sept. 14, 1882, Mrs. Henry George Papers, NYPL. George to E. R. Taylor, Nov. 20, 1881, Henry George Papers, NYPL. Helen Taylor to Mrs. Henry George, April 27, 1884, and Feb. 8, 1885, Mrs. Henry George Papers, NYPL. Henry George Papers, NYPL: George to Shaw, Sept. 12, 1882; Sept. 21, 1882; Sept. 26, 1882.

31. Henry George Papers, NYPL: Helen Taylor to George, Oct. 17, 1882; Percy William Bunting to George, Dec. 29, 1882; J. E. Symes to George, Nov. 22, 1883; George to McClatchy, March 28, 1883 (copy); George to Mrs. George, Jan. 15, 1884, and Jan. 19, 1884; Max Müller to George, Jan. 23, 1884.

32. Durant to George, Oct. 27, 1890, Henry George Papers, NYPL. Ashley to Seligman, May 2, 1890, Seligman Papers, CUL. Stead to Albert Shaw, Jan. 8, 1891, Albert Shaw Papers, NYPL. William Booth to George, Jan. 14, 1893, Henry George Papers, NYPL.

33. Blatchford to A. M. Thompson, undated, and Christmas Day, 1901, Robert Blatchford Letters, MCL.

34. Blatchford to Thompson, Sept., 1885, May 11, 1886, and one undated, Blatchford Letters, MCL.

35. Blatchford to John Burns, June 11, 1894, Burns Papers, BM46288. Stead to Shaw, Dec. 14, 1894, Albert Shaw Papers, NYPL. Blatchford to Thompson, undated, Blatchford Letters, MCL.

36. Cf. Thomas F. Bayard to Consular Officers of the United States, Sept. 20, 1886, Misc. Papers, NYPL. MCCP, Oct. 31, 1888, and July 28, 1897, MCL.

37. Andrew Reid to Edward Bellamy, Feb. 12, 1895, Bellamy Papers, HCL. Plato Draculis to William Shaw, May 5, 1890, William Shaw Papers, CUL. Albert Shaw Papers, NYPL: Stead to Shaw, Feb. 19, 1894; Jan. 4, 1894; May 23, 1894.

38. W. H. Dircks, reader's report on Hugh B. Philpott, "The Story of the London School Board," BERG. C. W. Sutton to F. Marquis, May 1, 1909, Autograph Collection, MCL.

VIII. FIGHTING ECCLESIASTICS

1. Augustus Jessopp to Mr. Laurence, March 17, 1893, Misc. Papers, NYPL. Darwin to the Reverend Mr. Hoare, July 18, 1876, M. F. Hales Autograph Collection, LC.

2. Bright to Gladstone, Jan. 26, 1874, Gladstone Papers, BM44113. Henry George Papers, NYPL: George to Francis Shaw, Sept. 12, 1882, Sept. 21, 1882, Aug. 15, 1882; Stewart Headlam to George, Sept. 25, 1882; Webb to George, March 8, 1889.

3. Manchester and Salford Sanitary Association MS Minute Book, Sept. 15, 1890, MCL. Thomas Hughes to Mrs. Carpenter, March 24, 1887, Hughes Letters, BERG. Stead to Shaw, Sept. 24, 1892, and April 21, 1894, Albert Shaw Papers, NYPL.

4. Henry Austin Bruce to Thomas Binney, Sept. 14, 1870, Gratz Collection, HSP. NYPL: Gladstone to Carnegie, March 8, 1892, and March 9, 1892, Carnegie Collection; Gladstone to Carnegie, July 3, 1891 (photostat), Misc. Papers. Archbishop Benson to Charles H. Brooks, Nov. 12, 1888, Archbishops of Canterbury Letters, PML.

5. George Wyndham Kennion to H. Harrison, Jan. 28, 1895, Ecclesiastical Letters, JRL841. Catherine Booth to George, Jan. 26, 1887, Henry George Papers, NYPL. Herbert Mills to A. R. Wallace, April 20, and April 23, 1889, Wallace Papers, BM46440. Henrietta O. Barnett to Davenport, May 8, 1896, Sir William Bromley Davenport Papers, JRL.

6. Thomas Dawson to George, July 17, 1883, Henry George Papers, NYPL. Joseph Chipchase to W. Boyden, March 24, 1879, Ecclesiastical Letters, JRL857. S. R. Crockett to T. Fisher Unwin, Nov. 24, 1893, Unwin Papers, BERG. Stead to Shaw, March 31, 1894, June 11, 1892, June 10, 1891, Albert Shaw Papers, NYPL. H. J. B. Heath to George, Jan. 18, 1885, Henry George Papers, NYPL.

7. Henley to Anna, undated, Henley Papers, PML. BERG: John Henry Newman to E. G. A. Holmes, Aug. 13, 1875, Newman Letters; Ouida to unnamed correspondent, Feb. 18, 1890, Ouida Letters; Swinburne to Gosse, April 6, 1877, Swinburne Letters. William Holman Hunt to Mary Millais, July 30, 1890, Millais Papers, PML. William Holman Hunt to Stanley Withers, April 8, 1885, Withers Collection, MCL. Christ in Art Collection, NYPL.

8. BERG: Darwin to unnamed French correspondent, Feb. 28, 1879, Darwin Letters (italics added); Swinburne to Paul Hamilton Hayne, May 2, 1877, Swinburne Letters. Bernard Shaw to Hamlin Garland, Dec. 29, 1904, Henry George, Jr., Papers, NYPL. Conway Papers, CUL: Annie Besant to Mrs. Conway, May 4, 1875; Mrs. Besant to Moncure Conway, Dec. 3, 1885. Leonard Huxley to William Knight, Nov. 19, 1900, Knight Papers, PML. John Fiske to his mother, Jan. 12, 1874, Fiske Papers, LC.

9. Ruskin to Margaret A. Bell, postmarked April 15, 1867, Ruskin Letters, PML. W. Copland, autobiographical letter, Twentieth Century New Testament Papers, JRL750. Edmund Gosse to Stedman, Feb. 21, 1880, Stedman Papers, CUL. Hunt to Millais, May 29, 1891, Millais Papers, PML. Angell, typescript reminiscences, p. 2, Oral History Project, CUL. W. H. G. Bagshawe to F. W. Bagshawe, July 26, 1886, Bagshawe Papers, JRL. G. Tyrrell to

Cobden-Sanderson, April 27, 1900, Cobden-Sanderson Papers, PML. Cf. A. R. Wallace to William Knight, Aug. 28, no year, Knight Papers, PML.

10. Bradlaugh to Kate Field, Aug. 10, 1872, Kate Field Papers, BPL. Anthony Autograph Collection, NYPL: Bradlaugh to Conway, April 11, 1878; Bradlaugh to R. J. Hinton, Sept. 19, 1873. Bradlaugh to W. Holmsly, Feb. 22, 1883, Dreer Collection, HSP. Emily S. Thompson to Moncure Conway, July 4, 1883. H. Bradlaugh Bonner to Conway, Nov., 1893 (printed form letter), Conway Papers, CUL.

11. Cardinal Newman to Knight, Jan. 7, 1887, Newman Letters, PML. Samuel Autliff to W. Griffith, Jan. 25, 1882, Ecclesiastical Letters, JRL861. C. A. W. Reade to Sir Elkanah Armitage, May, 1876 (copy), Armitage Papers, Chetham's Library. Congleton Town Mission, printed circular, 1897, Sir William Bromley Davênport Papers, JRL.

12. Kingsley to Boome, Dec. 21, 1870, American Academy of Arts and Letters Collection, LC. R. T. Booth to Dr. Browne, March 4, 1883, Temperance Collection, JRL863. William Booth to George, Jan. 14, 1893, Henry George Papers, NYPL. Tolstoy to G. T. Sadler, Dec. 16, 1898, Autograph Letters, JRL740. Tolstoy to Maude, June 25, 1901, Tolstoy Letters, CUL. Kingsley to unnamed correspondent, July 28, 1868, Kingsley Letters, BERG. Prince of Wales to Miss Kingsley, Jan. 24, 1875, Rulers of England Collection, PML. Benson to Gladstone, Dec. 18, 1882, Gladstone Papers, BM44109. Dickens to Fonblanque, March 13, 1843, Dickens Letters, BERG.

13. Twentieth Century New Testament Papers, JRL750: Mrs. Higgs, MS note book; Stead to Malan, June 2, 1891, and April 14, 1891; Mrs. Higgs to Malan, April 25, 1891; circular letters.

14. Ibid.: undated autobiographical letters of Mrs. Higgs, S. Elizabeth Mee, E. D. Girdlestone, Henry Bazett; Malan to Leonard, May 11, 1893.

15. Ibid.: circular letter, Dec. 17, 1893; circular letter, May 18, 1894; Malan to a few of his fellow workers, March 15, 1894; circular letter, Oct. 23, 1895; circular letter, Feb. 25, 1897; Malan to Mrs. Higgs, Nov. 6, 1891; Florence E. Booth to Mrs. Higgs, May 16, 1905.

16. Protestant Alliance, printed circular, 1892, Bagshawe Papers, JRL. Charles Kingsley to Stepleton, Sept. 13, 1853, Kingsley Letters, Parrish Collection, PUL. Dickens Letters, BERG: Dickens to W. W. Story, Aug. 1, 1863; Dickens to W. F. de Cerjat, Jan. 4, 1869. Anthony Collection, NYPL: James Anthony Froude to Dr. Holland, Oct. 17, no year; Samuel Smiles to unnamed correspondent, Sept. 3, 1873.

17. Santayana to Abbot, April 30, 1887, Santayana Letters, CUL. A. D. Bagshawe to W. H. Bagshawe, Sept. 20, 1888, Bagshawe Papers, JRL.

18. Bowker, MS journal, Oct. 31, 1881, NYPL. Cardinal Manning to Lord Ronald Gower, Dec. 4, 1889, Joan of Arc Collection, CUL. Lionel Johnson to unnamed correspondent, Jan. 14, 1896, Johnson Letters, BERG. Henry E. Manning to Sneyd, Dec. 8, 1836, Ralph Sneyd Papers, JRL. NYPL: George to Ford, June 22, 1882, (letter book), Henry George Papers; Stead to Shaw, June 6, 1891, Albert Shaw Papers.

19. Robert William Dale to Benjamin Green, Dec. 11, 1875, Stanley Withers Collection, MCL. J. G. Greenhough, autobiographical sketch, Ecclesiastical Letters, JRL861. William Booth to Edward Massie, Jan. 12, 1891, Brothers Autograph Collection, MCL. William Booth to W. H. G. Bagshawe, Sept. 18, 1888, Bagshawe Papers, JRL.

20. Robert Burns to Robert Cleghorn, March 31, 1788, Misc. Papers,

NYPL. J. Pollitt, *Religion in Manchester, Being Fourteen Articles Reprinted from the Oldham Chronicle* (Manchester, 1879), p. 5. Bowker, MS journal, Oct. 7, 1880, NYPL.

21. Plato Draculis to William Shaw, Jan. 16, 1891, William Shaw Papers, CUL. Bowker, MS journal, April 8, 1881, NYPL. Robert Williams Buchanan to John Le Sage, March 21, 1892, Buchanan Letters, BERG. W. D. Stephens to J. H. Hildred, June 12, 1882, Temperance Collection, JRL863.

22. Herbert Mills to A. R. Wallace, April 20 and April 23, 1889, Wallace Papers, BM46440. Charles Kingsley to Ludlow, March 25, 1851, Kingsley Letters, BERG. Julius Charles Hare to Connop Thirlwall, Aug. 22, 1853 (photostat), Thirlwall Papers, CUL. Thomas Hughes to Mac, Dec. 29, 1892, Hughes Letters, Parrish Collection, PUL.

23. Kingsley to unnamed correspondent, April 27, 1859, Kingsley Letters, PML. Kingsley to unnamed correspondent, Sept. 2, 1870, Josiah Gilbert Holland Papers, NYPL. James Fraser to Charles Rowley, Jan. 10, 1877, Autograph Collection, MCL. Edward Vansittart Neale to Seligman, March 21, 1885. J. M. Ludlow to Seligman, Oct. 29, 1885, Seligman Papers, CUL.

24. Bright to John Allen, Nov. 21, 1868, Bright Letters, PUL. George Gissing to Ellen Gissing, Nov. 13, 1887, Gissing Letters, BERG. George David Boyle to William Knight, Jan. 10, 1894, Knight Papers, PML. G. K. Chesterton, reader's report, Sept. 27, 1899, on A. R. Carman, "The Preparation of Ryerson Embury," Unwin Papers, BERG.

IX. POLITICIANS UNDER PRESSURE

1. Thomas Clarkson to Mrs. M. A. Rawson, April 15, 1833, Rawson Papers, JRL415. Thomas Hughes to unnamed correspondent, undated, Hughes Letters, BERG.

2. Thomas Hughes to unnamed correspondent, June 14, 1866, Shirley Brooks Papers, NYPL. Newspaper clipping, Salford *Chronicle,* May 30, 1891, Manchester Ship Canal Papers, Chetham's Library. Carlyle to unnamed correspondent, July 24, 1855, Carlyle Letters, BERG. Dickens Letters, BERG: Dickens to Sir Joseph Paxton, March 1, 1857; Dickens to S. Perkes, Nov. 29, 1866; Dickens to Trollope, Sept. 13, 1868. Dickens to Arthur, Sept. 6, 1867, Dickens Letters, Free Library of Philadelphia. Kipling to Richard Harding Davis, Jan. 3, 1893, Kipling Letters, PML.

3. Sidney Webb to John Burns, Nov. 14, 1889, Burns Papers, BM46288. Stead to Shaw, April 2, 1892, Albert Shaw Papers, NYPL. Benjamin Bryan to Bagshawe, Dec. 4, 1891, Bagshawe Papers, JRL. Joseph Chamberlain to Moreton Frewen, Oct. 15, 1894, Frewen Papers, LC. Thomas Snape to W. Boyden, March 20, 1894, Ecclesiastical Letters, JRL858. Millais Papers, PML: Stafford H. Northcote to Sir John Millais, Feb. 8, 1883; Arthur Balfour to Millais, July 12, 1894. John Foster Fraser to Stephen Crane, Whit Monday, 1900, Crane Papers, CUL. Sir Frank Lockwood to Arthur Symonds, June 25, 1887, Stanley Withers Collection, MCL. William Bromley Davenport Papers, JRL.

4. Thomas Bazley to J. B. Smith, Nov. 30, 1868, J. B. Smith Papers, MCL. J. P. Gledstone to Mrs. Sydney Howard Gay, Aug. 23, 1876, Gay Papers, CUL. Josephine Butler to Gladstone, April, 1877, Gladstone Papers, BM44454.

5. A. H. Gibson, MS autobiography, JRL867. F. W. Newman to Epes

Sargent, May 2, 1872, Newman Letters, BPL. Frances Power Cobbe to Lydia
E. Becker, Aug. 5, no year, National Union of Women's Suffrage Societies
Papers, MCL. Henry George Papers, NYPL: Helen Taylor to George, Jan.
7, 1883; George to Walker, March 27, 1883; Davitt to George, Nov. 1,
1885.

6. J. Y. W. Mac Alister to C. W. Sutton, July 9, 1900, Autograph Collection, MCL. T. H. Farrer, Memorandum of Jan. 29, 1880, Board of Trade
Papers (13), bundle 12, PRO. MCL: J. B. Smith to Sampson Lloyd, Feb. 8,
1871 (draft), J. B. Smith Papers; MCCP, Feb. 28, 1881, Feb. 9, 1881, April
20, 1886. John Burns Papers, BM46288: John Black to John Burns, Jan.
23, 1894; Leslie Davie to John Burns, Jan. 8, 1894; Charles Leech to John
Burns, Jan. 8 1894. Copy of resolution passed at a meeting of the Technical
Instruction Committee, Feb. 26, 1897, Sir William Bromley Davenport
Papers, JRL.

7. Francis W. Newman to Dr. Gourby, July 2, 1870, Raffles Collection,
JRL381. Joseph Chamberlain to Henry George, Jan. 5, 1880, George Papers,
NYPL. Frewen Papers, LC: Arthur Balfour to Moreton Frewen, July 24,
1888; Chamberlain to Frewen, July 23, 1888. John Morley to J. A. Spender,
March 11, 1892, Spender Papers, BM46391. H. R. Fox Bourne to H. J. Wilson,
Feb. 10, 1898 (letter pasted in pamphlet on *The Bechuana Troubles*), JRL.
Beatrice Webb to John Burns, Feb. 21, 1894, Burns Papers, BM46288.

8. Charles S. Parnell to William Tallack, April 20, 1885, Tallack Papers,
BM38835. George Butler to T. Stamford Raffles, Oct. 13, 1880, Raffles Papers,
JRL374. Joseph Chamberlain to William Gladstone, June 16, 1880, Gladstone
Papers, BM44125. Manchester *Examiner and Times*, April 17, 1885.

9. Robert Curzon to Walter Sneyd, Dec. 30, 1865, Walter Sneyd Papers,
JRL. John Bright to J. S. Henslow, Dec. 30, 1845, Bright Letters, PUL. John
Bright to W. H. Roberts, May 21, 1853, Lee Kohns Collection, NYPL. Bright
to C. Edward Lester, Jan. 9, 1867, Bright Letters, LC. Bright to John Allen,
Nov. 21, 1868, Bright Letters, PUL.

10. BERG: G. J. Holyoake to T. Fisher Unwin, Oct. 25, 1893, Unwin Papers; Gissing MS diary, May 10, 1888, and Gissing to Algernon Gissing,
May 17, 1888, Gissing Letters. Stead to Albert Shaw, March 3, 1894, Albert
Shaw Papers, NYPL. Unwin Papers, BERG: E. J. Hardy to Unwin, undated; W. H. Chesson to Unwin, April 29, 1897. T. B. Aldrich to Julius
Chambers, Jan. 25, 1898, DeCoursey Fales Collection, NYPL.

11. William Morris to Gladstone, Nov. 7, 1879, Gladstone Papers,
BM44461. Farmers' Memorial, Nov. 27, 1882, Gladstone Papers, BM44479.
Gladstone Papers, BM44303: Stead to Gladstone, June 17, 1892; Gladstone
to Stead, Aug. 23, 1888; Stead to Gladstone, April 15, 1897.

12. Gladstone to William Farr, Dec. 21, 1832, Farr Papers, JRL339.
Gladstone to unnamed correspondent, June 29, 1889, Lee Kohns Collection, NYPL. Gladstone to unnamed correspondent, June 16, 1890, Gladstone Letters, New-York Historical Society. Gladstone to H. B. Holding,
May 23, 1890 (facsimile), Henry George, Jr., Papers, NYPL. Gladstone to
Woods, Nov. 4, 1893, Thornton Autograph Collection, BM37725. Gladstone to J. Davies, Oct. 16, 1890, and April 22, 1891, Gladstone Letters,
Chetham's Library.

13. Albert Shaw Papers, NYPL: Stead to Shaw, Feb. 21, 1891, and June
23, 1894; Shaw to Richard Watson Gilder, Oct. 12, 1894. Joseph Chamberlain to Gladstone, Feb. 2, 1886, Gladstone Papers, BM44126. Bright to Glad-

stone, April 16, 1873, Gladsone Papers, BM44113. Chamberlain to Gladstone, April 16, 1877, Gladstone Papers, BM44125.

14. Gladstone to Sir Henry Ponsonby, Dec. 28, 1880, and Oct. 18, 1892, Ponsonby Papers, BM45724. Chamberlain to Gladstone, Dec. 17, 1881, and Oct. 18, 1883, Gladstone Papers, BM44125. Henry Hyndman to Henry George, April 5, no year, Henry George Papers, NYPL. Newspaper clipping, letter to the editor of *Advertiser*, Feb. 10, 1888, Bagshawe Papers, JRL. Joseph Chamberlain to unidentified correspondent, undated, Misc. Papers, NYPL. Bagshawe Papers, JRL: Frederick Fowler to Bagshawe, Dec. 3, 1883; J. Wood to Bagshawe, Nov. 2, 1885. John Temple Leader to Walter Sneyd, Nov. 19, 1885, Walter Sneyd Papers, JRL.

15. Chamberlain to the editor of the *Daily News*, Feb. 4, 1885 (copy), Gladstone Papers, BM44126. Arthur Balfour to Frank Banfield, Aug. 18, 1893, Autograph Collection of Prime Ministers, PML. Balfour to Knight, Oct. 27, 1898, Knight Papers, PML. Lord Rosebery to Unwin, Oct. 30, 1899, Unwin Papers, BERG. Lord Selborne to J. M. Libbey, Dec. 15, 1882, Misc. Papers, NYPL. Lord Northbrook to Earle, Oct. 1, 1882, Raffles Collection, JRL367. Sir Charles Dilke to Gladstone, Feb. 3, 1885, Gladstone Papers, BM44149. S. H. Butcher to William Knight, Feb. 3, 1904, Knight Papers, PML. Cf. Sir John Gorst to Lady Bective, Aug. 4, 1898, National Union of Women's Suffrage Societies Papers, MCL. Gladstone to Joseph Chamberlain, Dec. 10, 1883, Gladstone Papers, BM44125. Chamberlain to Gladstone, Feb. 7, 1885, Gladstone Papers, BM44126.

16. Chamberlain to Bright, March 28, 1875, and May 14, 1878, Bright Papers, BM43387. Chamberlain to Andrew Carnegie, Sept. 9, 1887, Carnegie Autograph Collection, NYPL. Chamberlain to Sir John Millais, Feb. 23, 1890, Millais Papers, PML. Sir Charles Dilke to Chamberlain, April 20, 1893 (copy), Dilke Papers, BM43953. Chamberlain to George, Aug. 12, 1882, Henry George Papers, NYPL. Chamberlain to E. Routledge, May 15, 1886, BM45918.

17. Chamberlain to Gladstone, Feb. 7, 1885, Gladstone Papers, BM44126. Carnegie Autograph Collection, NYPL: Chamberlain to Carnegie, Nov. 6, no year; Chamberlain to H. G. Reid, undated. Chamberlain to Henry George, Jan. 5, 1880, George Papers, NYPL. Chamberlain to Frewen, Oct. 15, 1894, Frewen Papers, LC. William Morris to John Burns, Oct. 27, 1885, Burns Papers, BM46288. George to Thomas Walker, March 27, 1883, Henry George Papers, NYPL.

18. Lord Randolph Churchill to W. Wilkinson, April 4, 1883, BM45918. NYPL: Disraeli to Sa, May Day, 1845, Lee Kohns Autograph Collection; Disraeli to T. Hodgskin, May 22, 1845, Misc. Papers; John Bigelow, MS diary, June 13, 1870, and July 7, 1870.

19. Churchill to Gladstone, June 16, 1883, Gladstone Papers, BM44481. Gladstone to Chamberlain, Sept. 9, 1885 (copy), Gladstone Papers, BM44126. Bagshawe to J. Wood, Nov. 13, 1885, Bagshawe Papers, JRL. Balfour to William Knight, March 13, 1886, Knight Papers, PML. Moreton Frewen to Mrs. Frewen, Feb. 4 1888, Frewen Papers, LC. Sir Horace Plunkett to Bourke Cockran, April 25, 1902; and Moreton Frewen to Cockran, Oct. 23, 1904, Cockran Papers, NYPL.

20. Chamberlain to Gladstone, Feb. 3, 1885, Gladstone Papers, BM44126. H. S. Foxwell to Seligman, Nov. 24, 1895, Seligman Papers, CUL. Keir Hardie to John Burns, May 23, 1891, Burns Papers, BM46288. Thomas

Walker to Henry George, Aug. 24, 1885, Henry George Papers, NYPL. Thomas D. Bolton, Election Address, June 21, 1886, Bagshawe Papers, JRL.

21. Joseph Henry Shorthouse to George Baker, Nov. 1, 1882, Shorthouse Letters, PML. A. Commins to Miss Winstanley, Feb. 1, 1889, Brothers Autograph Collection, MCL. JRL: Broadsheet on *Some Great Tory Reforms*, Bagshawe Papers; Broadsheet on *Mines and Labour Legislation*, Sir William Bromley Davenport Papers; election circular for F. G. Barnes, Bagshawe Papers; Sir William Bromley Davenport to the electors of the Macclesfield Division of the County of Chester, July 8, 1895, Davenport Papers.

22. Queen Victoria to Sir John Millais, Oct. 16, 1881, Millais Papers, PML. George Brooks to Sir William Bromley Davenport, March 12, 1896, and Joseph Chamberlain to Davenport, Jan. 22, 1906, Sir William Bromley Davenport Papers, JRL.

23. Richmond Smith, MS lectures on politics and constitutional history of England, Lecture 26, May 11, 1882, New-York Historical Society. *Review of Reviews*, V (1892), 570. Sir James Ramsden to T. S. Raffles, Oct. 18, 1878, Raffles Collection, JRL383. L. H. Blunden to Seligman, Dec. 27, 1893, Seligman Papers, CUL. Newspaper clipping, *The Telephone*, March 23, 1891, Manchester Ship Canal Papers, Chetham's Library. BERG: George Gissing to Algernon Gissing, Nov. 22, 1892, and Gissing to Morley Roberts, Aug. 2, 1900, Gissing Letters; Thomas Hardy to Edward Clodd, May 17, 1902, Hardy Letters.

24. John Blood to H. W. Hollis, Oct. 9, 1876, Walter Sneyd Papers, JRL. W. Williams to Sir Henry Roscoe, Dec. 23, 1901, Roscoe Papers, JRL963. Edward Peacock, MS diary, April 18, 1876, JRL125. H. C. Rothery to T. S. Raffles, July 2, 1878, Raffles Collection, JRL383. J. C. Fowler to unnamed correspondent, Dec. 11, 1875, Raffles Collection, JRL376. Thomas Barwick Lloyd Baker to Mrs. Josephine Lowell, July 7, 1880, Baker Letters, NYPL.

25. William Bromley Davenport Papers, JRL: newspaper clippings, Coventry *Standard*, Sept. 12, 1879; Birmingham *Daily Gazette*, Oct. 24, 1873.

26. Sir Louis Mallet to David Wells, Feb. 20, 1873, Wells Papers, LC. John Bright to Gladstone, Jan. 17, 1875, Gladstone Papers, BM44113.

27. Mrs. Josephine Butler to Aaron Powell, Feb. 17, 1880, S. H. Gay Papers, CUL. James Bryce to Albert Shaw, Jan. 3, 1886, Albert Shaw Papers, NYPL. Mrs. Annie Besant to Moncure Conway, Dec. 28, 1886, Conway Papers, CUL. W. T. Stead to Albert Shaw, Feb. 14, 1891, and Feb. 21, 1891, Albert Shaw Papers, NYPL. Richard Cobden to R. Ward, July 15, 1849, Cobden Letters, PML. Herbert Spencer to Moncure Conway, Dec. 12, 1893, and Dec. 13, 1893, Conway Papers, CUL. Thomas Barwick Lloyd Baker Letters, NYPL: Baker to Mrs. Josephine Shaw Lowell, June 13, 1879; July 18, 1879; April 23, 1881. NYPL: Duke of Argyll to J. Schoenhopf, Nov. 7, 1893, Lee Kohns Autograph Collection; Auberon Herbert to F. G. Fleay, Nov. 16, 1889 (letterhead), Great Britain, Autographs. Auberon Herbert to William Knight, Jan. 9, no year, and June 17, no year, Knight Papers, PML.

28. Herbert Spencer to Andrew Carnegie, March 7, 1885, Carnegie Collection, NYPL. Spencer to Moncure Conway, Jan. 10, 1894, Conway Papers, CUL. Cf. Ernest Benn to Nicholas Murray Butler, March 10, 1931, and Dec. 28, 1934, Butler Papers, CUL. Herbert Spencer to J. M. Libbey, Dec. 1, 1882, Misc. Papers, NYPL. Herbert Spencer to Courtland Palmer, March

30, 1882, American Academy of Arts and Letters Collection, LC. Knight Papers, PML: Herbert Spencer to William Knight, July 19, 1893, Nov. 5, 1894, Oct. 12, 1896; W. Troughton to Knight, Dec. 16, 1900. CUL: Herbert Spencer to Appleton, Dec. 28, 1896, Ripley Hitchcock Papers; Spencer to Conway, July 17, 1898, Conway Papers.

X. SCRAPPING THE OLD

1. John Burns, MS diary, May 25, 1888, BM46310. A. R. Wallace to William Tallack, April 20, 1899, Tallack Papers, BM38835. E. Girdlestone to A. R. Wallace, Jan. 13, 1909, Wallace Papers, BM46440. Hammersmith League Papers, Jan. 6, 1893, BM45893. Edward Carpenter, typescript autobiographical notes, p. 82, JRL1171.
2. Newspaper clipping, Birmingham *Morning News,* Sept. 24, 1874, William Bromley Davenport Papers, JRL. George Eliot, MS diary, Feb. 28, 1879, and March 29, 1879, BERG.
3. Hyndman to George, March 27, 1883, Henry George Papers, NYPL. Hammersmith League Papers, July 15, 1888, BM45892. Carpenter, typescript autobiographical notes, p. 79, JRL1171.
4. George Gissing to Algernon Gissing, April 24, 1881, Gissing Letters, BERG. George to Ford, Dec. 28, 1881 (letter book), Henry George Papers, NYPL. MCCP, June 25, 1879, and July 25, 1879, MCL. George to Ford, Dec. 28, 1881 (letter book), Henry George Papers, NYPL.
5. Hyndman to George, March 14, 1883, Nov., 1882 (?), Henry George Papers, NYPL. Hyndman to Richard Hawkin, Sept. 20, 1904, Hawkin Papers, JRL1040.
6. Hyndman to unnamed correspondent, June 24, 1884, Autograph Collection, MCL.
7. Carpenter, typescript autobiographical notes, pp. 72, 74, JRL1171. Henry C. Allen to A. R. Wallace, Nov. 3, 1883, Wallace Papers, BM46440.
8. Hyndman to George, Jan. 4, 1883, and March 14, 1883 (?), Henry George Papers, NYPL.
9. NYPL: George to Ford, March 9, 1882 (letter book), and George to Mrs. George, June 2, 1882, Henry George Papers; Henry George, Jr., to Francis G. Shaw, March 12, 1882, Henry George, Jr., Papers; Headlam to George, Sept. 25, 1882, and George to Walker, June 26, 1884, Henry George Papers.
10. CUL: Gosse to Stedman, Aug. 6, 1876, Stedman Papers; William Morris to Mr. Groze (?), undated, Autograph Collection; Morris to Emma Lazarus, Jan. 12, 1884, Lazarus Letters.
11. Stanley Withers Collection, MCL: Robert Louis Stevenson to Stanley Withers, March 23, 1886; Swinburne to Withers, May 13, 1886; Meredith to Withers, April 3, 1886; Thomas Hardy to Withers, April 22, 1886. Hammersmith League Papers, June 30, 1884, BM45891.
12. Morris to Mr. Spencer of Bradford, June 25, 1884, Autograph Collection, MCL. Morris to Emma Lazarus, April 21, 1884, Lazarus Papers, CUL.
13. William Morris to Mr. Spencer of Bradford, March 31, 1884, and June 25, 1884, Autograph Collection, MCL. George to Mrs. George, Nov. 17, 1884, Henry George Papers, NYPL. Hammersmith League Papers, Jan. 7, 1885, and Jan. 15, 1885, BM45891.
14. Edward Aveling to Seligman, Nov. 23, 1886, and one undated, Selig-

man Papers, CUL. Edward Carpenter, typescript autobiographical notes, p. 75, JRL1171. George Gissing Letters, BERG: Gissing to Ellen Gissing, Nov. 22, 1885; Gissing to Algernon Gissing, Sept. 22, 1885. Morris to Cobden-Sanderson, Jan. 24, 1885, Morris Letters, PML.

15. Morris to John Burns, Oct. 27, 1885, Burns Papers, BM46288. Hammersmith League Papers, BM45891–BM45892: Sept. 27, 1885; Nov. 15, 1885; Jan. 10, 1886; March 11, 1888; April 22, 1888; July 20, 1888; May 23, 1886; July 25, 1886; July 4, 1886.

16. W. C. H., *Confessions of an Anarchist* (London, 1906), p. 90. Hammersmith League Papers, BM45891–BM45892: June 6, 1886; March 27, 1887; June 19, 1887; May 13, 1888.

17. Bernard Shaw to Walter Crane, March 13, 1900, Bernard Shaw Letters, BERG. Hammersmith League Papers, Nov. 21, 1890, and Oct. 16, 1896, BM45893. May Morris to John Quinn, Oct. 17, 1910, Quinn Transcripts, NYPL. John Burns, MS diary, April 8, 1888, BM46310. BERG: Swinburne to Walter Watts-Dunton, Aug. 3, 1896, Swinburne Letters; Edmund Gosse to Edward Marsh, Aug. 17, 1899, Marsh Papers.

18. Andreas Scheu to A. R. Wallace, Feb. 3, 1909, Wallace Papers, BM46440. Stead to Shaw, April 15, 1891, Albert Shaw Papers, NYPL.

19. Conway Papers, CUL: Annie Besant to Mrs. Conway, May 4, 1875; Annie Besant to Moncure Conway, Dec. 28, 1886. John Burns, MS diary, March 26, 1888, BM46310. Annie Besant to Mrs. Conway, Jan. 2, 1888, Conway Papers, CUL. Annie Besant to Cobden-Sanderson, July 10, 1889, Cobden-Sanderson Papers, PML. Stead to Shaw, March 31, 1891, Albert Shaw Papers, NYPL. Annie Besant to Kate Field, April 10, 1891, Kate Field Papers, BPL. Annie Besant to T. Fisher Unwin, May 28, 1893, Unwin Papers, BERG.

20. Bernard Shaw to Mansfield, March 27, 1895, Bernard Shaw Letters, Free Library of Philadelphia. Henry Arthur Jones to Nicholas Murray Butler, 1921, Butler Papers, CUL. Bernard Shaw to Edward Marsh, April 1, 1937, Marsh Papers, BERG. Shaw to F. H. Evans, Aug. 27, 1895, and Shaw to Trebitsch, May 15, 1904, Bernard Shaw Letters, BERG. Henry James to Henley, May 26, 1879, Henley Papers, PML. William Archer to Brander Matthews, Jan. 16, 1895, Brander Matthews Papers, CUL. Reader's report on Bernard Shaw, "Love among the Artists," Unwin Papers, BERG.

21. Bernard Shaw to Hamlin Garland, Dec. 29, 1904, Henry George, Jr., Papers, NYPL. Bernard Shaw Letters, Free Library of Philadelphia: Bernard Shaw to Richard Mansfield, Feb. 22, 1895; Bernard Shaw to Mrs. Mansfield, March 19, 1898. Bernard Shaw to Sidney Darle, Jr., March 20, 1902, Bernard Shaw Letters, Folger Shakespeare Library. Bernard Shaw Letters, BERG: Bernard Shaw to Trebitsch, July 7, 1902; July 2, 1905; Nov. 18, 1902; Oct. 7, 1903. Bernard Shaw to Frank Harris, May 24, 1919, Shaw Letters, PML.

22. Bernard Shaw Letters, BERG: Bernard Shaw to Trebitsch, Dec. 10, 1902; Dec. 26, 1902; Feb. 21, 1903. Beatrice Webb to C. W. Sutton, March 14, 1913, Autograph Collection, MCL.

23. Bernard Shaw Letters, BERG: Bernard Shaw to Trebitsch, March 31, 1903, and Feb. 23, 1903. Ernest Dowson to Moore, June 14, 1889, Dowson Letters, PML. Albert Shaw to Herbert Baxter Adams, March 25, 1897 (letter book), Albert Shaw Papers, NYPL. *Economic Journal*, I (1891), 13.

24. Sidney Webb to John Burns, March 5, 1891, Burns Papers, BM46288.

Seligman Papers, CUL: Sidney Webb to Seligman, Jan. 9, 1891; June 22, 1895; Dec. 10, 1896; March 21, 1897; Nov. 25, 1897; March 10, 1898.

25. Sidney Webb to John Burns, Feb. 21, 1894, Burns Papers, BM46288. Sidney Webb to Seligman, June 20, 1895, and March 14, 1906, Seligman Papers, CUL. James Bryce to Emily Tuckerman, Mar. 18, 1898, Misc. Papers, NYPL. Stead to Albert Shaw, March 16, 1898, and Albert Shaw to Stead, April, 1898 (letter book), Albert Shaw Papers, NYPL.

26. Edward R. Pease to Seligman, July 19, 1895, Seligman Papers, CUL. Bernard Shaw to Albert Shaw, undated, and William Clarke to Albert Shaw, Jan. 15, 1889, Albert Shaw Papers, NYPL. Edith Nesbit to J. B. Pinker, Nov. 28, 1902, Nesbit Letters, BERG. William Archer to Brander Matthews, Jan. 4, 1897, Brander Matthews Papers, CUL. Bernard Shaw to Salt, Oct. 30, 1919, Bernard Shaw Letters, BERG. J. C. Durant to George, May 15, 1892, Henry George Papers, NYPL.

27. Ernest Benn to Nicholas Murray Butler, Dec. 24, 1931, Butler Papers, CUL. Cf. Duke of Argyll to Mrs. Millais, Feb. 24, 1884, Millais Papers, PML. John Burns to Champion, Feb. 11, 1892, Seligman Collection, CUL. John Burns to Mrs. Cobden-Sanderson, undated, Cobden-Sanderson Papers, PML. John Burns, MS diary, Nov. 22, 1888, BM46310.

XI. THE FAILURE OF A CAMPAIGN

1. Henry George Papers, NYPL: Hyndman to George, Jan. 9, 1882 (?); March 27, 1883; April 6, 1883. Leyton Williams to Seligman, Aug. 24, 1886, Seligman Papers, CUL. Sidney Webb to George, March 8, 1889, Henry George Papers, NYPL. William Shaw Papers, CUL: Plato Draculis to William Shaw, Oct. 17, 1889; Jan. 17, 1890; June 18, 1896; Nov. 29, 1896; July 2, 1894; March 5, 1897. Edward Carpenter, typescript autobiographical notes, pp. 78–79, JRL1171.

2. George Gissing Letters, BERG: Gissing to Margaret Gissing, Feb. 15, 1886; Gissing to Ellen Gissing, March 6, 1886, and March 14, 1886. JRL: John Temple Leader to Walter Sneyd, Dec. 21, 1887, Walter Sneyd Papers; William Procter to Sir William Bromley Davenport, May 23, 1895, Sir William Bromley Davenport Papers.

3. Edward Carpenter, typescript autobiographical notes, p. 82, JRL1171. Stead to Gladstone, Nov. 4, 1887, Gladstone Papers, BM44303. John Burns, MS diary, April 10, 1888, BM46310. Marie Corelli to unnamed correspondent, Aug. 4, 1886, Haggard Papers, CUL.

4. W. Duignan to A. R. Wallace, Sept. 1, 1882, Wallace Papers, BM46440. Burns, MS diary, June 23, 1888, and Sept. 5, 1888, BM46310. Theodore Roosevelt on Burns, in Atlantic Monthly, April, 1895, p. 555.

5. Carpenter, typescript autobiographical notes, p. 81, JRL1171. Newspaper clipping, Macclesfield Courier, May 21, 1888, and H. Sandford to Davenport, March 25, 1895, Sir William Bromley Davenport Papers, JRL. W. T. Stead to Albert Shaw, July 6, 1892, Albert Shaw Papers, and Moreton Frewen to Bourke Cockran, Aug. 25, 1895, Cockran Papers, NYPL.

6. Eleanor Marx Aveling to Burns, Aug. 6, 1895, and Aug. 8, 1895, Burns Papers, BM46288. Carpenter, typescript autobiographical notes, pp. 82, 96, JRL1171. Blatchford to Palmer, undated, Blatchford Letters, MCL. Bernard Shaw to Burns, Sept. 11, 1903, Burns Papers, BM46288.

7. Sir Norman Angell, typescript reminiscences, p. 16, Oral History Project, CUL. Besant to John Burns, Nov. 28, 1887, Burns Papers, BM46288. Bernard Shaw to Trebitsch, March 18, 1905, and Bernard Shaw to editor of *Evening Standard*, March 23, 1927, Bernard Shaw Letters, BERG. Gissing to Margaret Gissing, Sept. 29, 1889, Gissing Letters, BERG. Gilchrist to Kineton Parkes, Sept. 26, 1891 and one undated, Gilchrist Letters, NYPL. Blatchford to Thompson, March 29, 1885, Blatchford Letters, MCL. Annie Besant to Mrs. John Burns, Jan. 20, 1888, Burns Papers, BM46288.

8. Benjamin Ingham to G. Whitefield, Jan. 10, 1743, Raffles Collection, JRL344. Henry Ellis to William Frey, July 4, 1886, Frey Papers, NYPL. Stead to Albert Shaw, Nov. 24, 1894, and Robert Donald to Albert Shaw, Oct. 13, 1894, Albert Shaw Papers, NYPL. Annie Besant to Burns, April 9, 1889, and July 29, 1889, Burns Papers, BM46288. Burns, MS diary, Oct. 2, 1888, and Dec. 20, 1888, BM46310.

9. Hyndman to George, Jan. 9, 1882 (?), Henry George Papers, NYPL. John Stuart Mill to unnamed correspondent, March 2, 1835, Raffles Collection, JRL349.

10. Blatchford Letters, MCL: Blatchford to Thompson, Sept., 1894; Blatchford to Palmer, undated; Blatchford to Mrs. Bruce Glasier, March 8, 1897 (copy); Blatchford to Bruce Glasier, Feb. 26, 1897, and Oct. 19, 1901 (copies).

11. Burns Papers, BM46288: Beatrice Webb to Burns, April 7, 1896 (?); William Campbell to Burns, Nov. 7, 1890; Eleanor Marx Aveling to Champion, Jan. 3, 1890. E. Bernstein to Unwin, Oct. 25, 1897, Unwin Papers, BERG. Bernard Shaw to Burns, Aug. 12, 1892, and May 28, 1897, Burns Papers, BM46288.

12. Glasier to Blatchford, Oct. 23, 1901 (copy), Blatchford Papers, MCL. Michael Davitt to William O'Brien, Feb, 28, 1894, Davitt Letters, NLI. John Regan to John Burns, April 15, 1895, Burns Papers, BM46288. Stewart Headlam to Mrs. Cobden-Sanderson, Nov. 21, 1903, Cobden-Sanderson Papers, PML. Hyndman to Richard Hawkin, Aug. 25, 1904, and Aug. 31, 1904, Hawkin Papers, JRL1040.

13. John Burns, MS diary, May 12, 1888, and April 15, 1888, BM46310. Draculis to William Shaw, April 7, 1892, William Shaw Papers, CUL. Carpenter, typescript autobiographical notes, p. 81, JRL1171. Bernard Shaw to Hamlin Garland, Dec. 29, 1904, Henry George, Jr., Papers, NYPL.

14. John Burns, MS diary, April 9, 1888, BM46310. Cf. J. Middleton Murry to Borden, April 1, 1933, Misc. Papers, NYPL.

15. William Cobbett to Thomas Jefferson, Nov. 2, 1792, Cobbett Letters, PML. Gissing Letters, BERG: Gissing to Algernon Gissing, Aug. 6, 1895; Sept. 8, 1895; Nov. 13, 1876. *The Queen, The Lady's Newspaper and Court Chronicle*, CII (Oct. 2, 1897), 608.

16. The operative cotton spinners and self-actor minders in your employ to the manufacturers of Ashton and its neighbourhood, Aug., 1859 (printed letter), Rylands Papers, JRL1185.

17. John Bright to Edward Pierce, Jan. 17, 1886, Bright Letters, HCL. T. H. Farrer to Thomson Hankey, Feb. 22, 1885, and Aug. 18, 1887, Misc. Papers, NYPL. Thomson Hankey to David Wells, Aug. 19, 1886, Wells Papers, LC. Bolton Factory Operatives' Protective Friendly Society, *Rules and Regulations* (no place, 1860), p. 2. Alfred Neild, MS recollections, pp. 10–11, JRL872.

18. E. T. Craig to A. R. Wallace, March 8, 1884, Wallace Papers, BM46440.
John Bright to George Mitchell, Dec. 20, 1878, Bright Papers, BM43389.
19. Wigan workers to John Rylands, March 29, 1869, Rylands Papers,
JRL1185. Burns, MS diary, Sept. 9, 1888, BM46310.
20. Kipling to Hitchcock, Jan. 17, 1897, Kipling Letters, BERG. Cf.
Ralph Sneyd to Henry Vincent, Dec. 4, 1831, Ralph Sneyd Papers, JRL.
George Gissing to Ellen Gissing, May 13, 1888, Gissing Letters; MS diary,
March 17, 1889, BERG. Burns, MS diary, Sept. 13, 1888, and Aug. 13, 1888,
BM46310. Plato Draculis to William Shaw, April 20, 1891, William Shaw
Papers, CUL.
21. *Economist*, XXIX (April 15, 1871), 440. Burns, MS diary, April 11,
1888, BM46310. Francis Place to unnamed correspondent, Sept. 29, 1840,
Anti-Corn Law League Papers, MCL. Plato Draculis to William Shaw, Feb.
26, 1892, William Shaw Papers, CUL. Goldwin Smith to Andrew Carnegie,
April 18, 1893, Carnegie Collection, NYPL. Carpenter, typescript autobiographical notes, p. 79, JRL1171.

XII. SCHEMES EVERYWHERE

1. F. W. Farrar, MS article on Lord Shaftesbury, PML. Robert L. Stanton, MS journal, March 1, 1879, NYPL.
2. Thomas Hughes to Octavius R. Wilkinson, Feb. 4, 1885, Parrish Collection, PUL. May Morris to John Quinn, July 17, 1912, Quinn Transcripts,
NYPL. Henry George to Francis Taylor, March, 1882 (?), Henry George
Papers, NYPL.
3. F. W. Newman to Epes Sargent, Oct. 24, 1875, and Feb. 11, 1876, Newman Letters, BPL.
4. John Bright to John T. Middlemore, Jan. 31, 1875, Bright Letters,
PUL. Thomas Hughes to unidentified correspondent, March 25, 1864, Misc.
Papers, NYPL. George Gissing to Margaret Gissing, Feb. 4, 1887, and Gis-
sing to Algernon Gissing, Jan. 30, 1884, Gissing Letters, BERG. London
Working Men's Association, printed circular, Lord Chamberlain 2 (100),
PRO.
5. W. M. Rossetti to Anne Gilchrist, June 26, 1885, W. M. Rossetti Letters,
CUL. Mrs. Humphry Ward to Mr. Yorke, Aug. 30, 1905, Annie Russell
Papers, NYPL. Mrs. Ward to Elizabeth Jordan, March 7, 1908, Elizabeth
Jordan Papers, NYPL. Percy Alden to Sir William Bromley Davenport,
Feb. 25, 1897, Davenport Papers, JRL. F. W. Farrar, MS article on Lord
Shaftesbury, PML. Sir William Willis to Bagshawe, Nov. 1, 1889, Bagshawe
Papers, JRL.
6. John Stuart Mill to John Nichol, July 16, 1868, Mill Letters, PML.
Gissing to Algernon Gissing, Jan. 29, 1893, Gissing Letters, BERG. Florence
Nightingale to M. J. Loane, Sept. 9, 1895, and Amy Hughes to Florence
Nightingale, Sept. 30, 1893, Nightingale Collection, Teachers College
Library, Columbia University. William Farr to F. O. Ward, Sept. 15, 1854,
Autograph Collection, JRL341. Stead to Albert Shaw, Aug. 27, 1892, Albert
Shaw Papers, NYPL.
7. Ernest Dowson to Moore, 1896 (?), Dowson Letters, PML. C. R. Drys-
dale to Gladstone, June 15, 1877, Gladstone Papers, BM44454. Bernard
Shaw to unnamed correspondent, March 6, 1890, Bernard Shaw Letters,
BERG. Sir William Wilson Hunter to Moncure Conway, April 14, 1884,

Anthony Autograph Collection, NYPL. F. S. Pitt-Taylor to A. R. Wallace, Oct. 7, 1899, Wallace Papers, BM46440. John Nichol to William Knight, Jan. 26, 1892, Knight Papers, PML.

8. George Jacob Holyoake, MS speech, Aug. 17, 1901, Anthony Autograph Collection, NYPL. William J. Ashley to Seligman, July 15, 1889, and Sept. 15, 1889, Seligman Papers, CUL. William Leys to Campbell-Bannerman, Feb. 18, 1899, Campbell-Bannerman Papers, BM41234.

9. Henry W. Macrosty to Seligman, Aug. 20, 1897, Seligman Papers, CUL. Charles Leech to John Burns, Dec. 2, 1893, John Burns Papers, BM46288.

10. Seligman Papers, CUL: H. S. Foxwell to Seligman, June 23, 1909; C. F. Bastable to Seligman, Aug. 8, 1892, Aug. 17, 1892, May 9, 1894; Alfred Marshall to Seligman, Nov. 21, 1895; L. H. Blunden to Seligman, July 12, 1894. J. C. Durant to George, March 30, 1886, Henry George Papers, NYPL. W. T. Stead to Albert Shaw, Dec. 28, 1892, Albert Shaw Papers, NYPL. Seligman Papers, CUL: T. H. Elliott to Seligman, Nov. 23, 1895; Foxwell to Seligman, Nov. 24, 1895.

11. Moreton Frewen, printed address, 1892, Frewen Papers, LC. Seligman Papers, CUL: Worthington C. Ford to Seligman, Nov. 6, 1887; Jesse Seligman to Seligman, Dec. 12, 1891; Foxwell to Seligman, March 12, 1893, April 20, 1897. Charles Dickens to S. Perkes, Nov. 29, 1866, Dickens Letters, BERG. Arnold Bennett to George Sturt, Jan. 31, 1897, Bennett Letters, BERG. NYPL: Stead to Albert Shaw, Jan. 30, 1894, Albert Shaw Papers; James E. Thorold Rogers to J. M. Libbey, Nov. 21, no year, Misc. Papers; Thomson Hankey to David A Wells, March 21, 1882, Wells Papers. Lord Playfair to C. S. Fairchild, Sept. 17, 1895, Autograph Collection, New-York Historical Society. Rudyard Kipling to Ripley Hitchcock, Aug. 28, 1896, Kipling Letters, BERG. Winston Churchill to Bourke Cockran, Aug. 31, 1896, and Nov. 5, 1896, Cockran Papers, NYPL.

12. Gissing to Algernon Gissing, Nov. 24, 1895, Gissing Letters, BERG. Edward Garnett, MS reader's report, Feb. 16, 1898, Unwin Papers, BERG.

13. Thomas Hughes to Mrs. Price, Nov. 13, 1892, DeCoursey Fales Collection, NYPL. J. H. Howell to Moreton Frewen, Jan. 12, 1887, Frewen Papers, LC. Printed circular for *A Farmer's Year*, and Joseph Chamberlain to H. Rider Haggard, Aug. 1, 1903, Haggard Papers, CUL. Haggard to J. B. Paton, Feb. 11, 1901, Haggard Letters, HCL. Haggard to unidentified correspondent, May 5, 1915, Haggard Letters, BERG.

14. Arthur Young to Fanny Burney, July 18, 1792, Young Letters, PML. Edward William Cooke to B. R. Green, Nov. 19, 1867, Misc. Papers, NYPL. Thomas Carlyle to A. J. Scott, Aug. 5, 1856, Carlyle Letters, BERG. Rossetti to Mrs. William Cowper, undated, Rossetti Letters, PML. Edward Lear to Mrs. Kerr, undated, Raffles Collection, JRL360. Marie Corelli to Steve Massett, Oct. 31, 1892, Coykendall Collection, CUL. John Lockwood Kipling to Elkin Mathews, June 25, 1902, Kipling Letters, BERG. Edwin Waugh to Samuel Buckley, Aug. 12, 1885, Waugh Papers, MCL.

15. Edward Nicholson to William Frey, June 2, 1888, William Frey Papers, NYPL. Gissing to Algernon Gissing, Aug. 1, 1894, Gissing Letters, BERG.

16. Newspaper clipping, Oct. 24, 1873, and Birmingham *Gazette,* Dec. 10, 1875, William Bromley Davenport Papers, JRL.

17. Helen Taylor to Henry George, Dec. 13, 1891, Henry George Papers, NYPL. Jesse Collings to A. R. Wallace, Jan. 10, 1882, and J. S. Blackie to

Wallace, July 21, 1882, Wallace Papers, BM46440. Newspaper clipping, Coventry *Standard,* Jan. 21, 1881, William Bromley Davenport Papers, JRL.
18. Joseph Arch to Gladstone, Nov. 11, 1879, Gladstone Papers, BM44461. F. W. Newman to Epes Sargent, Oct. 24, 1875, Newman Letters, BPL. F. W. Newman to Alexander Strahan, Aug. 5, 1879, Misc. Papers, NYPL. George Burgess to Joseph Smith, May 19, 1880, and Joseph Smith to George Burgess, July 19, 1879, Burgess Papers, NYPL. Oldham Working Men's Branch of the Land Tenure Reform Association, Printed circular, Stanley Papers, JRL1095. T. C. Leslie to unidentified correspondent, July 14, 1874, General MSS Collection, CUL.
19. Edward Lyulph Stanley to Arthur S. Symonds, May 31, 1874, Stanley Withers Collection, MCL. Frederic Impey to A. R. Wallace, Feb. 19, 1886, Wallace Papers, BM46440. Thomas Ellis to Campbell-Bannerman, Feb. 6, 1899, Campbell-Bannerman Papers, BM41234. Newspaper clipping, *Times,* Oct. 21, 1899, Sir Henry Roscoe Papers, JRL963.
20. John Stuart Mill to John Nichol, Dec. 29, 1870, Mill Letters, PML. Amelia B. Edwards to Lydia E. Becker, Oct. 15, 1887, National Union of Women's Suffrage Societies Papers, MCL. George Gissing to Ellen Gissing, Feb. 3, 1882, Gissing Letters, BERG. Frank Newdigate to Walter Sneyd, April 7, 1888, Walter Sneyd Papers, JRL. Mrs. Israel Zangwill to Annie Russell, Jan. 21, 1909, Annie Russell Papers, NYPL.
21. Harriet Beecher Stowe to George Eliot, May 25, 1869, Stowe Letters, BERG. Mary A. Estlin to William Lloyd Garrison, April 27, 1875, Garrison Papers, BPL. Charles Dickens, MS speech, April 30, 1870, Charles Dickens Papers, JRL725.
22. John Stuart Mill to Florence Nightingale, Sept. 10, 1860 (draft), Mill Letters, BERG. Florence Nightingale to John Stuart Mill, Aug. 11, 1867, E. T. Cooke Papers, BM39927. James E. Thorold Rogers to unnamed correspondent, undated, Anthony Autograph Collection, NYPL. J. Nichol to William Lloyd Garrison, Aug., 1872, Garrison Papers, BPL.
23. National Union of Women's Suffrage Societies Papers, MCL: Emily Davies to Lydia E. Becker, Feb. 4, 1867, and Feb. 9, 1867; Leonard Courtney to Lydia E. Becker, Nov. 23, 1885. Sir Charles Dilke to Gladstone, April 12, 1884, Gladstone Papers, BM44149. Stead to Albert Shaw, April 27, 1892, Albert Shaw Papers, NYPL. Mary A. Estlin to Mrs. S. H. Gay, May 13, 1876, Gay Papers, CUL. John Morley to Cobden-Sanderson, Nov. 22, 1906, Cobden-Sanderson Papers, PML. Lord Brougham and Vaux to Lady Bective, July 18, 1899, and Marquis of Crew to Lady Bective, July 19, 1899, National Union of Women's Suffrage Societies Papers, MCL. Frederick William Holls to L. J. Maxse, Dec. 22, 1898, Holls Papers, CUL. Stead to Holls, Jan. 27, 1891, Stead Letters, HCL.
24. J. M. Ludlow to Seligman, Oct. 29, 1885, Seligman Papers, CUL. N. P. Gilman to George Jacob Holyoake, March 25, 1892, Unwin Papers, BERG. Plato Draculis to William Shaw, Jan. 16, 1891, William Shaw Papers, CUL. Hyndman to George, Jan. 4, 1883, and George to Mrs. George, Dec. 2, 1884, Henry George Papers, NYPL. Walter Crane to Hamlin Garland, Dec. 20, 1904, Henry George, Jr., Papers, NYPL. Hammersmith League Papers, Feb. 5, 1888, BM45891.
25. Henry George Papers, NYPL: Thomas Walker to George, Aug. 30, 1884; George to Walker, Sept. 9, 1884; Sidney Webb to George, March 8, 1889. John Paul to Henry George, Jr., July 15, 1898, and Bernard Shaw to Hamlin Garland, Dec. 29, 1904, Henry George, Jr., Papers, NYPL. Helen

Taylor to Mrs. Henry George, April 27, 1884, Mrs. Henry George Papers, NYPL. Hyndman to George, April 6, 1883, Henry George Papers, NYPL.

XIII. SCHOOLS AS WEAPONS

1. Cobden to William Neild, Sept. 30, 1838, Neild Papers, JRL868. Cobden to J. B. Smith, Oct. 28, 1853, J. B. Smith Papers, MCL. W. C. Macready to George L. Duyckinck, Feb. 25, 1859, Duyckinck Papers, NYPL. John Bright to Henry Vincent, July 19, 1866, Bright Letters, HCL. George Gissing to Algernon Gissing, Nov. 9, 1878, Nov. 13, 1876, Gissing Letters, BERG. William Ewart to Edward Edwards, March 31, 1849, Edwards Papers, MCL.

2. Prince Albert to Lord Ellesmere, July 3, 1856, Autograph Collection, PML. Denmark Hill Grammar School, *Prospectus,* 1849, in JRL380. BERG: Thomas Hughes to unnamed correspondent, Aug. 3, 1893, and Nov. 3, 1895, Hughes Letters; Thomas Arnold to Girdlestone, Oct. 28, 1840, Thomas Arnold Letters.

3. Mr. Bosworth's Academy, *Prospectus,* Dec., 1831, in JRL373. London University, *Prospectus,* undated, in JRL373. William E. Channing to James Yates, Nov. 29, 1828, Gaskell Collection, JRL732. Lord Denman to S. F. Rawson, Aug. 26, 1831, Raffles Collection, JRL364. *Substance of the Report of a Committee of the Trustees for Educational Purposes Under the Will of the Late John Owens, on the General Character and Plan of the College* (Manchester, 1850), p. 9.

4. S. C. Hall to Thomas Raffles, June, 1852, Raffles Collection, JRL359. Robert Chambers to Alexander Henry and others, Oct. 6, 1860, Dreer Collection, HSP.

5. Curzon to Sneyd, July 11, 1870, Walter Sneyd Papers, JRL. Bright to Northy, Dec. 25, 1871, Bright Papers, BM44877. Nightingale to A. Bourne, July 19, 1884, Nightingale Letters, Teachers College Library, Columbia University. C. O. Shepard to F. W. Seward, June 14, 1878, Consular Letters from Bradford, NA.

6. G. H. Rendall, *Inaugural Address Delivered at the Opening of University College, Liverpool, Saturday, 14th January, 1882,* pp. 5–6. Gladstone to Henry Roscoe, June 30, 1884, and Mundella to Roscoe, June 30, 1884, Sir Henry Roscoe Papers, JRL963.

7. Matthew Arnold to the acting editor of the *Pall Mall Gazette,* Jan. 13, 1886, E. T. Cook Papers, BM39927. Sir Lyon Playfair, address of April 27, 1888, Polytechnic Young Men's Christian Institute, *Syllabus and Prospectus, 1888–1889.*

8. James Bryce, MS article on commercial education, pp. 3–4, Bryce Papers, PML. Newspaper clippings, Sir Henry Roscoe Papers, JRL963.

9. Matthew Arnold Letters, PML: Matthew Arnold to Millais, Feb. 13, 1888, and one postmarked Sept. 15, 1884; Arnold to William Knight, March 11, 1881. James Bryce to Albert Shaw, Nov. 8, 1902, Albert Shaw Papers, NYPL. MCCP, Nov. 29, 1882, MCL.

10. *Ibid.,* July 29, 1889, Sept. 25, 1889, Feb. 17, 1890. J. W. Spencer to Davenport, March 7, 1899, Sir William Bromley Davenport Papers, JRL. Borough of Congleton, Technical Instruction Committee, *Prospectus of Classes Fifth Session, 1897–98,* p. 4. Sir H. H. Johnston to E. M. Bowdler Sharpe, Oct 2, 1905, BM42181.

11. William Brewer to unnamed correspondent, May 26, 1870, Raffles Col

lection, JRL373. John Bigelow, MS diary, May 21, 1870, NYPL. Caroline Herford to John Ruskin, March 8, 1887, Ruskin Letters, CUL. J. B. Smith to Sampson Lloyd, Feb. 8, 1871 (draft), J. B. Smith Papers, MCL. Examination questions in Ernest Jones Papers, CUL. Roscoe to Lydia E. Becker, July 14, 1887, National Union of Women's Suffrage Societies Papers, MCL. Elizabeth Blackwell to Barbara Bodichon, July 10, 1881 (?), Blackwell Letters, CUL. Newspaper clippings in Mrs. Dunlap Hopkins Papers, New-York Historical Society. Frederic Harrison to Unwin, Nov. 1, 1894, Unwin Papers, BERG.

12. Bright to T. H. Green, March 19, 1861, Bright Letters, PUL. Lincoln Steffens to Joseph Steffens, Aug. 28, 1892, and Lincoln Steffens to Frederick M. Willis, Aug. 29, 1892, Steffens Papers, CUL. Lord Zouche to Sneyd, Dec. 5, 1872, Walter Sneyd Papers, JRL. A. Sidgwick to Cobden-Sanderson, March 18, 1903, Cobden-Sanderson Papers, PML.

13. Seligman Papers, CUL: William A. S. Hewins to Seligman, May 11, 1895, Dec. 10, 1895, Oct. 30, 1896; Sidney Webb to Seligman, March 8, 1896, and Dec. 10, 1896; Foxwell to Seligman, Jan. 6, 1906; W. J. Ashley to Seligman, Jan. 20, 1887, Nov. 3, 1890, Nov. 9, 1890, Dec. 13, 1890.

14. Thomas Ashton to J. B. Smith, March 23, 1870, J. B. Smith Papers, MCL. Foxwell to Seligman, May 23, 1898, Seligman Papers, CUL. MCCP, May 14, 1879, MCL. Ashley to Seligman, Aug. 27, 1901, Seligman Papers, CUL.

15. Society for the Promotion of Scientific Industry, *Catalogue of the Exhibition of Appliances for the Economical Consumption of Fuel, Peel Park, 1874* (Manchester, 1874). *Times,* Aug. 4, 1904.

16. Newspaper clippings, Sir Henry Roscoe Papers, JRL963. Henry Sweet to unnamed correspondent, March 21, 1908, Misc. Papers, NYPL. Alfred Marshall to William Knight, Jan. 4, 1887, Knight Papers, PML. Gladstone to E. T. Cook, Dec. 25, 1889, Misc. Papers, NYPL. Hughes to Moran, April 24, 1868, Thomas Hughes Letters, Parrish Collection, PUL. Lord Curzon to Davenport, April 23, 1907, Sir William Bromley Davenport Papers, JRL. General Walker to William Knight, March 13, 1888, American Autograph Collection, PML. Ashley to Seligman, March 2, 1909, Seligman Papers, CUL.

XIV. A FAITH IN DOUBT

1. H. G. Wells to W. E. Henley, Feb. 4, 1900, Henley Papers, PML. Robert Hyde Greg to Edward Davies Davenport, July 9, 1846, Edward Davies Davenport Papers, JRL. T. Perronet Thompson to John Ballantyne, Jan. 19, 1839, and J. B. Smith to unnamed correspondent, March 13, 1839, Anti-Corn Law League Papers, MCL. Thompson to H. B. Peacock, Nov. 30, 1844, T. Perronet Thompson Letters, JRL1180. Adam Smith to Strahan, Oct. 26, 1780 (copy), Misc. Papers, NYPL. Samuel Smiles to John Bright, Sept. 23, 1879, Bright Papers, BM43389.

2. John Bowring to Archibald Prentice, Dec. 29, 1838, and Joseph Hume to James Chapman, July 12, 1839, Anti-Corn Law League Papers, MCL. Joseph Hume, form letter, March 22, 1841, Misc. Papers, NYPL. Cobden to Edward Davies Davenport, Dec. 26, 1845, Edward Davies Davenport Papers, JRL. John Bright to David Wells, Dec. 17, 1877, Wells Papers, LC.

3. Cobden to Firnley, April 10, 1835, Cobden Collection, JRL343. Richard Monckton Milnes to Carlyle, postmarked July 12, 1841, Autograph Collec-

tion, PML. Cobden to R. Morgan, Jan. 3, 1846, Anthony Autograph Collection, NYPL. Benjamin Stott, *Songs for the Millions, and Other Poems* (London, 1843), and Sir Thomas Bazley to John Evans, May 27, 1881, Autograph Collection, MCL. Thompson to Peacock, Nov. 30, 1844, and Dec. 14, 1844, Thompson Letters, JRL1180. Cobden to Edward Davies Davenport, April 5, 1845, and Dec. 26, 1845, Edward Davies Davenport Papers, JRL.

4. Carlyle to A. J. Scott, Dec. 5, 1845, Carlyle Letters, BERG. Bright to J. S. Henslow, Dec. 30, 1845, Bright Letters, PUL. Ralph Sneyd to Henry Vincent, Jan. 2, 1846, Ralph Sneyd Papers, JRL. Ebenezer Elliott to unnamed correspondent, Aug. 31, 1849 (photostat), Authors Club Collection, NYPL. J. B. Smith, typescript reminiscences, p. 1, MCL. Mrs. Cobden Unwin, MS speech, read by R. Cobden-Sanderson, June 29, 1946, Cobden-Sanderson Papers, PML. Cobden to C. Redding, Oct. 27, 1842, Cobden Letters, HCL. Cobden to J. B. Smith, Aug. 12, 1857, and Feb. 15, 1845, J. B. Smith Papers, MCL.

5. Charles Kingsley to Thomas Hughes, Sept. 11, 1854, Kingsley Letters, Parrish Collection, PUL. Cobden to J. B. Smith, Oct. 27, 1852, and Aug. 12, 1857, MCL. Cobden to Walmsley, Aug. 22, 1857, Cobden Letters, NYPL. Cobden to G. Rolston, Jan. 26, 1855, Seligman Collection, CUL. J. B. Smith Papers, MCL: Cobden to J. B. Smith, March 4, 1852; Oct. 26, 1852; Oct. 22, 1857; Dec. 10, 1857.

6. Thompson to Peacock, Jan. 3, 1854, Thompson Letters, JRL1180. MCCP, April, 1881, MCL. George Bancroft to Bright, Feb. 25, 1862, Misc. Papers, NYPL. Cobden to Smith, Dec. 20, 1864, and Jan. 6, 1865, J. B. Smith Papers, MCL. Cobden to Bradford R. Wood, Aug. 10, 1850, Gratz Collection, HSP. Cf. Gladstone to Wells, Jan. 5, 1870, Wells Papers, LC.

7. J. B. Smith Papers, MCL: J. B. Smith to Disraeli, Nov. 7, 1867 (copy); Disraeli to Smith, Nov. 25, 1867, and Feb. 9, 1868; Smith to Disraeli, May 8, 1868; W. Farr to J. B. Smith, May 27, 1868.

8. Michel Chevalier to Bright, Nov. 10, 1868, Bright Papers, BM43389. E. W. Watkin to Wells, Oct. 24, 1873, and W. H. Duncan to T. B. Potter, April 9, 1874, Wells Papers, LC. Marshall to Seligman, April 23, 1900, Seligman Papers, CUL. Thomas Bazley to Miss Smith, May 22, 1880, J. B. Smith Papers, MCL. MCCP, April 4, 1889, MCL.

9. Sir Louis Mallet to Bright, April 16, 1872, Bright Papers, BM43389. Thomas B. Potter to S. B. Ruggles, Oct. 14, 1880, Stauffer Collection, NYPL. Cf. F. J. Shaw to Arminius Vambéry, Nov. 24, 1922, Vambéry Papers, NYPL. Chevalier to Bright, March 7, 1876, Bright Papers, BM43389. MCCP, Nov. 22, 1876, MCL.

10. MCCP, Feb. 3, 1877, and Feb. 12, 1878, MCL.

11. *Ibid.*, Oct., 1879, and Sept. 24, 1879. Thomas Hughes to unnamed correspondent, Sept. 19, 1879, and Bright to Cyrus Field, Jan. 21, 1879, Anthony Collection, NYPL.

12. MCCP, Nov. 3, 1879, MCL. W. Price to A. R. Wallace, May 27, 1879, Wallace Papers, BM46440. Henry Fawcett to Wells, Jan. 31, 1877, and Sir Louis Mallet to Wells, Nov. 13, 1877, Wells Papers, LC. Jacob Behrens to C. O. Shepard, Nov. 16, 1877, Consular Letters from Bradford, NA. Bright to Edward L. Pierce, Jan. 10, 1883, Bright Letters, HCL. Edward Atkinson to Wells, Oct. 4, 1888, Atkinson Papers, and Joseph Smith to George Burgess, July 19, 1879, Burgess Papers, NYPL. Bright to Wells, Dec. 19, 1877, and Henry Ashworth to Wells, Dec. 18, 1878, Wells Papers, LC. C. O. Shepard to F. W. Seward, June 14, 1878, Consular Letters from Bradford, NA.

NOTES TO XIV: A FAITH IN DOUBT 367

13. J. C. Durant to George, Feb. 24, 1886, Henry George Papers, NYPL. Charles Nordhoff to Seligman, Nov. 14, 1888, Seligman Papers, CUL.

14. Gladstone to Bright, Sept. 29, 1881 (copy), Gladstone Papers, BM44113. Cobden-Sanderson Papers, PML: Sir Louis Mallet to Miss Cobden, Jan. 7, 1878; Gladstone to Miss Cobden, Oct. 24, 1881; John Bright to Miss Cobden, Oct. 31, 1881. Edmund Gosse to Brander Matthews, Jan. 27, 1882, Brander Matthews Papers, CUL.

15. Bright to Edward L. Pierce, Oct. 28, 1881, Bright Letters, HCL. Bright to Gladstone, Oct. 4, 1881, Gladstone Papers, BM44113. Dilke to Gladstone, Sept. 30, 1881, and Oct. 27, 1881, Gladstone Papers, BM44149. Lord Derby to A. G. Symonds, Nov. 16, 1881, Stanley Withers Collection, MCL. C. O. Shepard to Assistant Secretary of State, Aug. 4, 1881, Consular Letters from Bradford, NA. George Bradford to R. Gill, Nov. 7, 1884, Walter Sneyd Papers, JRL. Granville to Bright, Nov. 7, 1884, Bright Papers, BM43387. Archbishop Benson to Hamilton, March 14, 1885, Gladstone Papers, BM44109.

16. Frederick T. Mappin, electoral address, Nov. 6, 1885, Bagshawe Papers, JRL. T. B. Potter to Wells, June 22, 1873, Wells Papers, LC. Lord Iddesleigh to William Knight, June 14, 1886, Knight Papers, PML. Bright to Edward L. Pierce, Jan. 17, 1886, Bright Letters, HCL. MCCP, MCL: May 3, 1886; July 26, 1886; Nov. 1, 1886.

17. Newspaper clippings, Macclesfield *Courier*, July 10, 1886, and July 17, 1886, Sir William Bromley Davenport Papers, JRL. George to McClatchy, March 28, 1883 (copy), Henry George Papers, NYPL. Sir Louis Mallet to Moreton Frewen, Jan. 2, 1886, and May 6, 1889, Frewen Papers, LC. John Bright to Edward L. Pierce, Jan. 5, 1885, Bright Letters, HCL. M. E. Grant Duff to unidentified correspondent, Aug. 28, 1904, Anthony Collection, NYPL.

18. MCCP, MCL: April 25, 1887; Dec. 19, 1888; Jan. 3, 1889; Sept. 25, 1889; July 25, 1892. Balance sheet of funds collected during John Burns's imprisonment for the right of free speech, Burns Papers, BM46288. Bright to Richard Tangye, Nov. 17, 1886, BM44877. MCCP, June 29, 1887, MCL. Charles Francis Adams, Jr., to Wells, Jan. 26, 1887, Wells Papers, NYPL. Stead to Shaw, Aug. 30, 1892, Albert Shaw Papers, NYPL. CUL: Lincoln Steffens to Joseph Steffens, Aug. 7, 1892, Steffens Papers; Ashley to Seligman, Dec. 21, 1891, Seligman Papers. Kipling to Henley, Jan. 19, 1893, Henley Papers, PML.

19. Newspaper clipping, *Northern Whig*, Feb. 18, 1894, Mrs. Dunlap Hopkins Papers, New-York Historical Society. Lord Stanley to Davenport, March 3, 1895, and Feb. 25, 1895, Sir William Bromley Davenport Papers, JRL. James Edgcome to Frewen, April 6, 1887, Frewen Papers, LC. James Edgcome to Davenport, April 4, 1895, and July 6, 1895, Sir William Bromley Davenport Papers, JRL.

20. Cobden Club, printed letter, April 2, 1896, Cobden-Sanderson Papers, PML. C. P. Villiers to Bright, Jan. 3, 1884, Bright Papers, BM43386. MCCP, April 30, 1896, MCL. Mrs. Julie Schwabe to Unwin, Feb. 7, 1895, Unwin Papers, BERG.

21. E. Brookes to Davenport, Feb. 6, 1897, Sir William Bromley Davenport Papers, JRL.

22. Thomas Wardle to Davenport, March 27, 1896, *ibid*. William Pringle to Campbell-Bannerman, March 18, 1899, Campbell-Bannerman Papers, BM41234.

23. Henry Ashworth to J. B. Smith, Nov. 10, 1865, J. B. Smith Papers,

MCL. Farrer to Unwin, Jan. 16, 1899, and Harold Cox to Unwin, May 13, 1900, Unwin Papers, BERG. George to Walker, June 13, 1884, Henry George Papers, NYPL.

24. W. T. Stead to Frederick William Holls, June 27, 1903, Holls Papers, CUL. Bernard Shaw to Trebitsch, Sept. 18, 1903, Bernard Shaw Letters, BERG. Balfour to Joseph H. Choate, Aug. 12, 1903, Choate Papers, LC. Unwin Papers, BERG: Justin McCarthy to Unwin, June 30, 1903; June 27, 1903; Feb. 10, 1904. Bernard Shaw to Trebitsch, Oct. 7, 1903, Bernard Shaw Letters, BERG.

25. Bourke Cockran Papers, NYPL: Winston Churchill to Cockran, June 19, 1904; Dec. 12, 1903; May 31, 1904. Justin McCarthy to Unwin, March 17, 1904, Unwin Papers, BERG. F. Y. Edgeworth to Seligman, Sept. 14, no year, Seligman Papers, CUL: Winston Churchill to Cockran, May 31, 1904, and July 16, 1904, Cockran Papers, NYPL.

26. Ashley to Seligman, April 8, 1903, and Dec. 1, 1895, Seligman Papers, CUL. Knight Papers, PML: Joseph Chamberlain to William Knight, Nov. 28, 1903; Archbishop Davidson to Knight, July 20, no year; Balfour to Knight, Oct. 9, 1905. Winston Churchill to Cockran, July 16, 1904, Cockran Papers, NYPL.

27. Conrad Russell to Edward Marsh, Jan. 8, 1906, Marsh Papers, BERG. Winston Churchill to Cockran, June 5, 1906, Cockran Papers, NYPL.

28. Joseph Chamberlain to H. Rider Haggard, Aug. 1, 1903, Haggard Papers, CUL. Joseph Chamberlain to Davenport, Jan. 10, 1906, Sir William Bromley Davenport Papers, JRL. Thomas Maston to Bright, Feb. 5, 1879 (spelling altered), Bright Papers, BM43389. Goldwin Smith to Choate, Jan. 24, 1906, Choate Papers, LC. Philip Bright to Nicholas Murray Butler, March 1, 1932, April 6, 1931, Butler Papers, CUL. Sir George Gower to Cobden-Sanderson, Jan. 6, 1938, Cobden-Sanderson Papers, PML.

XV. OTHER ENGLANDS

1. Sir Louis Mallet to Samuel Ruggles, Sept. 7, 1869, Stauffer Collection, NYPL. Bright to unnamed correspondent, Jan. 25, 1846, Raffles Collection, JRL345. Cobden to Bradford R. Wood, Aug. 10, 1850, Gratz Collection, HSP. Thomas Paine, poem (MS copy), PML.

2. Cobden to Villiers, May 30, 1853, Anthony Autograph Collection, NYPL. Dickens to Frank Stone, Oct. 13, 1854, Dickens Letters, Free Library of Philadelphia. Bright to George C. Beckwith, July 7, 1855, Bright Letters, PUL. J. B. Smith Papers, MCL: Bright to Smith, Oct. 11, 1854, and Oct. 21, 1854; Cobden to Smith, Aug. 13, 1855, Oct. 23, 1855, Dec. 3, 1855, Oct. 3, 1855.

3. J. B. Smith Papers, MCL: Cobden to Smith, May 19, 1857; Aug. 8, 1857; Aug. 12, 1857. NYPL: Cobden to Walmsley, Aug. 22, 1857, Misc. Papers; Bright to Charles Bird, Sept. 10, 1857, Anthony Autograph Collection.

4. Smith to unnamed correspondent, Jan. 17, 1860, J. B. Smith Papers, MCL. Dickens to W. W. Story, Aug. 1, 1863, Dickens Letters, BERG. Robert Curzon to Walter Sneyd, July 16, 1866, Walter Sneyd Papers, JRL.

5. NYPL: Gladstone to Anthony Panizzi, Nov. 29, 1856 (facsimile), Misc. Papers; Bright to John Jaffray, Dec. 6, 1868, DeCoursey Fales Collection. Cf. Bright to Sir David Wedderburn, Feb. 10, 1874, Bright Letters, PUL.

6. F. W. Newman to Epes Sargent, Aug. 20, 1871, Newman Letters, BPL.

Sir Louis Mallet to Wells, Dec. 21, 1873, Wells Papers, LC. Beke Papers, JRL890.

7. Newspaper clipping, Birmingham *Gazette,* April 11, 1874, William Bromley Davenport Papers, JRL.

8. Gladstone to Stead, Sept. 21, 1876, Gladstone Papers, BM44303. Gladstone to Bright, Nov. 12, 1878, Bright Papers, BM43385. Mary Stoughton, MS diary, July 4, 1878, NYPL.

9. Newspaper clipping, Leamington Spa *Courier,* Dec. 6, 1879, William Bromley Davenport Papers, JRL. Chetham's Library: Charles E. Phillips to Mrs. John Davies, March 29, 1932; Maggs Brothers to Phillips, Nov. 27, 1931, Autograph Letters. Goldwin Smith to Gladstone, Nov. 13, 1877, Gladstone Papers, BM44303. Gladstone Papers, BM44454: Oscar Wilde to Gladstone, May 14, 1877; Herbert Spencer to Gladstone, June 17, 1877; Edward A. Freeman to Gladstone, June 29, 1877.

10. BPL: Henry Vincent to William Lloyd Garrison, July 11, 1876, and Sept. 30, 1876, Garrison Papers; Francis W. Newman to Epes Sargent, Nov. 2, 1878, and Jan. 20, 1879, Newman Letters. Francis W. Newman to Alexander Strahan, Oct. 3, 1877, Misc. Papers, NYPL. Goldwin Smith to Gladstone, Nov. 23, 1878, Gladstone Papers, BM44303. Elizabeth Blackwell to Barbara Bodichon, Dec. 2, 1878, Blackwell Letters, CUL. G. J. Holyoake to Bright, May 1, 1878, Bright Papers, BM43389. Disraeli to Dr. Mackenzie, Feb. 26, 1848, Gratz Collection, HSP.

11. H. Farnall to J. S. Blackie, Jan. 6, 1879, Blackie Papers, NLS. John Lockwood Kipling to General Maclagan, April 22, 1886, J. L. Kipling Letters, PML. J. P. Gledstone to Mrs. S. H. Gay, Oct. 11, 1897, S. H. Gay Papers, CUL. *Aborigines' Friend: Journal of the Aborigines Protection Society,* V (1896), 105, 45. James C. Carter to Bourke Cockran, Feb. 13, 1902, Cockran Papers, NYPL.

12. Cf. F. Y. Edgeworth to Seligman, Jan. 8, 1915, Seligman Papers, CUL. Charles George Gordon to Lord Cardwell, Oct. 26, 1877, in Alexander William Armour, *Notables and Autographs* (New York, 1939). Thomas Bazley to J. B. Smith, Nov. 14, 1861, Smith Papers, MCL. MCCP, Oct., 1879, MCL.

13. Henry Richard to unnamed correspondent, March 4, 1881, Ecclesiastical Autographs, JRL859. Barrington to Millais, 1881, Millais Papers, PML. Bright to Conway, April 9, 1885, Conway Papers, CUL. Thomson Hankey to Wells, Sept. 9, 1882, Wells Papers, NYPL. Herbert Spencer to Moncure Conway, July 17, 1898, Conway Papers, CUL. Wilfrid Scawen Blunt, *The Wind and the Whirlwind* (London, 1883), p. 37.

14. Millais Papers, PML: Sir William Harcourt to Millais, Sept. 15, 1882; Sir William Howard Russell to Millais, Nov. 23, 1882, and June 8, 1885.

15. Lady Gregory to John Quinn, May 6, 1912, Quinn Transcripts, NYPL. Tennyson to Whittier, May 4, 1885, Tennyson Letters, PML. Swinburne to the editor of the *St. James's Gazette,* March 29, 1888, Swinburne Letters, BERG. Andrew Lang to Brander Matthews, Feb. 11, 1885, Brander Matthews Papers, CUL. Annie Besant to Mrs. Conway, April 23, 1885, Conway Papers, CUL.

16. Chamberlain to Bright, April 10, 1885, Bright Papers, BM43387. Bright to E. L. Pierce, Jan. 10, 1883, and Jan. 5, 1885, Bright Letters, HCL. Bright to Conway, April 9, 1885, Conway Papers, CUL. Whittier to Bright, March 31, 1885, Whittier Letters, BERG.

17. *Times,* Sept. 5, 1882. Bowker, MS journal, April 21, 1881, NYPL.

H.M. Stanley to A. S. Sullivan, Jan. 11, 1885, Stanley Letters, New-York Historical Society. MCCP, MCL: March 29, 1883; May 20, 1885; Dec. 9, 1886; Nov. 14, 1892; Feb. 26, 1894.

18. Charles Gould, electoral address, Nov. 5, 1885, Bagshawe Papers, JRL. Newspaper clipping, June 26, 1886, Sir William Bromley Davenport Papers, JRL. George R. Parkin to R. U. Johnson, Oct. 9, 1914, Johnson Papers, NYPL. Herbert Spencer to Carnegie, Sept. 23, 1891, Carnegie Collection, NYPL.

19. Whittier to Bright, May 20, 1885, Whittier Letters, BERG. Ripon to Bright, Oct. 24, 1885, Bright Papers, BM43389. Gladstone, MS article on the future of the English-speaking races, Gladstone Papers, HCL.

20. Lord Chamberlain 2 (100), PRO: Memorandum on State Ceremonials; Banting & Sons to Sir Spencer Ponsonby Fane, April 1, 1887; C. B. Harness to Lord Lathom, March 24, 1887; Howell & James Ltd. to Lord Lathom, May 2, 1887; Sir Spencer Ponsonby Fane, circular letter, 1887.

21. J. Levey to Lord Lathom, April 4, 1887, *ibid.*

22. MCCP, MCL: Nov. 16, 1887; Jan. 30, 1888; April 27, 1891; Jan. 20, 1892. Circular of United Empire Trade League, June, 1891, Moreton Frewen Papers, LC.

XVI. IN THE TIME OF THE IMPERIALISTS

XVI. IN THE TIME OF THE IMPERIALISTS

1. Arthur Coke Burnell to Cotton, Feb. 23, 1882, Burnell Papers, JRL740. Florence Nightingale to Kegan Paul & Co., Aug. 30, 1891, Nightingale Letters, Teachers College Library, Columbia University. Nightingale to Kegan Paul & Co., Oct. 30, 1891, Autograph Collection, New-York Historical Society. Stead to Gladstone, Aug. 17, 1891, Gladstone Papers, BM44303.

2. Albert Shaw Papers, NYPL: Stead to Albert Shaw, Nov. 19, 1892, April 4, 1893, May 6, 1891; contemporary history examination, Jan. 17, 1891; Stead to Shaw, June 6, 1891; Percy L. Parker to Shaw, Feb. 19, 1896.

3. Stead to Gladstone, April 23, 1892, Gladstone Papers, BM44303. Kipling to Henley, undated, Henley Papers, PML. Kipling to Henley, Jan. 3, 1893, Kipling Letters, BERG. Albert Shaw to Stead, Oct. 25, 1895 (letter book), Albert Shaw Papers, NYPL.

4. Alfred Austin to Millais, Jan. 9, 1896, Millais Papers, PML. Alfred Austin Papers, CUL: Arthur Bigge to Austin, Jan. 5, 1896; Feb. 19, 1896; June 17, 1897. Stopford Brooke to William Knight, May 20, 1897, Knight Papers, PML. R. J. Muir to Unwin, June 1, 1902, Unwin Papers, BERG. Cf. Edmund Gosse to Stedman, Aug. 6, 1876, Stedman Papers, CUL. Alfred Austin to Lane, Feb. 18, 1898, DeCoursey Fales Collection, NYPL. Austin to Millais, June 17, 1896, Millais Papers, PML.

5. Henley Papers, PML: Henley to Lord Windsor, May 24, 1899; T. Durrant to Henley, May 25, 1898; George Wyndham to Mrs. Henley, July 27, 1903; Lord Roberts to Henley, Jan. 2, 1897, and Jan. 10, 1897; Milner to Henley, June 15, 1901. Henley to Brander Matthews, Nov. 28, 1885, Matthews Papers, CUL. Gosse to Henley, May 4, 1892, Henley Papers, PML.

6. Henley to Swinburne, 1870, Henley Letters, BERG. Henley Papers, PML: Henry James to Henley, May 26, 1879; Henley to Anna, undated; Oscar Wilde to Henley, undated; Kropotkin to Henley, Sept. 17, 1882; Thomas Hardy to Henley, Feb. 20, 1891. Edward Garnett, reader's report, Jan. 25, 1897, Unwin Papers, BERG. Henley to Lord Windsor, Oct. 16, 1896;

and George Meredith to Henley, March 24, 1898, Henley Papers, PML. Joseph Conrad to the chairman of the committee on the Henley memorial, Feb. 17, 1904, Conrad Letters, BERG.

7. Kipling to Sir Arthur Sullivan, May 14, 1898, Kipling Letters, BERG. W. S. Gilbert to Alfred Austin, Nov. 2, 1899, Gilbert & Sullivan Collection, PML. T. E. Brown to Henley, March 9, 1890, Henley Papers, PML. Kipling to William Canton, June 20, 1890, Kipling Letters, BERG. Kipling to Henley, 1890, Henley Papers, PML. John Lockwood Kipling to Bemrose, Dec. 20, 1898, English Autograph Collection, PML. Kipling to Edgar Bateman, Nov. 12, 1896, and Alice Fleming to Elkin Mathews, March 13, 1902, Kipling Letters, BERG.

8. Kipling to G. W. Black, April 10, 1908, and Kipling to Gosse, July 30, 1908, Kipling Letters, BERG. Kipling to Brander Matthews, Feb. 28, 1896, Brander Matthews Papers, CUL. Cf. Arnold Bennett to George Sturt, Feb. 8, 1897, Bennett Letters, BERG.

9. Unwin Papers, NYPL: M. A. S. Hume to Unwin, Oct. 28, 1896; H. F. Wilson, draft letter, 1898; G. Birkbeck Hill to Unwin, Feb. 14, 1896. Herbert Spencer to Conway, July 17, 1898, Conway Papers, CUL. Michael Davitt to "My Dear Admiral," April 22, 1892, and Davitt to William O'Brien, Oct. 28, 1898, Davitt Letters, NLI.

10. Albert Shaw Papers, NYPL: Albert Shaw to Percy Bunting, Jan. 3, 1896; Shaw to Stead, March 23, 1896, March 2, 1896, Dec. 30, 1895 (letter book). Henry James to Millais, Christmas, 1895, Millais Papers, PML. William Smart to Seligman, March 2, 1896, and Dec. 21, 1895, Seligman Papers, CUL. C. E. Norton to Conway, May 11, 1900, and May 8, 1898, Conway Papers, CUL. James Bryce to William Knight, Nov. 15, 1898, Knight Papers, PML. Carnegie to Albert Shaw, March 2, 1900, Albert Shaw Papers, NYPL.

11. Lord Coleridge to Unwin, June 13, 1900, Unwin Papers, BERG. Mark Twain to James Burton Pond, Oct. 19, 1899, Clemens Letters, BERG. Bryce to J. A. Spender, Nov. 9, 1899, Spender Papers, BM46391. John M. Robertson to Moncure Conway, Oct. 12, 1899, Conway Papers, CUL. Robert Buchanan to Unwin, Dec. 6, 1899, Unwin Papers, BERG. James Bryce to Spender, Dec. 26, 1899, Spender Papers, BM46391.

12. R. Brown to Davenport, Dec. 14, 1899, Sir William Bromley Davenport Papers, JRL. G. Birkbeck Hill to Unwin, Jan. 24, 1900, Unwin Papers, BERG. Walter Crane to Charles Rowley, Dec. 21, 1899, Autograph Collection, MCL. Bernard Shaw to Walter Crane, March 13, 1900, Bernard Shaw Letters, BERG.

13. Percy Bunting to Albert Shaw, Sept. 3, 1900, Albert Shaw Papers, NYPL. F. Greenwood to Spender, Jan. 1, 1900, Spender Papers, BM46391. Goldwin Smith to Bourke Cockran, Dec. 23, 1899, Cockran Papers, NYPL. Henry James to Brander Matthews, Aug. 22, 1914, Brander Matthews Papers, CUL.

14. Stead to Moncure Conway, Dec. 8, 1900, Conway Papers, CUL. Stead to Frederick William Holls, Oct. 21, 1899, and Oct. 19, 1900, Holls Papers, CUL. Stead to John E. Milholland, Dec. 22, 1900, Bourke Cockran Papers, NYPL. Burns to Stead, June 15, 1904 (draft), Burns Papers, BM46288. George Wyndham to W. E. Henley, Christmas, 1899, and Oct. 13, 1899, Henley Papers, PML.

15. Munro Smith to Seligman, Dec. 27, 1899, Seligman Papers, CUL. Kipling to Ralph, Feb. 14, 1900, Kipling Letters, PML. Henley to Lord Windsor,

March 18, 1901, Henley Papers, PML. James Bryce to Spender, Feb. 9, 1901, Spender Papers, BM46391. Countess of Aberdeen to Fisher Unwin, Oct. 17, 1900, Unwin Papers, BERG.

16. Newspaper clipping, *East Anglian Times*, Aug. 13, 1900, Henley Papers, PML. Frederick William Holls to Balfour, Dec. 8, 1900, Holls Papers, CUL. Goldwin Smith to Cockran, Nov. 10, 1899, Cockran Papers, NYPL. Goldwin Smith to Ordway, Nov. 7, 1901, Ordway Papers, NYPL. Balfour to Unwin, June 6, 1901, Unwin Papers, BERG. Arthur Conan Doyle to Coulson Kernahan, April 30, 1915, Haggard Papers, CUL. Wyndham to Henley, Feb. 4, 1900, Henley Papers, PML. Maffeo Pantaleoni to Seligman, Jan. 8, 1900, Seligman Papers, CUL. Mark Twain to William Dean Howells, Jan. 25, 1900, Clemens Letters, BERG.

17. Henry Higgs to Seligman, Feb. 3, 1900, Seligman Papers, CUL. Bryce to unnamed correspondent, undated, Anthony Autograph Collection, NYPL. Karl Blind, MS article on the Transvaal War, PML. J. L. Kipling to A. M. Poynter, July 25, no year, Anthony Autograph Collection, NYPL. Frederick William Holls to Theodore Lange, April 5, 1900, Holls Papers, CUL.

18. John Hay to Joseph Choate, Jan. 3, 1900, Choate Papers, LC. NYPL: Alfred Chasseaud to Bourke Cockran, March 16, 1900, Cockran Papers; Woman's South African League, Eliza Verplanck Richards Papers; Samuel Gompers to E. W. Ordway, Dec. 28, 1899, Ordway Papers. Holls to Lecky, Jan. 29, 1900, Holls Papers, CUL. NYPL: Albert Shaw to Stead, Feb. 6, 1900 (letter book), Albert Shaw Papers; "American woman" to Cockran, March 29, 1900, and John A. Joyce, poem dated Dec. 25, 1901, Cockran Papers.

19. Frederic Harrison to Mrs. Carnegie, Oct. 15, 1901, Carnegie Collection, NYPL. Memorandum on Frederic Harrison's visit to the United States in 1901, Holls Papers, CUL. Francis P. Fletcher-Vane to Catherine Welch, April 9, 1908, Anthony Autograph Collection, NYPL. William Watson to William Knight, June 17, 1901, Knight Papers, PML. Gissing to Morley Roberts, March 14, 1901, Gissing Letters, BERG.

20. Goldwin Smith to Cockran, Aug. 8, 1900, Cockran Papers, NYPL. Goldwin Smith to Conway, Nov. 11, 1902, Conway Papers, CUL. Cockran Papers, NYPL: Goldwin Smith to Cockran, May 25, 1900; June 4, 1900; March 23, 1902; Jan. 15, 1902. Ripon to Spender, Nov. 17, 1900, Spender Papers, BM46391.

21. Unwin Papers, BERG: W. H. Dircks, reader's report, Sept. 17, 1901, on Cronwright Schreiner's MS; Michael Davitt to Unwin, Aug. 31, 1900; Countess of Jersey to Unwin, Jan. 26, 1902; George Moore to Unwin, Nov. 17, 1902.

22. Goldwin Smith to Cockran, May 27, 1900, Cockran Papers, NYPL. Unwin Papers, BERG: H. D. Banning, reader's report, May 21, 1902, on E. D. Morel MS on Europe and West Africa; E. D. Morel to Unwin, June 1, 1902. Gosse to Marsh, May 6, 1903, Marsh Papers, BERG.

XVII. THE OTHER ISLAND

1. John Butler Yeats to John Quinn, Aug. 16, 1902, Quinn Transcripts NYPL. Sir Robert Peel to a deputation from the Manchester Chamber of Commerce, June 8, 1841, Harland Collection, MCL. Daniel O'Connell to Costello, Sept. 28, 1828, Stanley Withers Collection, MCL.

2. Disraeli to Sa, June 8, 1843, Lee Kohns Collection, NYPL. Ralph Sneyd to Henry Vincent, Feb. 20, 1844, Ralph Sneyd Papers, JRL. C. G. Berke to

NOTES TO XVII: OTHER ISLAND

Henry Raikes, Jan. 1, 1840, Raikes Papers, JRL1121. Daniel O'Connell to Walmsley, Jan. 17, 1837, Raffles Collection, JRL381. Daniel O'Connell to Edward Davies Davenport, March 26, 1844, Edward Davies Davenport Papers, JRL. Cobden to Firnely, April 10, 1835, Raffles Collection, JRL343. Farr Papers, JRL339: Gladstone to William Farr, Sept. 14, 1827; Sept. 25, 1828; Nov. 22, 1826.

3. E. Raikes to Henry Raikes, Feb. 14, 1833, Raikes Papers, JRL1121. Gladstone to J. H. Gray, July 27, 1848, Gladstone Letters, PML.

4. Thomas Carlyle to James Carlyle, July 17, 1849, Carlyle Letters, PML. Jane Barlow to Unwin, Aug. 23, 1894, and Nov. 17, 1894, Unwin Papers, BERG. Maria Edgeworth to Wilkie Collins, April 22, 1849, Edgeworth Letters, PML. Sir Charles Wood to Nassau Senior, Dec. 22, 1852, Misc. Papers, NYPL. Bright to E. K. Tenisson, Oct. 1, 1849, and Bright to S. Powlett Scrape, Nov. 9, 1849, Bright Letters, PUL.

5. T. Harvey Ashcroft to Thomas Raffles, Raffles Collection, JRL372. Robert O'Driscoll to O'Donovan Rossa, Sept. 28, 1863, and John S. O'Connor to O'Donovan Rossa, Sept. 18, 1863, O'Donovan Rossa Papers, NYPL. John and Jane Chambers to Mrs. Chambers, March 20, 1796, Autograph Collection, New-York Historical Society. Philadelphia Committee to O'Connell, Jan. 29, 1838 (printed), Dreer Collection, HSP. Pierrepont Edwards to Denis Godley, March 18, 1867 (copy), Fenian Papers, BM43742. Lord Hardinge to Lord Clare, Aug. 15, 1848, Clare Papers, JRL. Dickens to W. F. de Cerjat, Jan. 4, 1869, Dickens Letters, BERG. AE to John Quinn, July 8, 1914, Quinn Transcripts, NYPL.

6. Lord Clarendon to unnamed correspondent, Jan. 19, 1852, Raffles Collection, JRL364. Bright to Smith, Oct. 11, 1852, J. B. Smith Papers, MCL. James Stephens to Michael Doheny, Jan. 1, 1858, Margaret McKim Maloney Collection, NYPL.

7. O'Donovan Rossa Papers, NYPL: James Stephens to John O'Mahony, March 5, 1860; James Cantwell to John O'Mahony, Aug. 19, 1860; Thomas Clarke Luby to John O'Mahony, Aug. 25, 1860; Michael Kerwin to John Barry, Dec. 27, 1869; Denis Mulcahy, Jr., to Thomas Clarke Luby, Aug. 6, 1860.

8. *Ibid.*: James Stephens to John O'Mahony, Feb. 25, 1861, March 13, 1863, Oct. 14, 1863; James Stephens to unnamed correspondent, Oct. 14, 1865; Thomas Kelly to William Halpin, March 12, 1867. Fenian Papers, BM43742: Report of the Committee upon Finance and Ways and Means, Sept. 7, 1867 (printed); Lord Monck to the Duke of Buckingham and Chandos, Dec. 26, 1867. Lord Monck to Duke of Buckingham and Chandos, July 4, 1868, Fenian Papers, BM41860.

9. See the pathetic correspondence between William Halpin and John O'Mahony, O'Donovan Rossa Papers, NYPL. *Ibid.*: Jeremiah O'Donovan Rossa to John O'Mahony, 1865; James Stephens to John O'Mahony, Feb. 10, 1866.

10. H. Hulme, MS recollections of Manchester about the period 1860, p. 19, JRL985. Alfred Neild, typescript recollections, pp. 34–35, JRL872. George Kelly to Sir J. A. Macdonald, Dec. 10, 1867 (copy), Fenian Papers, BM41860. Robert Curzon to Sneyd, Dec. 18, 1867, Walter Sneyd Papers, JRL. Dickens to Georgina Hogarth, March 15, 1867, Dickens Letters, BERG. William B. West to Hamilton Fish, June 25, 1870, Consular Letters from Dublin, NA.

11. Home Office 41 (23), PRO: A. F. O. L. to the Under Secretary of the War Office, May 31, 1870; James Fergusson to the Head Constable of Leeds, Aug. 22, 1868; Hicks Beach to the Mayor of Berwick on Tweed, Nov. 14, 1868; Hicks Beach to the Chief Constable of Preston, Oct. 1, 1868.

12. Duke of Buckingham and Chandos to Lord Monck, Dec. 28, 1867, Fenian Papers, BM41860. See Gladstone Letters to Bright, Bright Papers, BM43385. John Stuart Mill to R. Tabouelle, Feb. 26, 1868, Raffles Collection, JRL381.

13. Fanny Byrne to Bright, Jan. 14, 1866, Bright Papers, BM43389. Bright to Smith, Oct. 7, 1866, J. B. Smith Papers, MCL. Bright to Greeley, Nov. 28, 1866, Horace Greeley Papers, NYPL. John Mitchel to Greeley, March 11, 1866, English Autograph Collection, PML. Bright Papers, BM44877: Bright to Ernest Jones, Oct. 4, 1867; Bright to Northy, Dec. 26, 1867, and April 25, 1868. Bright to H. D. Hutton, Jan. 27, 1868, and Bright to Edward L. Pierce, Sept. 26, 1863, Bright Letters, PUL.

14. Bright to H. D. Hutton, Jan. 27, 1868, Bright Letters, PUL. MS discussion on Church and State, 1876, JRL199. Curzon to Sneyd, April 22, 1868, Walter Sneyd Papers, JRL. Ralph Sneyd Papers, JRL: Lady Lansdowne to Ralph Sneyd, May 6, 1869; Walter Sneyd to Ralph Sneyd, June 7, no year; Edward Cheney to Ralph Sneyd, March 4, 1869.

15. Dickens to Trollope, Sept. 13, 1868, Dickens Letters, BERG. Bright to J. M. Hare, April 18, 1848, Bright Letters, PUL. Gladstone to Thomas Binney, April 4, 1869, Gratz Collection, HSP. James Johnstone to Gladstone, April 10, 1872, Gladstone Papers, BM44434. Gladstone to A. W. Haddan, May 18, 1852, Gladstone Letters, PML. Gladstone to Dawson Burns, Jan. 11, 1897, Temperance Collection, JRL342.

16. Circular concerning meeting in support of Mr. Gladstone's resolution for disestablishing the Irish Church, held in Salford, April 22, 1868, Ernest Jones Papers, CUL. Goldwin Smith to Gladstone, March 22, 1868, Gladstone Papers, BM44303.

17. Bright to Northy, Dec, 27, 1869, Bright Papers, BM44877. Lady Lansdowne to Ralph Sneyd, Jan. 10, 1870, Ralph Sneyd Papers, and Lord Zouche to Walter Sneyd, July 17, 1870, Walter Sneyd Papers, JRL.

18. Bright to Northy, Dec. 27, 1869, Bright Papers, BM44877. George Errington to Gladstone, Aug. 11, 1877, Gladstone Papers, BM44454. G. E. Buckle to Frank MacDonagh, Feb. 14, 1918, Butt Papers, NLI.

XVIII. THE HEYDAY OF THE LAND AGITATION

1. Butt Papers, NLI: Butt to Callan, Aug. 31, 1872; memorandum, Dec. 27, 1873; William O'Brien, typescript reminiscences of Isaac Butt.

2. Bright to Gladstone, Jan. 17, 1875, Gladstone Papers, BM44113. Bright to Northy, Dec. 25, 1874, Bright Papers, BM44877. Butt to unnamed correspondent, May 31, 1877; John Barry to Frank MacDonagh, March 5, 1913, Butt Papers, NLI. Newspaper clipping, Leamington Spa *Courier*, Dec. 6, 1879, William Bromley Davenport Papers, JRL. Sir Henry Ponsonby to Sir Stafford Northcote, Jan. 29, 1881, Ponsonby Papers, BM45724. Henry W. Lucy to Unwin, Sept. 2, 1892, Unwin Papers, BERG.

3. Lord Mayor of Dublin to Cyrus Field, Feb. 24, 1880, Cyrus W. Field Collection, PML.

4. Henry Labouchere to Chamberlain, Dec. 17, 1880, Gladstone Papers,

BM44125. Irish National Land League, United States, Jan. 1, 1883, form letter, Thomas Addis Emmet Papers, AIHS. George to Ford, Feb. 4, 1882 (letter book), Henry George Papers, NYPL. Davitt to William O'Brien, June 20, 1899, Davitt Letters, NLI. Michael Davitt to John Boyle O'Reilly, Nov. 5, 1886, Emmet Papers, AIHS. Whittier to Bright, 1886, Whittier Letters, BERG.

5. George to Ford, Dec. 28, 1881 (letter book), Henry George Papers, NYPL. Home Office memorandum relating to Davitt, Oct. 7, 1873, Gladstone Papers, BM44144. Labouchere to Chamberlain, Dec. 17, 1880, Gladstone Papers, BM44125. Cf. George Budd to J. S. Blackie, Jan. 21, 1880, Blackie Papers, NLS. Labouchere to Chamberlain, Dec. 17, 1880, Gladstone Papers, BM44125.

6. Newspaper clipping, *Times,* Dec. 4, 1880, William Bromley Davenport Papers, JRL. Gladstone to Bright, Dec. 23, 1880 (copy), Gladstone Papers, BM44113. Gladstone Papers, BM44125: Chamberlain to Gladstone, Nov. 16, 1880; Dec. 14, 1881; Dec. 22, 1880.

7. Bright to Gladstone, Dec. 7, 1880, and Dec. 22, 1880, Gladstone Papers, BM44113.

8. Labouchere to Chamberlain, Dec. 17, 1880, Gladstone Papers, BM44125. Carpenter, typescript autobiographical notes, JRL1171. Newspaper clipping, *Morning Post,* Jan. 3, 1881, and poem in issue of Dec. 27, 1881, William Bromley Davenport Papers, JRL. John Temple Leader to Walter Sneyd, Jan. 31, 1881, and John R. Wood to Sneyd, Dec. 21, 1881, Walter Sneyd Papers, JRL.

9. G. W. Spencer Lyttelton to Stanley Withers, Sept. 11, 1882, Withers Collection, MCL. Gladstone to Broadhurst, Jan. 8, 1881, Gladstone Letters, PML. Darwin to Asher, Oct. 28, 1879, Darwin Letters, BERG. Darwin to Müller, Dec. 19, 1881 (photostat), Darwin Letters, NYPL. Rosebery to Blackie, Nov. 24, 1879, Blackie Papers, NLS. Gladstone to Bright, Sept. 29, 1881 (copy), Gladstone Papers, BM44113.

10. Balfour to Knight, April 22, 1881, Knight Papers, PML. Bright to Samuel A. Goddard, Aug. 5, 1881, Bright Letters, PUL. Bright to Northy, July 9, 1880, and May 16, 1881, Bright Papers, BM44877. Bright to H. Mac-Dermott, Nov. 23, 1884, Anthony Collection, NYPL. Reginald Cholmondeley to Sir John Millais, Nov. 4, 1881, Millais Papers, PML. S. G. Osborne to Bright, Nov. 18, 1881, Bright Papers, BM43389. Poem in William Bromley Davenport Papers, JRL.

11. Bright to Edward L. Pierce, Oct. 28, 1881, Bright Letters, HCL. NYPL: George to Ford, April 22, 1882 (letter book), Henry George Papers; William Black to R. R. Bowker, no date, Bowker Papers; W. P. Byles to Henry George, Jr., June 6, 1898, Henry George, Jr., Papers; George to Edward R. Taylor, Sept. 12, 1881; George to Thomas Briggs, Oct. 29, 1881; George to Ford, Nov. 10, 1881 (letter book), Henry George Papers; George to Harry George, Jan. 7, 1882, Henry George, Jr., Papers; Mrs. Henry George to her sons, Dec. 20, 1881, Henry George Papers. Bishop of Salford to Mayor of Manchester, May 12, 1882, Autograph Collection, MCL.

12. Henry George Papers, NYPL: George to Taylor, Jan. 1, 1882; George to Francis G. Shaw, April 28, 1882; George to Mrs. George, May 4, 1882; George to Ford, May 30, 1882 (letter book); George to Shaw, May 30, 1882, July 1, 1882; George to Ford, May 17, 1882 (letter book).

13. NYPL: George to Shaw, May 30, 1882, Henry George Papers; Henry

George, Jr., to Shaw, June 12, 1882, and Henry George, Jr., to grandmother, June 14, 1882, Henry George, Jr., Papers. Henry George Papers, NYPL: George to Shaw, May 30, 1882; George to Ford, June 8, 1882 (letter book); George to Briggs, June 9, 1882; George to Shaw, July 1, 1882; Davitt to George, Nov. 4, 1886.

14. Gladstone Papers, BM44125: Chamberlain to Gladstone, Dec. 17, 1881, and July 11, 1882; Gladstone to Chamberlain, Dec. 15, 1881 (copy).

15. Bright to Gladstone, Oct. 4, 1881, Gladstone Papers, BM44113. Lady Wilde to Miss Ford, Jan. 19, 1882, DeCoursey Fales Collection, NYPL.

16. George to Mrs. George, May 3, 1882, Henry George Papers, NYPL. Edward Caird to William Knight, Aug. 24, 1882, Knight Papers, PML. Bishop Nulty to George, Aug. 6, 1883, Henry George Papers, NYPL. Bright to H. MacDermott, Nov. 23, 1884, Anthony Autograph Collection, NYPL.

XIX. NO PARLIAMENT IN DUBLIN

1. William O' Brien, typescript reminiscences of Isaac Butt, NLI. S. H. Butcher to William Knight, July 5, 1888, Knight Papers, PML. Goldwin Smith to Gladstone, Aug. 4, 1881, Gladstone Papers, BM44303. Bright to Gladstone, Oct. 4, 1881, Gladstone Papers, BM44113. Julian Hawthorne, MS article on London, p. 30; Henry George to Francis Shaw, July 1, 1882, Henry George Papers, NYPL.

2. Edward Atkinson to Charles Nordhoff, June 10, 1883, Edward Atkinson Papers, NYPL. Henry George Papers, NYPL: A. R. Wallace to George, June 30, 1882; Hyndman to George, Jan. 9, 1882 (?); Davitt to George, Aug. 8, 1884. Michael Davitt, MS speech, 1886, NLI.

3. Mrs. Gladstone to Mrs. Carnegie, Feb. 27, 1885, Carnegie Collection, NYPL. Alfred Austin to Cracroft (?), July 1, 1885, Anthony Autograph Collection, NYPL. Gladstone to E. T. Cook, Dec. 18, 1895, E. T. Cook Papers, BM39927. Henry George Papers, NYPL: Davitt to George, Nov. 1, 1885; Rosebery to Mr. McGhee, Dec. 25, 1888, and Dec. 27, 1888.

4. Mrs. Shirley to Walter Sneyd, Dec. 15, 1885, and John Temple Leader to Sneyd, Jan. 14, 1886, Walter Sneyd Papers, JRL. Poem in William Bromley Davenport Papers, JRL. Swinburne to Paul H. Hayne, March 20, 1877 (copy), Misc. Papers, NYPL. Swinburne, poem in *Times*, July 1, 1886.

5. Liberal Unionist campaign literature in Bagshawe Papers, JRL. Sir Louis Mallet to Frewen, May 2, 1886, Frewen Papers, LC. S. H. Butcher to Knight, undated, and July 23, 1886, Knight Papers, PML. Newspaper clippings, Macclesfield *Courier*, June 26, 1886, and July 10, 1886, Sir William Bromley Davenport Papers, JRL.

6. Helen Taylor to Mrs. George, Aug. 26, 1886, Mrs. Henry George Papers, NYPL. Confidential memorandum submitted by Joseph Chamberlain to Cardinal Manning on Irish local government, April 25, 1886 (copy), Dilke Papers, BM43953. Gladstone Papers, BM44126: Chamberlain to Gladstone, Dec. 19, 1885, March 15, 1886, March 27, 1886; Gladstone to Chamberlain, March 27, 1886 (copy). Chamberlain to Bright, Feb. 5, 1886, Bright Papers, BM43387.

7. Gladstone to Bright, July 2, 1886 (copy), Gladstone Papers, BM44113. Hartington to Bright, March 26, 1886, Bright Papers, BM43387. Bright to Edward L. Pierce, Jan. 17, 1886, Bright Letters, HCL. Bright to Gladstone, May 13, 1886, Gladstone Papers, BM44113. Bright to Henry Bowie, July

22, 1869, Bright Letters, PUL. Bright to Northy, Dec. 26, 1883, Bright Papers, BM44877. Bright to Gladstone, May 13, 1886, Gladstone Papers, BM44113.

8. Northy to Bright, June 15, 1886 (copy), Bright Papers, BM44877. John Bright, electoral address, June 24, 1886, Bagshawe Papers, JRL. Cobden to Smith, Nov. 8, 1856, and Oct. 3, 1856, J. B. Smith Papers, MCL.

9. Cobden to Walmsley, Nov. 10, 1856, Cobden Letters, and Bright to Cyrus W. Field, Sept. 10, 1865, Cyrus W. Field Papers, NYPL. Bright to Northy, Nov. 18, 1872, Bright Papers, BM44877. Henry Vincent to William Lloyd Garrison, June 17, 1874, Garrison Papers, BPL. Bright to Sir David Wedderburn, Feb. 10, 1874, and Bright to Henry Hawkes, Nov. 4, 1874, Bright Letters, PUL. Bright to Gladstone, Dec. 4, 1880, Gladstone Papers, BM44113. Bright to Edward L. Pierce, Jan. 10, 1883, Bright Letters, HCL.

10. Bright Papers, BM44877: Bright to Northy, July 27, 1886, Dec. 27, 1886, Dec. 28, 1885; Gladstone to Northy, Dec. 11, 1886.

11. Chamberlain to Bright, May 15, 1886, Bright Papers, BM43387. Chamberlain to Carnegie, Aug. 17, 1887, Carnegie Collection, NYPL. F. W. Bagshawe to W. H. Bagshawe, April 10, 1886, and March 11, 1886, Bagshawe Papers, JRL. Chamberlain to Labouchere, May 2, 1886 (copy), Gladstone Papers, BM44126. Granville to Bright, May 6, 1877, Bright Papers, BM43387. Bright to Northy, July 27, 1886, Bright Papers, BM44877. Matthew Arnold to Carnegie, July 7, 1886, Carnegie Collection, NYPL. Annie Besant to Mrs. Conway, Dec. 3, 1885, and Besant to Moncure Conway, Dec. 28, 1886, Conway Papers, CUL.

12. Lord Carnarvon to Lewis, July 17, 1886, Gratz Collection, HSP. J. A. Froude to Stanley Withers, Nov. 13, 1887, Withers Collection, MCL. Wolseley to Campbell-Bannerman, Nov. 22, 1884, Campbell-Bannerman Papers, BM41232. Foxwell to Seligman, Nov. 24, 1895, Seligman Papers, CUL. Balfour to Frewen, Dec. 31, 1886, Moreton Frewen Papers, LC. Balfour to William Knight, Sept. 2, 1892, and Sept. 27, 1887, Knight Papers, PML. Balfour to Lord Latham, April 29, 1887, Lord Chamberlain 2 (100), PRO.

13. F. Schnadhorst to Northy, Jan. 1, 1887, Northy Papers, BM44877. Bryce to Albert Shaw, Dec. 16, 1887, Albert Shaw Papers, NYPL. Chamberlain to Carnegie, May 9, 1887, Carnegie Collection, NYPL. Bright to unnamed correspondent, May 24, 1888, Bright Letters, PML. Bright to Northy, June 22, 1887, Northy Papers, BM44877.

14. Gladstone to Stanley Withers, Jan. 20, 1887, Withers Collection, MCL. Carnegie Collection, NYPL: Gladstone to Carnegie, July 25, 1887, and July 1, 1887; private and confidential memorandum signed by Wolverton, Morley, and others. Gladstone to Carnegie, July 18, 1887, Misc. Papers, NYPL. Alfred Milner to Eugene Noel, Nov. 27, 1887, Milner Letters, BERG.

15. William Archer to Henley, Jan. 18, 1890, Henley Papers, PML. Helen Gilman Brown to her family, May 15, 1887, Brown Letters, Union Theological Seminary Library. John Temple Leader to Sneyd, Sept. 9, 1887, and Feb. 21, 1888, Walter Sneyd Papers, JRL. Gladstone to Millais, Sept. 25, 1887, Millais Papers, PML. Campbell-Bannerman to Donald Crawford, Nov. 16, 1889, Campbell-Bannerman Papers, BM41233. John Anthony Froude to John Stuart Blackie, Nov. 10, 1879, Blackie Papers, NLS. Froude to Withers, Nov. 13, 1887, Withers Collection, MCL.

16. S. H. Butcher to William Knight, July 23, 1886, Knight Papers, PML. John Dillon to Emmet, April 15, 1893, Emmet Papers, AIHS. Gladstone to

Carnegie, July 3, 1891 (photostat), Misc. Papers, NYPL. Harcourt to Carnegie, July 5, 1891, Carnegie Collection, NYPL.

17. Emmet Papers, AIHS: Thomas H. Grattan Esmonde to Eugene Kelly, July 9, 1881; James F. X. O'Brien to Emmet, July 13, 1891; William Louis Kelly to James S. Coleman, Sept. 4, 1891; Michael Corcoran to Emmet, July 14, 1891; Arthur O'Connor to J. P. Ryan, April 29, 1892. Gladstone to Carnegie, March 8, 1892, Carnegie Collection, NYPL.

18. Emmet Papers, AIHS: McCarthy and Dillon to Emmet (telegram), May 28, 1892; Dennis Flaherty to Eugene Kelly, June 11, 1892; Vincent Cody to Eugene Kelly, July 4, 1892; Timothy Moroney to Joseph P. Ryan, June 26, 1892.

19. NYPL: Harcourt to Carnegie, March 16, 1890, Carnegie Collection; Stead to Albert Shaw, June 22, 1892, July 1, 1892, Albert Shaw Papers; Frank Harris to unnamed correspondent, July 5, 1892, DeCoursey Fales Collection. Emmet Papers, AIHS: John Dillon to Eugene Kelly, July 15, 1892; Arthur O'Connor to J. P. Ryan, July 20, 1892; McCarthy to Emmet, Jan. 27, 1893, and Aug. 5, 1893. Davitt to William Clarke, Dec. 18, 1892, and Davitt to William O'Brien, postmarked Dec. 23, 1892, Davitt Letters, NLI.

20. General MSS Collection, CUL: Duke of Devonshire to unnamed correspondent, June 29, 1892; Chamberlain to R. M. Edgar, June 29, 1892; Salisbury to the moderator of the General Assembly of the Presbyterian Church of Ireland, March 30, 1893. C. F. Bastable to Seligman, Jan. 26, 1893, Seligman Papers, CUL. MCCP, Oct. 26, 1892, MCL.

21. Harold Frederic, MS diary, Feb. 13, 1893, LC. Notes used by Gladstone in the House of Commons when introducing the home rule bill of 1893, E. T. Cook Papers, BM39927. T. F. Bayard to David A. Wells, July 11, 1893, Wells Papers, NYPL. Sir Charles Gavan Duffy to Unwin, March 27, 1893, and April 5, 1893, Unwin Papers, BERG. Justin McCarthy to Mrs. Stephen Crane, Jan. 20, 1899, Stephen Crane Papers, CUL. Emmet Papers, AIHS: circular signed by Emmet, April 2, 1893; Emmet to W. G. Hines, May 13, 1893; J. F. Fox to J. P. Ryan, March 4, 1893; McCarthy, Dillon, Davitt, and others to Emmet, Feb. 18, 1893 (cable); Dillon to J. P. Ryan, May 26, 1893. Davitt to William O'Brien, Jan. 19, 1893, Davitt Letters, NLI.

22. Emmet Papers, AIHS: John B. Altgeld to Emmet, March 17, 1893 (copy); John J. Rich to Emmet, March 17, 1893 (copy); Robert J. Reynolds to Emmet, March 17, 1893 (copy); Emmet to Gladstone, March 29, 1893 (copy of telegram). Davitt to O'Brien, Aug. 9, 1893, and Aug. 25, 1896, Davitt Letters, NLI.

23. J. F. Fox to J. P. Ryan, March 4, 1893, Emmet Papers, AIHS. Salisbury to the Moderator of the General Assembly of the Presbyterian Church of Ireland, March 30, 1893, General MSS Collection, CUL. James Bryce to A. R. Wallace, 1884, Wallace Papers, BM46440. Lecky to Wilson, March 21, 1894, Lee Kohns Collection, NYPL. Jesse Macy to Albert Shaw, March 28, 1894, Albert Shaw Papers, NYPL. Swift McNeill to Unwin, April 5, 1894, and reader's report on McNeill, Unwin Papers, BERG.

24. F. W. Hirst to J. B. Clark, Aug. 11, 1911, J. B. Clark Papers, CUL. Cf. Nicholas Murray Butler to Seligman, July 2, 1910, Seligman Papers, CUL. Winston Churchill to Bourke Cockran, April 12, 1896, Cockran Papers, NYPL.

25. Lewis Carroll to Mrs. George Girdlestone Woodhouse, Aug. 2, 1897, Lewis Carroll Letters, BERG. Gladstone to W. W. Farr, Nov. 26, 1827, Farr

Papers, JRL339. Newspaper clipping, Tuam *Herald,* Sept. 15, 1894, Davitt Papers, NLI. O'Donovan Rossa, MS diary, 1895, NYPL. Bryce to William Knight, June 4, 1898, Knight Papers, PML.

XX. CONTENTIOUS MEN

1. Davitt to O'Brien, Oct. 17, 1893, Davitt Letters, NLI. Emmet Papers, AIHS: Edward Blake to Emmet, Nov. 14, 1893 (printed statement of financial needs); Blake to Emmet, Nov. 25, 1894; James T. Doyle to J. P. Ryan, Dec. 28, 1893; D. Rindan to Ryan, Dec. 18, 1893; Hugh McCaffrey to Ryan, Dec. 22, 1893; John F. Walsh to Blake, Feb. 9, 1894; Irish National Federation of America, July 3, 1895 (circular); Emmet to the friends of home rule for Ireland, 1895 (circular); Ryan to McCarthy, Dec. 9, 1893 (letter book).

2. Emmet Papers, AIHS: Thomas McGuire to Emmet, April 2, 1894; T. H. O'Donovan to Ryan, June 27, 1895; National Federation of America to McCarthy, 1893; Ryan to McCarthy, Sept. 1, 1895 (letter book).

3. Davitt to O'Brien, Oct. 12, 1892, Davitt Letters, NLI. John Tweetman to Emmet, Dec. 27, 1893, and McCarthy to Emmet, Jan. 12, 1894, Emmet Papers, AIHS.

4. McCarthy to Emmet, Aug. 6, 1894, Emmet Papers, AIHS. McCarthy inscription in Myra Hamilton autograph album, PML. Davitt Letters, NLI: Davitt to Jerome Bryce, Feb. 13, 1895 (photostat), and Davitt to William O'Brien, Feb. 15, 1894; Aug. 31, 1891; Sept. 21, 1894; Oct. 16, 1895.

5. Davitt to Henry George, Oct. 8, 1896, George Papers, NYPL. Alice Balfour to William Knight, July 17, 1892, Knight Papers, PML. Ernest Dowson to Moore, 1896, Dowson Letters, PML. Winston Churchill to Bourke Cockran, April 12, 1896, Cockran Papers, NYPL.

6. Sydney S. Pawling to Stephen Crane, Dec. 4, 1895, Crane Papers, CUL. George Wyndham to Henley, Dec. 18, 1900, and Feb. 10, 1901, Henley Papers, PML.

7. Wyndham to Henley, Dec. 29, 1901, and Jan. 25, 1903, Henley Papers, PML.

8. Cockran Papers, NYPL: Plunkett to Cockran, Feb. 12, 1898, April 30, 1898, Aug. 23, 1902, April 7, 1909; newspaper clipping, Plunkett to the editor of the *Times,* March 25, 1898.

9. Joseph Conrad to John Quinn, Oct. 16, 1918, and Plunkett to Quinn, April 13, 1920, Quinn Transcripts, NYPL. Plunkett to Finley Peter Dunne, Dec. 21, 1907, Dunne Papers, LC. Cockran Papers, NYPL: Plunkett to Cockran, Jan. 29, 1902; Oct. 23, 1901; Jan. 13, 1902; Feb. 25, 1902.

10. Cockran Papers, NYPL: Plunkett to Cockran, Sept. 14, 1898; Jan. 30, 1901; April 30, 1902; May 24, 1902; July 20, 1903. Wyndham to Henley, Jan. 25, 1903, Henley Papers, PML.

11. Plunkett to Seligman, March 5, 1904, Seligman Papers, CUL. Plunkett to Cockran, March 1, 1904, and April 9, 1904, Cockran Papers, NYPL. AE to Quinn, May, 1904, and J. B. Yeats to Quinn, Aug. 16, 1902, Quinn Transcripts, NYPL.

12. Dillon to Ryan, Oct. 24, 1897, Emmet Papers, AIHS. Cockran to Plunkett, Jan. 21, 1897 (copy), and Redmond to Cockran, Dec. 5, 1904, Cockran Papers, NYPL. Conrad to Quinn, Oct. 16, 1918, Quinn Transcripts, NYPL.

13. Edward Garnett, reader's report on Duffy MS, Nov. 24, 1896, Unwin

Papers, BERG. John A. Bright to Edward L. Pierce, Nov. 20, 1895, Bright Letters, HCL. Emmet Papers, AIHS: Dillon to Emmet, April 20, 1896; Dillon to Ryan, June 21, 1896, and May 25, 1896. Davitt to O'Brien, Dec. 21, 1894, Davitt Letters, NLI.

14. Davitt to Ryan, May 29, 1897, Emmet Papers, AIHS. Davitt Letters, NLI: Davitt to O'Brien, Nov. 18, 1898; Dec. 9, 1897; March 9, 1899, April 6, 1899. Cf. Davitt to George, March 19, 1884, Henry George Papers, NYPL.

15. Davitt to O'Brien, May 27, 1897, Davitt Letters, NLI. Emmet Papers, AIHS: Dillon to Ryan, April 1, 1898, and April 17, 1898; Samuel Young to Ryan, May 24, 1897. Yeats to Ellen O'Leary, Feb. 3, 1889, Yeats Letters, BERG. Davitt to O'Brien, Aug. 7, 1898, and Aug. 15, 1898, Davitt Letters, NLI.

16. Davitt Letters, NLI: Davitt to O'Brien, March 31, 1898; May 18, 1898; June 11, 1898. Moreton Frewen to Cockran, June 17, 1898, Cockran Papers, NYPL. Irish Federation of America (circular), Nov. 26, 1898, and Dec. 27, 1898, Emmet Papers, AIHS.

17. Davitt Letters, NLI: Davitt to O'Brien, June 24, 1898; Aug. 7, 1898; Jan. 18, 1900; April 6, 1899; Dec. 14, 1899. Emmet Papers, AIHS: United Irish League (printed circular); Davitt to Emmet, Jan. 12, 1899; Dillon to Emmet, March 26, 1899.

18. Dillon to Emmet, April 3, 1900, Emmet Papers, AIHS. Patrick Ford to Cockran, March 20, 1900, and March 24, 1900, Cockran Papers, NYPL. Yeats to William Knight, June 19, 1902, Knight Papers, PML.

19. Redmond to Cockran, March 31, 1900, March 23, 1904, and one undated, Cockran Papers, NYPL. T. W. Rolleston to Quinn, May 19, 1915, and Douglas Hyde to Quinn, Sept. 14, 1915, Quinn Transcripts, NYPL. Edward Garnett, reader's report on Hyde MS, June 14, 1898, Unwin Papers, BERG. Cf. Bernard Shaw to Salt, Oct. 3, 1917, Bernard Shaw Letters, BERG.

XXI. AFTER THE VICTORIANS

1. Macaulay to unidentified correspondent, Feb. 21, 1844, Macaulay Letters, BERG. William Allingham to Moncure Conway, Aug. 13, 1867, Conway Papers, CUL.

2. Dillon to Emmet, April 3, 1900, Emmet Papers, AIHS. Gladstone to Douglas Campbell, Oct. 17, 1892 (copy), Misc. Papers, NYPL. Sir Norman Angell, typescript reminiscences, pp. 27–28, Oral History Project, CUL.

3. Florence Nightingale to Buxton, Feb. 7, 1895, Nightingale Letters, New-York Historical Society. Cf. Bernard Shaw to Hamlin Garland, Dec. 29, 1904, Henry George, Jr., Papers, NYPL. Cf. John Bowring, *The Influence of Knowledge on Domestic and Social Happiness* (London, n.d.), p. 10.

4. F. Max Müller to George, Oct. 3, 1882, Henry George Papers, NYPL. William Graham to A. R. Wallace, April 3, 1884, Wallace Papers, BM46440.

5. Election circular, 1906, North Lambeth Parliamentary Election, Pink Papers, JRL310. Goldwin Smith to Joseph Choate, Jan. 24, 1906, Choate Papers, LC. Austen Chamberlain to Nicholas Murray Butler, March 2, 1931, Butler Papers, CUL. Stead to Albert Shaw, Jan. 19, 1894, Albert Shaw Papers, NYPL. Winston Churchill to Bourke Cockran, June 5, 1906, Cockran Papers, NYPL.

6. Lord Goderich to Carlyle, Aug. 3, 1854, Goderich Letters, PML. *Rules*

and *Regulations of the Bolton Factory Operatives' Protective Friendly Society, and Surrounding Neighbourhood* (Bolton, 1860).

7. NYPL: American Society in London to Queen Victoria on the occasion of the Jubilee of 1897, Misc. Papers; Plunkett to Bourke Cockran, Feb. 18, 1899, Cockran Papers. Plato E. Draculis to William Shaw, Oct. 5, 1895, William Shaw Papers, CUL. Cf. John Bright to John Benjamin Smith, Dec. 27, 1852, Smith Papers, MCL.

8. Bowker, MS journal, Feb. 9, 1881, NYPL. Arthur Bigge to Alfred Austin, Aug. 24, 1900, and Jan. 22, 1901, Alfred Austin Papers, CUL. Arthur J. Balfour to William Knight, Jan. 21, 1901, Knight Papers, PML.

9. Frederick William Holls to Andrew D. White, Feb. 6, 1901, Albert Shaw Papers, NYPL. Holls Papers, CUL: Holls to Valentine Chirol, Jan. 25, 1901; Holls to Balfour, Feb. 15, 1901; Holls to L. J. Maxse, Feb. 15, 1901. E. J. Hardy to T. Fisher Unwin, Jan. 29, 1901, Unwin Papers, BERG. Reginald Golding Bright to Annie Russell, March 19, 1901, Annie Russell Papers, NYPL. George Wyndham to W. E. Henley, Jan. 23, 1901, Henley Papers, PML.

10. Henry Adams to W. C. Ford, Feb. 2, 1899, and Feb. 28, 1899, Misc. Papers, NYPL. William L. Clowes to Unwin, Nov. 1, 1900, Unwin Papers, BERG. Israel Zangwill to Laurens Maynard, Dec. 20, 1900, Zangwill Letters, PML. NYPL: Frederic Shields to John Powell Lenox, Aug. 22, 1905, Christ in Art Collection; Stead to Albert Shaw, Jan. 18, 1910, Albert Shaw Papers.

11. Cf. James Bryce to William Knight, Dec. 5, 1897, Knight Papers, PML. Stead to Frederick William Holls, Feb. 10, 1903, Holls Papers, HCL. Percy W. Bunting to Albert Shaw, Oct. 25, 1901, Albert Shaw Papers, NYPL. Herbert Burrows to Moncure Conway, May 2, 1903, Conway Papers, CUL. A. H. D. Acland to J. A. Spender, March 11, 1906, Spender Papers, BM46391. Winston Churchill to Bourke Cockran, June 5, 1906, Cockran Papers, NYPL.

12. Moreton Frewen to Cockran, Oct. 10, 1901, Cockran Papers, NYPL. A. H. D. Acland to Spender, Feb. 25, 1902, Spender Papers, BM46391. Arthur W. Hutton to Unwin, Nov. 3, 1898, and Edward Jenks to Unwin, Feb. 9, 1901, Unwin Papers, BERG. S. G. Fenton to Moncure Conway, Feb. 6, 1898, Conway Papers, CUL. Matthew Arnold to Andrew Carnegie, March 5, 1885, Carnegie Collection, NYPL. Albert Shaw to W. T. Stead, July 1, 1895 (letter book), Albert Shaw Papers, NYPL. Lord Rosebery to William Knight, Oct. 31, 1897, Knight Papers, PML. Campbell-Bannerman Papers, BM41234: Lady Evelyn Ashley to Campbell-Bannerman, Feb. 10, 1899; Campbell-Bannerman to Isaac Hoyle, Feb. 14, 1899 (copy).

13. Robert Blatchford to Thompson, Dec., 1905, Blatchford Papers, MCL. Edward Carpenter to Richard Hawkin, Dec. 1, 1914, Hawkin Papers, JRL1040.

14. W. H. Dircks, reader's report, Aug. 28, 1901, and G. J. Holyoake to Unwin, Feb. 21, 1900, Unwin Papers, BERG. Robert Blatchford to John Burns, June 3, 1901, Burns Papers, BM46288. John Richardson to A. R. Wallace, Feb. 12, 1901, Wallace Papers, BM46440. Goldwin Smith to Moncure Conway, Nov. 11, 1902, and Dec. 20, 1902, Conway Papers, CUL. Conrad Russell to Edward Marsh, Jan. 25, 1904, Marsh Papers, BERG. Unwin Papers, BERG: Sidney Low to Unwin, Dec. 1, 1904, and Dec. 3, 1904; T. H. S. Escott to Unwin, April 26, 1904. May Morris to John Quinn, July 17, 1912, Quinn Transcripts, NYPL. Knight Papers, PML: Joseph Chamberlain

to William Knight, June 23, 1903; Sept. 25, 1903; May 26, 1904. A. Fenner Brockway to Algernon Lee, April 19, 1913, and H. W. Lee to Algernon Lee, May 15, 1913, Algernon Lee Papers, Tamiment Institute Library, New York.

15. Rudyard Kipling to Brander Matthews, March 4, 1919, and Sept. 20, 1914, Brander Matthews Papers, CUL. James Bryce to Mrs. Carnegie, June 14, 1915, Carnegie Collection, NYPL. Augustus John to John Quinn, April 20, 1917, Quinn Transcripts, NYPL.

BIBLIOGRAPHY OF
MANUSCRIPTS

UNITED KINGDOM

ENGLAND

Bodleian Library, Oxford

Lord Bryce; Richard Congreve

British Museum, London

Sir William J. Ashley; Annie Besant; John Bright; John Burns; Sir Henry Campbell-Bannerman; Joseph Chamberlain; Richard Cobden; Sir E. T. Cook; Sir Charles Dilke; Fenian MSS; William Ewart Gladstone; Hammersmith Socialist League; William Morris; Florence Nightingale; W. H. Northy; Sir Henry Ponsonby; James A. Spender; William Thomas Stead; William Tallack; Alfred Russel Wallace

Chetham's Hospital and Library, Manchester

Ernest Jones; Manchester Ship Canal MSS; Pitt Club

John Rylands Library, Manchester

Bagshawe Family MSS; Thomas Carlyle; Edward Carpenter; Clergymen's MSS; Robert Curzon (Lord Zouche) *; Edward Davies Davenport; William Bromley Davenport Family MSS; Charles Dickens; W. W. Farr; Elizabeth Gaskell; Richard Hawkin; Alfred Neild; William Neild; Florence Nightingale; W. D. Pink; Thomas Raffles; Henry Raikes; Mary Anne Rawson; Sir Henry Roscoe; John Ruskin; Ralph Sneyd *; Walter Sneyd *; Edward Lyulph Stanley; William Thomas Stead; Temperance MSS; Twentieth Century New Testament MSS

Manchester Central Library, Manchester

Anti-Corn Law League; Robert Blatchford; John Bright; Richard Cobden; Elizabeth Gaskell; John Harlan; Ernest Jones; Manchester Chamber of Commerce; Manchester Statistical Society; William Morris; National Union of

* Transferred to the library of University College of North Staffordshire, Keele, Stoke-on-Trent.

384   BIBLIOGRAPHY OF MANUSCRIPTS

Women's Suffrage Societies; Pitt Club; John Benjamin Smith; Stanley Withers

Public Record Office, London

Fenian MSS; Home Office MSS concerning the Distress of the Working Classes, 1878–1879; Home Office MSS concerning Disturbances, 1868–1871; Lord Chamberlain MSS concerning the Jubilee of 1887

Sheffield Central Library, Sheffield

Edward Carpenter

University College of North Staffordshire, Keele, Stoke-on-Trent

Robert Curzon (Lord Zouche); Ralph Sneyd; Walter Sneyd (formerly on deposit in the John Rylands Library)

University of Leeds' Library, Leeds

Sir Edmund Gosse

Victoria and Albert Museum, London

Thomas Carlyle; Charles Dickens

SCOTLAND

National Library of Scotland, Edinburgh

John Stuart Blackie; Thomas Carlyle

IRELAND

National Library of Ireland, Dublin

Isaac Butts; Michael Davitt; William O'Brien

UNITED STATES

CONNECTICUT

Yale University Library, New Haven

George Gissing

DISTRICT OF COLUMBIA

Folger Shakespeare Library, Washington

Marie Corelli; William Michael Rossetti; Bernard Shaw

Library of Congress, Washington

American Academy of Arts and Letters; John Bright; Robert Browning; Lord Bryce; Andrew Carnegie; Joseph H. Choate; John Fiske; Harold Frederic; Moreton Frewen; William Ewart Gladstone; Julia Ward Howe; Herbert Spencer; David Ames Wells

National Archives, Washington

United States Consular MSS

MASSACHUSETTS

Boston Public Library, Boston

Mellen Chamberlain; Kate Field; William Lloyd Garrison; Francis W. Newman; John Ruskin

Harvard College Library, Cambridge

Edward Bellamy; John Bright; Richard Cobden; William Ewart Gladstone; Thomas Hughes; James Russell Lowell; Charles Eliot Norton; John Endicott Peabody; John Ruskin; William Thomas Stead

Massachusetts Historical Society Library, Boston

Edward Atkinson; George Bancroft

NEW JERSEY

Princeton University Library, Princeton

John Bright; Lowes Dickinson; Thomas Hughes; Charles Kingsley; Morris L. Parrish; Sir Horace Plunkett; John Ruskin

NEW YORK

American Irish Historical Society, New York

Michael Davitt; John Dillon; Thomas Addis Emmet; Irish National Federation of America; Justin McCarthy

Columbia University Libraries, New York

Sir Norman Angell; Sir William J. Ashley; Alfred Austin; Edward Bellamy; Annie Besant; Elizabeth Blackwell; Lord Bryce; Nicholas Murray Butler; John Bates Clark; Moncure Conway; Frederick Coykendall; Stephen Crane; William Eleroy Curtis; Plato E. Draculis; William A. Dunning; Herbert Somerton Foxwell; Sydney Howard Gay; Sir Edmund Gosse; Sir Henry Rider Haggard; Ripley Hitchcock; Frederick William Holls; Thomas Hughes; Ernest Jones; Emma Lazarus; Alfred Marshall; Brander Matthews; William Morris; William Michael Rossetti; John Ruskin; George Santayana; Edwin R. A. Seligman; William Shaw; Herbert Spencer; Edmund Clarence Stedman; Lincoln Steffens; Sidney Webb (Lord Passfield)

Teachers College Library, Columbia University

Florence Nightingale

General Theological Seminary Library, New York

Clergymen's MSS; United States Episcopal Bishops MSS

New-York Historical Society, New York

James Buchanan; Mrs. Dunlap Hopkins

New York Public Library, New York

A. W. Anthony; George W. Arents Tobacco MSS; Edward Atkinson; Thomas Barwick Lloyd Baker; George Bancroft; John Bigelow; Richard Rogers Bowker; Shirley Brooks; Sir Percy W. Bunting; George Burgess; Andrew Carnegie; William Conant Church; Richard Cobden; Bourke Cockran; Michael Davitt; Mrs. Henry Draper; DeCoursey Fales; Fenian MSS; Cyrus W. Field; Moreton Frewen; William Frey; Henry George; Mrs. Henry George; Henry George, Jr.; Robert Murray Gilchrist; William Ewart Gladstone; Horace Greeley; Bolton Hall; Mary S. Harkness; Julian Hawthorne; Robert Underwood Johnson; Lee Kohns; Laura Jean Libby; James Russell Lowell;

James Miller McKim; Margaret McKim Maloney; Charles Nordhoff; Jeremiah O'Donovan Rossa; Edward W. Ordway; Sir Horace Plunkett; John Quinn Transcripts; John Ruskin; Annie Russell; Albert Shaw; Robert L. Stanton; William Thomas Stead; Mary Stoughton; Mrs. Humphry Ward; David Ames Wells

Berg Collection, New York Public Library

Arnold Bennett; Richard Doddridge Blackmore; John Bright; Thomas Carlyle; G. K. Chesterton; Pearl Craigie; Charles Dickens; Sir Charles Gavan Duffy; George Gissing; Sir Edmund Gosse; Sir Henry Rider Haggard; George Jacob Holyoake; Thomas Hughes; Charles Kingsley; Rudyard Kipling; Justin Mc-Carthy; Sir Edward Marsh; George Moore; William Morris; Florence Nightingale; Ouida [Louise de la Ramée]; John Ruskin; Bernard Shaw; T. Fisher Unwin

Pierpont Morgan Library, New York

Arthur J. Balfour; John Bright; Lord Bryce; Thomas Carlyle; Joseph Chamberlain; Clergymen's MSS; Thomas James Cobden-Sanderson; Charles Dickens; Ernest Dowson; Cyrus W. Field; Sir William Schwenck Gilbert and Sir Arthur Sullivan; William Ewart Gladstone; William Ernest Henley; Rudyard Kipling; William Knight; Sir John Millais; William Morris; Dante Gabriel Rossetti; John Ruskin; Herbert Spencer; Mrs. Humphry Ward; George Wyndham

Tamiment Institute Library, New York

Algernon Lee

Union Theological Seminary Library, New York

Helen Gilman Noyes Brown

PENNSYLVANIA

Free Library of Philadelphia, Philadelphia

Charles Dickens; Bernard Shaw

Historical Society of Pennsylvania, Philadelphia

James Buchanan; Ferdinand Julius Dreer; Simon Gratz; John Welsh

INDEX

Abolitionists, 70, 273-74

Aborigines' Protection Society, 132, 241-42

Achievements of Victorian reformers, 322-29

Acland, A. H. D., 327

Act of Union, 295, 306, 308

Adams, Charles Francis, quoted, 76

Adams, Henry, 21, 34, 217

Address Chiefly Directed to Those Who Occupy Influential Stations in Life (Bower), 76

Advertising, 32

AE (pseud. George William Russell), 83, 316, 318

Afghanistan, 240, 243, 245, 298

Africa, 246, 256; *see also* Boers; Boer War; Egypt; West Africa; Zulu War

Agnosticism, 117-18, 274

Agriculture: and Great Depression, 50-63; and reform efforts, 186-90; and free trade, 224, 227-28; conditions in Ireland, 314-16

Ainsworth, W. Harrison, 61

Alabama Claims, 239

Albert, Prince, 13, 195

Alexandria, 243, 245

Alice in Wonderland (Carroll), 98

Allingham, William, 14

Allotments and Small Holdings Association, 190

Altgeld, John B., quoted, 307

Amalgamated Society of Engineers, 43, 132, 184

Americans, and British drinking habits, 46; *see also* Irish-Americans; United States

Anarchists, 154

Angell, Sir Norman, 118, 168

Anglican Church of Ireland, 12, 25-26, 274-76

Anglicans, 123-25, 128

Anglo-American alliance, proposed during Spanish-American War, 319

Anglo-French Commercial Treaty of 1860, 216

Answers (journal), 101

Anti-Aggression League, 243

Anticipations (Wells), 77

Anti-Corn Law League, 215; *see also* Corn Laws

Anticruelty movement, 101

Anti-imperialism, 234-49, 250-64; *see also* Imperialism

Anti-Imperialist League (U.S.), 262

Antireformers, 70-72

Anti-Semitism, 177, 241

Applegarth, Robert, 42

Arch, Joseph, 61, 189, 226

Archer, William, quoted, 157

Argyll, Duke of, 144

Arnold, Matthew, 65-66, 69, 90, 299, 328; quoted, 80, 105-6; on education, 180, 195, 200-201, 202

Arnold, Thomas, 197

Art Journal, 198

Arts, in England, 33-34

Ashanti War, 238-39

Ashbourne Act, 294

Ashley, William J., 35, 108, 207, 208; quoted, 210; on trade, 226, 231

Ashton, 174

Asia, 29; *see also* Afghanistan; Burma; China; India; Japan

Asquith, Herbert, 328

Association of English Hop-Growers, 228

Astor, William Waldorf Astor, 1st Viscount, 58

Atheism, 101, 117-19, 156, 274

Atkinson, Edward, quoted, 293

Austin, Alfred, 252; quoted, 294

Australia, 226, 234, 257; and Ireland, 307-8, 310

Austria, 28, 29, 34, 237

Austro-Prussian War, 237
Austro-Sardinian War, 237
Aveling, Edward, 153, 169

Bagehot, Walter, 11, 14
Bagshawe, W. H. G., 118
Baker, Barwick (Thomas Barwick Lloyd
  Baker), 57, 68-69, 71, 77; quoted, 41-42,
  72, 143; and self-help, 144, 180
Balaklava, 80
Balfour, Alice, quoted, 312
Balfour, Arthur J., 132, 137, 230, 261; and
  Ireland, 285-86, 300-301, 309; as leader,
  312, 327
Balliol College, 206
Ballot, secret, 12; see also Franchise;
  Suffrage
Bancroft, George, 216-17
Bancroft, Marie Effie Wilton, Lady, 104
Bancroft, Sir Squire, 104
Bankruptcy, after 1873, 19-20
Baptists, view quoted, 119
Barnardo, Thomas, 72
Barnett, Henrietta O., 115
Barnett, Samuel, canon, 102-3, 181
Barnum, P. T., 46
Barrow-in-Furness, relief in, 36
Bastable, C. F., 185
Bastille, 149, 164
Bath and Wells, Bishop of, 115
Battersea Branch, Amalgamated Society
  of Engineers, 132, 184
Bax, Ernest Belfort, 171
Bazett, Henry, 122
Bazley, Sir Thomas, 218
Beaconsfield, Lady, 130
Beaconsfield, Lord, see Disraeli, Benjamin
Bear, William E., 54
Beesly, E., 71
Beke, Charles T., 239
Belgium, 28, 34, 202
Bellamy, Edward: and Looking Back-
  ward, 38, 90-91, 112, 155, 164; and Mrs.
  Mee, 122; for insurance, 184
Benn, Sir Ernest, quoted, 162
Bennett, Arnold, 34, 95, 104-5, 185-86,
  325
Benson, Edward White, 114-15, 128
Bernstein, Eduard, 171
Besant, Annie, 5, 75, 101, 118, 169, 244-
  45, 299; and birth control, 104, 183; and
  Fabians, 156-57, 159, 168
Besant, Sir Walter, 65
Bessemer, Sir Henry, 30
Bible, 127; see also New Testament

Bimetallic League, 186; see also Mono-
  metallic Association
Bimetallists, 71, 185-86
Binney, Thomas, 114
Birmingham, 35, 36, 136, 142, 187;
  Lowell in, 11, 78, 93; U.S. consul in,
  20, 29
Birmingham Fabian Society, 122
Birmingham, University of, 208, 210
Birth control, 101, 104, 156, 183-84
Bismarck, 8, 223-24, 238
Blackburn, conditions in, 36
Blackie, John Stuart, 106, 189
Blackmore, R. D., 51; quoted, 62
Blackwell, Elizabeth, 53, 66, 77, 181, 184;
  quoted, 19-20, 64; on women's educa-
  tion, 205; against Disraeli, 241
Blackwood, William, 94
Blackwood's, 94
Blanc, Louis, 94
Bland, Edith Nesbit, 162; quoted, 164
Bland, Hubert, 162, 171
Blatchford, Robert, 101, 167-68, 170, 328;
  quoted, 83, 94; influence of, 93, 106;
  and Merrie England, 109-11
Blavatsky, Helena Petrovna, 157
Blue Ribbon Missions, 46
Blunden, L. H., 185
Blunt, Wilfrid, 98; quoted, 243-44
Board of Trade, 142, 218-19, 229, 238
Bodleian Library, 54
Boers, 252, 261-62
Boer War, 77, 98, 171, 257-64, 328; and
  English trade, 229; victory at Majuba
  Hill, 243; and Irish, 320-21; and Vic-
  toria's death, 326
Bolton, conditions in, 36, 175, 325
Books, and reform, 102-12
Booth, Catherine, 125-26
Booth, Charles, 181
Booth, William, 100, 122, 125-26, 180, 193;
  influence of, 106; In Darkest England
  and the Way Out, 108-9; quoted, 120
Boston, George Gissing in, 30, 174
Bosworth's Academy, 197
Boucicault, Dion, 98
Bourne, H. R. Fox, 132
Bower, G. W., 76
Bowker, R. R., quoted, 31; diary of, 32
Bowring, Sir John, quoted, 33
Bradford, 21, 22, 149; U.S. consular re-
  ports from, 23-24, 28, 42-43, 64, 199,
  222, 224
Bradlaugh, Charles, 65, 75, 101, 118, 193;
  for birth control, 104, 183; and self-

Kipling, Rudyard (*Continued*)
man of imperialism, 254; and the Boer War, 260
Knight, William, 231
Kropotkin, Prince, 170, 253
Kruger, Stephanus Johannes Paulus, 261, 264

Labor, 35-49, 62-63, 140, 174-76, 179-86; and socialism, 122-24, 167-68; and free trade, 229
Labour Legislation, Labour Movements, and Labour Leaders (Howell), 323
Labour Party, founded, 171
Labour Representation Committee, 171, 328
Laissez-faire, 82
Lambeth Polytechnic Institute, 203
Lancashire: industry in, 18; trade in, 148
Lancaster, 25, 30
Land Acts, 316, 321; of 1870, 277, 278; of 1881, 286, 289, 290-91; of 1886 and 1903, 312
Land League, 280-82, 284, 286-90, 292, 296, 320
Land-Leaguers, The (Trollope), 281
Land Nationalisation Society, 116
Land reforms, 189, 323; in Ireland, 268, 276-77, 278-91, 294
Land Tenure Reform Association, 189
Landlordism, 50-63, 101, 189, 282
Landor, Walter Savage, 295; quoted, 120
Lang, Andrew, quoted, 244
Last Days of Pompeii, The (Bulwer-Lytton), 170
Latin America, 29; see also Venezuela
La Touche, Rose, 84
Lawlessness, in Ireland, 266-67; see also Violence
Leach, Charles, 46
Leader, John Temple, 58, 302
Leadership, among Edwardian reformers, 327
Lear, Edward, 187
Leeds, relief in, 36
Legislation, 142-43; see also Education Acts; Factory legislation; Land Acts
Leslie, Cliffe, 189
Levi, Leone, 45-46, 174-75
Liberal Party, 24-25, 52, 98, 151, 256; reform views of, 139-45; and Gladstone, 150, 296, 302; and socialists, 166-67; and workers, 176; rural policy of, 190; and free trade, 219, 224, 229;

rift in, 227-28; and Bright, 245, 298-99; and imperialism, 252; and the Irish Question, 274, 279, 282, 289, 308, 317; George on, 287; for reform, 324; and Redmond, 328
Liberal Unionists, 228, 232, 299, 300, 312; and free trade, 229; and Ireland, 313-14, 316, 321; and Boers, 320
Liberty and Property Defense League, 144
Libraries, in England, 196
Liebknecht, Wilhelm, 163-64
Liquor, 44-47
Limerick, meeting in, 319-20
Linguistic achievements of reformers, 324-25
Literature of reform, 75-76
Little Lord Fauntleroy, 67, 68, 78
Liverpool, 9, 36, 70, 87-88, 187; University College, 201
Lloyd George, David, 99, 185
Local-government reforms, 101-2, 323
Loch, Sir Charles, 109, 180
Lockyer, Sir Joseph Norman, 208
London, 29, 39, 75, 157, 174-75, 187
London (journal), 101, 169
London County Council, 132, 160
London Quarterly, 96
London School Board, 162
London School of Economics and Political Science, 206
London Society for the Prevention of Cruelty to Children, 182
London University, 197-98
Longfellow, Henry Wadsworth, 80, 90
Looking Backward (Bellamy), 38, 90, 112, 155, 164, 184
Lords, House of, 11, 47, 115, 129, 327; reform of, 227; rejection of home rule, 308
Louis XVI, 4
Louis Napoleon, 85
Louis-Philippe, 7
Love among the Artists (Shaw), 158
Lovett, William, 41
Lowell, James Russell, 11, 52, 93, 186-87; quoted, 78
Lorna Doone (Blackmore), 51
Lower Congo, 246
Ludlow, J. M., 43, 127-28, 184, 193
Lunn, Sir Henry, 23
Luton, depression in, 36

Macaulay, Thomas Babington, 79, 322, 324
McCarthy, Justin, 98, 230, 305-7, 310-12

Tess of the D'Urbervilles (Hardy), 62, 118, 142, 184, 188
Thackeray, William M., 182-83
Theosophy, 157
Third French Republic, 164, 219
Thirlwall, Connop, 274
Thompson, Alexander M., 110, 170
Thompson, Joseph, 14
Thompson, T. Perronet, 211, 213-14
Thomson, Daniel, 169
Thomson, James, 73
Thomson, Joseph, 246
"Three F's," the, 282-83, 286
Thyrza (Gissing), 135
Times (London), 97, 201, 245, 247, 303
Times (New York), 307
Tit-Bits (journal), 101
Tobacco, 47-48
Tolstoy, Leo, 92-93, 120
Tone, Wolfe, 318
Tories, 7, 10-11, 24, 131, 256; and Corn Laws, 6, 215; and Chamberlain, 136-317; reform views of, 139-45, 324; imperialism of, 253; and Gladstone, 256, 294, 301; and the Irish Question, 279, 282, 286, 295; and Arnold, 299; election of, 300; *see also* Conservative Party; Liberal Unionists
Towards Democracy (Carpenter), 92
Toynbee, Arnold, 66, 68, 181, 185, 287; influence of, 93
Toynbee Hall, 181
Trade, English, 21, 26-34; *see also* Free Trade
Trades unions, 12, 40, 42-44, 61, 160-61; members' opinions, 175; role of, 176; leaders' opinions, 184; and cooperatives, 193; reforms in, 323; *see also* Labor
Trades Union Congress, 12, 44, 176
Traditionalist attitudes, after 1867, 15-16
Trafalgar Square, demonstrations in, 75, 165-66
Training, classical and technical, 195-210 *passim*
Transvaal, 259, 261, 263
Trollope, Anthony, 11, 275, 281
Turkey, 25, 29, 235-36, 240
Twain, Mark, 11, 261-62; quoted, 258
Twentieth Century New Testament, The, 121
Tyler, Wat, 61
Typewriters, 31
Tyrrell, Father George, 118

Uganda, 246
Ulster, 295, 314
Unclassed, The (Gissing), 135
Unemployment problem, 20, 37-42, 174-76
Unions, trade, *see* Trades unions
Unionists, *see* Liberal Unionists
Unitarians, 115, 127
United Empire Trade League, 249
United Ireland (journal), 304
United Irish reform movement, 320
United Irishmen, at Vinegar Hill, 318
United Kingdom Alliance, 44
United States, 21, 27-34, 43, 52-54, 220-21; consular reports from Bradford, 23-24, 28, 42-43, 64, 199, 222, 224; workers in, 164; and domestics, 173-74; slaves in, 175, 191; and emigrants, 180; education in, 195-96, 201-2, 209-10; and free trade, 216-18, 226; and imperialism, 234, 256-57; Cobden's views of, 236; and Alabama dispute, 239; and Venezuela affair, 252, 256-57; for Boers, 262; and Fenians, 270, 286; representatives in Dublin, 271-72; English alliance and Irish, 318-20; reforms in, 322; and Victoria, 326; *see also* Irish-Americans
University College (Liverpool), 201
Unto This Last (Ruskin), 85, 87
Unwin, Mrs. Cobden, 215
Unwin, T. Fisher, 158, 230-31, 255, 264
Urban workers, schemes to help, 179-86

Vagrancy, in 1878, 41
Vegetarianism, 71, 180
Venezuela, and the U.S., 252, 256-57
Venice, 135
Venus of Milo, 103
Vere, Aubrey de, 124
Vermont, Kipling in, 33, 251
Victoria, 12, 13, 14, 30, 255; and Chamberlain, 136-37; and Disraeli, 141; subjects of, 165; 50th anniversary of accession of, 248; and Henley, 252; and Irish situation, 271, 275, 279; and Jubilee of 1897, 318; stand of on reforms, 325; death of, 326; *see also* Jubilee celebrations
Victoria University, 208
Villiers, Charles Pelham, 218, 228, 230, 235
Vincent, C. E. Howard, quoted, 249
Vinegar Hill Insurrection, 318
Violence, Irish, 266-67, 290, 295-96; and Edwardian reformers, 328-29